JONI MITCHELL

BOOKS BY MARK BEGO

The Captain & Tennille (1977)
Barry Manilow (1977)
The Doobie Brothers (1980)
Michael! [Jackson] (1984)
On The Road with Michael! [Jackson] (1984)
Madonna! (1985)
Rock Hudson: Public & Private (1986)
Sade! (1986)
Julian Lennon! (1986)
The Best of "Modern Screen" (1986)
Whitney! [Houston] (1986)
Cher! (1986)
Bette Midler: Outrageously Divine (1987)
The Linda Gray Story (1988)
TV Rock (1988)
Between the Lines [with Debbie Gibson] (1990)
Linda Ronstadt: It's So Easy (1990)
Ice Ice Ice: The Extraordinary Vanilla Ice Story (1991)
One Is the Loneliest Number [with Jimmy Greenspoon of Three Dog Night] (1991)
Madonna: Blonde Ambition (1992)
I'm a Believer: My Life of Music, Monkees, and Madness [with Micky Dolenz of The Monkees] (1993)
Country Hunks (1994)
Country Gals (1994)

Dancing in the Street: Confessions of a Motown Diva [with Martha Reeves of Martha and The Vandellas] (1994)
I Fall to Pieces: The Music and Life of Patsy Cline (1995)
Rock & Roll Almanac (1996)
Alan Jackson: Gone Country (1996)
Raised on Rock: The Autobiography of Elvis Presley's Step Brother [with David Stanley] (1996)
George Strait: The Story of a Country's Living Legend (1997)
Leonardo DiCaprio: Romantic Hero (1998)
LeAnn Rimes (1998)
Jewel (1998)
Matt Damon: Chasing a Dream (1998)
Will Smith: The Freshest Prince (1998)
Vince Gill (2000)
Madonna: Blonde Ambition (2000)
Aretha Franklin: Queen of Soul (2001)
The Marx Brothers (2001)
Cher: If You Believe (2001)
Bette Midler: Still Divine (2002)
Bonnie Raitt: Still in the Nick of Time (2003)
Julia Roberts: America's Sweetheart (2003)
Whitney Houston: Fall from Grace (2003)
Tina Turner: Break Every Rule (2003)
Joni Mitchell (2005)

JONI MITCHELL

MARK BEGO

TAYLOR TRADE PUBLISHING
Lanham • New York • Dallas • Boulder • Toronto • Oxford

Published by Taylor Trade Publishing
An imprint of The Rowman & Littlefield Publishing Group, Inc.
4501 Forbes Boulevard, Suite 200, Lanham, Maryland 20706

Distributed by NATIONAL BOOK NETWORK

Library of Congress Cataloging-in-Publication Data Available

ISBN 1-58979-134-7 (cloth : alk. paper)

♾ The paper used in this publication meets the minimum requirements of American
National Standard for Information Sciences—Permanence of Paper for Printed Library
Materials, ANSI/NISO Z39.48-1992.

Manufactured in the United States of America.

To Marcy MacDonald

My multimedia international cohort in journalistic crime

Acknowledgments

Thanks to

Anne Bego	Ruth Mueller
Bob and Mary Bego	Kärstin Painter
Michael Brecker	Mandy Phillips
Tom Cuddy	Ross Plotkin
Micky Dolenz	Melissa Porter
Gino Falzarano	David Salidor
Tisha Fein	Chrisona Schmidt
James Fitzgerald	Tony Seidl
Deborah Gibson	Scott Shannon
Susan Gilbert	Barbara Shelley
Raymond Griffis	Andy Skurow
Randy Jones	Mark Sokoloff
Michael McDonald	Ann Watt
Zach Martin	Beth Wernick
Scott Meyer	and Mary Wilson

Special thanks go to Christopher Gilman and the staff of the Palm restaurant in New York City (250 West 50th Street), for making me feel at home in Manhattan, and for including my portrait on their wall of celebrities.

Contents

PROLOGUE

Discussing Painting with Joni Mitchell,

In the fall of 1969, during my senior year in high school, I attended my first bona fide rock concert in downtown Detroit. It was the group Crosby, Stills, Nash, and Young at Masonic Auditorium. As the group came toward the end of its incredibly moving show, Graham Nash announced that they were going to be joined onstage by a dear friend of theirs, Miss Joni Mitchell.

She was a willowy girl with long blond hair and a guitar in her hands. When she took to the stage, the crowd burst into a thunderous round of applause, and she joined the harmonious quartet in the song "Get Together." The group also performed "Woodstock," Joni's composition that the foursome had recorded and turned into a hit. It was the most magical moment of the show. After years of being a music writer, I remember the concert as one of my all-time favorites.

At the time I knew of Joni's touching, insightful writing from hearing Buffy Sainte-Marie ("The Circle Game") and Judy Collins ("Both Sides Now") singing her songs. It was a wonderful introduction to her own distinctly touching performing.

During my senior year in college, Joni released *Court and Spark*. I loved the vinyl album so much that I also bought the eight-track tape version of it, so I could listen to it in my car. In the 1980s, when Walkman portable stereos came in vogue, I purchased *Court and Spark* in its cassette version so I could rollerskate down the streets of New York listening to it. Later that decade it became one of the first CDs I ever purchased.

In New York City in 1978, I became the nightlife editor of *Cue* magazine and was responsible for reviewing—among other venues—the jazz clubs in town. Around this time, Joni released my second favorite of her albums, the jazz-infused *Shadows and Light*. She provided my true entrée into jazz music. I wore out my vinyl version of that album from playing it so much. The featured saxophone player on that album was the very well respected Michael Brecker.

In 1980 I went to work for Michael Brecker and his brother, Randy Brecker. My friend Beth Wernick and I were the publicists for the Manhattan jazz club they owned at the time, which was named for the street it was located on: Seventh Avenue South. One night at the bar I told Michael Brecker how much I loved his sax playing on *Shadows and Light*, and he told me that the thing he admired the most about Joni Mitchell was her "total musicianship, no matter what genre of music she played in."

Album by album, I followed Joni Mitchell's growth as a performer. My love of her music grew from her folk-oriented era (*Ladies of the Canyon*), to her rock phase (*Court and Spark*), to her jazz era (*Mingus*), to her electronica jaunt (*Dog Eat Dog*), through her insightful storyteller phase (*Night Ride Home*). After my career had made the leap from magazine writing to book writing, editors constantly asked me what person I most wanted to write a book about or in collaboration with. Time and time again I would reel off my "wish list," which always seemed to include the name Joni Mitchell at the top. And repeatedly, for one reason or another, it was always passed over—*unless* I could talk Joni into working with me. I always felt that if I could just have a face-to-face meeting with her, I could talk her into it.

Much to my surprise, on February 28, 1996, I met Joni Mitchell and had a one-on-one conversation with her. Like so many things in life, it came about unexpectedly.

It was the day of the thirty-eighth annual Grammy Awards at the Shrine Auditorium in Los Angeles. I attended the event with my friend Barbara Shelley, who had volunteered to aid production assistant Tisha Fein, working backstage. In that way, both she and

I had "full access" backstage passes throughout the day. For television viewers, the Grammy Awards seem like a three-hour evening event that begins at 8:00 P.M. In reality, however, the majority of the awards are presented at a nontelevised event that takes place in the afternoon before the telecast. Traditionally, few major performers attend the afternoon event.

This particular year, Joni Mitchell was nominated for two awards in the categories of Best Pop Album and Best Recording Package for the album *Turbulent Indigo*. The category of Best Recording Package—the art director's award—was one of the awards presented in the early afternoon of the event.

Barbara and I arrived in time to see the nontelevised awards being handed out. The admission tickets allowed viewers and participants to help themselves to unreserved seating. We settled into two vacant seats in the very front row, approximately eight feet from the podium that was set up on stage right.

Within minutes of our having taken our seats, it was announced that the next award to be presented was the one for Best Recording Package. On the list of nominees was Joni's *Turbulent Indigo* album, which featured her self-portrait mimicking Vincent van Gogh's painting of himself with his ear bandaged. When the envelope was opened, the announced winner was Joni. What a thrill it was to be a mere eight feet away when Joni and her art direction partner, Robbie Cavolina, personally accepted.

Throughout her career, Joni has maintained that she never intended to become a singer or a recording artist. According to her, she was a painter who discovered she could sing and write songs, a profession that inadvertently eclipsed her career in the field of art. I too am a painter, who had an intended art career eclipsed by the discovery that I could also write. It was never my intention to become an author; my original goal was to become a famous painter. So, to see Joni receive this award—at such close proximity, no less—was especially exciting for me. And, knowing all about Joni's passion for painting and art, I realized how much this particular award meant to her.

Eventually Barbara Shelley decided to head to the backstage area, so she left me in the auditorium to watch the rest of the nontelevised awards and the beginning of the telecast. Finally, I decided to venture to the backstage area as well. Using the designated badge I wore around my neck on a chain, I gained access to the backstage area, which was populated by press interviewers, technical people, stagehands, and several stars and superstars. A massive tent was set up in the fenced-in backstage outdoor area, where VIPs could dine at a buffet, have a cocktail, watch the telecast on projection screen TVs, and socialize.

No sooner did I arrive backstage than I encountered an amazing sight. There, in the middle of the outdoor area, stood Joni Mitchell and another woman casually hanging out. As per typical Joni fashion, she was smoking a cigarette.

I literally froze in my tracks, like a deer caught in the headlights of an oncoming automobile. "Oh my God, there's Joni," I thought to myself. "Do I dare go up to her and introduce myself? Should I? Shouldn't I? Should I? Shouldn't I?" I debated in my mind for several seconds. Finally I figured, "Hey, it's now or never. What's the worst that could happen—that she would tell me to 'get lost?'"

I walked directly over to her and announced, "Hello Joni, my name is Mark Bego. I am the author of several books about rock stars, and I am also a painter. I just saw you win the Best Art Director award, and I wanted to congratulate you. As a painter, I know that this a very important award for you."

With her cigarette still in her hand, she looked me in the eyes with a pleasant smile on her face and said, "Thank you. What is your style?"

"My style?" I asked. "My book writing style?"

"Oh no, your painting style," she asked.

So used to speaking about my book career, I was momentarily startled to be discussing my painting with Joni Mitchell. I felt like Gauguin having a chat with van Gogh. "I would call it impressionist, or slightly primitive realist," I replied.

"What medium do you paint in?"

"Mainly acrylic on canvas."

"I prefer oils," she claimed.

"I have been dabbling in watercolors lately too."

"I like the effects that watercolors have. What is your subject matter?" Joni inquired.

"Well, it is sort of like your paintings. Sometimes still lifes and sometimes landscapes. Recently I did a portrait of Madonna—the singer. It's a painting."

As we conversed, her friend excused herself and went into the

VIP tent to get herself a drink. Joni and I continued our conversation, while she finished smoking her cigarette.

"What happened to me is that in high school, I started writing for my school newspaper and the local daily paper, and in time my writing career seemed to dominate my life," I explained.

"That's what happened to me and my music career," she admitted.

Throughout our ten minutes together, Joni was very friendly and seemed genuinely interested in talking about art with another painter. By the time her friend returned, the conversation had shifted to writing.

"I write biographies about celebrities," I said. "I was the cowriter of the autobiography that Micky Dolenz of the Monkees wrote called *I'm a Believer*. And I was the coauthor of Martha Reeves's book, *Dancing in the Streets* as well. But I have always wanted to do a book with you."

"This is Julie Larson, who works for my management company," Joni said, introducing her returned friend. "Why don't you exchange numbers, and let's discuss it."

Julie and I exchanged business cards, and I told her that I would send her some books and press material on myself.

"Again, congratulations on winning your Grammy Award," I told Joni, sensing that I had taken up enough of her time.

"Thank you so much," Joni said with a warm and genuine smile.

Whether or not I ever received the opportunity to write a book with her, for the rest of the evening, I was walking on clouds. Painting is such a solitary art form that it is rare for two painters to find themselves in each other's company, let alone have an uninterrupted conversation with each other about paint, techniques, and subject matter.

In her song "A Case of You," Joni sang that she was just a lonely painter, whose life was lived amid a box of her paints. Every time I think of our conversation at the Grammys that day, I am reminded of those lyrics.

When I returned to my house in Tucson, I put together a package of books and a biography of myself for Julie and sent it to her. I telephoned her but never heard back. In time I realized that were I ever to do a book about Joni, I would just have to proceed on my own. For the most part, writing—like painting—is also a solitary art.

Knowing that one day, one way or another—if I had my way (which I usually do)—I would be writing this book, I continued to gather material on Joni and attended every event that would put me proximity to her and her music. In 1998 I was on the grassy hill in front of the historic stage in Bethel, New York, when Joni finally made her "Woodstock" debut at the weekend-long festival known as A Day in the Garden. And I was in the audience when Mitchell sang in front of a full concert orchestra at the Greek Theatre in Los Angeles in 2001. In this way, in a bicoastal fashion, I have personally witnessed Joni at each phase of her astonishing career.

In 2003, Taylor Publishing gave me the opportunity to write my own book about Joni Mitchell, and it is the one that you now hold in your hands. As I started to write this book about my favorite songwriting pop music diva, I thought the only fitting way to pay tribute to the artistic side of her career was to paint a portrait of Joni as well. You will find my acrylic-on-canvas homage to the inspiring Joni in this book. Both the portrait and the biography are the works of art I have waited longest to create. Here's to Joni Mitchell: painter, writer, performer, and the most highly revered singer-songwriter of the rock era. In my mind, Joni, "You rock!"

INTRODUCTION

A Woman of Heart and Mind

Joni Mitchell is the ultimate female folk troubadour. For five decades she has personified the role of an arty, sophisticated, socially conscious folk/rock singer. Throughout twenty-three critically acclaimed albums she has mesmerized millions of fans with her words, music, and pure, soul-baring songs.

She has never been one to rest on her laurels. And she has never been a performer who is content to create music in just one idiom. In the mid 1970s when she stepped away from the acoustic guitar and piano-accompanied songs that made her famous, she added rock & roll electric guitars and drums to her music, to achieve her greatest commercial success.

Never content to simply repeat herself, she next added jazz-influenced songs to her repertoire. When some of her critics and fans balked at such a move, she simply ignored their bristling and followed her own heart. She is someone who hates to repeat herself. As she so eloquently and succinctly put it, no one ever called out to Vincent van Gogh to paint *Starry Night* over again.

Born in Canada, Joni first came to prominence as a songwriter, and she gained international attention when her song "Both Sides Now" was recorded in 1968 by Judy Collins, for whom it became a Top 10 hit. Her first album, *Joni Mitchell* (1968), was produced by David Crosby, and her affiliation with his group—Crosby, Stills, Nash, and Young—has been a thread throughout her career. The quartet recorded "Woodstock," her ode to the most famous rock festival in history, and several times she toured with the group as its opening act. Her controversial—and very "sexual revolution" era—separate love affairs with CSNY group members David Crosby and Graham Nash have long been the talk of the rock world.

Her second album, *Clouds* (1969), featured Joni's distinctive versions of her songs "Chelsea Morning" and "Both Sides Now." The following year, the album won her a Grammy Award as the Best Folk Performance, Female. While sharing a house in Laurel Canyon with Graham Nash, Joni recorded her third album, *Ladies of the Canyon*, which features her interpretation of "Circle Game" and her own haunting version of "Woodstock."

These four songs by Joni—"Both Sides Now," "Circle Game," "Chelsea Morning," and "Woodstock"—carried fresh nuances when she recorded them. Although covered by many other recording artists, Joni's songs recordings were considered the ultimate versions. Much of her initial success was due to perfect timing, as Joni was swept up in the whole troubadour movement of the early 1970s, which also catapulted Carole King and Carly Simon to prominence.

Her 1971 album *Blue* is considered her most brilliant acoustic folk recording. To this day it is a steadily selling album on CD and is viewed as a classic of the singer-songwriter genre. After a year's vacation from her career, Joni returned to the marketplace with *For the Roses*, her first album for David Geffen's Asylum Records. This album brought Joni her first Top 25 hit, "You Turn Me On I'm a Radio." Although she never openly courted mainstream pop radio success, the song broadened her growing audience.

Throughout these formative years, Joni continued to establish her reputation for being an incredibly gifted singer-songwriter who had yet to break through to widespread fame. That all changed with her multimillion-selling 1974 album, *Court and Spark*. By blending her trademark acoustic guitar and piano playing with a top-notch electric and jazz rock band, she broke through with her most commercial and appealing recording yet. Aided by the chart hits "Help Me" and "Free Man in Paris," the recording became her first Top 10 album. It also garnered her a Grammy Award for Best Arrangement Accompanying Vocalists, for the song "Down to You."

That same year she released her first live album, *Miles of Aisles*, including two new songs, "Jericho" and "Love or Money." The live version of her classic "Big Yellow Taxi" went on to become a big chart hit for her. During the following two years she released two more masterful albums, *The Hissing of Summer Lawns* (1975) and the jazz-influenced *Hejira* (1976).

During this period, Joni was seen in several high-profile rock & roll contexts, including Bob Dylan's famed tour, the Rolling Thunder Revue, and The Band's feature-film farewell concert performance, *The Last Waltz*.

Over the years, Joni continued to stretch and grow musically. She delved heavily into jazz with her albums *Don Juan's Reckless Daughter* (1977), *Mingus* (1979), and *Shadows and Light* (1980). The unfolding of her association with Charles Mingus is fascinating. Stricken with Lou Gehrig's disease and knowing that his time on earth was limited, jazz star Mingus enlisted Mitchell to put words to several of his songs and ultimately assured his musical immortality with a wider audience of fans. She spent time with Mingus and added poignant lyrics to four of his instrumental jazz songs. Inspired by his creativity, she added two of her own Mingus-inspired compositions. The resulting album, *Mingus*, features some of the most adventurous and complex music of her career. Released just months after the death of the jazz great, *Mingus* won her critical acclaim from some and questioning scorn from others.

Devotees of pure jazz were appalled by the idea that a hippie folk singer could suddenly consider herself a jazz artist of the same caliber as Charles Mingus. On the other side of the coin, many of Joni's folk/rock fans felt deserted by her foray into the arty world of jazz. This was the beginning of her somewhat thorny relationship with the press. Her concert tour late that year gave birth to her excellent live double album, *Shadows and Light*. The music on it emerged like a cross between a historic jazz performance and an eclectic rock concert. Players on the album include Pat Metheny, Michael Brecker, and Jaco Pastorious.

In the 1980s, Joni's creative output continued as she signed a recording contract with *Geffen Records* and released her 1982 album *Wild Things Run Fast*, on which she returned to a musical style that was closer to her folk and pop roots. It included her hit version of Elvis Presley's "(You're So Square) Baby, I Don't Care."

Although this song became her biggest chart hit in almost a decade (number 47), it didn't achieve the kind of rock success she was hoping for. The album is noted for Joni's rapprochement with pop music and a longing to capture her nostalgic love for the music of her youth.

On her 1985 album, *Dog Eat Dog*, Joni tried her hand at a "new wave" sound. In her quest to get involved in electronic synthesizer rock, she involved techno artist Thomas Dolby, who ultimately co-produced the album. Long acknowledged as the conscience of rock music, Joni recorded songs that blisteringly criticized current topics, including the thievery of televangelists ("Tax Free"), media manipulation ("Fiction"), and the politics of the starving in Africa ("Ethiopia"). She proved that her socially conscious lyrics had lost none of their sting. Ultimately, *Dog Eat Dog* has become heralded as Joni's most sustained rock recording.

In 1988 she released her fifteenth album, *Chalk Mark in a Rain Storm*, which featured an all-star supporting cast including Peter Gabriel, Willie Nelson, Tom Petty, Wendy and Lisa, Don Henley, Thomas Dolby, and Billy Idol. Late in the year, Joni was one of the star performers in Pink Floyd's historic staging of their rock opera *The Wall*, in front of the Berlin Wall in Germany.

Throughout the years, Joni's expressive artwork graced the covers of most of her albums. She became so revered as an artist that she even became chummy with legendary artist Georgia O'Keeffe, toward the end of the famed painter's long and fruitful life. Joni's friendship with O'Keeffe deepened her interest in her own painting and strengthened her desire to be taken seriously as a painter. Like O'Keeffe, Joni was taken by the serene beauty of the American Southwest, and she too became a semipermanent resident of New Mexico.

Her 1990s albums, *Night Ride Home* (1991) and *Turbulent Indigo* (1994), found her as classy and intricate as always. Never one to hide her complex feelings, Joni even criticized onetime friend Jackson Browne for alleged physical abuse of actress girlfriend Daryl Hannah on "Not to Blame," a song from *Turbulent Indigo*.

Showing up in unexpected places, Joni Mitchell appearances increased in the mid-1990s. Noteworthy 1990s performances included an electrifying concert at the Edmonton Folk Festival and a much-heralded radio broadcast concert in January 1995. She was also exposed to a whole new audience in 1995, when a remixed version of her 1960s hit "Big Yellow Taxi" was featured on the soundtrack and soundtrack album of the twenty-something hit TV series, *Friends*. In December 1995 Joni was awarded *Billboard* magazine's Century Award for consistently creating lasting music that helped define the sound of the twentieth century. In her fourth decade of recording, Joni Mitchell remains as creative and insightful as always with her singing and her writing.

In 1996, only months after winning her third and fourth Grammy Awards, her personal life made also made headlines. The daughter she had given up for adoption as a teenager had discovered that Joni was indeed her birth mother. After years of questions and doubts, she instantly found herself with a new role to play: mother and grandmother. Finally, after years of feeling an emotional hole in herself, she felt complete as a person.

In her own signature introspective way, as she had done throughout her career, the next album she recorded of all-new compositions, *Taming the Tiger* (1998), found her turning these startling new events into touching songs. The subjects she illuminated included sudden motherhood in her fifties, aging, contemplating a face-lift, and her lifelong arguments with her own mother. The year 1998 was also highlighted by a high-profile appearance on the site of the original musical festival, which she had immortalized in her ode to the event, "Woodstock." She also performed a series of concerts with longtime friend and compatriot Bob Dylan, including a double bill event at Madison Square Garden.

Her most recently recorded albums, *Both Sides Now* (2000) and *Travelogue* (2002), have added a whole new dimension to her fascinating musical career. On *Both Sides Now* Joni recorded nearly a whole album filled with jazz standards sung to a full orchestra. Taking selections from the songbooks of Ella Fitzgerald and Billie Holiday, she stepped away from the folk and rock sound of most of her recorded work and stretched out stylistically. On *Travelogue* she took twenty-two of her own favorite compositions and reinterpreted them—again with a lush full orchestra of musicians accompanying her vocals.

She has continued her quest for musical self-exploration, garnering critical accolades and solidifying her place in the spotlight time and time again. Yet many questions continue to circulate about Joni Mitchell, and many areas of her life and her career need to be illuminated and discussed:

- How did she feel about being a victim of the polio epidemic that swept Canada in the 1950s? Did it cause her to become introspective?
- What was her inspiration for her songs, from "The Circle Game" and "Both Sides Now" to her compositions from *Taming the Tiger*?
- What is the truth about her rumored love affairs with the individual members of Crosby, Stills, Nash, and Young, Jackson Browne, James Taylor, and others? How did she feel when *Rolling Stone* magazine named her Old Lady of the Year for her many high-profile affairs?
- What was behind her decision to delve into jazz music and to record her controversial, misunderstood album *Mingus*?
- What is behind her battles with the highly political Rock & Roll Hall of Fame, and what exactly fueled the deeply personal convictions that led her to snub the induction ceremony?
- After years of recording only her own songs, what caused Joni's sudden decision in 1998 to begin performing jazz standards from the songbooks of Etta James, Billie Holiday, and Sarah Vaughan?
- How did her art career suddenly get sidetracked, and what was behind her friendship with legendary painter Georgia O'Keeffe? Did it have a profound effect on Joni's own painting?
- What is the dynamic of her relationships with James Taylor, Bonnie Raitt, Linda Ronstadt, Bob Dylan, Peter Gabriel, Judy Collins, Tom Rush, ex-husband Larry Klein, and Thomas Dolby?
- Joni suddenly took on the role as a mother—in her fifties—when her long-lost daughter "Kelly" found her after thirty years and returned to play a key part in her life. What pressures drove her to give up her only child, and what was the heartbreak that came with her decision?
- Mitchell has created one of the richest catalogs of popular music ever recorded. It has garnered her one of the most

unique places in rock & roll history. What led to the creation of each of her songs, and where she is headed next in
her music?

Joni Mitchell has seemingly boundless creativity on which to
draw. Where does it come from? To find the answers to all of these
questions—and more—we must delve into her past in the frozen
extremes of northwestern Canada, where it all began.

1

Oh, Canada

Roberta Joan Anderson was born on November 7, 1943, in Fort McLeod, Alberta, Canada. Her mother, the former Myrtle Marguerite McKee, worked as a bank clerk and later became a schoolteacher. Her father, William Anderson, was a lieutenant in the Royal Canadian Air Force.

True artist that she is, Joni's first memories are those of colors and light. "Above my crib as a baby was a rolled-up blind," she recalls. "This was a poor household and they had those kind of blinds that came in beige and dark green. This one was dark green and it was perforated and cracked in a lot of places from frequent rolling. I can remember lying in my crib, seeing the filtered little stream of light and the fluffs of dust floating in it. I was 1½, and that's my earliest memory." (1)

The place she was born was highly unglamorous. According to her, "Fort MacLeod was coming out of the Great Depression and into the war. So every house was weathered-out and derelict looking with no paint on it. There had been a drought, too, so gardens were nonexistent. Some of the people who had no money for paint would try to brighten things up by stuccoing their houses with chicken feed and broken brown, green, and blue bottle glass. I was born materialistic, and from an early age I always liked to look at light through transparent colors, so when I was let out into the yards to play, I would collect the glass that had fallen off onto the ground. Coming back into the house on more than one occasion with my cheeks bulging, my mother would say, 'Open up,' and my mouth would be full of this broken colored glass. But I never cut myself." (1)

Fort McLeod is fifty miles from the U.S. border, north of Montana. It was a remote place to grow up, and it wasn't long before young Joanie—as she was called—learned to escape into her creativity to entertain herself. Her first means of artistic expression came from her small box of crayons, and the pictures she would color and draw. "Color is my first priority in the arts, before form or anything," she explains. "It's the spark. My mother said that as a child, before my verbs came in—at 14 or 15 months—I grabbed some oranges, put them on a purple scarf, gathered everybody in, and said, 'Pretty!' So color juxtaposition intrigued me. In the public-school system, I craved to have the box of 24 [crayon] colors. I only had the box of 8; we couldn't afford the box of 24. But the 24 had magenta and turquoise and chartreuse and gold and silver and blonds in it. Oh, I wanted the 24!" (2)

Hers was not an easy childhood. "I was a sickly child," explains Joni. "At three my appendix burst, and they rushed me to the hospital. Then I had German measles and red measles, one of which nearly killed me." (1)

After World War II ended and Bill Anderson left the military, he moved his family to Maidstone, Saskatchewan, thirty-four miles east of the Alberta border on Canada Highway 16, over three hundred miles north of the Montana border. Joni's father was the manager of a small grocery store. It was a town so small there was no running water. Joni's mother took a job as a schoolteacher: one room, all grades, no books.

Joni recalls Maidstone: "When the war ended, my father found us a little house by the highway with a picture window. And I think that set up a permanent longing to take off and go somewhere, in me. Things coming and going past that window left an impression upon me: here they come, where are they going?" (3)

The trains ran so close to the tiny Anderson house that Joni would sit in the window and wave to the railroad conductors and engineers as they went by. Later she revealed, "Several years ago, my mom and dad were at a party, and they met a conductor on that railroad. He said, 'The only thing I remember about Maidstone was that there was a house with big window where they left the Christmas tree lights up, and a little girl used to wave to me.' It was the same guy! So we had this ritual, he and I. It really makes you want to think that every prayer, every message we send eventually gets answered." (1)

"Joni grew up in a small town on the Canadian prairie," says Graham Nash of Mitchell's stark childhood in Maidstone in the mid-1940s. (3)

Joni described her life in Maidstone: "The town I lived in was a small third world town. The mail still came at Christmas on open wagons with sleigh runners." (4)

Although Joni loved pets, especially those of the feline variety, she remembers that cats were not allowed in the Anderson house. "My mother was too house-proud, because cats are hard on furniture and they piddle and scratch here and there. My mother was also a farm girl and cats were not indoor things: They were for the barn. But I knew every cat in my neighborhood." (5)

From an early age Joni was an individual thinker. Her history of questioning authority dates all the way back to her childhood and led to her disdain for Sunday school and organized religion. As she explains it, "I left the church because I loved stories from an early age, but I liked them to have some logic. And the story Adam and Eve didn't make any sense, so I contested it. Adam and Eve had two sons, Cain and Abel. And Cain killed Abel, and then he married. Who did he marry? Eve? My Sunday School teacher's response was to hurt my feelings in some way, and I took on a pouty attitude, and said, 'I'm not going back there.'" (6)

When little Joanie was six years old, the Anderson family moved to Saskatoon, Saskatchewan. Although Saskatoon is both the largest city in that province and the home of the University of Saskatchewan, it was not very cosmopolitan. However, by comparison to Maidstone, Saskatoon seemed as exciting as Paris. There were restaurants and music, and clubs and shops.

Her first and most natural form of creative expression was— and is—painting. As she explains, "In my early childhood, because I was creative—I was a painter always—I had difficulty playing with the other children in the neighborhood, just because my games they couldn't get in on." (7)

Joni's love of music also dates back to an early age. She recalls hearing music around the house as a child. The songs that she heard on records also had an influence on her. "Well, not everybody had a record player when I was a kid. It was a relatively poor community, so it was considered a luxury item that we had a record player. My father was a trumpet teacher, so he had one Leroy Anderson record and one Harry James record. And my mother had [Beethoven's] 'Moonlight Sonata' and all the rhapsodies. So the use of the trumpet and my penchant for classicism, that comes more from my parents' collection. I had *Alice in Wonderland* and *Tubby the Tuba*. And if you listen to this new record, the tuba is way up loud on the record. So that family record collection—my mother's, my father's and my two childhood records—shows up in this collection." (8)

Admits Joni, "The first record I bought was a piece of classical music. I saw a movie called *The Story of Three Loves*, and the theme was by Rachmaninoff, I think. Everytime it used to come on the radio it would drive me crazy. It was a 78 [rpm disc]. I mean . . . the first one that I loved and had to buy? *The Story of Three Loves*." (9)

Suddenly fascinated with music, when she was seven years old, Joni asked her parents if she could take piano lessons. Being a musician himself, her father wanted to nurture her love of music, so he bought her a spinet, off the back of a truck. And, for the next couple of years, she studied piano on it.

For a short time, it looked like she would be an accomplished keyboard player. However, as much as she loved the music, she didn't always love the lessons. Instead of concentrating on classical music, like her teacher instructed her to do, Joanie preferred to come up with her own songs.

Headstrong from an early age, the budding artist and musician later explained, "But, I still used to sit down and compose my own little melodies. That's what I wanted to do, to compose . . . I thought I was going to be a painter when I grew up, but I knew I could make up music. I heard it in my head. I always could do it, but it was discouraged." (4)

Joni was never one to follow the rules, and being told she could not do something only made her want to do it more. "You have to be able to go out on a limb," she explains. "To innovate, you have to have a certain kind of fearlessness. I think it helps if at an early age you got used to being shunned and you survived that. If you had to fight some things in your childhood, you now can stand alone." (10)

Unfortunately the woman who was hired to teach her to play

the spinet ruined the whole experience for Joni. "I had music killed by my piano teacher. She rapped my knuckles with a ruler, which was the way they thought—everybody in that era anyway. And [she] said, 'Why would you want to play by ear'—that's what they called composing—'when you could have the masters under your fingertips, when you could copy?' So you go to art school and innovation is everything, but in music, you're just a weird loner. So I have more of a painter's ego or approach, which is to make fresh, individuated stuff that has my blood in it on the tracks." (11) For several years, that ended Roberta Joan Anderson's interest in learning to play the piano.

Joni later explained that the final blow was the fact that the lessons were scheduled to take place at the same time as her favorite radio program. She laughingly says, "They conflicted with listening to *Wild Bill Hickok* on the radio, so I quit." (12)

In Saskatoon, her bouts with childhood illnesses escalated. She recalls, "At eight I had chickenpox and scarlet fever, plus the arbitrary tonsillitis." (1)

Her worst illness struck in 1952, when a polio epidemic swept through Canada, and young Joni fell victim to the potentially crippling disease. "I vividly remember the day I got polio. I was nine years old, and I dressed myself that morning in pegged gray slacks, a red and white gingham dress with a sailor collar, and a blue sweater. I looked in the mirror, and I don't know what I saw—dark circles under my eyes or a slight swelling in my face—but I said to myself, 'You look like a woman today.'" (1)

She recalls, "After I got outside, I was walking along with a school friend, and at the third block I sat down on this little lawn and said, 'I must have rheumatism,' because I'd seen my grandmother aching and having to be lifted out of bed, and I collapsed. They rushed me to the St. Paul's hospital in Saskatoon. The infectious part of the disease lasts two weeks, and it twisted my spine severely forward in a curvature called 'lordosis,' and then back to the right in a lateral curve called 'scoliosis,' so that I was unable to stand. One leg was impaired, but the muscles didn't atrophy, so there was no withering, thank God. I was put in the children's ward, and with Christmas rolling up it became apparent I wasn't going home. Someone sent me a coloring book with pictures of old-fashioned English carolers and the lyrics to all these Christmas carols. I had ulcers in my mouth that they'd come and swab [with] an antibacterial solution called 'gentian violet' and they'd leave the swabs behind, so I used the swabs to color the carolers purple. And I sang these carols to get my spirits up." (1)

Confined to the hospital throughout December, Joni was not allowed to go home for Christmas. "My mother came with a little mask on, and put a little Christmas tree in my room with some ornaments," Joan recalls. "The first night they allowed me to leave it lit an hour after 'lights out.' And I said to the little tree, 'I'm not a cripple,' and I said a prayer, some kind of pact, a barter with God for my legs, my singing." (1)

According to her, "If the disease spread to your lungs, you were doomed to pass the rest of your life reclining in an iron lung with your head sticking out. As I rose to make my walk, I could hear iron lungs wheezing in the background." (1)

Her bout with polio made her rely even more heavily on her budding creativity to entertain herself. As Joni explains it, "I guess I really started singing when I had polio. Neil [Young] and I both got polio in the same Canadian epidemic. I was nine and they put me in a polio ward over Christmas. They said I might not walk again, and . . . I wouldn't go for it. So I started to sing Christmas carols and I used to sing them real loud. When the nurse came into the room I would sing louder. The boy in the bed next to me, you know, used to complain. And I discovered I was a ham. That was the first time I started to sing to people." (9)

When she got out of the hospital, Joni was stubborn about not becoming a cripple for life. During her year-long rehabilitation program she rejected braces, corrective shoes, and a wheelchair.

Not only did she recover from the disease and its aftereffects, but she even became stronger. "Polio probably did me good. Otherwise I would have been an athlete. I lost my running skills, but translated them into something less fast and more graceful; I became a dancer. I believe convalescence in bed develops a strong inner life in a young child. I think it solidified me as an independent thinker. Nietzsche was a convalescent." (2)

Nevertheless, polio left effects on Joan's body. She explains, "The fact of the matter is that I was—I am—crippled from it, but I just pretended like it wasn't there. I got through my youth and my teens without any real problem—never missed a dance. I'm sure you can't say that all handicaps can be overcome by spirit, but I believe that a lot of them can." (13)

Frustrated by her health problems, Joni developed a habit that continues to this day—her addiction to cigarettes. Although she hid her smoking from her parents, she learned to ease the tensions in her young life by lighting up and having a puff of tobacco.

Throwing herself further into her artwork, young Joanie had quite an eye for art and fashion. "As a child, I harbored the idea of becoming a fashion designer. I drew cut-outs. I'd dress dollies. Through every class, my mother saved some of them, and they're really interesting to look at now. I made my own clothes. So, fashion was a thing that interested me in my early teens . . . I had my own column in the high school paper: 'Fads and Fashion.' It was pretty fluffy." (10)

She was clever as a young girl. She learned how to cut corners in classes that didn't interest her. "I always hated poetry as a child. I used to read *Classic [Illustrated] Comics* for my reports in school," she confesses. (12)

Even when she put her heart into something, it didn't always yield the results she wanted. For her seventh-grade teacher, Mr. Kratzman, she recalls, "I wrote this ambitious epic poem for his class . . . I got this thing back, and it was circled all over with red. He had written, 'Cliché, cliché, cliché,' and gave me a B. I read the poem of the kid next to me who got an A+, and it was terrible, so I stayed after school and said, 'Excuse me, but how come you give an A+ to that when you give me a B?' He said, 'Because that's as good as he's ever going to write. You can write much better than this. You tell me more interesting things when you tell me what you did over the weekend. By the way, how many times *did* you see *Black Beauty*?'" (12)

That same teacher, Arthur Kratzman, gave her some creative advice that always stuck with her. After favorably commenting on one of her drawings displayed at a PTA meeting, he said to her, "If you can paint with a brush, you can paint with words." (1)

In the mid-1950s, the world—particularly the United States and Canada—was changing culturally. On November 7, 1955, Joni turned twelve, an impressionable age. Until this point in time, popular music had been dominated by adult crooners and the remnants of the big band era. Suddenly North American teenagers were moving into the spotlight with their own music and their own style.

In 1955 the film *Rebel without a Cause* was released. It starred James Dean and Natalie Wood and was all about the growing subculture of North American teenagers. A film about teenagers driving hot cars and motorcycles, it turned James Dean into something previously unheard of in pop culture: a teen idol. This movie left a huge impression on Joni Mitchell and she later used some footage from it in her 1980 *Shadows and Light* concert video and album.

Right after filming his final scenes in the movie *Giant* in September 1955, James Dean was killed in a horrible car accident in California and instantly went from teen idol to immortalized teen icon.

And, the next year—1956—was even more crucial to the teenage generation. A new form of music—called rock & roll—became a huge mass-culturizing force. That was the year Elvis Presley burst onto the music scene. In 1956, Elvis Presley placed hit after hit on the *Billboard* magazine singles chart—nine of them in all. He held the number 1 position on the singles chart twenty-six weeks that year. As he became the biggest teenage singing idol in history, the rock & roll era was officially under way. Suddenly nothing that came before it, and nothing that came after it, would ever be the same.

Even in Saskatoon, Saskatchewan, teenage dances were all the rage. Frank Sinatra's style of music became something your parents might listen to on the radio. "Pop music was something else in that time," Joni recalls. "We're talking about the Fifties now. When I was thirteen, *The Hit Parade* [radio show] was one hour a day—four o'clock to five o'clock. On the weekends they'd do the Top Twenty. But the rest of the radio was Mantovani, country and western, a lot of radio journalism. Mostly country and western, which I wasn't crazy about. To me it was simplistic. Even as a child I liked more complex melody." (9)

She claims, "In my teens I loved to dance. That was my thing. I instigated a Wednesday night dance 'cause I could hardly make it to the weekends. For dancing I loved Chuck Berry. Ray Charles. 'What'd I Say.' I liked Elvis Presley. I liked the Everly Brothers." (9)

According to Graham Nash, "You know, Joni was always a rebel. She told me she used to sneak out to the wrong side of town for rock & roll dance contests. She really lived to dance. It's almost as if she was making up for lost time." (3)

During her postpolio years, she had one passion: "Rock & roll dancing." She further explains, "I had an added advantage that I was a night owl and that radio stations shut down about midnight locally and there was a strong broadcast from a station in Texas that would wave in and out, and you could hear songs that were coming that wouldn't be there for four months, so you almost had a crystal ball and you could predict the hits in the future in a miraculous way." (10)

These weren't just chaperoned high school dances that she attended at the time. Often her lust to dance and party all night took her to the rougher sides of Saskatoon. "I gravitated to the best dance halls from the age of 12 to the age of 16," she recalls. "Not that I liked beer, but we would go from time to time to the bootleggers . . . and the bootleggers were also brothels. Like any young black trumpet player in the South, like John Handy or any New Orleans musician who knew he was a musician at an early age, somehow I was drawn to where the music was best, and it's always in the roughest areas. And yet, the street had heart then, and a child, a baby, a clean-looking baby was not molested. If anything, they were very protective. First of all, they'd say, 'Get out of here,' or if I insisted on remaining, they'd make sure that someone saw me safely to the bus." (10)

Her experiences during this era enriched her view of the world. Even in potentially dangerous settings, she found herself protected—as though by guardian angels. "So, even the toughest areas," she recalls, "which I went to for the music and the booze or whatever, or to see people drinking, not necessarily because I cared to drink myself, to see life, were very protective and generous to me. My street experience was not anything like what the streets are now, with cocaine and white slavery and so on. But I [saw] a lot of life and [had] a lot of difficulty." (10)

In this way, she went from being a shy introvert into a fully developed party girl. "When I was a kid, I was a real 'good-time Charlie,'" she laughs. "As a matter of fact, *that* was my nickname." (14)

Meanwhile, her love of rock & roll and the revitalized energy that she received from dancing the nights away interpreted into greater creativity in school. For one of her classes, Joni composed an epic poem about the perils of show business. It was based on an article she had read in one of the gossipy fan magazines of the day. Joni explains, "I wrote a poem when I was 16. Having written this poem, why am I in this business? But we had to write a poem, right? It was supposed to be blank verse. So I was getting my hair done for some kind of prom deal, because that's the only time we'd go to the beauty parlor in those days. And I was sitting under the dryer, and they had stacks of movie star magazines. The reigning deities—the teen idols at that time—were Sandra Dee and Bobby Darin, who were newly married. So the tabloids were full of misadventures of their marriage. And I just felt so bad for them. And I remember thinking to myself, 'If somebody wrote this about me in the school paper, I would just die.' So, that's what triggered this poem that had to be turned in for assignment. It was called 'The Fishbowl.'" (7)

The confidence that she began to feel from her writing sparked her creativity more. According to her, "There's this tendency to court the new—people are just so afraid not to be hip. I used to start fads as a kid, wearing my father's tie to school, things like that, and I even had a column called 'Fads and Fashions' in the high school paper. I was hip to the hip at sixteen!" (15)

Being a sickly child who was then struck by polio might have broken other people. Instead of forcing her into a shell of depression, it made her want to live her life in an even more exciting fashion. "I was always a star," Mitchell remembers. "I'm not one of those kids that had a bad high school life. I was always invited to the [parties of the] pretty kids—the doors were opened to the things that most people come to this business wanting. But I always chose my friends. My mother said, 'You have the weirdest friends,' but I chose them with my heart." (7)

Art and music became her passion. She began listening to an even wider variety of music, not only rock & roll but jazz as well. Her love of drawing and painting was enhanced by her growing musical taste. "In high school, I was kind of like the school artist," says Joni. "I did backdrops for school plays, I was always involved in illustrating the yearbooks. I designed a UNICEF Christmas card for a guy who was like the school leader, the senior watchman. He reimbursed me with a Miles Davis album. Friends of mine who were older than me, and in college, began talking about Lambert, Hendricks and Ross as the hottest new sound in jazz. Their record flipped me out, but it was already out of print. I had to finally buy it off somebody and pay a lot, maybe fifteen dollars, which was unheard of at that time. But you couldn't get the record anywhere. Lambert, Hendricks and Ross were my Beatles. In high school, theirs was the record I wore thin, the one I knew all the words to." (16)

The trio composed of Dave Lambert, Jon Hendricks, and Annie Ross was all the rage during this era. Their fast-paced jazz singing and harmonizing on songs like "Cloudburst" and "Sermonette" were so influential to young Joni that she later recorded their songs "Twisted" and "Centerpiece" on two of her biggest-selling albums.

She also became a fan of jazz innovator Miles Davis. When asked what her favorite Miles Davis albums were, Joni replies, "*Sketches of Spain*. I must admit that it was much later than Miles really grabbed my attention, and *Nefertiti* and *In a Silent Way* became my all-time records in just any field of music. They were my private music. Somehow or other I kept that quite separate from my own music. I never thought of making that kind of music. I only thought of it as something sacred and unattainable." (17)

In the early 1960s, a whole new style of music grew out of the rock & roll era—folk music. People would gather and sing songs to the sound of the acoustic guitar. This became a further outlet for her musically. As she explains it, "There came to my home-town at college—I was still in high school—a different kind of party where people sat around and sang. It was a different way of partying than I was used to, which was dancing and drinking beer, and I kind of took to it. But a lot of the time there was no accompanist, no one seemed to play an instrument. So I got it in my mind that I wanted to learn to play guitar. Well, I borrowed a guitar from somebody, but the action was incredibly high. It was an old orchestral F-hole rhythm guitar, basically, and I couldn't press the strings down. My fingers were bleeding. It was intolerable." (10)

All of a sudden, Joni decided that she wanted a guitar of her own. Her mom and dad were less than supportive to her wishes for a new musical instrument. Reminisces Mitchell, "My parents—my mother in particular—said, 'Oh if we buy you a guitar, you'll just abandon it. You never follow anything up. It'll be just like the piano.' So I started saving up, but I couldn't save up fast enough. Guitars were fairly expensive. But I managed to scrape up $36 to buy myself a baritone ukulele. That's what I stayed on. About six months later, I was playing, accompanying some kind of bawdy drinking songs at a wiener roast, which was our teenage form of entertainment—go out in the bush with some beer and sit around a campfire and sing songs—when I was overheard by some—they seemed like old people, but they were young people, really. They were like, in their early 20s, and they worked for a television station in Prince Albert, Saskatchewan, and they thought I was really good. So they took off this moose hunting program—*Field and Stream* type of show which came on late in the evening—and they stuck me on. I'd be 18 at the time and playing this baritone ukulele for about an hour long." (10)

She had shifted from being a girl dancing with wild abandonment, to Elvis Presley and Chuck Berry records, to wanting to be a ukulele-playing singer of sad and often maudlin songs. As she remembers her transformation, Joni claims, "In the meantime, my friends, who knew me as a rock & roll dancer and kind of an *enjoyer,* found this change kind of hard to relate to, 'cause the songs at that time [were] folk songs and English ballads, and you know, women's English ballads are always 'the cruel mother,' and there's a lot of sorrow in them. But they had beautiful melodies, that was the thing, and I always loved melody. Melody is generally melancholy and sad, and the text that accompanies it must be the same." (10)

Looking back on her high school days, she explains, "I'm not sure I have a clear picture of myself. My identity, since it wasn't through the grade system, was that I was a good dancer and an artist. And also, I was very well dressed. I made a lot of my own clothes. I worked in ladies' wear and I modeled. I had access to sample clothes that were too fashionable for our community, and I could buy them cheaply. I would go hang out on the streets dressed to the 'T,' even in hat and gloves. I hung out downtown with Ukrainians and the Indians; they were more emotionally honest and they were better dancers. When I went back to my own neighborhood, I found that I had a provocative image. They thought I was loose because I always liked rowdies. I thought I was loose because I always liked rowdies. I thought the way the kids dance at my school was kind of, you know, funny. I remember a recurring statement on my report card—'Joan does not relate well.' I know that I was aloof. Perhaps some people thought that I was a snob." (9)

Through it all, she was simply trying to figure out who she was. "I didn't want people to think I was an egghead, so I became an anti-intellectual," she proclaims. (15)

In her high school yearbook, under her name—Joan Anderson—is her photo with an inscription that reads, "'You go to my head and you linger like a haunting refrain.' Not only does Joan's beauty leave one in a daze but also in Bowman her artistic talent is unequaled." (18)

Although she was clearly talented in both art and music, during her senior year in high school her grades in her other classes suffered. She had lost all interest in studying and homework. "I was a bad student. I finally flunked out in the twelfth grade. I went back after [the missed graduation] and picked up the subjects that I lost. I do have my high-school diploma—I figured I needed that much, just in case. College was not too interesting to me. The way I saw the educational system from an early age was that it taught you what to think, not how to think. There was no liberty, really, for free thinking. You were being trained to fit into a society where free thinking was a nuisance. I liked some of my teachers very much, but I had no interest in their subjects. So I would appease them—I think they perceived that I was not a dummy, although my report card didn't look like it. I would line the math room with ink drawings and portraits of the mathematicians. I did a tree of life for my biology teacher. I was always staying late at the school, down on my knees painting something." (9)

When she flunked out of school during her senior year, she did so without remorse and without guilt. What need did she have for geometry or history? She was not intending to be an intellectual. Roberta Joan Anderson had her sights on other goals: she was going to be a graphic artist. Vincent van Gogh and Pablo Picasso didn't need a high school diploma to prove they were painters or to be acknowledged as artistic geniuses. And neither did she.

2

Child with a Child: Pretending

Joni's life over the next two years took several unexpected turns as she struggled to find herself as an adult and searched for a way to express herself as an artist. First she needed to find a career goal and stay on target. For a while she seemed destined to make commercial art her career. She certainly had the artistic talent to become a successful commercial artist, but could she fit into a somewhat regimented field?

In her later life, her friends understood Joni's frustration and her need to find her own creative destiny. She told them her tales of artistic angst. According to Graham Nash, "Joni had this 'other worldly' view of what was possible in her life, and that she was definitely going to go out there and find it." (3)

Indeed she was on the right path in 1963 when—at the age of nineteen—she enrolled at the Alberta College of Art in Calgary. One of her main possessions at that time was a $36 baritone ukulele, which she had bought with some of the money that she made modeling dresses.

The rock & roll dancing "goodtime Charlie" incarnation of teenage Roberta Joan Anderson had evolved into a more maudlin, introspective folk singer persona.

Commenting on her own metamorphosis, she reveals, "So, this kind of joyous, fun-loving creature became this earnest character. This transformation had taken place, and I think a lot of people had a hard time with that transition. I know some of my best dance buddies would say, 'Put that thing down. We're gonna drag you onto the dance floor.' 'No, no, no,' I was clinging to it [the ukulele] in the corner, saying, 'Leave me alone.' I introverted into this intimate relationship with this stringed instrument." (10)

For a while, she was living out the embodiment of her dreams. To make extra money, Joni modeled in local clothing stores. "There were no fashion shows in the region. But I worked in dress shops in Saskatoon, and traveling salesmen came through town and hired 'wholesale models' locally, who were basically quick-change artists exhibiting clothes for retail buyers. You wore a black slip and changed behind a screen because you were a young woman working in a hotel room with a traveler, and you had to be a size eight. But the pay was pretty good, and that's how I got the money to go to art school." (1)

It wasn't long before Joni became disillusioned with art school. And she was uncertain about her role in life. Neither the conservative route with sororities and parties nor the teenage hoodlum route appealed to her. She wasn't sure where she belonged. "There came a split when I rejected sororities and that whole thing. I didn't go for that. But there also came a stage when my friends who were 'juvenile delinquents' suddenly became 'criminals.' They could go into very dull jobs or they could go into crime. Crime is very romantic in your youth. I suddenly thought, 'Here's where the romance ends. I don't see myself in jail.'" (9)

She saved some of the money she earned modeling dresses and bought her first guitar. She was primarily self-taught and eventually purchased instruction books to assist her in learning how to play the instrument properly. "When I was learning to play guitar, I got Pete Seeger's *How to Play Folk-Style Guitar*. I went straight to the Cotten picking. Your thumb went from the sixth string, fifth string, sixth string, fifth string . . . I couldn't do that, so I ended up playing mostly the sixth string but banging it into the fifth string. So Elizabeth Cotten definitely is an influence; it's me not being able to play like her. If I could have I would have, but good thing I couldn't because it came out original." (18)

She quickly developed her own unique way of guitar playing. She tuned her instrument differently than the standard players did. "In the beginning, I built the repertoire of the open major tunings that the old black blues guys came up with. It was only three or four. The simplest one is D modal [D A D G B D]; Neil Young uses that a lot. And then open G [D G D G B D], with the fifth string removed, which is all Keith Richards plays in. And open D [D A D F# A D]. Then going between them I started to get more 'modern' chords, for lack of a better word," she explains. (18)

For a while, Joni balanced her interests in painting and singing. "All my life I was waiting to study painting," she recalls. "When I got there, the teaching was as disappointing as the piano was. If you had any hand-eye control, and if you already knew how to render tonality and you'd made these simple observations, there was almost a prejudice levied against you, and it was considered that you should go into commercial art because, basically, the age of the camera had come, and Greenberg was king, and de Kooning, all the profs were pouring paint down inclined planes and they were basically resentful or prejudiced against someone who had drawing ability. I would say, out of 150 new students, there were only about four of us that had that. A lot of them had entered into art school, I think, for the lifestyle or the idea of becoming an artist, and the profs seemed to figure that they were better suited knowing nothing to be implanted with their love of abstract painting." (10)

Although she loved art and painting, she hated the regimentation in art school.

Quite by a twist of fate her mode of artistic expression shifted. While studying art in Alberta, she became very immersed in the budding folk music scene. Speaking of the "art versus music" crossroads she was at during this era, Joni recalls, "Well, I developed a prejudice towards it and a kind of rebellion, and I took to playing in the coffeehouses north of there in a city called Edmonton and one in Calgary called The Depression, and the two interests began to kind of conflict." (10)

Joni claims that her singing style came from parroting recordings by a pair of folksinging women who were influential in her life and her career. "You know, in the beginning I mimicked Joan Baez and Judy Collins. And, I thought of myself merely as a competent mimic. But, the idea of being a recording artist was not anywhere in my mind. Although as a painter I had the need to innovate. As a musician, it was just a hobby. So, I didn't think I had the gift to take it any further than that." (3)

From the very start, the music critics loved her. In a Calgary newspaper, Joni received her first mention in the press. In a piece entitled "Folk Singing Art Student," the aspiring singer was described as "Joni Anderson, a first year student at the Alberta College of Art, is relatively new in the folk music circuit. Joni Anderson is from Saskatoon where she had her start in folksinging. This resulted from her association with a folk singing group." (3)

Citing the drawbacks of pursuing an art career in Canada, Joni claimed, "The lack of classical training at the school, and also the fact that, in Canada, art was looked on more as a vocation than an important and great thing that it is. Truth and beauty? No, no, they viewed it more as a trade. It was stuck in between auto mechanics and cafeteria cooks in training." (10)

Consequently she abandoned her goal of becoming a commercial artist and firmly shifted her focus to folksinging.

Her flight from the Alberta School of Art started as a temporary journey east. She figured that this was just the kind of creative sojourn that she needed. In 1964, she boarded a train for Toronto. The event that drove her to make this journey was the Mariposa Folk Festival. Joni was determined to see a singer she was fascinated with, Buffy Sainte-Marie. While she rode the Ontario-bound train, she penned the first song of her long and prolific writing career: "Day after Day."

When she arrived in Toronto, she saw a world of opportunity for her singing, songwriting, and performing career. "I allowed my disappointment in the education offered me, to lead me to the East Coast where there were 17 thriving coffeehouses in Toronto." (10)

In the heart of downtown Toronto, the Yorkville district, there was a lively and vital folk music singing scene. Such performers as Tom Rush, Odetta, and Eric Andersen were among the up-and-coming stars who were seen in the Yorkville coffeehouses during this era. Along Yongue Street there was also a jazz scene, attracting Charles Mingus, Oscar Peterson, and Cannonball Adderly.

However, Toronto didn't spell instant success. Joni recalls, "When I got there, it cost $160 to get into the [musician's] union, which was a fortune for me, just an impossible goal. And there wasn't much 'scab' [nonunion] work around, and coffeehouse doors slammed in my face, and it was pretty insulting. There were some dues [to be paid] in that town." (10)

She took side jobs to supplement her income. "So I worked in women's wear, in a department store. I could barely make ends meet . . . And then I finally found a scab club in Toronto that allowed me to play. I played for a couple of months." (16)

Then, suddenly and in an unplanned fashion, her entire focus dramatically changed. "I was late to lose my virginity," she recalls. "I was 20, and it was a crush with a fellow painter, and I got pregnant immediately. To be pregnant and unmarried in 1964 was like you killed somebody." (1)

Joni decided to hide her pregnancy from her mom and dad, and being hundreds of miles away in Toronto helped her accomplish this goal. "The main thing was to protect my parents from the scandal. You had to. What [unwed pregnant] girls did: either you got married to cover it up or you went into a home. Abortion was unheard of. So, I entered onto the 'bad girls' trail, you know, which was a trail of shame and scandal. And, I had to kind of hide myself away." (3)

On February 19, 1965, Joni gave birth to a daughter she named "Kelly Dale Anderson." She nicknamed the baby "Kelly Green." But the happy mother–child relationship that should have happened at this point, did not. "I [became] an unwed mother, and all of the travail and the white-trash prejudice that accompanied that," she claims. (10)

The biggest challenge she faced was a financial one. "I kept trying to find some kind of circumstance where I could stay with her." (19) If she was going to continue to keep Kelly with her, she had to earn a living. She was barely making ends meet, and she had to go back to work. "Two weeks after I gave birth to my daughter, I again went looking for work, because I had to put her into a foster home—and I was penniless at the time." (3)

Joni needed a quick influx of money and/or a man to support her and Kelly. She met the man she would marry at one of the nonunion clubs in town, the Penny Farthing. He was singing his version of Bob Dylan's "Mr. Tambourine Man." She walked up to him after his set, and they found that they had a lot in common. As she explains it, "In 1965, I was playing in the cellar where they kept the Canadian talent and where the imported American talent played upstairs. And, I met a folk singer named Chuck Mitchell. I was at an indecisive time in my life, and he was a strong force." (10)

According to her, "We quickly became friends, and he said that he could get me work in the States. So, with that optimism, I went and took a few gigs down there . . . my child was in the foster home, and he said he would marry me. I was emotionally weak, with a lot of things pulling me in all sorts of unattractive directions. And this was a strong pull in a certain direction, and somewhat of a solution. So, we married each other, for all the wrong reasons." (3)

Joni's wedding day was an event she would never forget. "We had no money," she explains. "I made my wedding dress, and I made the bridesmaids' dresses. One of my bridesmaids was his sister Celia, who I barely knew. I barely knew *any* of these people." (3)

Joni and Chuck were married in an outdoor ceremony in his parents' backyard in Rochester, Michigan, in June 1965, four months after Kelly's birth. The photos from the wedding depict Joni as a willowy bride with long blond hair. The guests sat in rented chairs arranged under a shady tree on a warm Michigan afternoon. Joni sat under the trees with her acoustic guitar and entertained the assembled wedding guests with one of her own songs. From the outside it seemed idyllic and destined to be true love. She smiled brightly, hoping that this marriage would spell happier days ahead for her, her daughter Kelly, and her new husband. But the smiles and congratulatory bouquets barely masked the sadness that lay beneath the emotional surface of Joni's fragile world.

In spite of the wonderful-looking wedding photos, what was going on in Joni's mind that day was something totally different. "When I walked down the aisle, brandishing my daisies, [I was] thinking, 'I can get out of this.'" She instinctively knew that the dreamy wedding under the shady trees—with its pristine white tablecloths and the rented folding chairs—presented a false picture of what was to be. According to Joni, "The moment we were married, he intimated strongly that he had no interest in raising another man's child—so I was trapped." (3)

Joni and Chuck promptly resumed their aspiring folksinging careers. It was in the Detroit coffeehouses that the young singer first billed herself as Joni Mitchell. "Chuck insisted that we be a [singing] duo. But, we were totally unsuited to be a duo. He made more money with me than he did without me. And, he held the purse strings—completely. Because we were young and attractive, we were remade into kind of Detroit's golden couple. So, we were living a lie, and I don't like to live a lie. We tried to make the best of moments, and I looked relatively happy. But, I felt like I had been betrayed. It was very difficult for me, so I began to write. I think I started writing just to develop my own private world. Also, because I was disturbed." (3)

At this point in her career, was Joni expecting the success she ultimately achieved? According to her, "I never thought that far ahead. I never expected me to have this degree of success," she later claimed. "It was a hobby that mushroomed. I was grateful to make one record. All I knew was, whatever it was that I felt was the weak link in the previous project gave me my inspiration for the next one. I wrote poetry and I painted all my life. I always wanted to play music and dabbled with it, but I never thought of putting them all together. It never occurred to me. It wasn't until Dylan began to write poetic songs that it occurred to me you could actually sing those poems." (9)

"It was not a marriage made in heaven. He was relatively well educated. He was in contempt of my lack of education and also my illiteracy. I did all my book reviews [in school] from Classic Comic Books, and I had a kind of contempt for what I called pseudo-intellectuals, and in a way I was right. I mean, I was developing as an original, unschooled thinker, and I had the gift of the blarney." (10)

"We still scrambled for work. As a couple, I think we were making fifteen dollars a night," Joni recalls of their financial situation. (16) Finally Joni came to the realization that she was ill prepared to be a mother at this time. And furthermore, Chuck wasn't interested in raising the child with her. Finally she came to a heartbreaking conclusion: she would allow Kelly to be adopted. According to her, "It says in the notes, on the adoptive papers, 'Mother had very difficult time signing this.' A piece of me was missing. Right after that of course I began to write . . . It left a hole in me." (20)

During this era, Joni met several lifelong friends. She met singer-songwriter Neil Young for the first time in the winter of 1965. As she recalls, "I was married to Chuck Mitchell at the time. We came to Winnipeg, playing this Fourth Dimension [folk] circuit. We were there over Christmas. I remember putting up this

Christmas tree in our hotel room. Neil, you know, was this rock & roller who was coming around to folk music through Bob Dylan. Of course. Anyway, Neil came out to the club, and we liked him immediately. He was the same way he is now—this offhanded, dry wit. And you know what his ambition was at the time? He wanted a hearse, and a chicken farm. And when you think of it, what he's done with his dream is not that far off. He just added a few buffalo. And a fleet of antique cars. He's always been pretty true to his vision." (9)

It was becoming known among their circle of friends that Joni and Chuck Mitchell were running something of a creative commune in their apartment. There would be a revolving door of folk singers "crashing" at the Mitchells' Motor City pad. Recalls Joni, "In Detroit, everybody was kind of scuffling, and we had a big apartment, Chuck and I, so we billeted a lot of artists. Eric Andersen stayed there, and Tom Rush stayed there. It was a fifth floor walk-up in the black district, basically, it was two white blocks, Wayne [State University] campus housing. The rent was really cheap, and we had three or four bedrooms in this old place. So, artists stayed with us frequently. I was just beginning to write, and Tom, I think, first carried off 'Urge for Going.' So, he played that around, and the next time he came to play the club The Chessman, he said, 'You got anything else?' and I played him some songs. It was usually the one that I thought was too feminine, a little too light for a man to sing, that I withheld—'Any more?' 'Well, yes, this one, but it's not right for you'—'The Circle Game' or something. 'That's the one I want!' So, he'd cart that off, and in that way the songs became known in places that I hadn't gone. There were no records." (10) In this way, Joni's songs became well known before anyone knew who she was.

Meanwhile, she and Chuck had their distinct differences. According to her, "He liked Cape Cod, English furniture and was more cultured. I was just a rampant adolescent." (12)

Working in the Detroit coffeehouses, they were billed as the singing duo: Joni and Chuck Mitchell. Through their opening act gigs, they met several of the headlining acts who came through the Motor City.

In very short time, Joni and Chuck had become chummy with the likes of folk stars Eric Andersen, Ramblin' Jack Elliott, and Tom Rush. Joni recalled that she learned a lot while hanging out with this elite group. "Eric started teaching me open tunings, an open G, a drop D. For some reason, once I got the open tunings I began to get the harmonic sophistication that my musical fountain inside was excited by. Once I got some interesting chords to play with, my writing began to come," she reveals. (16)

Looking back on this 1966–1967 era, Joni claims that a deep chasm lay between her and Chuck. She knew it was a bad union taking a turn for the worse. As she recalls, "I was anti-intellectual to the max. Basically, I liked to dance and paint and that was about it. As far as serious discussions went, I found them boring. To see teenagers sitting around trying to solve the problems of the world, I figured—all things considered—I'd rather be dancing. My husband was different. He had an education, a degree in literature. Chuck always said that you couldn't write unless you read. He considered me an illiterate, and he didn't give me a great deal of encouragement regarding my writing. But Tom Rush did." (16)

Thanks to the fact that Tom Rush and Eric Andersen encouraged her and told her how much they loved her songs, she began to spread her own creative wings. As her songwriting grew stronger and her reputation spread, her songs showed up in unexpected places.

At a March 1967 concert, Joni proudly introduced her song "Urge for Going" by explaining, "It's currently on the Country Hit Parade. However, I don't think it really is a country song, if you can classify songs. As a matter of fact, it's Number 13 with a 'Bullet.' That means it's moving up rapidly. It's by a fellow named George Hamilton IV. The song is [written] by me, but he does it, with Chet Atkins and a whole Nashville chorus and a Carter Family–type and all sort of people and a recitation and electric rock & roll mandolin. But originally the song went like this . . . " (10) "Urge for Going" by Hamilton became a number 7 hit on the country chart in *Billboard*.

On their 1967 *So Much for Dreaming* album, the folk duo Ian and Sylvia recorded their version of "The Circle Game" on Vanguard Records. In June of that year, Buffy Sainte-Marie included Mitchell's songs "Song to a Seagull" and "The Circle Game" on her *Fire and Fleet and Candlelight* album, also on Vanguard. The folk/rock group Fairport Convention recorded its own version of "I Don't Know Where I Stand" and "Chelsea Morning" on their debut album.

While Joni's songs were starting to make her famous, Chuck Mitchell was less than supportive. Chuck considered Joni his inferior and discouraged her efforts. According to her, "I had no ambition to make a career of it at all. Of course, once I began to write my own songs, I was slightly ambitious for them. I was a stage door mother to them. I wanted to display them. I thought that this was a superior work to selling women's wear, which was all I was really trained for. I had a grade 12 education. So, waitressing, hairdressing, that was about all [I was qualified to do]. This was slightly more lucrative and a lot more fun at the club level." (10)

The biggest contribution Chuck Mitchell made to Joni's career was to help her set up her own music publishing company to sublicense recording rights, which paid her royalties for having her songs appear on other people's albums and for her songs being played on the radio.

According to Joni, "The one thing I had was my own publishing company. Chuck and I set up two publishing companies. That was at his instigation. That was very insightful." (10) She named her company Siquomb Publishing. It stood for "She Is Queen Undisputedly Of Mind Beauty."

Chuck also discounted Joni's wealth of life experiences. "I think at 21 I was quite old. 'Both Sides Now' is like an old person reflecting back on their life. My live had been very hard. I had gone through a lot of life. When . . . I wrote 'Both Sides Now,' he said to me, 'Oh, what do you know about life?' I'd gone through a lot of disease and personal pain. Even as a child. I'd had three bouts of death. I was not unaware of my mortality. But somehow, still, I was very young for my age, in spite of my experience," she proclaims. (10)

Joni knew that she didn't need Chuck onstage or as a songwriter. "We never were a full-fledged duo. I'm a bad learner, see. I bypassed the educational system. I learn by a process more like osmosis. It's by inspiration and desire. So when we would try to work up songs together, we would bang into differences of opinion. Some people say, 'Oh Joan, that's just because you're lazy.' But in a way, more than laziness, it's a kind of block that runs all through my rebellious personality. If someone tries to teach me a part that I don't find particularly interesting, it won't stick. I'll end up doing what I wanted to do in the first place, and then they're annoyed. We had a difference of opinion in material. It was more like two people on-stage at the same time, sometimes singing to-gether. We had a difficult time." (9)

Chuck Mitchell admitted, "She always had a strong visceral sense of what to do. She knew she was beginning to happen and needed out." (21)

Some of Joni's finest, best-crafted songs were written years be-fore she entered a recording studio. There are videotapes of her performing several of her greatest compositions on local television shows. "Both Sides Now" and "The Circle Game" both dated back to 1967.

According to Joni, "'Both Sides Now' was one of the first songs. I was meditating on fantasy and reality. Childlike optimism and adult reality. This was the work of my childhood's end." (3)

Chuck Mitchell claimed, "She was into her Magic Princess trip. Her first hits were for people who were frustrated, unhappy and also living in a fantasy world." (21)

The fantasy world she was creating in her songs was to escape from what was going on in her personal life. She knew she had to get away from Chuck Mitchell. Their marriage had been a big mis-take from the very beginning. His offer of marriage had simply been a rope thrown to a drowning woman. Well, she was no longer feeling either desperate or drowning. Finally it was time for her to strike out on her own. First she ended the singing duo.

"As my work began to mature," she explains, "I began to long for my own growth. I felt that I couldn't grow with Chuck, that we would never grow together, that I had to separate myself from the duo, that I had to become an individual in order to grow." (3)

With that, she played her first dates as a solo act in Detroit. One critic at the time wrote of Joni, "She is a beautiful woman. Her voice and her acoustic guitar are free, pure instruments in them-selves; there is additional beauty in the way she uses them to con-vey such a full range of emotions. But if she knew only three chords, her performance would be justified by her songs alone. As a songwriter, she plays yang to Bob Dylan's yin, equaling him in richness and profusion of imagery and surpassing him in concise-ness and direction." (22)

Since she was in the mood to make changes, why not go all the way? "As soon as the duo dissolved, the marriage dissolved," she recalls. (3)

Knowing when to leave is helpful at parties—and when it comes to ending a marriage. According to Joni, "I was in the middle of a poker game some place in Michigan late in the evening, and I turned to a stranger, basically, next to me, and I said, 'I'm leaving my husband tonight. Will you help me?' We rented a U-Haul truck. We drove back to Detroit. I had polio, and a lot of muscles in my back are deteriorated. So, you can imagine the will. I separated what I considered was a fair split, 50 percent of the furniture, and the stranger and I hauled it on our own backs down a fifth floor walk-up in the middle of the night, and I moved out." (10)

She left Chuck half of the furniture and his individual belongings, and she never looked back. The only part he played in her life from that point onward was as subject matter for her songwriting.

With her baby in a foster family and her marriage from Chuck dissolved, it was time for Joni to begin to concentrate on finding herself and defining her own creative fire. New York City represented a whole new creative phase in her solo career. She left Detroit and headed to the place in which the folk music scene was centered: Greenwich Village.

3

The Circle Game

In 1967 New York City was a whole new oyster for Joni, just waiting to be cracked. Singing her deeply personal, highly intellectual and emotional songs, accompanying herself on acoustic guitar, at first it seemed like an unlikely long shot. When she arrived in Manhattan, she began her uphill struggle of finding work.

She moved to the Big Apple and took a tiny one-bedroom apartment in the Chelsea district of the city. This setting was the inspiration for one of her favorite early compositions, "Chelsea Morning." She recalls of her tiny abode: "I papered the bedroom with rolls of aluminum foil and hung an American flag in the window. It was my Independence Day celebration." (12)

"Chelsea Morning" was one of the first truly joyous songs that Joni composed, reflecting the sense of newness and abandonment that she felt on her own in the big city. Another of her significant compositions to come from this brief New York era was the equally upbeat and jubilant "Night in the City."

Joni had written several new songs about her recent somber life experiences. Especially touching were the ballads "I Had a King" and "Little Green." It is acknowledged that the song "I Had a King" is about Chuck, that his "rusted carriage" in the song refers to his automobile, and that the country he carried her off to for marriage was Detroit.

According to her, "The song 'I Had a King' kind of tells a bit of the aftermath of that. I moved to New York. I moved to West 16th Street, and I set out looking for work in that area." (10) In "I Had a King," she sang of a "king" who married her but could not hold her, emotionally or physically. The only thing that she kept from Chuck Mitchell was his last name.

Another poignant song she wrote during this era was "Little Green," in which she sings about the baby she gave up for adoption, whom she nicknamed Kelly Green. "Little Green" went right for the heartstrings. Joni acknowledged writing this sad and beautiful song from the depth of her emotions. "I had to bottom out," she recalls. "I had lost my child, and I was grieving a tremendous loss. At the same time, I found myself swept in this tremendous popularity. That had a lot to do with my introspection and my deepening." (15)

At first, she recalls, she found New York City an uphill struggle: "I had difficulty initially in finding work in clubs. But I had a kind of a circuit on the Eastern seaboard from Miami to Boston, and a little bit of the Midwest around the Detroit area. New York was difficult without a record. The major clubs were hard to crack until some people started singing my songs. When Buffy and Tom Rush initially began to play [them], then the circuit that they played on opened up to me because they were kind of a herald of the writer of these songs. So, 'Circle Game' and 'Urge for Going,' [Dave] Van Ronk with [his jazz version of] 'Both Sides Now' and 'Chelsea Morning,' all helped to make club work possible for me." (10)

As Joni's songwriting career began to take off, she was amazed by the reactions of her old friends from Saskatoon. "When I first started making all this sensitive music, my old friends back home could not believe it. They didn't know—where did this depressed person come from? Along the way, I had gone through some pretty hard deals and it did introvert me. But it just so happened that my most introverted period coincided with the peak of my success." (14)

Joni found that friends from her past—who had known rock & roll dancing teenage Joni Anderson—were now amazed by her transformation into the singer of sad ballads. This feeling became the basis for the lyrics to her most famous song from this era, "Both Sides Now." In the context of the song, she sings of running

41

into old friends and hearing them tell her that she has "changed." The lyrics of this song struck a chord in everyone who heard it—including Tom Rush and Judy Collins.

Joni's biggest stroke of luck came when Judy recorded her own rendition of Mitchell's "Both Sides Now" on her 1967 album, *Wildflowers*. According to Collins, "The first time I heard 'Both Sides Now' was on the phone in 1967 during the middle of the night. I got a call from Tom Rush, who was very excited. Tom, a great fan of Joni's, had earlier introduced me to her fine song, 'The Circle Game.' 'Joni has a new song, and I want you to hear it. I think you'll love it.' He put Joni on the phone, and she sang 'Both Sides Now.' I immediately fell in love with the song and knew it was classic. I had to sing it." (23)

Recalls Judy's record producer buddy David Anderle, "Judy [Collins] taught me something which I haven't forgotten to this day. If you don't write a song, pick a song that either sounds like you wrote it or it was written for you. Period. At that time she was only just starting to write herself, and she was absolutely impeccable in choosing young songwriters. She talked to me about this young Canadian named Joni Mitchell, and she introduced me to Leonard Cohen." (24)

Judy was very supportive of Joni's budding career, and because of the success of "Both Sides Now," both Collins and Mitchell were thrust into the spotlight. Since Judy was known as a folk singer, that label stuck to Joni as well.

Joni is very sensitive about being referred to as a folk singer. She argues that this label is limiting and defines only a small part of her career. "I would say I was a folk singer from 1963 until '65. '65, when I crossed the border, I began to write. Once I began to write, my vocal style changed. My [Joan] Baez/Judy Collins influence disappeared. Almost immediately when I had my own words to sing, my own voice appeared." (10)

According to her, "I came into the game looking like a folk singer but I was really playing classical art songs. Those weren't like the chords that folkies played. But I looked like a folk singer, like the girl with the guitar. And at that point I had already been a lover of classical music in my preteens, a rock & roll dancer in high school, and I had discovered jazz. So folk music was easy and I needed money for art school just because we were all on student's wages. It wasn't until I was 21 and the desire to compose and create—came back." (11)

One of the most exciting boosts in Joni's career came when she was invited to the legendary Newport Folk Festival in Newport, Rhode Island—by none other than her idol, Judy Collins. However, when the day came, Joni was crestfallen when Collins unceremoniously stood her up.

Mitchell explains, "Judy Collins called me up. She was supposed to take me. Al Kooper had put us in touch and we were supposed to meet and go. Well, Judy stood me up, and she was my hero—it was kinda heartbreaking. I waited and waited and waited and she never came to pick me up to take me to Newport." (16)

Says Joni, "The following day I got a phone call from her in Newport. She said she felt I should be there. I guess she felt bad about standing me [up]." (12)

On the phone, Joni recalls, "She said somebody had sung one of my songs in a workshop. It was a terrible rendition, she said, but people went crazy. Judy really felt I should be at Newport, so she game me instructions on how to get there." (16)

To make up for the slight, on July 16, 1967, Judy invited Joni to participate in an afternoon songwriters' workshop along with Leonard Cohen, Judy Collins, Janis Ian, David Blue, Mike Settle, Tom Paxton, and Eric Andersen. Then, later that day, Judy invited Joni onstage to sing with her amid her set. "I went to the Newport Folk Festival," she recalls of that exciting day. "When I played there, I got a large roar [of recognition from the crowd], and it made me incredibly nervous. That night, my girlfriend Jane, who was road-managing for me, and I went to a party at one of those old mansions. Standing at the gate was like being at Studio 54 in New York. People all over the place who couldn't get in. A guard asked us for credentials. I kind of waxed pensive and backed down. Jane, who was always trying to get me to use my existential edge, said, 'Do you know who she is?' Well, she said my name and these kids standing there at the gate went, 'Aaaah!' and sucked their breath in. My heart started to beat like crazy. I turned and ran in the other direction like some crazed animal. I ran, and I ran, and I ran. I must've run about five blocks before I realized how strange the reaction was." (16)

Due to her performance that day with Judy Collins, everyone

who saw her onstage at the Newport Folk Festival knew her by sight. Since Joni was not used to being recognized as a "famous" figure, she simply freaked out at her first taste of face recognition. According to her, "It pumped me so full of adrenalin, I bolted like a deer. I came back to Janie and said, 'I'm so embarrassed, man, why did I do that?' It's a mystery to me." (9) For Joni, it was a completely unique and bizarre experience.

Meanwhile, back in New York, Joni found that audiences who loved Judy Collins, Tom Rush, and Buffy Sainte-Marie were coming to see her. She recalls, "People were starting to record my songs; I drew [paying audiences] even though I didn't have a record out. I really felt self-sufficient. I was working constantly, every night, and I was trying to build up a bank account because I didn't think it was going to last too long. I thought I was going to have to go back into what I knew, which was women's wear. Become a buyer for a department store. But I was going to go on with it as long as I could." (9)

Once Judy Collins's recording of "Both Sides Now" took off, Joni experienced a sudden surge of popularity. In New York she was slowly establishing a name for herself in the coffeehouses and folk clubs around Bleecker Street. Clubs like Folk City and the Bitter End provided the perfect platform for her to showcase her singing and her songs. Although it was the tail end of the 1960s folk scene, she was able to tap into it. Eventually her first three albums attested to the simplistic and deeply personal material she was singing at the time.

But for the time being, landing a recording contract was still a way off. Joni honed her craft, singing her songs like "The Circle Game," "Both Sides Now," and "Urge for Going." And she was successful, almost instantly. Booking herself on the folk club circuit, she worked forty weeks a year and banked $400 as a cushion if anything went wrong. It wasn't long before she built her own following and booked herself on the folk music circuit around the country.

"I wasn't keen waiting for my big break or anything," she claims. "As a matter of fact, I entered into the game thinking that this was the tail end of the era. The minimum wage at that time was $36 a week, you could barely eat and pay your rent on it, and I was able to make about $300 a week in the clubs. Traveling, of course, ate up some of it. But I had no manager, I had no agent, I had no liens on me. So I viewed it initially as a way to get a little nest egg ahead, and then I would fall back on salesmanship. I would go back into women's wear. My idea of a little bit ahead was, the rent paid and enough for the next month, like, $400 in the bank. That's probably the richest I ever felt, because after I had my recording deal, I had a lot of people on my payroll, and unless you're an arena artist, it's a lot of work, and everything you do is self-promotion." (10)

Although she had started out as a slightly timid performer, she soon came out of her shell on stage. "In some ways I had more confidence," says Joni. "I was outspoken. I enjoyed performing. I loved the compliments I received when I came off-stage. Everything seemed to be proportionate to me. I had $400 in the bank. I thought I was *filthy rich*. I liked the liberty of it all. I liked the idea that I was going to North Carolina, visiting all these mysterious states. I used to tell long, rambling tales on-stage. It was very casual." (9)

As Joni achieved fame in folksinging circles, she encountered the other women in her same league, as well as several legends in the business. From the very start Joni found that not all women in the music business are friendly towards other female singers.

Joni happily reports, "Linda Ronstadt was always kind to me. She makes friendships with women easily. And Bonnie Raitt is a sweetheart and a good old girl." (12)

She was thrilled the first time she met her idol, Joan Baez. However, Joan felt uncomfortable in her presence. "Oh, she was horrible. She was always supercompetitive and threatened by me," says Joni. (14)

According to Mitchell, even in later years, "She managed, whenever possible, to cut my set back one song when we played together." (12)

Joni amusingly points out, "It's funny about women in song. The classic example of misunderstanding was between Laura Nyro and Janis Joplin. Laura invited Janis over to dinner. Unbeknownst to Janis, Laura's favorite food was tuna fish and pink champagne, which she served. Janis got all huffy about it, it was as if Laura had prepared this tacky food in her tacky honor." (12)

The year 1967 was a time of changes in the music industry. The sounds of Motown were a hot hit-making force in the pop and rock world—with the Supremes, Martha and the Vandellas, and the Temptations scoring hit after hit. It was the year that *More of the Monkees* was one of the biggest-selling number 1 albums of the year. In June of that year, the Beatles released *Sgt. Pepper's Lonely Hearts Club Band*, and suddenly the "psychedelic" sound was the hot new thing on the charts. Could the decidedly folk sound of Joni Mitchell find its way to prominence in this atmosphere?

The year she moved to Manhattan, Joni still had no idea where all of this was leading. Could she land a record deal of her own? If so, would it be a one-shot deal, or could she actually turn this into a career? Joni had no clue. There were no guarantees. She recounts, "None of us had any grandiose ideas about the kind of success that we received. In those days it was really a long shot. Especially for a Canadian. I remember my mother talking to a neighbor who asked, 'Where is Joan living?' And she said, 'In New York; she's a musician.' And they went, 'Ohh, you poor woman.' It was hard for them to relate." (9)

By that autumn, Joni Mitchell was making a name for herself in music circles, but she needed help in taking her career to the next level—a manager to take over her concert booking and find her a record deal.

It just so happened that in 1967, a young agent by the name of David Geffen was working at the famed talent agency, William Morris. At the time Geffen was working primarily with comedians on the company's roster. Several people in the business sought out his advice. Among those who contacted Geffen for advice was Joel Dean, the employee of a management company called Chartoff-Winkler. The company's clients at the time included Jackie Mason and the comedy team of Jerry Stiller and Anne Meara.

Dean signed Native American folk singer Buffy Sainte-Marie for management in an attempt to branch out of the comedy field and get involved in the music scene.

When Dean asked Geffen to recommend agents to hire to expand their music division, he suggested a coworker at William Morris: Elliot Roberts. At the time Roberts was languishing in a secretarial job in the William Morris theater department. Born Elliot Rabinowitz in the Bronx, he changed his last name to Roberts to fit into the show business realm. However, his name wasn't the only thing that needed to be smoothed out for success. His brutally honest criticism of his clients sometimes got him into trouble.

In his first month of working at Chartoff-Winkler, Elliot pissed off just about every comedian on the company's roster. However, he had a keen ear for music and hit it off with Buffy Sainte-Marie, who convinced Roberts that he should go down to Greenwich Village to hear a certain folk singer/songwriter she admired. Buffy had fallen in love with one of Joni's compositions, "The Circle Game," which she had recorded.

Joni was set to perform at a small club called the Café Au Go Go as the opening act for headliner Richie Havens and the middle act, a comedian. That evening at the club, twenty-four-year-old Joni took center stage, her long blond hair flowing, and her sensitive songs were presented at their simple and highly effective best. Elliot was knocked out by what he saw that night.

After her set at the Café Au Go Go, Roberts introduced himself to Joni and asked if she had a personal manager. He was shocked find that she did not have representation and was doing her own bookings.

Joni told Roberts, "I'm leaving tomorrow for Detroit." She was on her way out of town on a three-and-a-half week tour, beginning in the college town of Ann Arbor, Michigan.

Elliot told her, "Listen, I'll go with you. I've got nothing to hold me down. I'll meet you at the airport tomorrow, and I'll do the tour with you. After three weeks, let's see how you feel. If you want me to manage you, I will. If you don't I won't." (25)

They met at the airport the next day, and together they flew to Detroit. One of the first things Elliot negotiated for Mitchell was her divorce from Chuck Mitchell, and the reclamation of her music publishing rights she had originally agreed to split with Chuck. This was a major step that cleared paths for her personally and professionally.

On this particular tour of American club dates, Joni found herself heading south to Florida, while Elliot headed to Los Angeles to nail down a recording contract for her. According to him, "We did a month of clubs. Joni went to Coconut Grove and met David Crosby, and in the meantime I went to California alone to meet with Mo Ostin at Warner Brothers [Records] to get Joni a record deal." (26)

Joni recalls, "I was singing in Coconut Grove, Florida, at the Gaslight South. I hadn't made a record yet, but Joe Boyd had taken me to England with the Incredible String Band and I'd done some work in little coffeehouses there. I'd come back all Carnaby Street, with false eyelashes, sequined belts, flashed out." (26)

David Crosby first found fame as a member of the highly successful rock group the Byrds. The group scored a string of hit singles, including "Turn, Turn, Turn" and "My Back Pages." However, he left the Byrds in October 1967 after a dispute with his band mates. In his temporary sabbatical from active recording, he bought a boat called the *Mayan,* where he lived for a long period of his life. According to him, "I got the *Mayan* for $22,500, which I borrowed from Peter Tork, who was flush with Monkees money. It's the best spent money I ever spent. The *Mayan* stands for the good things in my life: health, sanity, and freedom—all the positive values." (26) David intended to go down to Florida, buy a yacht, and sail it back to Los Angeles and live on it.

At the same time that David purchased his dream boat, Mitchell arrived in town to perform at the Gaslight South. Joni recalls, "David had just purchased the boat that he loved. I remember being introduced to him and thinking he reminded me of Yosemite Sam. I used to secretly call him 'Yosemite Sam' in my mind. I don't think I ever called him that to his face, but I might have. He mistakenly thought I wrote the song called 'Dawntreader' for him and [he] was thinking of naming his boat *Dawntreader*. He ended up keeping the original name, *Mayan*, which was good because it had a history already. I guess people identify songs with songs that you write and think you wrote them just for them." (26)

Joni recalls falling for David Crosby's laid-back, big-hearted charm: "He was tanned. He was straight. He was clearing out his boat, and it was going to be the beginning of a new life for him. He was paranoid about his hair, I remember. Having long hair in a short hair society. He had a wonderful sense of humor. Crosby has enthusiasm like no one else. He can make you feel like a million bucks. Or, he can bring you down with the same force." (9)

In addition to being attracted to her sexually, David was "blown away" by Joni's musical talent. Says Mitchell, "David was wonderful company and a great appreciator. When it comes to expressing infectious enthusiasm, he is probably the most capable person I know. His eyes were like star sapphires to me. When he laughed, they seemed to twinkle like no one else's and so I fell into his merry company and we rode bikes around Coconut Grove and the winds were warm and at night we'd go down and listen to the masts clinking down on the pier. It was a lovely period and soon we became romantically involved." (26)

Joni found Crosby refreshingly unpretentious. In that way, he encouraged her to just let loose and be herself, apart from the conventions of fad or fashion of the time. She explains, "I had just come back from London. That was during the Twiggy/Viva era, and I remember I wore a lot of make-up. I think I even had on false eyelashes at the time. And Crosby was from his scrub-faced California culture, so one of his first projects in our relationship was to encourage me to let go of all of this elaborate war paint. It was a great liberation, to get up in the morning and wash your face . . . and not have to do anything else." (9)

Elliot Roberts recalls, "She called up to say she was coming back with David Crosby and David was going to produce her first album. They showed up at my office in New York and David looked as he looks now: he had long hair flowing to his shoulder, he had the trademark mustache. He looked just like he did on his Byrds album covers. He was the first hippie that I met in that era. He didn't talk very much. He seemed slightly paranoid." (26)

While in Los Angeles, Elliot Roberts had successfully negotiated a recording contract for Joni with Reprise Records, a division of Warner Bros. Records. Company executive Mo Ostin personally signed her to the label in December 1967. With that, it was off to the West Coast for Ms. Mitchell.

Joni recalls, "A friend found an old book that said, 'Ask anyone in Hollywood where the craziest people live, and they'll tell you Laurel Canyon. Ask anyone in Laurel Canyon, and they'll tell you Lookout Mountain [Avenue].' So we went to Lookout Mountain. When I moved [there], there were no sidewalks, it smelled of eucalyptus, and the air was filled with the sound of young bands practicing." (27)

Says Roberts: "The three of us went to California to start on Joni's album and stayed at B. Mitchell Reid's house; I slept on the floor in the basement on a mattress and David slept in the big bed with the little woman." (26)

B. Mitchell Reid was known around the Los Angeles area as one of the top rock & roll disc jockeys. He had "drive time" shows on local stations KRLA and KMPC. Living in Laurel Canyon, his house became one of the most popular crash pads in the neighborhood. When friends came to visit, Crosby would have Joni perform so that his musical peers could hear his new girlfriend. Recalls Elliot Roberts, "David invited some people over one day. I remember Cass [Elliot of the Mamas & Papas] was there, John Sebastian, Michelle Phillips, about seven or eight people, all heavy players. David says, 'Joan,' and called Joni out. She was upstairs and came down with her guitar and she played eight or nine of the best songs ever written." (26)

David Crosby was proud of Joni's very personal songs, and her endearing ability to just pick up a guitar and sing them in a room full of strangers. One afternoon Crosby and Mitchell showed up at actor Peter Fonda's house, and David had Joni perform an impromptu acoustic set of her songs for the actor. According to Fonda, "Joni was fabulous. I was just bowled over by this fabulous person with a wonderful voice and a great style. Lovely." (26)

Not only were the performers present impressed, but B. Mitchell Reid was blown away too. Says Roberts, "The next day B. Mitchell Reid talked about it on the radio, how this girl in town named Joni Mitchell that's recording an album and there's nothing he can play now, but whenever this album comes out, it's going to be one of the great albums of all time." (26)

Joni explains, "When it came time to make my record, David did me a solid favor for which I am eternally grateful, because the way you enter the game in this business is usually the way you stay. It takes a lot to break typecasting and the way you come into the game is crucial, which was something I didn't realize at the time. In retrospect, I didn't realize the importance of it. David put me into the game at a certain level and helped me keep control of my work, which I do to this day. In those days I resembled a folk singer to the untrained ear and David knew that there was only one record company that was even interested in someone who resembled a folk singer. What David and Elliot did was make me look like the 'New Movement.' The record company was going to 'folk rock' me up and David thought that would be a tragedy, that my music should be recorded the way I wrote it. He appreciated it the way it was and since he had been in the premier folk rock group [the Byrds], he could go to the record company with some authority and say, 'I'm going to produce her' and the trick was that he was not going to 'produce' me at all! The way David put it, he'd produce me minimally." (26)

John Haeny, the recording engineer for Elektra Records, was one of the many cross-pollinating characters who lived in Laurel Canyon during this highly creative era. He lived on Ridpath Road at the time. An incredible who's who list of characters were in and out of the area, many of them contributing to each other's albums in one way or another. Haeny was personally responsible for introducing several of them to each other. He also, secretly, and suddenly, became involved in the creation of the *Joni Mitchell* debut album.

According to Haeny, "Also at the Ridpath house I introduced Judy [Collins] to Stephen Stills, and that resulted in their romance, and their romance resulted in Stephen writing 'Suite: Judy Blue Eyes' [for the *Crosby, Stills, and Nash* album]. Carole King was in and out of Ridpath—it was a dog owned by Carole and [her husband] Gerry Goffin that sired my dog Niki's first litter of puppies. Neil Young was around. I was at some friend's house with David Crosby—we were all in a pack, you know, all buddies then—and somebody had brought a tape of a young girl that nobody knew much about, except Judy had discovered her as a songwriter, and it was Joni Mitchell. Joni was living on the next road up from Kirkwood. David was producing her first album. The people who recorded it were basically incompetent, and the tapes were a mess. David was having serious problems with the mix. I was exclusive to Elektra, but David came to me and asked would I sneak out and remix. We did it in the dead of the night in a little studio at Sunset Sound. I didn't have a written contract with Jac [Holtzman of Elektra Records], but it was a violation. Years later Jac told me he had always known I did it. There wasn't much going on that Jac didn't know about: he was a fox. He let it go because he knew Joni was important." (24)

Newly located in Laurel Canyon, Joni found herself in a hotbed of musical activity. The whole canyon was inhabited by rock & roll royalty. She was surrounded by the famous, the not so famous, and the wannabe famous. It was in this creative communal atmosphere that Joni began recording her debut album.

4

Song to a Seagull

Finally Joni began to share her songwriting and her distinctive singing with a wider audience via her recorded albums. She was, and is, a confessional writer with a tendency to compose songs illuminating her deepest thoughts—whether they were popular at the time, or not. From the very beginning, her albums have been composed of songs that expressed what was going on in her personal life and/or what she observed going on in the world around her. That became her trademark.

At first, her albums were diaries set to music and lyrics. At times she masqueraded her feelings and her subject matter in her creative prose. At other times she confronted her subject matter by exposing and hitting her targets with direct bull's-eyes. They described exactly what was going on in her life—figuratively, literally, or indirectly as an observer.

In this way, each of Joni's original albums represented a specific chapter in her life. As she grew and evolved as a person and as a musician, so did her album releases. In this way, she has never chased or sought commercial appeal. She never lusted for a hit single. She never aimed for a gold or platinum album. She simply wrote and sang what she felt, and she let the public find her as it chose.

Joni proceeded to plot her course in life as though she knew she was destined to accomplish great things creatively. From time to time, just to make certain she was on the right path, she consulted gypsy fortune-tellers. "In 1968 somebody in the Village prophesied that I would one day be very famous. I thought he just wanted to be nice to me. I thanked him but didn't believe a word." (28) Little did she know, but the gypsy knew exactly what he was talking about. Furthermore, throughout her career, her music was filled with images of Tarot cards, fortune-tellers, and soothsayers.

In March 1968, Elektra Records released the album *The Circle Game* by Tom Rush. The singer chose songs by three of the brightest and most aspiring new folk songwriters around: Joni Mitchell ("The Circle Game," "Urge for Going," and "Tin Angel"), James Taylor ("Something in the Way She Moves" and "Sunshine Sunshine"), and Jackson Browne ("Shadow Dream Song"). Tom had an instinct for recognizing talent. It wasn't long before all three of them became huge stars as singer-songwriters. And both Taylor and Browne became intimate friends of Joni's.

But at the time, David Crosby was the main man in her life— her lover, her producer, and her mentor. Her association with Crosby elevated her to a rare echelon of the rock world. She recalls, "Crosby is the most into my music of any outsider I've ever met. He also has very good judgement, and gets a very good sound out of me in the studio. He's taught me a lot of things about recording, and he's managed to get that stage presence on the album." (29) He delighted in getting his friends high on marijuana and either have Joni sing live or play tracks from her forthcoming album.

Finally, in March 1968 the *Joni Mitchell* album was released. Minimally produced by David Crosby, it benefited from his association with the project. Joni played her own piano and guitar, and Stephen Stills is featured on bass. In the United States, the album peaked at number 189 on the *Billboard* charts. It was not a huge sales hit, but it put Joni firmly on the map.

On this album, Joni's unadorned and intricate but simple guitar-led songs weave a mesmerizing tapestry of emotions. On the first casual listening, it seems like a pleasant folk-rock album of delicately textured music. However, as Mitchell draws you into her spellbinding storytelling, you are compelled to delve further into her insightful lyrics. The songs tell tales about her own life and loves.

From the very start, on this album you can tell that Mitchell is an artist as well as a gifted songwriter. In her painterly fashion, the self-composed music on Joni's first album was a vivid palette with many references to colors and colorful images, from the brown walls of "I Had a King," to the flashing colored lights of "Night in the City," to the autumn reds and summer greens of "Marcie," to the blue tongues of "Sisotowbell Lane." The album sparkles with images of gemstones, like the lime green peridots and periwinkle blue medallions of "The Dawntreader," to the precious yellow amber stones of "Cactus Tree."

Joni took the opportunity on her evocative debut release to make it into something of a "concept" album. Originally released as a two-sided vinyl disc, she subtitled side 1 of it "I Came to the City." The five songs speak of her urban adventures and misadventures and refer to Detroit, New York City, London, and finally Los Angeles. On the flip side, which she titled "Out of the City and Down to the Seaside," she sings of ships, and tales of sailors and of the sea.

The album opens with Joni's insightful song of independence: "I Had a King." She describes Chuck Mitchell as a man in "dripdry" paisley shirts, who calls her "crazy" and "blind." She describes him as being emotionally chilly and negative. She sings of their inability to see eye to eye on life, and the fact that her key no longer fits his door. Is there a chance of reconciliation? Can they ever be together? According to Joni, they "never can." The song is a brilliant ode to knowing when to get up and simply walk away from a derisive relationship. Joni sounds resolute and intensely conviction filled as she sings the stinging lyrics.

In direct contrast, in the song "Michael from Mountains," Joni sings of an enchanting lover who stops to play in the oil-streaked puddles of rain that he encounters in the city. There are images of cheery suns in bright paintings, and cats that run to the door when they hear your key enter the lock. This is the kind of love affair Mitchell clearly preferred.

Her New York City experience is brilliantly captured in the song "Night in the City," a song with a slightly giddy honky-tonk sound. She sings of the colors waltzing to the music that pours out of doorways. She weaves an enchanting picture of Manhattan by night.

In the song "Marcie," Joni sings of her sorrow, and the fact that she needs a man in her life. The "Marcie" that Mitchell sings of is a woman who is feeling lonely in the gray city. As she walks past the shipyards on the Hudson River with her bag of peaches, she experiences the redness of anger and the greenness of jealousy. In reality, it is Joni singing of her own lack of romance in her New York period—prior to meeting David Crosby. Joni confirms, "Marcie is a real girl, she lives in London. I used her name because I wanted a two-syllable name. But I'm the girl in all these songs." (30)

"Nathan La Franeer" is a quirky ballad about the limousine driver Joni hired to drive her to the airport. In this moody song, Nathan the "coach" driver furrows his eyebrows and looks disapprovingly at Joni in the rearview mirror. A little vignette that Mitchell wrote on the way to the airport, she describes Nathan as a grumbling man who asks for another dollar, as he looks her over resentfully. This was the first of many everyday experiences Joni described in her career. She has the ability to turn an ordinary taxicab ride into a haunting and insightful character study.

On the subject of her observant writing, as personified in the song "Nathan La Franeer," Mitchell explains, "In a pure anonymous encounter you find a world alive and full of character." (21)

The second five songs come under the umbrella heading of "Part Two: Out of the City and Down to the Seaside." The first song on this "side" is the hippie-like optimism of "Sisotowbell Lane." She sings of eating muffins and berries, and rocking in a rocking chair against a backdrop of woodlands and grasslands from her seat on Sisotowbell Lane.

On "The Dawntreader," Joni weaves a scenario under the sea, of the wreckage of a once opulent ship. A treasure of peridot jewelry and blue medals lie on the sea floor, where dolphins and colonies of mermaids swim by the placid setting where the sea wreckage lies. A man beckons her to come to him from the tourist sites and the city's neon lights, down to the sea. In the context of the song she rhapsodizes about "dreams" of "a baby" that haunt her like the sound of children laughing combined with sounds of the sea. This song creates a rich and beautiful vision of satin clothes billowing in the wind and the sound of the riggings of a boat.

"Pirate of Penance" is another stylish tale of a sailor and his affair with a dancer in a smoky seaport bar. When the sailor is accused of murdering a man, the dancer holds the key to the crime, for it is she who saw him last. Singing in multiple tracks, Mitchell lyrically portrays both characters, "Penance" and "the Dancer."

"Song to a Seagull" finds Joni longing to soar like a seabird. Instead, she came to the island of Manhattan, where she lived amid a cacophony of noise on a sea of cobblestones and concrete. She laments that she wants her dreams to soar on the wings of seagulls. It is from this song that the phrase "Out of the City and Down to the Seaside" comes.

On the final song on this album, "Cactus Tree," Joni sings harmony vocals to her own voice. The song is clearly about seafaring David Crosby and his courtship of her. He is the man who beckons her to him—offering amber beads from California. He takes her out on his schooner, and he calls out to her from three thousand miles away—approximately the distance from Los Angeles to New York City. While he is entreating her to come to California to live with him, she is busy being "free" and leading an artist's lifestyle.

According to Joni, there was a definite chronology to this album. "The first song, 'I Had a King,' is about the break-up of my marriage. The album does tell a story, though not necessarily in chronological order. Certainly, the songs aren't placed in the order that I wrote them. As we were working on it, songs came up that would fit in. And since it was finished, I've written others that could go into the sequence too." (30)

David Cleary of the *All Music Guide* claims, "What sets this release apart from those of other confession-style singer/songwriters of the time is the craft, subtlety, and evocative power of Mitchell's lyrics and harmonic style. Numbers such as 'Marcie,' 'Michael from Mountains,' 'The Dawntreader,' and 'The Pirate of Penance' effectively utilize sophisticated chord progressions rarely found in this genre. Verses are substantive and highly charged, exhibiting careful workmanship . . . This excellent debut is well worth hearing." (31)

Mitchell claims that at first, people mistakenly thought she was merely a part of the early 1960s folkie/protest song era, like Peter, Paul, and Mary. "When I first came out, I appeared to be a spinoff of something that was going out of vogue, which was like a poor man's Baez or Judy Collins," she claims. "The old thing was folk, and the new thing was folk/rock. Nobody wanted to sign me, because I appeared to be part of this old thing that was dying, but musicians could see that I was a musician." (14)

The truth was that Joni's music and singing style had something that the other ladies of folk music did not. Unlike the other reigning folk music divas, like Joan Baez, Buffy Sainte-Marie, or Mary Travers of Peter, Paul, and Mary, she did not write music of protest. She had a mesmerizing and highly crafted style all her own.

Although it had been a couple of years—and many life experiences later—the advice that her teacher Mr. Kratzman gave Joni was still with her, so much so that in the liner notes to her first album say, "This album is dedicated to Mr. Kratzman, who taught me to love words." (32)

The album cover features original artwork by Joni. A brightly colored pen-and-ink drawing, it contains lush floral designs, a city photograph, and the sketch of a sailboat placidly sailing the sea at sunset. The seagulls that fly in the sky on the album cover form the words "Song to a Seagull." Her name appears above in burgundy-colored letters. Although the actual title of this album is *Joni Mitchell*, it has been erroneously called *Song to a Seagull* in many publications throughout the years.

When the *Joni Mitchell* album was released, she was the latest singing star to come out of the percolating Los Angeles music scene. Before long several other hopeful singers and songwriters gravitated toward her neighborhood in hopes of being discovered as well. Some came for the music. Some came for the partying. Some came for both.

During the summer of 1968 another of Joni's contemporaries, Jackson Browne, gravitated toward the Laurel Canyon area of Los Angeles. The Laurel Canyon road stretches from Sunset Boulevard in the West Hollywood area, up the Hollywood Hills, across Mulholland Drive, and into the Valley. On the Hollywood side of the mountain-crossing road are several roadways and houses that seem to hang from the hills. Partially because of its proximity to the Sunset Strip, Laurel Canyon was known as a hotbed of undiscovered musical talent. There was a lot of creative cross-pollination between the talents there in the late 1960s and early 1970s, and Joni Mitchell was in the middle of it.

Describing the communal scene in the Laurel Canyon area in a cover story on Linda Ronstadt, *Time* magazine explained, "Colonies of rock musicians were forming in the Los Angeles subdivisions of Laurel Canyon, Echo Park and Venice. Glenn Frey drifted in from Royal Oak, Michigan. Don Henley was a North Texas State English major before he decided to move west. They eventually formed the supergroup the Eagles. Before long everyone knew Jackson Browne and Bonnie Raitt, who had grown up around L.A. Neil Young, Joni Mitchell, and Stephen Stills lived near the top of Laurel Canyon, Frank Zappa in an old Tom Mix house a short walk away." (33) Also in the area at the time were Micky Dolenz and Peter Tork of the Monkees, Carole King, Lee Michaels, and the Turtles.

Explaining the communal feeling of the L.A. music scene at the time, said Linda Ronstadt, "We were all learning about drugs, philosophy, and music. Everything was exciting." (33)

Remembering the living situation in Los Angeles during this era, Jackson Browne claims that to this day he romanticizes this innocent era of sex and drugs and rock & roll. Jackson recalls, "There was a house in the Hollywood Hills that was owned by Peter Tork. He had all this money from being in the Monkees, and he was a freak. I saw Hendrix play in the pool house, with Peter's girlfriend, Ren, playing drums, naked. It was wild! At that particular house, there was an abundance of beautiful woman. Everyone slept with everybody, and nobody wore any clothes. It was . . . paradise. I really feel bad that that world's gone, irretrievably, because I really had a great time." (34)

It was one big orgy of sex and drugs and rock & roll. Says Jackson, "These beautiful chicks from Peter Tork's house, they kept coming over with these big bowls of fruit and dope and shit. They'd fuck us in the pool. We'd wake up and see this beautiful 16-year-old flower child who only knew how to say 'fave rave,' with a bowl of fruit, get you incredibly high and take you downstairs and go swimming." (35) According to Browne, he did a lot of hanging out at Peter Tork's house. Two other frequent guests *chez* Tork that year were David Crosby and Stephen Stills—who had recently departed Buffalo Springfield. And, according to Joni, she was the one who put Crosby, Stills, Graham Nash, and Neil Young together in the first place.

"I introduced those guys to each other," she claims, "because we used to jam when they were in the throes of their musical courtship. You've got an Englishman and a Southerner and a Californian boy and a Canadian trying to get an accent blend, and they ended up with this twang and a nasal thing." (29)

While the boys of Laurel Canyon were harmonizing and partying, Joni was busier than ever working on her career. That year she appeared on three different shows on Canada's CBC-TV: *The Way It Is*, *This Hour Has Seven Days*, and *Mon Pays, Mes Chançons*. She played January and April gigs at the Riverboat Coffeehouse in Toronto. She also had spring appearances in Cambridge, Massachusetts; Crouse College in Syracuse, New York; Le Hibou in Ottawa; and Swarthmore College in Swarthmore, Pennsylvania.

Finally on June 4, 1968, Joni headlined at the Troubadour club in Los Angeles, her first L.A. public appearance. She appeared for six days at the club, through June 9, with the singing duo of Hedge and Bonnie also on the bill. From June 10 to June 16, she headlined the Troubadour for another six days, this time with Dave Van Ronk as the supporting act.

When the *Joni Mitchell* album was released, no one was more proud of it than David Crosby. He proclaimed of his new protégée/girlfriend and her insightful lyrics, "I think she had more understanding than most people do—of human beings. She had already been through some hard things. And what makes human beings 'get with' them is paying dues. [It's] sort of like, you arrive here as a boulder, and you knock corners off yourself until you get smooth like a river stone. And, she was already starting to get smooth." (3)

According to Elliot Roberts, "David [Crosby] set it up so that when the album finally came out, everyone in L.A. was aware of Joni Mitchell. The first club date we played, at the Troubadour, was standing room only for four nights, two shows a night." (26)

In addition, Reprise Records rented a huge billboard on Sunset Boulevard, with a large photograph of Joni on the left side. On the right it read: "JONI MITCHELL. May Change Your Mind, with Reprise Album 6393."

The Troubadour was the perfect place in Los Angeles for Joni to promote her first album. David Geffen and Elliot Roberts knew that this was a gathering place for the young talent in town, where Joni would be seen by the who's who of the industry.

The Troubadour, on Santa Monica Boulevard, has long been the ultimate showcase club for aspiring singer/songwriters hoping to snag a recording deal. It was often filled with young hopefuls and record company executives on the lookout for the "next big" singing sensation. The late folk singer Jim Croce once said of the scene at the club, "The Troubadour was one of the most unique and respected places to play. There would be Cadillacs and Porsches parked outside, and inside it was one big wild party. People would be doing drugs and trying to get picked up, while young talent was being revealed on its stage. There was no club that was more influential during the '60s and '70s for promoting new talent than the Troubadour. If you were lucky enough to get a gig there then you had a shot at getting discovered and getting signed to a recording contract." (36)

David Geffen explains, "Elliot [Roberts] became wildly excited about Joni. And, he introduced me to her, and I became her agent. It was the beginning of her career, it was the beginning of our careers." (3)

It was at the Troubadour that Geffen either discovered and/or promoted all of his star acts. There he first became associated with Linda Ronstadt, whom he later signed to his record label. On one occasion, she sang with a handful of musicians she had met there, who included Glenn Frey and Don Henley. Geffen had Frey and Henley form their own band, which he christened "the Eagles." Another Troubadour singer/songwriter Geffen signed became one of his most famous acts: Jackson Browne. Since he and Elliot Roberts had gone into business together, Geffen also had a hand in shaping Joni Mitchell's career as well. In addition, Geffen and Roberts ended up managing the career of Crosby, Stills, Nash, and Young.

Explaining the club scene during this exciting era, Jackson recalls, "The Troubadour was the big thing then, but I'll tell you something, I don't really think there was ever [a] songwriter's scene around the Troubadour. It was like Bob Dylan said, 'You probably call it folk music, but it's not.' It wasn't folk music at the Troubadour, and nobody thought of it as folk. People came in with a full band. They'd come and they'd get record deals and they'd go. A lot of them were real corny. And flashy, too. If you hung out there long enough, you could almost chart someone's progress. You'd see them one day by themselves, and the next day with two or three people they'd be forming a band. Like J. D. Souther and Glenn Frey began playing there as a duo, and eventually you'd hear J. D. go up there by himself. And then a couple of weeks later Glenn would be in rehearsal with these other guys and they'd become the Eagles." (16)

After the Troubadour engagement, also in June 1968, Joni appeared at the Mariposa Folk Festival in Innes Lake, Ontario. On July 3 she returned to Manhattan to headline six dates at the Bitter End, with the duo of Bunky and Jake on the bill with her. On August 14 she shared the bill with Arlo Guthrie at the Wollman Skating Rink in Central Park in New York City, as part of the Schaefer Music Festival.

The music critics loved Joni from the start. Her Troubadour engagement really set the wheels in motion for her. From this point on, she was known as part of the "California music scene." According to Stephen Holden of the *New York Times*, "She was always more poetic than most of her peers. Even in the early songs like 'The Circle Game' and 'Both Sides Now,' there was a construction of images and structure to her work, and ingenuity of imagery that nobody else had." (3)

On August 8, 1968, she performed at the Philadelphia Folk Festival in Upper Salford, Pennsylvania, at Old Pool Farm. In September she was off to England, where she played the Revolution Club in London. She was also featured on the BBC Radio 1 *Top Gear* show. On September 28, 1968, Joni performed at Festival Hall in London on a program billed as "An Evening of Contemporary Song." Also on the bill that evening were Al Stewart and Fairport Convention.

October found her on both coasts of the United States, playing Bovard Hall at the University of Southern California on October 4, and in New York City on October 23 she began a six-day engagement at the Bitter End. From October 31 to November 3, Joni played a four-day booking at the Main Point in Philadelphia.

On November 8 she played at the Hunter College Auditorium in New York City. November 17 found her back at the Mariposa Folk Festival at Innes Lake, Ontario. And on November 23, she and Tim Hardin headlined at Brooklyn College in Brooklyn, New York.

And finally, on December 28, 1968, Joni was one of the performers at the Miami Pop Festival in Hallandale, Florida. Also on the bill were Marvin Gaye, Three Dog Night, and Fleetwood Mac.

As 1968 came to an end, bookings were already falling into

place for the beginning of 1969. For Mitchell, it turned out to be the beginning of a forty-week series of concert performances across the country. In 1969 she played at rock music festivals in Newport, Atlanta, Big Sur, New York, and Monterey, and opened for Crosby, Stills, and Nash. Joni Mitchell was clearly on her way to mainstream success.

5

Clouds

The year 1969 was a highly volatile time in the United States. NASA put a man on the moon. *Hair* was the big hippie musical hit on Broadway. The Vietnam War was raging and gaining increased unpopularity. The Beatles released *Abbey Road* and the Supremes were singing "Someday We'll Be Together." It was also the year of the most famous rock festival of all: Woodstock. Joni Mitchell was an exciting new voice to listen to, and she was in the middle of all of it.

It was a transitional period for Mitchell. She was about to change her singing style and her lover. Recording sessions for Joni's second album, *Clouds*, were already under way. However, this time around David Crosby was not serving as the producer of this album—Joni was.

It was the era of "free love," and everyone in Laurel Canyon was busy cross-pollinating musically and experimenting sexually. For the time being, Joni and David Crosby were a hot couple. He was mainly known as the ex-Byrds singing star. But in 1969 he was about to make an even bigger splash as one third of the group Crosby, Stills, and Nash—later adding Neil Young to the group.

Joni's affair with David Crosby ended in the beginning of 1969. Reportedly Mitchell found David to be much too possessive. She had a career to maintain and focus on, and she felt smothered by life with him.

Apparently they were having their differences and he was seeing other girls on the side. Another barb came when he gave an interview to *Rolling Stone* magazine and stated, "Joni Mitchell is about as modest as Mussolini." (36)

Then Graham Nash reentered Joni's life, and suddenly there was a love triangle in full blossom. As Joni explains it, "I was living with David. Graham and I had had a kind of ill-fated beginning of a romance because we had met in Ontario, when I was playing one club in Ottawa, and the Hollies were playing another. We finally got together in Winnipeg. He ended up at David's place and I was staying with David until my house was ready. Graham came down sick in David's house and I took him to my new house to play Florence Nightingale. At first it wasn't really for romance's sake; he was sick and I still had some domestic chops because I hadn't been trained to be a celebrity. I had been trained to be a regular Frau. I took him home and was looking after him and I got attached—here was a mess. What was I going to say? I'm kind of going with David and sort of staked claims, but I'd written all these independent songs, trying to explain my position to him: that I'm still in an independent mode. But I got really attached to Graham and I guess that's the first time that I could pair bond." (26)

It was a sticky situation; however, David was not someone who was exclusive when it came to love and sex either. He too had fallen in love with someone else, Christine Hinton.

Recalls Graham Nash, "I camped out with Crosby and then I rekindled my relationship with Joan, whom I'd met a couple of years earlier in Canada. There was a party at David's house and Joni was there. I was already totally intrigued and in love with this woman and she invited me home. I went with her and I didn't leave for a couple of years. It was a cute little house. That was an incredible time for me, probably the most intensely creative, free, and special time I've ever experienced. Not only was I in love with Joni, but I was in love with David and Stephen [Stills], and I was in love with the music and I'd taken a giant chance." (26)

David Crosby later explained, "The thing with Joni and Graham was that I felt great about it. I wanted to be with Christine. I know I was happy with her and Joan was a very turbulent girl and not an easy person to be in a relationship with, particularly then. I was very happy for them. They were in love and it was cool. Graham was then—and is now—my best friend and I didn't feel any jealousy about it. I loved him and I loved her and couldn't see being angry at two people I loved for loving each other. That just didn't make a lot of sense to me." (26)

With the money she made from her recording deal and her touring, Joni purchased her own house in Laurel Canyon, which she shared with Graham Nash and two cats. Theirs was a homey existence of singing and hanging out with their neighbors, who included Mama Cass, David Crosby, and Stephen Stills. Nash loved the incredible pies she baked—especially the rhubarb ones. When *Rolling Stone* magazine came to visit the star couple, reporter Happy Traum described "[Joni's] isolated, wood-hewed home, surrounded by stained Tiffany glass windows, oak-beam wooden floors, a Priestly piano, a grandfather clock, and a black cat named Hunter, a nine-year-old tom." (37)

Joni and Graham became an inseparable couple. "I just remember her as being Graham Nash's girlfriend," says Micky Dolenz of the Monkees, who was a fellow resident of Laurel Canyon. (38)

Not only were they in love with each other, but their love inspired them to write some of the finest music of their careers. According to Nash, "['Our House' was] written for Joni, about her house that we shared in Laurel Canyon, on Lookout Mountain. It was written on her piano. Such a charming house. She had a collection of multi-colored glass in the window that would catch the light—the 'fiery gems.' There was a fireplace, and two cats in the yard. It was like a family snapshot, a portrait of our life together." (39)

All three sides of this lovers triangle turned around and set their experiences to music. The song "Willy" was written by Joni, using her nickname for Graham. Nash penned "Our House" about his cozy—but brief—life with her. And David Crosby wrote the song "Guinnevere" in part about Joni. He later wrote and recorded the song "Triad" about the triangle of tangled love in which he and Graham and Joni found themselves. Another song Joni wrote about her love affair with Graham was "My Old Man."

As her love affair with Graham grew, a lot of songwriting creativity blossomed. According to Graham, "It was an intense time of 'who's' gonna get to the piano first, 'who's' gonna fill up the space with their music first. I mean, we had two very creative writers living in the same space. And it was an interesting clash of 'I want to get as close to you as possible'/'Leave me alone to create.'" (3)

Says Joni, of their writerly Dashiell Hammett/Lillian Hellman life together, "Graham and I have been the source of many songs for one another. A lot of beautiful music came from it, and a lot of beautiful times came from it." (3)

The household they had together was unique. Graham was fascinated with the way Joni could sit for hours writing a song as if she were channeling it. He would try to get her attention, but she wouldn't hear him. She was *that* deeply involved in her songwriting.

Mitchell began the year headlining at the Troubadour. She played a six-day engagement there from January 21 to 26. It kicked off her most exciting year yet. On February 1, 1969, Joni made her debut at Carnegie Hall in New York City, announcing when she took the stage, "It's a long way from Saskatoon, Saskatchewan, to Carnegie Hall!" Onstage that night she played all of the songs that made her a star and introduced several yet-to-be-released compositions, including "Morning Morgantown."

Recalls her proud boyfriend, Graham Nash, "The audience at Carnegie Hall were ecstatic that Joni was there. I think it was jammed to the rafters. It was Joan's 'coming out' in a really big way. She brought her parents from Canada. This was a big deal. She was magnificent that night. She had reached a place in her career that was undisputable." (3)

Says Joni, "Well, Carnegie Hall the first time around was quite an event on so many levels." One of her fans made a huge cardboard heart emblazoned with the words "Dear Joni: New York Loves You." The singer was deeply touched: "'New York Loves You, Joni,' It was wonderful!" (3)

On March 15 Joni returned to Saskatoon to play the Centennial Auditorium in her former Canadian hometown. And on March 28 and 29 she headlined the Unicorn Coffee House in Boston. This was an important engagement, since she met James Taylor for the first time.

Continuing to tour the East Coast, she appeared at Queens College in New York on March 30, Sargent Gymnasium at Boston University on April 11, and Kresge Auditorium in Boston at the Massachusetts Institute of Technology on April 18. On April 20 she headlined at the Academy of Music in Philadelphia with Jerry Jeff Walker as the opening act. Then she performed a two-date gig at Bill Graham's famed Fillmore East in Greenwich Village, April 25 and 26. Her college tour continued to Wesleyan University in Middletown, Connecticut, on April 27.

On May 1, 1969, Joni was one of the guest stars on the *Johnny Cash Show*, a network TV special on ABC. The program was taped in Nashville and broadcast in June. One of her most important friendships came out of this TV appearance. Bob Dylan was another musical guest on the program, and he and Joni became lifelong friends from that meeting. She felt that her music gained a positive influence from Dylan. She had never dreamed that her lyrics could be written as though she was addressing one person—telling her story in songs and phrasing things as if it was a one-to-one statement. She claimed that Bob Dylan's music taught her that was possible. It was a big thrill for her to finally meet him and work with him on the TV show.

She continued to tour, and from May 20 to 25, she played another six-day engagement at the Troubadour in L.A. On June 26, 1969, Joni was a guest on Mama Cass Elliot's network television special. On July 7 she appeared at the Southern Illinois University in Edwardsville, Illinois. She sang at the Mississippi River Festival, and her performance was later broadcast as a PBS special, *The Sounds of Summer*, on August 3. On July 12 she was in concert at the Memorial Stadium in Mount Vernon, New York, as part of the Uncola Music Festival, and on July 19 she was again at the Newport Folk Festival in Newport, Rhode Island. Joni and Tim Hardin were booked to perform on July 23 at Wollman Skating Rink in Central Park, but they were rained out. Instead Hardin and Mitchell gave their midtown Manhattan concert the following night.

Her other concert performances that important summer included a return to the Mariposa Folk Festival at the end of July. On August 1, she took part in the Atlantic City Pop Festival, at the Atlantic City Race Track. Then on August 15, Joni was the opening act for Crosby, Stills, Nash, and Young at the Auditorium Theater in Chicago. It was a historic event, as it was the newly formed quartet's debut live concert. This set a precedent for a major event that came that month: Woodstock.

Joni was booked as the opening act to this singing quartet, for whom the term "supergroup" was coined. As a trio, their debut album—*Crosby, Stills & Nash*—was a million-selling success. When Neil Young was added to the lineup, the stakes went up even farther. Putting Mitchell on the bill as well made this one of the hottest concert tours of the year.

Along comes the Woodstock Music Festival in upstate New York. On August 17, 1969, Joni was invited to be one of the many acts to appear. Crosby, Stills, Nash, and Young were invited to perform that day as well. However, Joni was booked for her first really major network TV interview on the *Dick Cavett Show* in New York.

Recalls Joni, "We got to the airport [in New York City], but in the meantime, Woodstock has been declared a national disaster area, and there was no way in. David Geffen took me into the city. Elliot Roberts was with the boys [Crosby, Stills, Nash, and Young], and they rented a plane, and they got to go and I didn't. I watched it on television. I was not allowed to go because I had to do the *Dick Cavett Show* the following day." (26)

David Geffen explains, "The headline in the *New York Times* said '400,000 People Sitting in Mud.' So, I said to Elliot [Roberts], 'You go. I'm staying here.' Joni Mitchell and I stayed at my apartment in New York, where she wrote the song 'Woodstock,' having never been to Woodstock. She was with me. Then they heard the song, they recorded it, and it became the anthem for Woodstock." (26)

For Joni, it was the one performance of her career that should have been. Although she had played several other high-profile music festivals throughout this era, Woodstock was the biggest, the most important, and the most famous of all. When it became an important concert album—and then a massively successful documentary film in 1970—its fame grew to legendary proportions.

Sensing that she was missing out on something really major, Joni sat down and wrote the song that was forever welded to the legend of the music festival: "Woodstock." The song begins with Joni singing of a chance encounter with a child of God, which was uncharacteristically religious for Mitchell at this stage of her life. Her brilliant lyrics tell of the "peace and love" credo behind the music festival. The writing process also helped Joni get over her pangs of jealousy caused by wanting to be there with her singing buddies.

"I was put in the position of being a kid who couldn't make it [to the concert]," she remembers. "So I was glued to the [TV] media [coverage]. And at the time I was going through a born-again Christian trip—not that I went to church. I'd given up Christianity at a very early age in Sunday school. But suddenly as performers, we were in the position of having so many people look to us for leadership. For some unknown reason I took it seriously, and decided I needed a guide and leaned on God. So I was a little 'God mad' at the time. Woodstock, for some reason, impressed me as a being a modern miracle, like a modern-day fishes and loaves story. For a herd of people that large to cooperate so well it was pretty remarkable, and there was tremendous optimism. So I wrote the song 'Woodstock' out of these feelings." (39)

Joan had a lot to be jealous of. Woodstock was a great convergence between established superstar acts and lesser-known singers. In the star category were Jefferson Airplane, Joan Baez, the Who, Joe Cocker, Sly and the Family Stone, Jimi Hendrix, John Sebastian, and Crosby, Stills, Nash, and Young. On the other side of the coin, several singing stars got their lucky break by being part of the Woodstock lineup, including Melanie, Richie Havens, and Santana.

The next day, Crosby, Stills, Nash, and Young showed up in New York City with Grace Slick of Jefferson Airplane, and they all shared Joni's appearance on Cavett's program. As Mitchell explains it, "They crashed the *Dick Cavett Show*. It hurt. It was like I was the grounded daughter, but the boys get to go. Most of the song was written on the last night of the [festival], out of frustration of being disallowed to go." (26)

The *Dick Cavett Show*, which was broadcast the following day, on August 19, became a whole Woodstock theme episode. The look on Joni's face betrays her envy as she sits listening to David Crosby and her boyfriend Graham Nash tell the TV cameras what an awesome historic musical event Woodstock had become.

Naturally, since she was on tour with them through the rest of the summer and fall, she played the song "Woodstock" for them. She recalls, "CS&N heard it later and asked permission to record it." (26) The rest is history.

The song "Woodstock" was recorded for Crosby, Stills, Nash, and Young's album *Déjà Vu*, and it became a huge hit for them, as well as the signature song of their career. Furthermore, it crystallized the message behind the Woodstock phenomenon. When it came time for the documentary film version of the festival, David Geffen was determined to make sure that it was used as the theme song.

According to Geffen, "As for the movie, I would not allow them to use the footage of Crosby, Stills, Nash & Young in the movie unless they used Joni's song with Crosby, Stills, Nash & Young singing it as the theme of the movie. That's how that happened. The producers were either going to give me what I wanted or that was it. And since I represented a lot of important artists on Warner Brothers and Atlantic and Elektra Records, they just weren't going to fuck with me. So, they pretty much did what I wanted." (26) Joni did not get to attend Woodstock, but because of her song, she has forever been considered a part of the project.

On August 25, 1969, Crosby, Stills, Nash, and Young began a seven-day engagement at an open-air venue, the Greek Theatre, in the Hollywood Hills of Los Angeles—and Joni opened the show. The next big festival that Mitchell and "the boys" played together was the Big Sur Folk Festival in Big Sur, California. Like Woodstock, Big Sur was also filmed as a documentary, and there is footage in it of Crosby, Stills, Nash, Young, and Mitchell singing the hippie era song of peace: "Get Together."

While Joni was at the 1969 Big Sur Music Festival, she met a musician and craftsman who was a dulcimer maker. She was fascinated with the odd and ancient traditional string instrument, along the lines of an autoharp. She loved it so much she bought one for herself.

"I had never seen one played," she confessed. "Traditionally it's picked with a quill, and it's a very delicate thing that sits across your knee. The only instrument I had ever had across my knee was a bongo drum, so when I started to play the dulcimer, I beat it. I just slapped it with my hands." (18) She went on to add it to her instrumental repertoire.

Throughout the fall, Joni continued to tour with "the boys" and had solo performances as well. On October 19, 1969, Joni was the special guest artist at the Gala Fiftieth Anniversary Concert by the Los Angeles Philharmonic Orchestra.

In October 1969, Joni's second album, *Clouds*, was released on Reprise Records. It contained Mitchell's own versions of her now famous compositions "Chelsea Morning" and "Both Sides Now." The album was a big hit, peaking at number 31 on the *Billboard* charts in the United States.

The reviews for *Clouds* were mainly glowing. In England, rock critic Mark Williams in the *International News* claimed that *Clouds* was not as successful an effort as *Joni Mitchell* had been "despite her gorgeous voice, which she knows how to control and to apply to her own compositions to maximum effect." *Melody Maker* called her "a great talent, and this album more than confirms it!" *Disc* magazine praised her "brilliant poignancy." (29)

The *Clouds* album opens with the one track that was not produced by Joni Mitchell. Most likely to appease the record company, the song "Tin Angel" was produced by Paul Rothchild. Rothchild gained a reputation for producing rock women, and he was particularly successful working with Janis Joplin (*Pearl*), Bonnie Raitt (*Home Plate*), and Bette Midler (*The Rose*).

Immediately, there is an audible difference between *Joni Mitchell* and *Clouds*—an attempt to establish a warm feeling to the recordings. Like her debut album, there are almost no instruments on this album but guitar and voice. The one exception is the eerie calliope sound on "Roses Blue." On "Tin Angel" particularly, there are several intricate sounds. Apparently Rothchild's technique was influential with the rest of the recordings. From the very start "Tin Angel" effectively sets the tone for many multilayered tracks on the album.

"Tin Angel" finds Joni pensively singing about moving on from the memories of her past, to the love she suddenly found "today" in a café on Bleecker Street in Greenwich Village. One of her songs from her days in New York City, the track had previously been recorded by Tim Rush on his 1969 *The Circle Game* album. It is both touching and beautiful.

"Chelsea Morning" is the first of Joni's truly joyous songs. Reflecting the giddy feeling of newness that she experienced when she moved to Manhattan, "Chelsea Morning" expressed Joni's happy freedom after her marriage to Chuck.

This song inspired many people who were in their teenage years or early adulthood. When the future First Lady Hillary Clinton was a college student, "Chelsea Morning" was one of her favorite songs. It was such a favorite of hers, in fact, that when she gave birth to her daughter, she and Bill Clinton named the child "Chelsea."

"I Don't Know Where I Stand" is another pensive song of love. This time around, Joni sings of apprehension over a relationship in which she is in the middle. It is sung simply, and without any additional instruments but her own guitar. Hauntingly she weaves a beautiful spell of a beautiful idyllic morning, clouded in doubts.

"That Song about the Midway" finds Joni addressing the object of her love—presumably Graham Nash. She sings about meeting him a year ago, playing guitar—and exhibiting some traits of an angel, some traits of a devil. Clearly she is deeply in love with the man she addresses in the song.

"Roses Blue" brings to life Joni's visits to fortune-tellers. Against the sound of a calliope or a hurdy-gurdy, she sings of Tarot card readings and astrology readings. She tells the story of "Rose," who has gotten involved with the occult, from zodiac to Zen. A mesmerizing song of black magic and spells, Joni creates an eerie and dark ode of high priestesses and dark religions, in this mysterious and chillingly evocative tune.

"The Gallery" is another vignette-like story song of Joni's. Throughout her career, she has written about all sorts of people she encounters in her life. Instead of taking a snapshot of them, or drawing a sketch of them, she instead writes a song about them. Here she sings a ballad about the girlfriend of an artist and a gallery owner. She has the understanding to put up with his moods, and she inspires his artwork.

"I Think I Understand" is a slow ballad about Joni feeling that she has finally found her path in life. Her eloquent poetry and her unique sense of imagery make this a genuine gem in an album of beautifully insightful music. Likewise, "Songs to Aging Children Come" is her coming-of-age song. She sings of the sad beauty of wanting to hold on to her child-like innocence, while moving forward in her life. Sung with a haunting double track of her own voice, this song is an incredibly effective medieval-sounding track, very much like the kind of song that Kate Bush—of "Wuthering Heights" fame—would later make popular.

"The Fiddle and the Drum" is a rare excursion into the political arena for Joni. It strongly indicts America for fighting an unpopular war in Vietnam. Without speaking of the Vietnam conflict itself, in this a capella song she wonders why the United States has traded the fiddles of peaceful joy for the drum—an instrument that is used to march soldiers off to war.

The album fittingly ends with Joni's greatest songwriting hit: "Both Sides Now." A simple guitar-led ballad, this is a beautiful revelation for fans of Judy Collins's version of the song. Both recordings have their undeniable charm, but this more simple one is a beautiful performance all its own. This is the first of three completely different recordings of this song that Joni has released in her career. In many ways, this is the simplest and the best.

The *Clouds* album package is another piece of Joni's artwork. Another artist-singer from this era, Cat Stevens, also designed the majority of his album covers. But Joni was the first to use her albums to promote her artwork from the very start. For *Clouds*, she painted a portrait of herself, holding a bright orange tiger lily next to her face. Behind her is a vibrant yellow sunset in the horizon. In the distance is a castle that looks like Chateau Frontenac in Quebec. In the liner notes to the album, Joni dedicated the LP to her mother—using her maiden name: Sadie J. McKee.

Looking back on this era Joni identified a progression since her first album. "My artwork, at the time I made the first album, was still very concerned with childhood," she says. "It was full of the remnants of fairy tales and fantasia. My songs still make references to fairy tales. They referred to kings and queens. Mind you, that was also part of the times, and I pay colonial allegiance to Queen Lizzy. But suddenly I realized that I was preoccupied with the things of my girlhood and I was twenty-four years old. I remember being at the Philadelphia Folk Festival and having this sensation. It was like falling to earth. It was about the time of my second album [*Clouds*]. It's almost as if I'd had my head in the clouds long enough. And then there was a plummeting into the earth, tinged with a little bit of apprehension and fear. Shortly after that, everything began to change. There were fewer adjectives to my poetry. Fewer curlicues to my drawing. Everything began to get more bold, and solid in a way." (9)

According to Joni, *Clouds* was a product of the era in which it was recorded. "The things that I look back on and sort of shrug off, maybe in a weak moment—*grimace* over—are the parts when I see myself imitating something else. Affectations as opposed to style. It's very hard to be true to yourself. For instance, I don't care too much for the second album I made [*Clouds*]. I like the first one, the first one's honest. *Blue* is an honest album. *Clouds* has some honest moments on it, but at the time, I was singing a lot with Crosby, Stills, Nash & Young, and *they* had a style, out of necessity, to blend with one another. They had a way of affecting vowel sounds so that when they sang together, they would sing like a unit. I picked up on that and there's a lot of that on the album. I find it now kind of irritating to listen to, in the same way I find a lot of Black affectations irritating. White singers sounding like they come from deep Georgia, you know? It always seems ridiculous to me. It always seemed to me that a great singer—now we're talking about excellence, not popularity—but a great singer would sing close to his or her own speaking voice." (9)

Joni elaborates, "I liked the sound of my voice and my guitar on that first record because I wasn't influenced by anything. But on the second album, I'd been singing a lot with CSN—I introduced those guys to each other—because we used to jam when they were in the throes of their musical courtship. You've got an Englishman and a Southerner and a California boy and a Canadian trying to get an accent blend, and they ended up with this twang and a nasal thing which I also ended up singing my second record in. I mean, 90% of the singers in this business pretend they're Southern Blacks, and I didn't want to fall into that pitfall of losing my natural song-speech." (1)

Mitchell was now an A-list star in musical circles. She was meeting the crème de la crème of the rock world. She recalls, "I met Jimi Hendrix at the Capitol Theatre in Ottawa, and after his set, he came down, and he brought a big reel-to-reel tape recorder. He introduced himself very shyly and said, 'Would you mind if I taped your show?' I said, 'Not at all.' And later that evening, we went back, we were staying at the same hotel. He and his drummer, Mitch [Mitchell], the three of us were talking. It was so innocent. But management, all they saw was three hippies. We were outcasts anyway. A Black hippie! Two men and a woman in the same room . . . So they kept telling us to play lower. It was a very creative, special night. We were playing like children." (20)

Said Joni of Jimi, "His main concern at that time was that he wanted to drop the phallic aspects of his showmanship. The big, flamboyant dick stuff was offensive to him, and he wanted to stop it. But every time he tried, he told me, the audience would boo. He wanted to take a different kind of band out with a brass section. O.K., in three words: 'Sensitive. Shy. Sweet.'" (20)

On November 1, 1969, Joni performed at Centennial Auditorium in Saskatoon. That month found her taping the *Tom Jones Show* for TV, as well as a concert at California State University in Fullerton. On November 29, she performed an afternoon show at Alden Memorial Auditorium, and that night performed at the College of Holy Cross, both in Worcester, Massachusetts. On December 5 she was at Symphony Hall in Boston. She ended the year with college campus concert appearances in Hartford, Springfield, Cambridge, and Boston.

During 1969, Joni Mitchell was *the* hot new girl to watch on the music scene. Her association with Crosby, Stills, Nash, and Young, as well as her left-handed association with the whole Woodstock phenomenon, proved to be a brilliant springboard for her career. The fact that *Clouds* was a widely successful Top 40 album put her right where she needed to be to soar even farther.

6

Ladies of the Canyon

As the 1970s began, Joni found herself in a great position. She was living a fast-paced life—both in her personal life with Graham Nash and in her solo career. Before long, everyone was wanting to record her compositions. While many of her songs seemed to have a life of their own, she was also becoming a bona fide rock superstar—via the popularity of *Clouds*. Her next album, *Ladies of the Canyon*, was completely recorded—"in the can," as they say in the record business.

She had already begun writing songs for her next album, which she was to entitle *Blue*. She said at the time, "I'm going through a change as an artist. I'm beginning to write on the piano, which is a much freer instrument, and I want to learn the concertina and the violin." (40)

At this point in her career, by the time Joni's albums were released, they were not a representation of what was going on in her life at that time as much as a product of what was going on in her personal life six to nine months earlier.

In January 1970 Joni left Los Angeles and traveled around Europe for a year. She had a lot to think about, especially her relationship with Graham Nash. Where was it going? Where did she want it go?

One of the most insightful songs that she recorded for *Ladies in the Canyon* was "Willy," which Joni lovingly wrote about Graham Nash. The lyrics of the song carry Joni's doubts and fears regarding the relationship—in spite of the fact that she deeply loves him. In it she claims that Nash is at once her "child" and her "father." He is both the cause of her "joy" and the cause of her "sorrow." She also claims in the lyrics that he does not think that their love is true because he cannot hear the wedding bells ringing.

In the January 27, 1970, issue of *Look* magazine, Joni received her first major national American press coverage. In a story called "Joni Mitchell: Songs for Aging Children," she was portrayed by writer Gerald Astor as the ultimate hippie princess. "Sorrow is so easy to express and yet so hard to tell," she told the writer. "I'm supposed to take a year off until I get a new motivation. Used to be I couldn't wait until I would do my latest song." (41) Now she couldn't wait to get out of town.

The article also pointed out that "as part of the stoned generation, she's smoked her pot." Joni was then quoted as replying, "Grass: it sits you down on your fanny. You can't do anything but see things. It shows you your God. But if you make drugs your God, that's bad." (41)

It was truly the era of sex and drugs and rock & roll. Joni is the first to admit that the drugs part of that equation somehow eluded her. With the exception of a marijuana joint here and there, she was not into the drug scene. On the other hand, many of her fellow musicians—especially David Crosby—got deeply involved in substance abuse. According to her, she lived a bit under a rock when it came to harder drugs: "I was in the industry for a long time before I had any idea of what drugs people were doing. I mean, I'd say, 'Geez, he looks awfully skinny. Why doesn't he have an appetite?' I was very, very sheltered by Elliot Roberts and Crosby, Stills, and Nash, when I first entered the business." (16)

Said Joni in January 1970, as she was preparing for her year in Europe, "When you know you're going back on the road there's so many things to do—every minute becomes vital—and my writing suffers. As a woman, I have a responsibility to my home, and it takes me a week to get the house re-perking." (40) She seemed to comprise a dichotomy between a gypsy and a housewife. This year the gypsy in her soul won out, and off to Europe she flew.

In 1970, she abandoned formal touring but performed at several significant venues. On February 17, 1970, Joni appeared in concert at Royal Albert Hall in London. During her onstage banter with the audience she announced that she was discontinuing all public performances. It was the first time Joni declared that she was through with the music business. Yet over the years she managed to "come back" from every attempt to retire, time and time again.

So respected was she by her peers that the accolades began at an early stage. On March 11, 1970, Joni won her first Grammy Award, in the category of Best Folk Performance, Female, for the *Clouds* album. It was solid validation that she had officially arrived in the eyes of the recording industry.

Meanwhile, Joni was on her European sabbatical. When she left on her trip, one of the things she took with her was the dulcimer that she had purchased at the Big Sur music festival. She explains, "I bought it, and I took off to Europe carrying a flute and this dulcimer because it was very light for backpacking around Europe. I wrote most of *Blue* on it." (18)

On her 1970 European trek she did not have a guitar with her. "I was craving a guitar so badly in Greece," she recalls. "The junta had repressed the [Greek] population at that time. They were not allowed public meeting; they were not allowed any kind of boisterous or colorful expression. The military was sitting on their souls, and even the poets had to move around. We found this floating poet's gathering place, and there was an apple crate of a guitar there that people played. I bought it off them for 50 bucks and sat in the Athens underground with transvestites and, you know, the underbelly running around—and it was like a romance. It was a terrible guitar, but I hadn't played one for so long, and I began slapping it because I had been slapping this dulcimer. That's when I noticed that my style had changed." (18)

According to her, "When I'm playing the guitar, I hear it as an orchestra: the top three strings being my horn section, the bottom three being cello, viola, and bass—the bass being indicated but not rooted." (18)

While writing the songs that would be recorded on her *Blue* album, Joni delved into her darker, decidedly bluer emotional side. She knew she loved Graham, and she knew she had to leave him. It caused her to feel a deep sadness that fueled some of the most insightful music of her career.

In April she was on Crete, where she was visited by James Taylor. He was a key character in this particular year's transitional course.

While Joni was in Europe, that same month, Crosby, Stills, Nash, and Young's version of Joni's song "Woodstock" peaked at number 11 on the U.S. singles charts. After that, Joni was forever linked with their success, their legendary career, and the whole Woodstock phenomenon.

It was also during April 1970 that Joni's third album, *Ladies of the Canyon*, was released. She had recorded it during her affair with Graham Nash. Literally a product of her time spent in Laurel Canyon, it carries an overall feeling of lightness and the optimism of love.

Musically, the major difference between *Ladies of the Canyon* and Joni's previous two albums was the fact that her music was now accompanied by the sounds of other musicians, and by her own piano and dulcimer playing. The overall sound is much more varied, and she is accompanied by several top-notch players, including Paul Horn on the clarinet and flute. It was refreshing to hear Joni progress out of the folk guitar mode, accompanied by the cello and saxophone of some of the tracks.

The album opens with an optimistic song about small-town life, with "Morning Morgantown." The chirpy, piano-led song brings to mind Joni's childhood in Maidstone on the Saskatchewan plains. It is a charming, light song out of Joni's songbook circa 1967. It sets the tone for a varied, multifaceted album.

In "For Free" Joni sings autobiographically about her position in the music business. She examines the irony of singing and playing music for a living. Here she is—in the context of the song—traveling around the world in limousines, escorted in and out of concert halls. At the same time, she encounters a clarinet player on a city street corner and finds that he too is a master of music. While people were paying cash to hear her play music, on the street corner people were bustling by this lone and unemployed musician, and they ignored the mastery of his work. Who is more talented? she seems to be asking us. "She" who is paid or "he" who plays for free?

The song "Conversation" is about a flirtation with a married man. She flirts with him, but if she encounters him in public—in a café—she can only glance in his direction without making eye contact. This is another of her songs dating back to 1967. She had been so prolific over the last four years that she was just now catching up to recording some of them.

The hippie-like ballad "Ladies of the Canyon" is about the life she lived in Laurel Canyon with Graham Nash. Here she essays three of the women who populate that star-filled neighborhood. She sings of Trina, who wears Native American jewelry. She is an artist who loves antique furniture and decorates with lace. Annie invites you in for a bite to eat, maybe some brownies, while her cats and her children run about. Estrella is something of a gypsy songstress in her shawls, amid beveled glass mirrors. These three women are distinctive hippie "Ladies of the Canyon." This is a perfect peace and love character study. As in all of her songs, the lyrics in this period piece of poetry are cleverly constructed and sung her in a deeply heartfelt fashion.

The song "Willy," Joni's song for Graham Nash, is sad and simple. Singing to the lone piano, Joni pours her heart out about him and counts the ways she loves him. The pervasive sadness to the song lets one know she is contemplating leaving him. This has the sound of a moth resisting the all too attractive flame of love.

In the song "The Arrangement," she sings of a slow suicide—or a desolate drug overdose—on the thirty-third floor of a high-rise building. With a jazzy piano solo in the middle of it, Joni opens up a bit as a musician. Looking back over Joni's career, many critics cite this song as the first evidence of her venturing into jazz, which occupied so much of her career. This unique song is a preview of brilliant things to come.

Joni herself traces her first jazz singing to this particular recording. "It started, I would say, back on *Ladies of the Canyon*. There was one song, 'The Arrangement,' which was a predecessor which had a bit of that voicing—post-Stravinsky modern open voicing—and in the chordal patterns, too. It's been very organic. It definitely wasn't rock & roll voicing or movement." (42) It definitely was a sparkling preview of coming attractions from Ms. Mitchell.

Likewise, on "Rainy Night House," Joni's piano playing is hauntingly beautiful. Musically she is stretching out here. She sings of taking a taxi ride to the house of a friend's mother. The friend is a male rock star, or as Joni describes him: he is a "holy man" who is heard on FM radio. They make love in his affluent mother's bed. Again she shows mastery for using the piano effectively to carry her intricate storytelling. In this odd but effective vignette about one of her brief love affairs, she demonstrates her ability to see even the simplest detail and report her observations vividly to music.

The song "The Priest" is another story of a chance encounter. However, in this case, Joni is entertaining the affectionate advances of a priest she's met in an airport bar. This song echoes her ambivalence toward religion and uses metaphors of sermons, contradictions, hymns, and confessions. The lyrics imply that she has sex with the priest—in thought if not in deed.

"Blue Boy" is a creative song about a woman sculptor. She has the "Blue Boy" pose for her and makes a granite statue of him for her garden; along the way seduces him as well. Although their love affair died, whenever she looks out into her garden, she sees his granite image, as fresh as when she first laid eyes upon him in the flesh.

Ladies of the Canyon ends with a triple whammy of three of Joni Mitchell's most famous and perennial songs: "Big Yellow Taxi," "Woodstock," and "The Circle Game." The joyous song "Big Yellow Taxi" was Joni's first big hit as a performer.

During a trip to Hawaii, Joni was shocked to see that America's tropical paradise state—especially Honolulu—looked like anywhere else in the United States. It inspired her to write her most famous song, about how they "paved" over several pieces of "paradise" in an effort to put up an eyesore of a "parking lot." The resulting song, "Big Yellow Taxi," remains her most endearing hit.

The final pair of songs are the definitive versions of two songs that made Joni a star as a songwriter. While the Crosby, Stills, Nash, and Young version of "Woodstock" is a soaring harmonic masterpiece, Joni's interpretation is a simpler, more haunting version of the song. She slows down the pace and gives the song a mysterious treatment. The affecting multitracked background voices—a chorus of Joni—makes this a riveting classic.

This charming smorgasbord of an album ends with an optimistic version of "The Circle Game." Already Buffy Sainte-Marie and Tom Rush had made the song one of their trademark songs. However, Joni's has a childlike charm all its own.

Here she has a slightly off-key chorus of voices behind her that add to the guitar-led around-the-campfire approach, and she crystallizes the sing-along effect that this song still has in concerts.

Again, Joni used her album cover as a platform to promote her artwork. For *Ladies of the Canyon* Mitchell drew a pen-and-ink silhouette of herself in a shawl and in the pattern of her shawl is a landscape of houses on Laurel Canyon.

The reviews for *Ladies of the Canyon* were consistently glowing. It created a new high-water mark in her short but exceptional recording career. According to David Cleary in the *All Music Guide* this album is "another 'essential listen' in Mitchell's recorded canon . . . a wonderfully varied release . . . arrangements here are more colorful and complex than before . . . Mitchell sings more clearly and expressively than on prior albums, most strikingly so on 'Woodstock.'" (43)

When it was released, it was an even bigger hit for Joni. *Ladies of the Canyon* peaked at number 27 in the United States and became her first in a long string of gold records. In the United Kingdom, it made it all the way to number 8. The song "Big Yellow Taxi" was released as a single and hit number 67 in the United States and made it to number 11 in Great Britain.

While she was in Europe, Joni thought about her relationship with Graham Nash. As much in love as Joni and Graham were, something told Mitchell that she needed to get out of this relationship. Graham wanted a wife. Mitchell was too independent to give up her freedom so quickly. The end of the affair came in the summer of 1970.

She flew back to America and told him it was over. Joni explains, "I had sworn my heart to Graham in a way I didn't think was possible for myself. And he wanted me to marry him. I had agreed to it. And then I just started thinking: My grandmother was a frustrated poet and musician, and she kicked the kitchen door off of the hinges, on the farm. And, I thought about my paternal grandmother who wept for the last time in her life at 14 behind some barn because she wanted a piano, and [was told], 'Dry your eyes you silly girl, you'll never have a piano.' And I thought, 'Maybe I'm the one who has the gene that has to make it happen for these two women.' As much as I loved and cared for Graham, I just thought, 'I'm gonna end up like my grandmother, kicking the door off the hinges.' It's like: 'I better not!' And it broke my heart." (3)

She had to soar as a musician in her own right and didn't have time spend as a housewife. She had music to compose and art to create. According to Graham, "The day before the Fillmore East show in June 1970, I broke up with Joni and my whole world fell apart. The afternoon of that show I wrote this song ["Simple Man"] and that evening I performed it for the first time, with Joni sitting in the audience. I don't know how I got through that." (39)

He recalls their final farewell: "I remember getting a telegram from Greece from Joan, the last line of which was: 'If you hold sand too tightly in your hand, it will run through your fingers.' It was Joan's way of saying 'goodbye' to me." (3)

That spring, James Taylor visited Joni on Crete. Together they spent much of the year in London. By 1970 James Taylor had several accomplishments under his belt. First, he was one of the lucky performers to be discovered by and signed to a recording deal by none other than the Beatles. When the Fab Four established their own record company, Apple Records, in 1968, Taylor was signed to the prestigious label, along with Badfinger ("Come and Get It") and Mary Hopkins ("Those Were the Days").

The following year, James moved to Warner Bros. Records and recorded his breakthrough album, *Sweet Baby James*. It was heralded as one of the most frank and autobiographically revealing LPs ever recorded. Especially touching was the song "Fire and Rain," which became Taylor's first big hit.

In addition to his wonderful, revealing songwriting style, he also had a reputation for being self-destructive, suicidal, and a recovering heroin addict. Although it was the height of the whole hippie/Woodstock pot-smoking era, heroin carried with it the stigma that it was the drug of choice of people who were truly out to destroy their own lives.

His personal demons were deeply ingrained. In fact, when he was only seventeen years old, James Taylor was admitted to a Massachusetts mental institution. Part of his path back to wellness came in the form of his songwriting.

When Joni met and became involved with James, he had gotten off of heroin and had been satisfying his cravings for the illegal drug by shooting up methadone. He was chronically depressed, and he felt that his life was again spiraling out of control. Taylor later explained, "It's an amazing downhill slide. It's fast, too, but the initial thing is trying to get away from a feeling that you cannot control that in any way you cannot express. That's the basis for most addictions. Either it's anger or fear or a combination of the two. The other thing about addiction is that it's consistent. What the junkie is looking for when he picks up his syringe or goes out to cop [purchase heroin] is something that will be the same every time and that it will completely supersede all other goings-on. And smack [heroin] does that." (36)

What James needed, circa 1969–1970, was something positive to focus on while he was trying to shake his heroin addiction and shooting methadone. At the time he was overwhelmed by events in his life that he could not control, and he felt like he was on the verge of a serious nervous breakdown.

Now that he was a rock musician of note, there were young women who were interested in him sexually, mainly groupies who were looking to have sex with a rock star, and not the kind of women he could actually have a relationship with.

What he needed was an affair of the heart. He needed someone to love and to be loved by in return. At exactly the right moment he found just such a person. Voila! Joni Mitchell!

At the time, Joni was unhappy about her impending breakup with Graham. In late 1970, Mitchell's and Taylor's paths seemed destined to cross. They were both regular performers at the Troubadour in Los Angeles, and before they became acquainted, they were aware of each other and each other's music. When a mutual friend introduced them, James felt that Joni represented a new beginning for him. According to Taylor, "When I first heard Joni's music, you know, I was amazed. It was truly unique." (3) In addition to the other pressures that were swirling in his life, he experienced the sudden weight of instant fame that came when "Fire and Rain" hit number 1 in August of that same year.

Mitchell was intelligent, creative, and eloquent. She impressed him in ways that no one else had, up to this point. Instantly smitten, he wrote her love letters and poems. She was most impressed with the attention he lavished on her. James was twenty-two at the time, and Joni was twenty-six. They were both young and free, and destined to become two of the biggest hit-making superstars of the era.

She later explained of James, "He wasn't very well known when I first met him, but the things I did hear were a bit conflicting. But I fell for him right away because he was very easygoing and free-spirited. We shared a lot of similar interests and common ground." (36)

By 1970, the affair between James Taylor and Joni Mitchell was in full swing. They seemed very much in love, and according to James, they paralleled each other sexually. "She's so sensual and free with her body. She's like a goddess: a goddess of love. A real true goddess. Being with Joni is so pleasurable. We share a lot of common ground. We've very compatible," he claimed at the time. (36)

They did all sorts of things together. They made love. They made music. And they seemed perfect for each other. While Joni's affair with James Taylor was in full blossom in 1970, she explored her sad side and wrote songs for her acclaimed confessional album, *Blue.*

On August 29, 1970, Joni was one of the headliners at the Isle of Wight Festival, which was held at the East Afton Farm, Godshill, on the Isle of Wight off the coast of England. It was originally hoped that the Isle of Wight Rock Festival could be exploited as Woodstock had been the year before. There were certainly enough A-list acts on the bill to make a great album. To make certain that this wasn't an opportunity missed, the festival was not only recorded for an album but was filmed for a potential documentary movie as well.

The head of Elektra Records, Jac Holtzman, recalls, "During the last week of August, 1970, Ahmet [Ertegun of Atlantic Records] and I were in London to discuss recording the Isle of Wight festival, the big European outdoor festival of the summer, featuring Jimi Hendrix—twelve days before he 'O.D.'d; Emerson, Lake and Palmer; Joni Mitchell; Kris Kristofferson; Miles Davis; Tiny Tim; to name a few, and The Doors—with the bearded and bulky Jim Morrison." (24)

When Jimi Hendrix and Jim Morrison died of drug-related causes, the Isle of Wight Festival album rights were frozen in litigation. It was years before either was released in a major way. Some artists released their performances from that very successful festival on albums, including *The Who: Live at the Isle of Wight Festival 1970* and Jimi Hendrix's *Blue Wild Angel Live at the Isle of Wight.* Both the album *Message to Love: The Isle of Wight Festival* and the movie of the same name are currently available, on CD and DVD; they were finally released in 1995. Joni's performances of "Woodstock" and "Big Yellow Taxi" are captured on these audio/visual packages.

At the festival there were several mishaps onstage. Even Joni's usually quiet performance was punctuated by a man jumping onstage during her set. Among other pronouncements, he yelled out to the crowd, "This is a hippie concentration camp!" (44)

It turned out to be a former yoga instructor of Joni's, apparently with a few too many mind-altering substances flowing through his veins. According to Joni, "I go and sit at the piano and this guy I know from the caves at Matala, Yogi Joe, he taught me my first yoga lesson, he leaps up on the stage. He gives me the 'Victory' sign, he sits at my feet and starts to play the congas with terrible time. He looks up at me and says, 'Spirit of Matala, Joni.' I bend down off mike and say, 'This is entirely inappropriate, Joe.' It was [the song] 'Woodstock,' of all songs to be singing, because this was so different, it was a war zone out there. At the end of 'Woodstock' Yogi Joe springs up, grabs the microphone and yells, 'It's desolation row and we're all doomed!' or something to this effect. A couple of guards grab him. The crowd then stand up and scream 'They've got one of ours!' And they're moving forward." (29)

Joni was visibly shaken but regained her composure and continued her show, singing her recently released song about Graham Nash, "Willy," and a song she had written for her forthcoming *Blue* album, entitled "California." Having shown the crowd that she could not be deterred by the rantings of the madman who had leapt onstage, she was cheered on through four encores. Among the songs she sang for them during her encores was an enlivened version of "Big Yellow Taxi."

Although she was still on something of a sabbatical from touring, many of her performances—with and without James Taylor—were key ones. On October 9, 1970, Joni was presented in concert on BBC2 TV. The title of the program, which emanated from London, was *Joni Mitchell Sings Joni Mitchell*. On October 16 she was back in Vancouver, British Columbia, to perform at a benefit for the environmentalist group Greenpeace. That event was held at the PNE Coliseum in Vancouver. During her set, she was joined on stage by a surprise guest: James Taylor.

On October 29, 1970, James Taylor and Joni Mitchell performed together at Royal Albert Hall in London. Since they were romantically linked, James's manager/producer, Peter Asher, felt that it would be a perfect career move for both of them. The concert turned out to be a magical event and was broadcast on BBC radio. It was later released as a bootleg album, which can still be found under the title *In Perfect Harmony* or *You Close Your Eyes.*

During the concert, Mitchell prefaced her performance of the song "The Gallery" by explaining on stage, "This next song is a little play, a little soliloquy. It's about an artist's old lady. I play the part of that old lady. There's one thing that kind of holds true of artists, and that is they're connoisseurs of beauty, you know, and that's what this song is about, it's about an artist who runs around the countryside connoisseuring lots of beauties." (45)

To kick things up a notch, in October 1970, the group Matthews Southern Comfort hit number 1 in England with their own recording of Joni's "Woodstock." On both sides of the Atlantic, Mitchell would forever be closely associated with the Woodstock Music Festival. Ironically, it was the music festival that she never actually attended.

November 7 found Mitchell and Taylor together in Princeton, New Jersey. James was performing at Dillon Gymnasium at Princeton University. Joni joined him onstage during the encore and accompanied him on the song "You Can Close Your Eyes," which they had recorded together.

A week later, on November 13, Joni attended a Frank Zappa concert at the Fillmore East in New York City. She ended up sitting in on his set during the second show. Right afterward, she returned to England, where she based herself that autumn and winter.

On November 28, 1970, Joni performed a solo concert at London's Royal Festival Hall. Previously just a guitar and vocal act, she was now alternating between guitar, piano, and dulcimer. Reviewing her appearance for *New Music Express*, Nick Logan found her nervousness defeating much of her performance. She was reportedly having trouble staying on pitch, and when she couldn't get her guitar tuned right, she appeared flustered. Instead of being alienating, however, her audience rooted for her. As her second set ended with her version of "Woodstock," according to Logan, "hearing her emotionally shrilling about getting back to the garden, you realize that no other interpreter will ever convey what she means by the phrase." (46)

When she appeared for still another encore, Joni performed "The Circle Game." Then she introduced a surprise guest to join her for that song. For the first time that fall, it wasn't James Taylor. Much to the surprise of everyone, it was ex-boyfriend Graham Nash, who happened to be in London at that time. The crowd loved it.

Reviewing the same concert, *Sounds* magazine reported, "Few performers today can strike such a rapport with an audience, yet few others are prepared to expose themselves, their private loves and fears, to the public gaze. Unlike her countryman Leonard Cohen and other contemporaries who enact their emotions against a background of human desperation, Joni sings of hope, of love and joy. Of dignity and despair." (29)

In December 1970, Joni went to Paris to record an hour-long concert to be broadcast on the twentieth of the month on BBC Radio 1. She was joined in song by James Taylor. During the broadcast, the show's producer referred to Taylor as the man Joni was "stepping out with at the time." (29)

The concert was a big hit and became a popular bootleg recording, under the title *For Free*. During that concert she sang much of her popular material from the past and present, including "The Priest," "The Gallery," "The Circle Game," and "That Song about the Midway." She also previewed new songs that would be included on her *Blue* album—including "My Old Man," "The River," "A Case of You," "California," and "Carey."

Joni was such a big hit in England in 1970, that when *Melody Maker* magazine tallied its year-end reader's poll, she was named the Top Female Singer of the Year. Also on the list that year were Sandy Denny, Grace Slick, Janis Joplin, Aretha Franklin, Christine Perfect (McVie)—soon to be part of Fleetwood Mac—Judy Collins, Laura Nyro, and Joan Baez. How interesting to note that Mitchell—who was often compared to Collins and Baez—was now ranked higher in popularity than her two former idols.

In London Joni and James partied and hung out with mutual friends. However, their relationship was about to change. When they returned to Los Angeles together in early 1971, they both had new albums to record. Mitchell and Taylor were so involved in each other's careers that they both appeared on three songs on the other's album. James can be heard on Joni's *Blue* album on the guitar for three of the songs: "A Case of You," "All I Want," and "California." The album was recorded at A&M Studios on La Brea just south of Sunset Boulevard. They were still very much in love and involved with each other. It is assumed that the song "All I Want" is a love song addressed to James Taylor.

At that same time, also at A&M Studios, Carole King was recording her breakthrough album, *Tapestry*. While she was there she invited James and Joni to record a song with her. The song this session yielded was the chilling "Will You Still Love Me Tomorrow." Coyly, Joni and James were credited in the album liner notes as "The Mitchell/Taylor Boy-and-Girl Chorus."

According to James Taylor, he had been friends with Carole for a year: "[Musician Danny] Kootch[mar], introduced us in 1969, just around the time she was starting to perform her songs herself (people in the biz had treasured her demos for years). We recorded together, toured together, shared a band and hung out. She gave me my only Number One single. Those were remarkable days in Laurel Canyon. Joni [Mitchell], Jackson [Browne], CSNY, The Eagles, Carole King . . . exceptional was commonplace. The record industry was a labor of love in the service of the music. It was a hoot. We laughed, we cried." (47)

Simultaneously, James was working on his *Mud Slide Slim and the Blue Horizon* album, and he was looking for songs. When he played acoustic guitar on Carole King's recording of her composition "You've Got a Friend," he asked her if he could record it on his album as well. She agreed that he could. When he recorded his version of the song, Joni came into the studio and sang the background vocals. She is also heard singing background vocals on the tracks "Love Has Brought Me Around" and "Long Ago and Far Away." Joni's voice is especially prominent on the featured harmony vocals of "Long Ago and Far Away."

Carole's version of her own composition, "Will You Still Love Me Tomorrow," is absolutely beautiful. It was originally written as a hit for the Shirelles. The voices of Carole, James, and Joni are all beautifully distinctive on this incredible harmony performance. When Carole's album was released in 1971, it was an instant success. It hit number 1 and stayed there for fifteen weeks. It was on the *Billboard* charts for years, and for the majority of the 1970s it was the biggest-selling album in record history. Ironically, this was Joni's only appearance on an album that reached number 1 in the United States. Furthermore, that same year, James Taylor's recording of Carole's "You've Got a Friend," with background vocals by Joni, also hit number 1 in the United States—the first and only number 1 hit he scored in his long career. This also marks Joni's only appearance on a song that hit the top of the singles charts.

For a long time, James Taylor and Joni Mitchell were the ideal rock & roll couple. However, once they returned to Los Angeles, it wasn't long before their love affair began to unravel. The sudden success of his career turned Taylor into an instantly recognizable singing star. Several young women began to flirt with him, and, unaccustomed to the spotlight of stardom, he developed quite the roving eye as well.

When they were out in public in Los Angeles, Joni became very aware that James was watching all of the pretty girls who were eyeing him. Arguments and jealousy soon destroyed their union.

Reportedly, James Taylor was the man Joni Mitchell thought she would end up married to and settling down with. After all, they had so much in common. They were the world's premiere songwriters of sensitive lyrics and confessional ballads. They hung out in the same circles, and they seemed made for each other. However, when Joni had to start looking over her shoulder to see which pretty girl James was now eyeing, it all crumbled.

Joni's indignation over his constant flirting with other women caused James to break off their love affair suddenly. The breakup was swift and anything but amicable. Joni was devastated. She felt both humiliated and betrayed. However, the hurt that she felt at the hands of James fueled several of her most famous compositions on her next couple albums.

When Joni was asked by *Maclean's* magazine in 1974 if her career had benefited at all from her affair with James Taylor, she claimed that it had not. "I don't think so, not in the time that James and I were spending together anyway. He was a total unknown, for one thing; maybe I helped his career? . . . But I do think that when creative people come together, the stimulus of the relationship is bound to show. The rock & roll industry is very incestuous, you know, we have all interacted and we have all been the source of many songs for one another. We have all been close at one time or another, and I think that a lot of beautiful music came from it. A lot of beautiful times came from it, too, through that mutual understanding. A lot of pain too, because, inevitably, different relationships broke up." (48)

Jerry Garcia, the lead singer of the Grateful Dead, once proclaimed, "Both of them were big innovators in the modern folk movement. I could listen to Joni's albums over and over and keep finding new things in her music every time I put it on. And the same can be said about James Taylor. And the times they sang together were very uplifting moments. Everybody who was into the whole thing of the peace-and-love movement in the '60s bought their albums. They were the two artists we could all relate to because they were doing drugs, making love and living the lives every hippie out there could only in their dreams. Hey, we were all a bit screwed up during that period. So when Joni and James sang about how fucked-up their lives were, it sure hit home. Listening to their music was spiritual. It was almost along the lines of being therapeutic." (36)

To bury her hurt, Joni almost instantly threw herself into a fling with Lothario-like actor Warren Beatty—a notorious womanizer. Her short-lived affair with Beatty temporarily assuaged the pain that James Taylor caused her. She refused to speak to Taylor for years and seemed to cringe at the mention of his name. This cold war between the two of them lasted until the 1980s, when there was finally enough distance between them to have some perspective on the relationship. From time to time their paths crossed. But the bitter feelings and hurtful songs from Joni to James became a huge part in the legend of Mitchell's most deeply personal music from this era.

7

Blue

At this point in time the careers of Joni Mitchell, Linda Ronstadt, the Eagles, Laura Nyro, Carly Simon, Jackson Browne, John David Souther, and Crosby, Stills, Nash, and Young were becoming closely knitted together. Each of these acts was either managed by David Geffen and/or Elliot Roberts or signed to label deals orchestrated by Geffen. And, in time, many of them—including Joni—were signed to record labels owned and run by Geffen. On several occasions these artists appeared on each other's albums as guest musicians and singers. In a way, it was very incestuous.

In the 1990s there was a running joke that everyone on the planet had "six degrees of separation from Kevin Bacon." Well, circa 1971, it seemed that everyone in the Los Angeles music scene had "two degrees of separation from Joni Mitchell." Furthermore, all of these acts also had something to do with the Troubadour in the West Hollywood area. That was where Geffen either discovered new acts or showcased the acts that he had signed—just as he had with Joni.

During Joni's ascent to pop stardom, Troubadour owner Doug Weston saw several talented aspiring singers on his stage. One he had been watching for a while was Jackson Browne. Doug noted that he was becoming an impressive performer. In September

1969, Linda Ronstadt was about to headline a week at the club, and an opening act was needed. It was Doug who offered Browne the gig—just the boost that his fledgling career needed.

In the audience that night was David Crosby. Jackson was especially excited since David was in one of his all-time favorite groups: the Byrds. That was the year that David became a singing star with Crosby, Stills, and Nash, and he was also a record producer. Because of Crosby's role in the *Joni Mitchell/Song to a Seagull* album the previous year, he was also a bona fide record producer.

Jackson was completely blown away by the fact that Crosby had been in the audience. Not only had he been there through Browne's set, he was very greatly impressed by what he heard. In fact, he told Jackson backstage at the Troubadour that night, that he wanted to be the producer of Browne's first album. David found Browne to be an exciting singer and songwriter. He had had the same feelings the first time he had heard Joni perform in Florida.

Months later, David Crosby bragged to *Rolling Stone* magazine of this new singer whom he was interested in producing an album for: Jackson Browne. Said Crosby, "The cat just sings rings around most people, and he's got songs that'll make your hair stand on end." (49) In spite of the backstage promise from Crosby, the proposed album production deal was never to be made. But, the compliment was an affirmation to Browne.

In autumn 1969, Jackson Browne had a new song he had written, called "Jamaica Say You Will." In February 1970 he recorded an acetate demo of this new song, with John David Souther on drums, and Glenn Frey and Ned Doheny backing him.

When Jackson figured out that Joni Mitchell, Laura Nyro, and Crosby, Stills, and Nash were all managed by one person, twenty-eight-year-old rock manager David Geffen, he made a very clever and aggressive move. Jackson packaged up an eight-by-ten-inch glossy black-and-white photo of himself, a copy of "Jamaica Say You Will," and an impassioned letter which began, "I am writing to you out of respect for the artists you represent." (50)

The package was delivered to David Geffen's management office on Sunset Boulevard. Geffen received the package, opened it, glanced at it, looked at the photo, and tossed it into the wastebasket. After he had left the office, his secretary emptied the wastebasket and caught a glimpse of young Jackson Browne. She liked what she saw, and she fished the demo and the letter out as well.

She took the package home, listened to the acetate recording, and loved the song and the singer she heard.

The next day she brought the letter, the acetate, and the photo back to the office and presented them to her boss, telling him she thought Jackson was very good, and Geffen should at least give it a listen. On her insistence, he did exactly that, and he was instantly impressed with the performance and the song he heard.

He was so impressed that he picked up the phone to reach Jackson immediately. Unfortunately Browne had left town. As he was later to recount, "I went to Colorado. From there I was gonna go to New Mexico and check out the communes." (35)

When Jackson returned to Los Angeles, he called Geffen back, and an audition was set up. Browne provided David Geffen with a one-man show, and David loved what he heard and saw. Shortly thereafter, it was announced that David Geffen was to be his new manager. It wasn't long before Browne was integrated into the circle of musical artists managed by the Geffen/Roberts team.

While all of this was going on, David Geffen also managed Laura Nyro. Joni and Laura both started out as singer-songwriters. As sensitive and passionate women, they both were able to transform their personal emotions into touching songs. While Joni entered the business as a guitar player, Laura was exclusively a pianist. When David Geffen first started working with her, he was able to get her a record deal on Columbia Records. Her albums, including *The First Songs*, *Christmas and the Beads of Sweat*, and *Eli and the Thirteenth Confession,* were all classics of the female singer-songwriter genre. She reached her zenith as a performer on the album *It's Gonna Take a Miracle*, which she recorded with the group Labelle—Patti LaBelle, Sarah Dash, and Nona Hendryx.

Paralleling Joni, Laura's songs—as recorded by other people—scored bigger hits than she did. "Stoney End" became a big hit for Barbara Streisand. Three Dog Night had a huge hit with "Eli's Coming." And the Fifth Dimension recorded eight of her songs, including "Stoned Soul Picnic," "Time and Love," and "Sweet Blindness." Eventually everyone did, from the Supremes and Labelle, to Blood, Sweat, and Tears.

Also paralleling Joni, Laura went through a period of adjustment in the recording studio when it came time to instructing other musicians as to what they were to play on her songs. Both Mitchell and Nyro knew what they heard in their heads. But sometimes communicating these ideas proved daunting.

Joni explains, "It used to be embarrassing to myself and to Laura Nyro in particular, to play with technical musicians in the early days. It would embarrass us that we were lacking in a knowledgeable way, and that we would give instructions to players in terms of metaphors—either color descriptions or painterly descriptions. That feeling of embarrassment persisted until one day when I turned on the television in the middle of the film *Never on Sunday*. The scene was this: there's a drunken American, I guess it's Melina Mercouri's wedding, and he's yelling at the band in his intellectual manner, saying, 'You're not musicians! You can't even read!' And the bouzouki player or guitar player, he's a sensitive guy, and he suddenly stops playing because he's injured by the belief that the American's words might be true. And he locks himself in the bathroom. Mercouri's upset and says, 'Now look what you've done, you've ruined my wedding!'—I'm paraphrasing the scene—and she's standing outside the bathroom door, wondering how she's going to restore this musician's confidence, until finally she knocks and says, 'It's okay! The birds don't read either!' And he comes out elated and goes back to the bandstand. That's how I felt, before and then afterward." (51)

In June 1971, Joni's fourth album, *Blue*, was released. It reached number 15 in the United States and number 3 in England. Eventually it was certified platinum for selling over a million copies in the United States. It instantly became a brilliant new high-water mark for her.

"I remember when *Blue* was first recorded that was the first really confession kind of writing," she recalls. "It was like nothing left to lose, let's spit it out, and when it was finished I went over to a friend's house and Kris Kristofferson was there. I played it. He said, 'Joni, save something for yourself.' It was hard for him to look at it. There was an odd sense of respect, like it was a Diane Arbus photo book or something. I've heard some of the writing called that, and yet I find it hard to relate to those images. These are not strange people in the basement of apartment buildings. These are *all* of us." (29)

She had dug deep inside herself and created a masterpiece. Joni admits, "*Blue* was the first of my confessional albums, and it was an attempt to say, 'You want to worship me? Well, okay, I'm just like you. I'm a lonely person.' Because that's all we have in common. Happily married, there are still lonely moments. Loneliness is the main thing we have in common with animals. Unfortunately, we have this ability to perceive more strongly—unlike, say, the coyote, who's born and sits in the bushes until one day his mother bites his nose to the bone and says, 'I'm not feeding you anymore!' And then sends him cruelly out into the world to be on his own. We all suffer for our loneliness, but at the time of *Blue* our pop stars never admitted these things. Now, I'm a public person, and my life's an open book." (51)

The breakup with Graham Nash, the hopeless love she felt for James Taylor, the festering pain of having given up her only child were all channeled into this classic album. "*Blue* was really a turning point in a lot of ways. As *Court and Spark* was a turning point later on," Mitchell explains. "In the state that I was at in my inquiry about life and direction and relationships, I perceived a lot of hate in my heart. You know, 'I hate you some, I love you when I forget about me.' I perceived my inability to love at that point. And it horrified me." (9)

Another thing on her mind was her stature as a singing star. She was worshiped by her fans at this point. But was she worthy of worship? If people wanted to look up to her, she wanted them to know what they were looking up to see. On *Blue*, she served her emotions on a black vinyl platter for all to see.

According to her, "I have, on occasion, sacrificed myself and my own emotional makeup, singing 'I'm selfish and I'm sad,' for instance. There are 'not attractive' things in the context of rock & roll. It's the antithesis of rock & roll—which is: 'Honey, I'm a lover and I'm *bad*!' You don't go saying these other things in pop circles because they're liable to bring terrible results: unpopularity. Which is what you don't want. When I started doing this 'confessional reporting,' partially it was artistic integrity, and partially I wanted to sabotage any worship that was setting up around me. If I was being worshiped, something was wrong. If you're worshiping things, it means you're not really leading a full life. It's healthy to admire, all of my musical growth has come out of admiration. But to worship, that's taking it too far. You've got to get yourself together if you do that." (51)

When she was asked, several years later, what she considered her most sincere and directed album, Joni answered *Blue*, which she views "as the purest one of all." (52) And indeed that is what it is: pure blue emotion.

Blue opens with the most optimistic song on the album, the up-tempo "All I Want." Joni joyously proclaims her love and devotion to the man she loves, and what the love she feels for him inspires her to do. She sings of wanting to write love letters to him, knit sweaters for him, and do a dance of happiness for him. However, she also sings of loving him some and hating him some. It sounds suspiciously like she is debating about how she should fit him into her life—like the mixed feelings she felt for Graham Nash. While she loved him dearly, she also needed to wander. This song seems to perfectly express the emotional debate she was having at the time. James Taylor plays the guitar on this song of love.

Women identified with this song, and female singers were especially drawn to it. According to Mary Wilson of the Supremes, "Joni's song 'All I Want' is one of my all-time favorite songs that I recorded with the group. It appears on our album *The Supremes Produced and Arranged by Jimmy Webb* [Motown Records, 1973], and it remains a favorite of mine to this day. It is sensitive and beautiful, and it perfectly describes the feeling of being truly in love with someone." (53)

On a slower ballad of devotion, "My Old Man," Joni sings of the man she loves as someone who sings in the park, walks in the rain, and sometimes makes her crazy. Still she loves him. This is her first big piano-driven ballad. It shows off her newly revived keyboard proficiency with beautiful results. Obviously written about Graham Nash, she defends her position of not wanting to marry him by lyrically claiming that a piece of paper from city hall is not what makes a union. On "My Old Man" Joni affirms her position of not wanting to get married to prove her love.

Then the album takes a sudden turn toward the deep end of the blues. A song left over from her 1967 era, "Little Green" is emotionally devastating. Here she sings about the child she gave up for adoption. It is a mother's song of longing. Since she nicknamed her baby "Kelly Green," she uses that metaphor for the child she never saw grow up. Accompanying herself on lone guitar, she daydreams about the little girl's life. Sometimes there would be crocuses and blossoms and birthday clothes, and other days there would be tears and pain. Joni missed all of them. This is the most emotionally wrenching song of Joni's career. It is nearly impossible to hear this song without shedding a tear.

Joni once said, "If I express a truthful emotion that is pure and honest, then I consider the poem a success." (21) That is so true in the case of "Little Green." This is a masterpiece of despair.

Right afterward Joni shifts gears to her European adventures, as she sings a song about a character she met in Greece named Carey. Mitchell explains of this amusing song, "I'd say that I was born with a gift of metaphor—which you can translate into any of the arts quite nicely—and a love of color: color for the eyes, color for the ears. And I like colorful people. Some of the people that have remained in my life entered my life in a colorful way. Carey Raditz blew out of a restaurant in Greece, literally. Kaboom! I heard, facing the sunset. I turned around and this guy is blowing out the door of this restaurant. He was a cook; he lit a gas stove and it exploded. Burned all the red hair off himself right through his white Indian turban. I went, 'That was an interesting entrance—I'll take note of that.'" (2) On "Carey" Joni is accompanied on bass and guitar by her buddy Stephen Stills.

"Blue" is said to be about James Taylor and his inward sadness. Joni sings pensively about his habit for burying his own blues in syringes, booze, and sex. Her singing is again devastating as she explores the dark and sad side of being in love. Accompanying herself on the piano, Joni sings with a world-weary sadness. In the song she tries to offer him moral support to navigate thorough the "waves." She tells him "I love you," but is it enough? "Blue" is both intense and beautiful to listen to, as Joni pours her heart out in song.

As she sat in a park in Paris, Joni wrote a postcard of a song devoted to the place she had left behind: "California." Toward the end of her European adventure, she longed to go to her adopted home on the West Coast of the United States. Although she considered herself to be a member of the "counterculture" there, in the song she claimed that she would even kiss a cop on Sunset Boulevard, she so longed for California.

Explains Joni, "I wrote a song called 'California'—it was written in Europe—and it was longing for that kind of creative climate where we did drop around with our songs to play, but that kind of thing happened prior to success. After success everybody became—whether they'll admit it or not—very much into their own particular creative process. For myself, my work began to encompass other kinds of music outside of the L.A. circle." (42)

In the pensive but up-tempo song "This Flight Tonight," Joni sings of the trip she is making. Should she be leaving or should she have them turn this plane around? On the airplane she rides in class. She wears her headphones, sips champagne, and wonders about the lover she has left behind: is his heater on, is his car fixed, and what will she find when she gets back?

"River" is another intense song of the blues. Accompanied by her lone piano, Joni sings of wanting to run away. She wants to make a lot of money and then retreat. She is sad that the love she has found—presumably Graham Nash—is the one she has to leave. Here she claims she wants to strap on ice skates and disappear down her frozen river of despair. Since this song speaks of the bleakness of winter and the fact that the lyrics state "Christmas is coming," the song "River" has become associated with that holiday. However in this song it is more of a chilling winter reference.

"A Case of You" is another intoxicating Joni Mitchell classic. As a storyteller she takes the listener to a specific scene. She sings of sitting in a bar and drawing a map of Canada on a cocktail napkin, and wondering what her next move will be. Clearly this is the song she wrote when she made up her mind to take some time off and leave the craziness of the music business behind. She wonders if she should just seclude herself somewhere and go back to her art career, as she looks at herself as a solitary painter who is lost in her box of paints. Accompanying herself on the guitar, she apparently wonders if she should just go back to Graham, since he is in her blood and in her heart.

"The Last Time I Saw Richard" is clearly about Chuck Mitchell. When she sings about last seeing him in Detroit in 1968, you know she is surveying her life since leaving him behind. Accompanying herself on the piano, she sings of his melancholy moods and skepticism. Chuck had moved on with his life, and in this song Joni sings of his new life with his new wife. She wonders if the choices she has made in her life—post Chuck—have been the right ones.

Although there are a few upbeat songs on the album, like "Carey," "All I Want," and "California," Blue is essentially a musical exploration of extreme sadness. It completely expressed the way that she felt at the time she ran away to Europe. She was able to crystallize her thoughts and her emotions into one incredible album. To this day it stands up as one of the most significant and effective collections of songs in her entire career.

The reviews were glowing, and *Blue* cemented Joni Mitchell's fame as one of the most insightful and emotionally revealing songwriters and singers around. Lynn Kellermann in *The Music Gig* wrote, "*Blue*, a very private album is a study of a woman torn between unfettered freedom and traditional love, seeking perspective once more on foreign shores. It was [her] first total lapse into self-scrutiny, staged before the public eye. Despite *Blue's* intimacy, Mitchell was so perfect in her lyric, so vivid in her universal portrayal of desperate love . . . that she never once detached the listener. If anything, the feeling was almost sinful, intrusive, the sensation one would get from reading someone's personal diary and relating it into their own lives." (54)

In the *All Music Guide*, Jason Ankeny writes, "Sad, spare and beautiful, *Blue* is the quintessential confessional singer/songwriter album. Forthright and poetic, Mitchell's songs are raw nerves, tales of love and loss . . . etched with stunning complexity; even tracks like 'All I Want,' 'My Old Man,' and 'Carey'—the brightest most hopeful moments on the record—are darkened by bittersweet moments of sorrow and loneliness . . . Mitchell's music moves beyond the constraints of acoustic folk into more intricate and diverse territory . . . *Blue* remains a watershed." (43)

Although the *Blue* album branded Joni with the moniker of "confessional songwriter," she complained that she didn't feel that she was being all that self-examining and self-revealing. In 1997 she claimed, "I don't think of myself as confessional. That's a name that was put on me. The confessional poets like [Sylvia] Plath, whom I read later when they started calling me 'confessional,' most of their stuff seemed contrived to me, and not as greatly honest as it was touted to be. I never wanted to act the part of the poet with pearls of language and wisdom falling from my lips. The first time I met Prince, he said, 'Are you tired, or are you hungry?' It was some grammatical error—still sounds right to me. The point is not to confess. I've always used the songwriting process as a self-analysis of sorts. Like the *Blue* album—people were kind of shocked at the intimacy. It was peculiar in the pop arena at the time, because you were supposed to portray yourself as bigger than life. I remember thinking, 'Well, if they're going to worship me, they should know who they're worshiping." (55)

Blue was such an influential album that it brought further hero worship. Elliot Roberts was in awe of her. He claimed, "We all looked at Joan as the seer because she was the most intelligent of writers. She was one of the first people I ever knew who always considered herself an artist. . . . You could see that her philosophy of longevity, of being an artist, would, in the long run, end up making you more money than if you tried to take advantage." (2)

Unlike her contemporaries, Carole King ("I Feel the Earth Move"), Carly Simon ("That's the Way I Always Heard It Should Be"), and Melanie ("Candles in the Rain"), Joni did not produce any really big hit singles and couldn't care less. In her mind, she wasn't in the business of producing songs for Top 40 radio.

Both "Carey" and "California" were pulled from the *Blue* album as singles, but only one of them really made the charts. In September 1971 "Carey" hit number 93 on the pop singles chart in America, according to *Billboard* magazine. Naturally this frustrated her record company and her managers: Geffen and Roberts.

There was constant pressure from Reprise Records for her to "please" write and record a hit single for the radio. According to Elliot Roberts, "Editing a song to make it a single was not in her vocabulary. I would remind her when she made a heavy left turn not to expect to sell . . . and the response was always the same: 'I appreciate it, thank you. *Let's do it this way.*'" (2)

In 1971, Joni decided that she had to get out of Los Angeles and she packed her bags for Canada. She ended up purchasing a hideaway for herself in Vancouver, British Columbia. For the next several months she meditated, got back to nature, and took a good hard look at her life and her career. While there, she also wrote the songs for what was going to be her next album.

One of her very rare public appearances in 1971 was in Vancouver. Around the time of the release of the Crosby, Stills, Nash, and Young double album, *Four Way Street*, the quartet had its first big breakup. While Neil Young was busy with his solo career, and while they were in a bit of a tiff with Stephen Stills, David Crosby and Graham Nash hit the concert road as a duet. It was at the Queen Elizabeth Theater in Vancouver that Joni made a surprise guest appearance during the duo's September 10 concert.

The success of the *Blue* album was undeniable and indelible. It became a defining album in her career. It had taken three varied albums to lead up to this moment of songwriting proficiency and emotion-charged singing. Because of *Blue*, Joni Mitchell was at a new peak of success in the record business. In her career she was a growing and evolving musician. And in her personal life she again found herself at still another crossroad.

8

For the Roses

J oni Mitchell's first five albums chronicle her life and her loves from 1967 to 1972. The song "I Had a King" deftly dismissed her marriage to Chuck Mitchell. "Little Green" was the story of her lost daughter "Kelly." And "River" was how she felt about running away from a possible marriage to Graham Nash.

Her debut quintet of albums celebrated her three most significant love affairs at that time. *Joni Mitchell [Song to a Seagull]* was recorded while she was in love with David Crosby. *Clouds* was recorded as she ended her affair with Crosby and began her relationship with Graham Nash. *Ladies of the Canyon* was recorded while she was living blissfully with Graham in Laurel Canyon. *Blue* was recorded amid her heartbreak over Graham, and her affair with James Taylor—featuring him on several of its tracks. *For the Roses* was the album that she used to vent her frustrations during the breakup with Taylor. And lyrically she expressed her feelings about her sojourn to the woods of British Columbia.

Regarding her sabbatical from life in the fast lane, Joni explained, "At a certain point, I actually tried to move back to Canada, into the bush. My idea was to follow my advice and get back to nature. I built a house that I thought would function with or without electricity. I was going to grow gardens and everything." (9)

She reveals, "Most of *For the Roses* was written there." (9) It was an album on which she was able to vent her pain and her disillusionment: "The hippie dream seemed to be collapsing," she recalls. (12)

Being a million-selling, Grammy Award–winning recording artist suddenly seemed to be a hollow achievement. Fame had also brought a sense of pressure and went against her basically shy nature. However, she was such a concert draw that she now had to perform in huge theaters and arenas. By retreating to the woods of British Columbia, she sought to become creatively renewed in a back-to-nature sort of way.

According to Joni, "I liked playing in small clubs the best, still do. I really like holding the attention of thirty or forty people. I never liked the roar of the big crowd. I could never adjust to the sound of people gasping at the mere mention of my name. It horrified me. And I also knew how fickle people could be. I knew they were buying an illusion, and I thought, 'Maybe they should know a little more about who I am.' I wanted to believe that the attention I was getting was for me. I didn't want there to be such a gulf between who I presented and who I was. David Geffen used to tell me that I was the only star he ever met who wanted to be ordinary. I never wanted to be a star. I didn't like entering a room with all eyes on me. I still don't like the attention of a birthday party. I prefer Christmas, which is everybody's holiday." (16)

One of the things that preyed on her mind while she was in British Columbia was her failed romance with James Taylor. She loved him, but she couldn't deal with his drug-enhanced mood swings and infidelity. When she was with Taylor the previous year, *Rolling Stone* magazine writer Jules Siegel put the spotlight on what life was like around them at the time. He observed from backstage one night: "A joint was lighted and passed around. Joni strummed his guitar. She was wearing a grey woollen knitted long dress and a hand-knitted scarf. 'I spend a lot of time on planes. It's a good time to knit.' The drummer brought out a small vial that looked like a miniature sweet cream bottle and contained cocaine. He horned the white powder from a tiny silver spoon. The room became crystal sharp. Joni was crisp and glistening as she stroked the guitar. It was time for James to go on stage. He picked up the guitar and ran his fingers lightly over the strings and frowned. 'Joni, did you re-tune my guitar?' She blushed, made a small 'O' and put her hand to her mouth." (56) Now it seemed she couldn't even smoke a joint backstage without it making the news.

Vignettes like this ran through her head while she sat in the woods and penned songs about James Taylor for her next album. Songs like "For the Roses," "Cold Blue Steel and Sweet Fire," "The Blonde in the Bleachers," "Electricity," "See You Sometime," and "Woman of Heart and Mind" were all written about her love for James, and the frustration and aggravation she felt from him.

"Around the time of *For the Roses*, there was an adjustment period to be made, and that album was that adjustment period," she explains. "*For the Roses* was a time of withdrawal from society, and intense self-examination. Maybe I don't handle adrenaline very well, but even the applause was hard. I know I have adrenal problems now [1988], and I'm hypoglycemic—but back then I didn't. So my animal sense was to run offstage! Many a night I would be out on-stage, and the intimacy of the songs against the raucousness of this huge beast—that is an audience—felt very weird. I was not David to that Goliath. Fight or flight? I took off in flight, a strange reaction. I didn't know anyone else who did that. I had to adjust to the din of that much attention. So, *For the Roses* was written in retreat, and it's nearly all piano songs. I was building a house in the northern British Columbia forest, with the rustle of the arbutus trees at night finding its way into the music. There was moonlight coming back on black water; it was a very solitary period. It was melancholy exile; there was a sense of failure to it." (51)

While she was there, she started reading philosophy books and thinking about the meaning of life. She recalls of this era, "I moved up into the Canadian back bush to a small sanctuary where I could be alone, I lived with kerosene [lamps], stayed away from electricity for about a year. I turned to nature. I was going down, and with that came a tremendous sense of knowing nothing. Western psychology might call it 'a nervous breakdown,' but in certain cultures they call it a 'shamonic conversion.' I read nearly every psychological book that I could lay my hands on, and threw them all against the wall, basically. But, depression can be the sand that makes the pearl. Most of my best work came out of it. If you get rid of the demons or the disturbing things, if you get rid of them then the angels fly off too." (3)

Meanwhile, back in Los Angeles and New York City, the times

were a-changing. At this point, what was going on in Jackson Browne's career bore a direct effect on Joni's career, since they were both managed by David Geffen. When Geffen felt that Jackson Browne was ready for a record deal, he made appointments with the top people at the New York record labels. First on the list was Clive Davis, who at the time was the head of Columbia Records—which was also Laura Nyro's and Bob Dylan's label.

In Davis's Manhattan office, Geffen had Jackson take his guitar out and sing his new composition, "Doctor My Eyes." In the middle of Browne's performance, Clive's secretary came in and whispered something to him. Apologizing, Davis told David and Jackson that he had to take this call and would be right back. Geffen went crazy with anger. How could he be treated this way?

"Pack up your guitar," David instructed the young balladeer.

"What?" said a startled Jackson.

"Pack up your guitar, we're leaving," Geffen insisted.

"We don't have to do that," said Browne.

"Just do what I tell you," he instructed his client. (25) And, with that, he left.

The next appointment was with Ahmet Ertegun of Atlantic Records. In terms of enthusiasm, his audition in Ertegun's office failed to elicit a record deal.

When Geffen pressured Ertegun to sign Browne, claiming, "You'll make a lot of money," Ertegun said, "You know what, David, I have a lot of money. Why don't you start a record company and then you'll have a lot of money?" (25)

Right then and there, Geffen told Ertegun, if he gave him his own distribution and manufacturing deal, he would split the profits 50/50 and start his own record label. Ertegun agreed, and so was born Geffen's first record label, Asylum Records. It was named "Asylum" because Geffen felt that the Laurel Canyon enclave that Joni and the rest of her "pack" were all living in was a bit of an "insane asylum." It was the perfect deal for him. He wouldn't have to lay out any money, and he would sign Jackson as his first recording act. Then he could lure his other acts—including Joni—to sign with the label.

On his debut album, *Jackson Browne*, the big Top 10 hit single it produced was a song called "Doctor My Eyes," which featured David Crosby and Graham Nash singing background vocals. Then

Geffen signed Linda Ronstadt's backup band, christened them the Eagles, and signed them to Asylum too. During this same era Geffen added Linda Ronstadt to the Asylum Records as well. Her debut album on the label was called *Don't Cry Now*.

With the completion of her *Blue* album, Joni's contract with Reprise Records had lapsed. David Geffen orchestrated her signing to his own Asylum Records, keeping himself and Elliot Roberts as her managers. Joni's first album for the label was *For the Roses*.

At this point, David Geffen had a great house in Los Angeles. He loved to entertain and often he had houseguests. During this period, Geffen invited Jackson to move into his house on Alto Cedro Drive, where he lived for several months. David gave him money for food and clothes. He couldn't have his new star not dressing like a star. On a couple of occasions Jackson invited his buddies John David Souther and Glenn Frey over for a swim. The trio ended up skinny dipping in David's swimming pool.

It was a whole new lifestyle for Jackson Browne. He would hang out at Geffen's mansion in the Beverly Glen area of Los Angeles, adjacent to Beverly Hills. Jackson would swim in the pool there, write songs, and play music. He even showcased his talent before songwriting stars Jimmy Webb and Laura Nyro. Geffen was clearly grooming him for pop music stardom.

For a while, Joni's sabbatical in the north woods of British Columbia was good for her. But after several months of swatting mosquitoes and reading by a kerosene lamp, she had had enough of its romantic charm. Finally she was ready to return to civilization. According to her, "I found that I was too spoiled already. I had too much choice. I could take the more difficult, old-fashion way for a short period of time, but the idea of doing it forever would not work. I have reclusive fits, though, all the time. Not that it isn't rewarding, you know. It is, I mean, I do it for myself first, but I don't want to do it for myself only. I feel I can still share my work with people and they appreciate it. I guess it is my calling." (9)

When Joni Mitchell was ready to return to Los Angeles, she lived at Geffen's house as well. She recalls, "When I came back, I came to stay with David Geffen as a guest, and I was kind of 'The Woman Who Came to Dinner.' I ended up staying on for a while." (3)

David Geffen remembers, "We were roommates. For me, it was

a very heady time, you know. I had just signed Bob Dylan, and I was dating Cher. You know, it was very tumultuous and a lot of fun and '70s." (3)

It was a busy first year for Asylum Records. First there was Jackson Browne's album. Then the Eagles released their self-titled debut album. They scored a hit with a song cowritten by Jackson and Glenn Frey called "Take It Easy." And Joni Mitchell had already written the majority of the songs for her debut album on the label, *For the Roses*—released later that year.

Once the long-awaited *Jackson Browne* album was in the stores, the troubadour hit the road on another high-profile concert tour, with another of David Geffen's artists: Joni Mitchell. The four-month trek took the duo on several stops through the United States and Europe.

It was not only the beginning of Jackson's most successful push into the mainstream of the music business, it was also the beginning of his brief love affair with Joni. Browne was on something of a trail of heartbreak too. He had ventured to New York City in 1969, where he played guitar and had an affair with rock singer Nico of Velvet Underground fame. He was devastated when she broke up with him. His first major tour in 1970 was with another Geffen leading lady, Laura Nyro. He had an affair with her as well. On the rebound, Jackson and Joni toured together for four months, beginning in February 1972. The tour kicked off at the Paramount Theater in Seattle on February 16, Masonic Temple in Detroit on February 18, and Chicago's Arie Crown Theater on February 21.

When Browne was later asked if this was a hindrance, being the opening act for the most successful woman of her genre, he argued that it was a blessing. "No, no, it was incredible . . . That was what they call a 'break,' because I don't think I could have attempted to play for a better audience . . . more suited to me," claimed Jackson. (57) The fact that he and Joni were lovers at the time only intensified the whole affair.

One of the most memorable dates on this tour was playing Carnegie Hall on the bill with Joni Mitchell on February 23, 1972. This honor was not lost on Jackson. The following night, he had his own gig out of town. It was a return to the East Coast stronghold of his popularity: Stony Brook.

On the stage that night at Stony Brook, Jackson spoke of having played Carnegie Hall the previous evening. "I'm not telling you that to impress you or anything. When you play in a big city everybody from the record company comes around and greases you to make you feel that you're on the job: 'You sold five records yesterday, kid.' So the only way to get through that is to annihilate yourself and see how long you remain standing. That's what I did. Woke up this morning at 11 with all the lights on," he claimed of his post–Carnegie Hall partying. (58)

The Joni and Jackson show then continued on to Massey Hall in Toronto, the Music Hall in Boston, Constitution Hall in Washington, the Academy of Music in Philadelphia, Tulane University in New Orleans, the Berkeley Community Theater in Berkeley, the Dorothy Chandler Pavilion in Los Angeles, and Queen Elizabeth Hall in Vancouver.

For the first time since writing "The Fiddle and the Drum," Joni flexed her celebrity power by entering into the political arena. On April 15, 1972, she performed at the Los Angeles Forum at a fund-raising benefit concert for George McGovern's presidential campaign. On April 28, 1972, she was on the bill with James Taylor and Paul Simon for another McGovern fund-raising concert at the Cleveland Arena in Cleveland, Ohio.

On May 3, 1972, Joni and Jackson Browne headlined the Odeon Theatre in Manchester, England. On May 5 and 6, they performed at Royal Festival Hall in London. Joni's reviews were raves. She may have thought she was going to escape from "idol worship," but it was back again, and in full form. Catching their act at Festival Hall in London on May 6, 1972, Mike Watts wrote of the concert in *Melody Maker*: "There was Jackson Browne, Joni Mitchell and this third malignant presence on stage, which manifested itself by a series of whistles, screeches and boots in the PA system, whose volume level was skittish to the point of perversity." In spite of the technical problems, Watts worshiped at her feet. He called her a "high priestess, virginal and vulnerable, not to be vilified . . . the mood of her performances tends to be excessively devotional. When she sits down at the piano, one knows the song is going to be melancholic, and when she takes up the guitar, only slightly less down beat. She becomes not just a performer but some kind of icon." (59)

On May 9, 1972, they performed at Jahrhunderthalle in Frankfurt, Germany. On May 26 Joni was on the BBC2 TV broadcast *In*

Concert BBC in London. The next day Penny Valentine interviewed Joni in London for a big feature article to be published in two parts in *Sounds* magazine's June 3 and 10 issues.

After the tour ended in England in the summer, Browne visited friend and musician Albert Lee, who lived outside of London, in Blackheath. When they made plans to get together on the telephone, Jackson told Lee that he was going to be bringing a friend with him. That was fine with him. Lee had no idea at the time that the friend was going to turn out be one of the hottest female singing sensations in the business—Joni Mitchell.

According to Albert, Jackson exuded more ease and self-confidence than usual. He had a Top 10 hit, a critically acclaimed debut album, and a romantic involvement with Joni. Lee noted that day, "He seemed really enamored with her." (50)

Joni's 1972 touring continued with a June 15 concert at the Olympia Theatre in Paris, June 18 at Waikiki Shell in Honolulu, and a return to the Mariposa Folk Festival in Toronto on July 15.

In fall 1972 Jackson started recording tracks for his second album. One of his last collaborations with Joni was her playing the electric piano on the recording of "Sing My Songs to Me." Jackson's affair with Joni ended when another young woman came into his life.

Jackson's longtime friends were all abuzz over his affair with Joni. Browne's singer-songwriter friend Steve Noonan was especially curious. According to him, "I remember saying to Jackson, 'Gee, tell me about Joni Mitchell,' and him saying, 'I don't want to talk about it.'" (50)

Jackson's love affair with Joni burned out rather quickly. Pamela Poland, an aspiring Los Angeles singer and one of Jackson's friends, hypothesized, "With Joni it was again the thing where she embodied all the things that he was in the process of developing. He was also in the process of developing them, but she was ahead of him. She'd certainly been involved in the music business longer. She had more deep-rooted awareness of the business . . . a popularity that couldn't be denied, that is attractive in itself, and a strong devotion to her own to her own artistry . . . Unfortunately it became conflicting. And then, beyond the conflict, the even more unfortunate thing is that it became too heavy for Jackson to be with someone who was so much more prolific than

Few singer-songwriters can rival the musical impact that Joni Mitchell has had
in her career. Her twenty-five albums span five decades of some of the most insightful and personal music ever recorded.

With albums like *Court and Spark*, *The Hissing of Summer Lawns*, and *Don Juan's Reckless Daughter*, Joni expanded her musical scope into jazz fusion and world music styles.

(Photo: Norman Seeff for Asylum Records/MJB Photo Archives)

Joni in the late 1970s adopted a more sophisticated musical style and personal
look. She wanted to grow beyond her initial hippie goddess phase.

One of the most appealing things about Joni Mitchell's music is that she is not
only brilliant at writing touching personal music, but she knows
how to sing lively rock & roll as well.

he. She was creative in so many ways, and it came out of her so easily, that to face his own struggle with his craft, his own slowness with his craft—to have those two mirrored against each other—I think was very painful for him." (50)

For whatever reason, Jackson's love affair with Joni Mitchell was over. Was the problem that they were too much alike? They came out of the same Laurel Canyon circle of friends, and they were seeking to capture the same kind of audience, musically. Perhaps the problem was that they were just too similar for it to work.

According to author Tom King in *The Operator,* a biography of David Geffen, "Joni Mitchell's romance with Jackson Browne was short-lived and had an ugly ending. Unlike her previous relationships with Graham Nash and David Crosby, she was not the one to end this one. Browne broke it off." (25)

Looking back on his string of love affairs gone wrong, including his affair with Joni, Jackson stated, "I got my heart crushed about eight times in a row. It would happen every two years or so; I'd forget and fall in love." (35) This was pretty much the end of Joni's friendship with Jackson as well.

Unlike her split from James or Jackson, Joni always maintained an amicable friendship with Graham Nash. In fact, her artistic sense was something she instilled and nurtured in Graham. "My relationship with Graham is a great enduring one. We lived together for some time—we were married, you might say. The time Graham and I were together was a highly productive period for me as an artist. I painted a great deal, and the bulk of my best drawings were done in '69 and '70 when we were together. To contend with this hyperactive woman, Graham tried his hand at several things: painting, stained glass. And finally he came to the camera. I feel he's not just a good photographer, he's a great one. His work was so lyrical. Some of his pictures are worth a thousand words. Even after we broke up, Graham made a gift of a very fine camera and a book of Cartier-Bresson photographs. He gave the gift back to me. Even though the romance ended, the creative aspect of our relationship has continued to branch out." (9)

Because of Graham's gift to her, Joni began to dabble in photography as well. On November 10, 1972, at the Gallery of Photography in Vancouver, Joni attended the opening of a photographic exhibition that included her photos, as well as the photographs of Graham Nash and Joel Bernstein. The exhibit ran through November 29.

In December 1972 Joni's fifth album, *For the Roses*, was released. It was her first for Asylum Records. No less than half of the twelve songs on the album were the musical recriminations toward her ex-lover—in this case, James Taylor. She chose several different approaches to addressing the sadness and loss she felt over him. These six songs were interleaved into six other songs that addressed other topics—including her relationship with her parents, her self-imposed vacation in the wilderness, and even a chirpy song about a radio. Again, the entire album was produced by Joni and recorded at A&M Studios in Hollywood.

The *For the Roses* album opens with the song "Banquet," in which she surveys the fate of people in the world. Some people—like herself—come down to hang out at the beach to refresh themselves, watching people water ski and picnic. While some turn to heroin (like James Taylor) and others turn to Jesus, she wonders what it all really means.

On the song "Cold Blue Steel and Sweet Fire," accompanying herself on guitar, Joni surveys the insanity of scoring and shooting up heroin. The cold blue steel is obviously a syringe, and the sweet fire is the feeling of the drug coursing into one's veins. She sings of blood stains on the bathroom sink and the desolation of a junkie who is "scoring" a fix. In this case, it's obviously James. This is her first foray into having a full jazz/rock band sound behind her. The lyrics are intoxicatingly dark and depressing, but the music is beautiful to behold. This is Joni's "Stairway to Heaven." She weaves a spellbinding musical tale, complete with the jazzy clarinet of Tom Scott.

The song "Barangrill" finds Joni sitting in a British Columbia bar and restaurant and describes the people she encounters there. Amid her sojourn to Canada, Joni was looking for the meaning of life—her life in particular. On "Barangrill," Joni has an epiphany while the waitresses pause to discuss their favorite cocktails, Singapore Slings and Zombies. According to her, "Sometimes it takes a personal crisis to turn you on the spiritual path. During your childhood and your teens you go through many crises. Everybody should go through it, it's a good experience. You go through a re-evaluation of yourself. Anybody with a smile on their face is enlightened. Everybody knows more than you. I walked into a restaurant a while back, and I saw three waitresses and thought they were all wearing black diamond earrings. While going through some guru books, it said that some people look to Mecca, some to the Cross, and some to the City National Bank. But I decided they were all wrong. It was happening right here in the restaurant." (60)

"Lesson in Survival" finds Joni singing to her lone piano about what she sees back in British Columbia: grilling salmon and the cold green ocean beyond the bay. "Let the Wind Carry Me" finds Joni talking about her disapproving parents, who around this time were wondering what their only daughter was doing with her life, running around the world chasing her rock & roll dreams.

"For the Roses" finds Joni criticizing James Taylor for the way he handles his life. Now that his image is on giant TV screens, he seems to be someone totally different than the young man she originally met. He was once struggling, but now everything he does is first class. She sits among the arbutus trees in the forest and thinks she hears the din of applause for her ex-lover, on a stage somewhere.

On "See You Sometime" Joni wonders what James is up to tonight. She calls him callous and "jive." Is he on a stage somewhere? Is he in his hotel room? Are his arms wrapped around some groupie? She claims that she is not ready to get married and change her last name. Still, in spite of the pain he caused her, she would like to see him again.

The song "Electricity" finds Joni again wondering what went wrong in her relationship with James. They once loved so easily and so nicely, in and out of the spotlights. Yet it all slipped through her fingers—like some emotional short-circuit.

The next song on the album is a change of pace for Joni, as subject matter and stylistically. If one were to pick a song in the Joni Mitchell songbook that has a country flavor, it is clearly the rhythmic and extremely catchy "You Turn Me On I'm a Radio." Using Bob Dylan–style storytelling, Joni weaves a musical confection of likening her love to the music that pours out of the AM radio. In actuality, this was a song that Joni was talked into writing.

Recalls David Geffen, "I kept telling Joni to write a hit, and she was always kind of making fun of me about the idea that she should have a hit. But I wanted her to sell a lot of records. I remember when she sang it to me. You know, I mean, it was almost with a—kind of like—making fun of my attempt for her to write a hit record." (3)

According to Joni at the time, "I wrote a song called 'You Turn Me On I'm a Radio' out of blatant commercial. I just thought—you know, I thought that it would have a certain amount of disc jockey appeal since it was full of things like the 'recording tower,' and you know, 'call me at the station,' and everything. And it was sort of just my peculiar warped sense of humor." (3)

This was one of Joni's first forays into coming up with a song by committee—with her playing leader of the band. She explains, "I've never had a hit record in America, so I got together with some friends and we decided we were going to make this a hit—conjure up this bit of magic for AM radio, destined to appeal to DJs. Graham [Nash] and David [Crosby] came, and Neil [Young] lent his band and he came and played some guitar, and somehow it just didn't work. There were too many chefs, you know. We had a terrific evening, a lot of fun, and the track is nice, but it's like when you do a movie with a cast of thousands. Somehow I prefer movies with unknowns. So I'm going to start looking for people who are untried, who have a different kind on enthusiasm that comes from wanting to support the artist." (29)

"The Blonde in the Bleachers" is the first song of Joni's where she really attempted to get a more rock & roll sound in her recording. In this case she has Stephen Stills on multiple tracks as a whole rock band. This is also the first time she has drums on one of her songs. In the lyrics of the song, a blonde groupie beckons to James from the audience, follows him home, and beds him. In this song, Joni basically asks him, "What's up with that?" She understands that the idea of James being monogamous would go against the macho credo of a hardcore rock & roll man. Still, she isn't buying it here.

On "Woman of Heart and Mind" she chides Taylor for coming to her like she was more of his mother than his lover. Addressed right at James, she tells him that nothing keeps him high long enough, and when he comes down from his latest "fix," he finds everything in life—including her love—disappointing. She tells him that he can go and "fuck" his "strangers," and essentially that he can go and fuck himself as well.

The last song on *For the Roses*, "Judgment of the Moon and

Stars (Ludwig's Tune)," is about Ludwig van Beethoven. Joni explains, "While looking for a guru, I found a book on the spiritual development of Beethoven. I wrote him a song, and was gonna call it 'Roll Over Beethoven Revisited,' but I decided to call it 'Ludwig's Tune.' No disrespect intended." (60)

She likens her job of squeezing songs out of the sounds that piano wires and hammers make to the similar life of Beethoven. She abstractly refers to "broken" trees—signifying the black ebony wooden keys of the piano—and ivory from elephants to signify the white keys. On the song, amid her poetic singing, she plays the lone piano and crafts one of her most beautiful, jazzy recordings to date. It is a preview of musical attractions to come.

When Joni was writing songs for her fifth album, *For the Roses*, she had a lot of issues on her mind. Reeling from a series of failed romances and feeling disillusioned with music business in general, she used her songwriting to express her deepest feelings.

Although she never came out and pinned individual songs to the hurt feelings she felt for specific ex-lovers, it is generally perceived that several of the songs included on *For the Roses* were meant to vent the pain and the rage she felt against James Taylor. Critics, fans, and the press have long pegged several of the songs as directly aimed at James.

She admitted in the 1970s, "I'm a confronter by nature. I have a tendency to confront my relationships much more often than people would care. I'm always being told that I talk too much. It's not like I like to, but I habitually confront before I escape. Rather than go out and try to drown my sorrows or something, I'll wallow and muddle through them. My friends thought for a long time that this was done out of some act of masochism. I began to believe it myself. But at this time in my life, I would say that it has paid some dividend. By confronting those things and thinking them through as deeply as my limited intelligence would allow, there's a certain richness that comes in time. Even psychiatrists—'mind whores' for the most part—don't have a healthy attitude toward depression. They get bored with it. I think their problem is they need to be deeply depressed." (9)

According to Joni, the title of her album, *For the Roses*, referred to her feeling that her race to sell records was as exploitive as a horse running at the track, for the horseshoe-shaped arrangement of roses that is placed on the winning horse. This is her sense of humor about the music business. According to her, "The title it-self was facetious. I wanted to use a drawing of a horse's ass for the album cover. I did use it for a billboard ad. It was my joke on the Sunset Strip, the huge drawing of a horse with cars and glamour girls, and it had a balloon coming out of the horse's mouth which said, 'For the Roses.' But nobody got the message." (51)

Instead, the cover of *For the Roses* was a portrait of Joni taken by her photographer friend Joel Bernstein. It depicts her sitting on a bluff in the British Columbia woods, looking over a placid lake or bay down below. On the inside is another of shot of Joni—nude. She is photographed from the back, standing on a boulder on the rocky Canadian coast. She looks something like Venus rising from the sea in a Botticelli painting.

The nude shot of Joni caused quite a stir—especially with her parents. According to her, "I remember my mother putting on glasses to scrutinize it more closely. Then my father said, 'Myrtle, people do things like this these days.' Which was a great attitude. It was the most innocent of nudes, kind of like a Botticelli pose. It was meant to express that line: 'I'm looking way out at the ocean, love to see that green water in motion, there's this reef around me.' Joel Bernstein is the only photographer I would feel comfortable enough to take off my clothes for. It was part of our concept for the cover when we were going to call the album *Judgment of the Moon and Stars*. We were originally going to set the [nude] photograph in a circle and replace the daylight sky with the starry starry night, so it would be like a Magritte. At the time, no one was paying homage to Magritte. Then Elliot said, 'Joan, how would you like to see $5.98 plastered across your ass?' So it became the inside [photo]." (9)

Right after the album was released, from December 16 to 19, 1972, Joni played four sold-out nights at the Troubadour in Los Angeles—two shows a night. She was presented with a huge bouquet of red roses and then she entertained her audiences with nearly two and a half hours of music and between-song stories.

The press reviews for this latest album were wonderful and en-thusiastic. Stephen Davis in *Rolling Stone* raved about it, claiming, "Her appeal is in the subtle texture of her toughness, and her readiness to tell secrets and make obscure and difficult feelings lucid and vocal. She breaks your heart and makes you tentatively smile. She is the leading lady in a personal pageant of Heavy Duty romance. The poetry of her love songs sets her almost on some other planet . . . *For the Roses* is constructed like the cleverest of novels—stories within stories within stories." (61)

Lynn Kellerman in *Music Gig* called it "the next logical step toward maturation. Mitchell tackles more worldly subjects; 'Cold Blue Steel, Sweet Fire' traces the excessiveness of the junkie's world. *For the Roses* scorns the selfless superstar, the manufactured god . . . each tune flowed smoothly into the other, the concept complete, the introduction of jazz influence making it all the more intriguing, but never alienating." (54)

David Cleary in *All Music Guide* wrote, "Lyrics here are among Mitchell's best, continuing in the vein of gripping honest and heartfelt depth exhibited on *Blue*. As always there are selections about relationship problems such as 'Lesson in Survival,' 'See You Sometime,' and perhaps the best of all her songs in this genre, 'Woman of Heart and Mind.' More than a bridge between great albums, this excellent disc is a top notch listen in its own right." (43)

Some people criticized Joni for blasting James Taylor so strongly in her songwriting. Others—especially women—cheered Mitchell's courage for singing about the unfair way men treat the women they are in relationships with. According to concert promoter Myra Dorfman, "If you read between the lines of a lot of material that Joni put out after they [Mitchell and Taylor] broke up, it was pretty easy to figure out that a lot of the heartache and pain that were prevalent in her songs was because of the rough time she went through after her relationship with Taylor. And it really hit home because so many women, myself included, went through tough relationships and could relate to everything Joni was singing about. No woman had challenged males before the way Joni did in her songs. Today we have people like Alanis Morrissette and Tori Amos singing about how shitty men treat women, but Joni was the first person to do this. She paved the way for the whole women's movement in popular music, and a lot of it came out because of the heartache she went through when she was involved with James Taylor." (36)

At the beginning of her recording career, Joni Mitchell was the darling of Rolling Stone magazine. Then suddenly the publication turned on her. One Rolling Stone article from that year quoted a publicist in Hollywood who snidely claimed, "It's all so very incestuous:

musically, socially, romantically. Graham used to be Joni Mitchell's old man, after David Crosby, and before James Taylor." (29)

The frosting on the cake came in *Rolling Stone's* year-end issue giving Joni Mitchell the Old Lady of the Year award. It included a chart intimating that she had slept with half of the music business. Joni Mitchell was represented as a pair of lips pursed in a kiss. Lines were drawn to the names of Graham Nash (identified as a broken heart), David Crosby (broken heart), and gay David Geffen (erroneously identified with kisses). Also on the list were supposed lovers like her band member Russ Kunkel and her buddy Stephen Stills.

She tried hard to dismiss it. "I never saw it. The people that were involved in it called up to console me. My victims called first. That took some of the sting out of it. It was ludicrous. I mean, even when they were drawing all these broken-hearted lines out of my life and my ability to love well, I wasn't so unique. There was a lot of affection in those relationships. The fact that I couldn't stay in them for one reason or another was very *painful* to me. The men involved are good people. I'm fond of them to this day. We have a mutual affection, even though we've gone to new relationships. Certainly there are pockets of hurt that come. You come a little battered out of a relationship that doesn't go on forever. I don't live in bitterness." (9)

Looking back at it Joni recalls, "I think I was called 'Old Lady of the Year'—some facetious thing that was hurtful." Did she care at the time? According to her, "Yeah, of course I did, unfortunately." (55)

Angela Bowie, author of the book *Pop Sex*, claims, "It was well known in London in the early 1970s, that every time she came to town, it was on the arm of a new male singing star. David Crosby, Graham Nash, James Taylor, Jackson Browne. While I was exploring at the time with bisexuality, Joni was busy changing the sexual mores of society as well. In the past, it was *de rigueur* that male rock stars would have a series of girls on their arms. Never before had a female rock star had multiple affairs so publicly, like there was nothing even remotely questionable about such behavior. It was like Joni was saying, 'If no one thinks twice about the guys behaving like this, then why shouldn't I behave the same way?' My hat was off to her. Joni's disinterest in the subject hearkens to other artists I have known who liked to test the water with a little intimate hanky-panky. But that was supposed to be for male rock stars, until Joni Mitchell, Cher, and Barbra Streisand remolded behavior for divas!" (62)

When the publication snidely dubbed her Old Lady of the Year, it riled her fans. "This was a total crock of shit," exclaims Angela, who was married to David Bowie at the time. "This was just Jan Wenner and the male writers at *Rolling Stone* setting up a sexual double standard for her to work around. Did they do a chart on who Jimmy Page was sleeping with? Did they chart a trail of Elton John's 'rent boys'? Was Rod Stewart's trail of ex-lovers a separate graph? Hell no. No wonder Joni didn't speak to the magazine for several years. Instead of showing how 'hip' and 'contemporary' the writers of *Rolling Stone* were, they instead illustrated how chauvinistic they still were." (62)

Joni was mad at the publication for quite some time, and for many years refused to grant interviews. "It was a low blow, and it was unfair," she complained. "I was not abnormally promiscuous, especially within the context of the free love experiment, so to be turned on by my peer group and made an example made me aware that the whore/Madonna thing had not been abolished by that experiment. People who were legitimately on the list, like Graham Nash, were gonna call and complain, but then they figured it would fan the flame." (63)

Furthermore, she was tired of the publication second-guessing which of her boyfriends her songs were written for. "Assumptions were made in interpreting the lyrics that this was about so-and-so. All that nonsense that destroys the ability of the listener to identify with the song. Plus, they were misinterpretations. So that was painful and unnecessary, and *Rolling Stone* had a policy for years after that to get me," she claimed. (63)

Years later she was still smarting from that particular press mention. "They portrayed me as this heartbreaker. They say that about Madonna now, and it gives her a certain distinction. But I don't know. A heart is something people need," said Joni. (12)

Regardless of what *Rolling Stone* was publishing about her love life, her record sales were going through the roof. By the end of December *For the Roses* was already certified gold and it was well on its way to platinum. In the United States, the tongue-in-cheek single, "You Turn Me On I'm a Radio" became her biggest radio single to date, peaking at number 25 in *Billboard* in January 1973.

Stimulated by her first bona fide hit, her album hit number 11 in the United States.

The year 1973 was to be a big one for her. She was about to produce her biggest album ever, and she was finally about to find a lasting love. Conveniently, the band that would bring her the greatest success also brought her next lover.

9

Court and Spark

While she was recording *For the Roses*, Joni Mitchell came on an interesting new idea. She had explored being a solo guitar player and piano player on previous albums. As she wrote and recorded the song "You Turn Me On I'm a Radio" with David Crosby, Graham Nash, and several other musicians present, it struck her that what she needed was a band of her own to interact with, to perform with, and to record with. This concept and the top-notch band that she came up with converged to create the most widely satisfying single album of her entire career: *Court and Spark*.

The year 1973 was largely spent coming up with this new musical direction. She did very little touring that year—logging only two benefits as her entire public performance schedule. On April 15 she was part of the St. James Benefit in Montreal, Quebec. On August 11–12, she was one of the acts performing at the Topanga Canyon Corral in Los Angeles, California. It was a benefit to stop the construction of condominium apartments in Topanga Canyon, and the bill featured Joni, Neil Young, and the Eagles, two shows per day.

Much of her income now came from songwriting royalties. She was famous for providing songs for a diverse number of singers. Her song "Both Sides Now," for example, was recorded by several song stylists, including Frank Sinatra, Bing Crosby, and even jazz singer Cleo Laine. In late 1973 the group Nazareth released a version of "This Flight Tonight" as a single and placed it at number 11 on the British pop charts. Even when Joni wasn't actively touring that year, her music was out there representing her and earning her cash.

Something else was occupying her mind that year. She was working on crystallizing a fuller sound and recording a new album. How does someone of Joni Mitchell's stature find her own rock band? Place an ad in the trades? Enlist old friends and hope for the best? Or just discover them? Fortunately, the latter scenario yielded a new direction for her.

As she explained, "There were no drummers or bass players that could play my music. I tried the same sections that Carole King and James Taylor were using. I couldn't get on the airwaves, because there was no bass and drums on [my records], so I had incentive, but everything they added was arbitrary. They were imposing style on something without seeing what the something was that they were playing to. I thought, 'They're putting big, dark polka dots along the bottom of the music, and fence posts.' I'd end up trying to tell them how to play, and they'd say, 'Isn't that cute, she was telling me how to play my ax, and I've played with James Brown . . .' So it was difficult as a female to guide males into playing [what I wanted], and to make observations in regard to the music that they had not made. Finally a drummer said, 'Joni, you're going to have to play with jazz musicians.' So I started scouting the clubs." (18)

Then, she just happened to find herself at the right place at the right time. "One night I went down to the Baked Potato [a jazz club in Los Angeles] to hear the L.A. Express play. I knew Tom Scott, I'd done some work on *For the Roses* with him. When I heard the band, I was very enthusiastic, and I asked them to play on my next session. When they got in the studio, it was the same problem. They didn't really know how heavy to play, and I was used to being the whole orchestra. Many nights I would be very discouraged. But one night we suddenly overcame the obstacles. The next thing we knew, we were all aware we were making something quite unique." (9)

She claims that jazz musicians best understood the music she wanted to produce: "I had no choice but to go with jazz musicians. I tried to play with all of the rock bands . . . when we made our transition from folk to folk/rock. They couldn't play my music because it's so eccentric. They would try, but the straight-ahead 2/4 rock & roll running through it would steamroller right over a bar of 3/4. My music had all these little eccentricities in it, and it would just not feel right to me . . . People used to call my harmony weird. In context of today's [1990s] music, it's really not weird, but it is much broader polyphonic harmony." (10)

Finally, Mitchell felt that she was really hitting her stride as a musician: "I found the L.A. Express, but that was for my sixth album [*Court and Spark*]. It took me that long!" (18)

For the first time she felt that she was working with musicians who understood her unconventional way of communicating the sounds she wanted to hear on the tracks. "Tom Scott was also very open to metaphorical instruction on *Court and Spark*, I'd say, 'You're playing the Doppler effect: just give me straight lines.' And he was a great sport. It was an exciting project, that record with Tom," she claims. (51)

If Joni initially heard songs in her head, how did she finally get them down on paper? According to her, "I sang all the counter-melody to a scribe, who wrote it out. So anything that's added is my composition. In a few exceptions I'll cut a player loose, but then I'll edit him, move him around, so even though he's given me free lines, I'm still collaging them into place." (18)

How was this change in musicality so different? Joni explains, "Well, I started singing folk songs because it was a great way to begin. By the time I began to write my own music, I would say I was no longer a folksinger, although I looked like one because I was a girl with a guitar. The music I heard in me was harmonically and rhythmically much more complex, which you can hear as I began to overdub—like for instance, on *Court and Spark*. Even though we used an orchestra on that record, everything you hear is my composition, not an arrangement by someone imposed on my composition." (64)

She also confirms that many of the songs she recorded that year were left over from her retreat in the woods, including "Free Man in Paris." "*Court and Spark* still contains a lot of songs written up in Canada. The song 'Court and Spark' itself was written up on my land there. It deals with a story based on Vancouver and the Sunshine coast," she says. (9)

However, in the process she found a new source of inspiration—in addition to the excitement of playing with a new jazz ensemble. Circa 1974 the L.A. Express consisted of Tom Scott on woodwinds and reeds, Robben Ford on electric guitar, Max Bennett on bass, Larry Nash playing piano, and John Guerin on drums. She and Guerin instantly hit it off during these recording sessions, and for the next couple of years, it seemed that Joni had found lasting love.

The recording sessions were going very well, and several guest stars showed up to appear on the album and/or dropped in to have a listen. But not everyone understood what she was trying to accomplish by combining elements of folk and rock and jazz on the same album. "When I was recording *Court and Spark* at A&M Studios, John Lennon was recording across the hall. He came in one night. I played him a few tracks. Being a working-class lad, he said all he liked was simple rock & roll, and anything too orchestrated was too sophisticated [didn't interest him]. He was very drunk." (65)

She recalls, "I knew I wanted to write literature in the pop arena, and in a way, I was really punished for it. Even by John Lennon. He told me that I was 'the product of my own over-education'—and remember, I only have a twelfth-grade education. He said, 'Why do you let other people have your hits for you? You want a hit, don't you? Put some fiddles on it.' He said this about *Court and Spark*, mind you." (14)

Lennon wasn't the only one who didn't understand the direction Joni was heading musically. "Right at the time I made *Court and Spark*, which was my most successful album, David Geffen was trying to sign Dylan for what turned out to be the *Planet Waves* L.P. project. David and I were sharing a house. I'd been working on *Court and Spark* under his nose, and maybe he heard it through too many stages, but I knew I was making something special. I was so excited the night I finished it. There were a bunch of people there, including Dylan. I played *Court and Spark* for everyone, and Bobby fell asleep and snored all the way through it. When the record came to the end, the people went, 'Huh?' Then they played *Planet Waves* and everybody jumped up and down. There was so much enthusiasm. Now, *Planet Waves* wasn't one of Bobby's best projects, and I hadn't expected it to be a competitive situation, but for the first time in my career I felt this sibling rivalry. It was an ordinary record for Bobby, a transitional piece, and yet everybody was cheering. Finally, one of the women took me aside and said, 'Don't pay them any attention. Those boys have no ears.'" (16)

Prior to the album's release, Joni hit the concert road. She alternated between formal concert halls and theaters and college campuses across America. She toured with her new band, the L.A. Express. They would be the opening act, there would be an intermission, and then they would come back as Joni's band. On January 18 she headlined the Kiel Opera House in St. Louis, Missouri. From there it was on to South Bend, Urbana, Chicago, Ann Arbor, Philadelphia, Boston, Ithaca, and New York City. In Manhattan she played at Avery Fisher Hall on February 5, and the next night it was on to Radio City Music Hall.

Chuck Pulin wrote a review of Joni's concert at Radio City Music Hall for *Sounds* magazine. In it he observed, "The Radio City Music Hall audience, made up largely of teenage girls, sat with idolatry expressions, almost cooing with joy. The male section of the audience seemed to compromise dates or boyfriends or elder brothers, but in any event the New York gals jumped or danced with joy, running up to the front of the stage with flowers for Joni. Her piano was so bedecked with flowers it seemed it would collapse under the weight, and during her two-hour set many wept, while others cried out, 'We love you Joni!'" (66)

From February 7 to March 11, it was one prestigious music hall after another—from Boston to Cleveland, Philadelphia to Sacramento and points in between. The tour also included the Dorothy Chandler Pavilion in Los Angeles. Then it was off to the Pacific Northwest, where she performed at the Civic Auditorium in Portland, Oregon, on March 11. The next night she was one of the headliners at the kickoff to the Crosby, Stills, Nash, and Young reunion tour at the Seattle Center Arena. Whatever creative problems the foursome had in the previous year or so, they buried their differences and hit the road. Recalls Graham, "Stephen Stills liked that. It was enormously satisfying for him to have the Beach Boys, Santana, The Band, Joni Mitchell open for us. That was quite something." With regard to the quartet's reconciliation, Nash explained, "When we started the first album, we were all in love, and everything was sunny. And then just before the second album, Joni and me split up, Neil got divorced from his wife, Stephen hadn't seen Judy [Collins] in months, and the week before we were due to start, David's lady, Christine, was killed in a [car] crash. That's the difference between CSN and CSNY. It started out real weird." (67)

Finally, in March 1974, the album she had previewed in so many concerts was released. And what a worthwhile wait it had been. Fortunately Joni didn't take John Lennon's advice and put fiddles on it. Instead she followed her own instincts and put a lot of jazz on it. The resulting album, *Court and Spark*, was unlike any of the albums she had released before it.

First, there was the trio of Scott, Guerin, and Bennett from L.A. Express. Then the jazz factor was intensified by adding Joe Sample and Wilton Felder of the Jazz Crusaders to many of the songs. Larry Carlton and Chuck Findley were among the additional jazz masters included on this album, which became known as a milestone in Joni's career.

From the very first piano notes of the opening track—"Court and Spark"—it is a fuller, richer, more confident Joni. Instead of coming across like the pained narrator, she sounds strong and in command. Since much of her best music has to do with singing about love, or that pain that love causes, it is good to find her in a position of courting and sparking. She was clearly enjoying her more developed, fuller sound. There are many layers to the sound and lots of musical interludes—like those she began to experiment with on *For the Roses*. In the lyrics of the song she claims that she finds it impossible to get Los Angeles—the city of the "fallen" angels—out of her system.

On the breezy, up-tempo "Help Me," she sings of her love affair with Guerin. She fears that she is falling in love too fast, an emotion she is all too familiar with. With Guerin's drums driving the track and lyrics of love that can be universally identified with, "Help Me" became a Mitchell trademark song. Here she claims that she loves being in love, but she also loves her freedom. This is a recurring theme in her music.

"Free Man in Paris," featuring José Feliciano as guest guitarist, is a musical ode about her friend and manager, David Geffen. In a lighthearted, amusing story she tells of how on this Paris trip he is not saddled with deciding anyone's career fate—at least for a few days. She speaks about his taking a break from feeding the star-making machinery of show business. To make this song even more poignant, two of Geffen's star clients sang the background vocals: David Crosby and Graham Nash.

Explains Joni, "Here's how I look at my songs, and it's very simple: I feel that the melodies, if they're 'born' first, require words with the same melodic inflections that English has in its spoken forms. So I'm singing with an ear for the music and meter of the spoken word. And then from jazz I took the liberty to not necessarily nail the downbeats all the time. I enjoy dialogue, and I'm a big talker, and my music helps me be a listener too. Besides the 'confessional' assumption, people assume that everything I write is autobiographical. If I sing in the first person, they think it's all about me. With a song like 'Free Man in Paris,' they attribute almost every word of the song to my personal life, somehow missing the setups of 'He said' and 'She said.' Certainly most of the song is eyewitness accounting, but many of the characters I write about—even if their tone is entirely first-person—have nothing to do with my own life in the intimate sense. It's more like dramatic recitation or theatrical soliloquy." (51)

On "People's Parties" and "Same Situation" Joni again writes about personal experiences, touching on feelings and emotions everyone can relate to and identify with. On "People's Parties," Joni sings of laughing her way through her sadness, surrounded by a myriad of fascinating characters at a cocktail event. And on "Same Situation," she prays for the kind of relationship she can rely on—as she weighs out "beauty" and "imperfections." She has spent much of her life "tethered" to the telephone, waiting for one man or another to call her. Will her prayer for a man who is both "strong" and "sincere" ever be answered?

The upbeat and percolating "Car on a Hill" finds Joni awaiting the arrival of her lover's automobile. A thoughtful and moody jazz-influenced piece, this is a song that Joni always thought would have made a better single than what the record company thought. It is a beautiful musical suite all to itself.

Again, with Guerin's snappy drum work, Joni and her new-found band take this medium tempo song to stirring heights. In the middle of the song, Joni blends her voice into the jazz instrumentals and becomes an instrument herself. The musical interludes strengthen the track and show off Mitchell at her most chanteuse-like. It is slow, thoughtful, and gorgeous. Here she lyri-

cally essays the emotionally hollow 1970s habit of going to the local pickup bar and looking for love in all the wrong places. But in
the end, she surmises it all comes "Down to You."

"Down to You" is a sheer masterpiece, and a lot of the magic
comes from the arrangement. Never before has Joni's piano playing been treated as a jazz solo. If ever her father should have been
proud of buying that spinet off of the back of the truck when she
was a child, it was on this song.

On the song "Just Like This Train," Joni speaks in frank terms
about her lovers like they were the boxcars of an emotional railroad. In pure Joni fashion, it is clearly she who is the engine driving this railroad of love. She admonishes one of the men she
sings of by attacking his vanity. She even wickedly hurls some
hair-loss voodoo in his direction.

According to her, "That was intentionally mean. 'I hope your
hairline recedes.' That was mean. That was the meanest I ever got,
though," she admits. "You should've heard the first draft for
'Carey'! Oh, that was a mean song. I wrote it for this guy's birthday. He was very mean to me, but he was a character and I liked
him anyway. He just picked on me unnecessarily. It could have
been anyone, any woman. So for his birthday I wrote him this
song and after every verse said, 'Oh, you're a mean old daddy but I
like you.' It had a few stings. I'm a double Scorpio, you know. Supposedly that makes me a stinger. I think I've pulled a lot of
punches, considering what the stars endowed me with." (68) It is
suspected that the hairline in question here is David Geffen's.

For "Raised on Robbery" Joni and her new band kick up the
excitement to tell another of Joni's bar stories, with Robbie
Robertson of The Band guesting on electric guitar. With saxophones wailing, "Raised on Robbery" is an edgier version of
"Barangrill." While that had a more relaxed, late afternoon feeling
to it, this song is more of a drunken brawl scenario, set to music.
Here Joni lyrically sings the part of a bawdy woman in a bar, trying to "hook up" with a man who will buy her a drink and listen
to her jumbled life story.

On the moody and slow "Trouble Child" Joni addresses an
overprivileged friend who has landed in trouble again for
overindulging. Here Joni speaks directly to a person who is
bedridden and isolated and feeling distraught. She looks at the se-

rious side of madness. And on the next track, "Twisted," she looks at the amusing side of being thought of as crazy. It's almost as though with these two distinctly different tracks, she has looked at "madness" from both sides now.

The album ends on a high note with the loony, loopy "Twisted." This marked the first time Joni ever recorded a song written by someone else—Annie Ross and Wardell Gray. Originally it was Annie Ross's jazzy rendition of this song—about going nuts—that brought it to prominence in the 1950s. This was taken from Joni's favorite jazz vocal group when she was a teenager, and she is absolutely delightful singing this goofy medium-tempo song. To take the levity to a new level, the comedy team of Cheech and Chong guest-star on the track—quipping a couple of one-liners about Joni's degree of craziness. This song, which basically asks the listener, Am I nuts? is the perfect and amusing way to end Joni's most developed and richest-sounding album to date. Was she nuts? No, just crazy like a fox!

On *Court and Spark*, Joni returned to doing her own cover art work. In this instance, it was a pencil sketch of mountains and clouds on a creamy beige background. After two albums that featured her photograph on the cover, she was back to promoting her own vastly creative artistry, both on the record and on the cover.

The reviews for *Court and Spark* were ecstatic. Michael Watts in *Melody Maker* claimed, "Of all the female writers and singers postdating Joan Baez in pop music, Joni Mitchell seems to have arrived at the most complete definition of herself as an artist. True, she's not witty, like Dory Previn, as sophisticated as Bette Midler or La Streisand, not as stylistically far-ranging as Carole King, but few other rock musicians, male or female, have so refined personal expression that it succeeds as genuine art." (69)

In the *All Music Guide*, Jason Ankeny proclaimed, "Mitchell reached her commercial high point with *Court and Spark*, a remarkably deft fusion of folk, pop, and jazz . . . a concept record exploring the roles of honesty and trust in relationships . . . smart, smooth and assured from the first note to the last." (43)

Jon Landau in *Rolling Stone* praised it by writing, "On *Court and Spark* the music is less a reinforcement of the lyrics and more of a counterpoint to them. An album about the individual struggling with notions of freedom, it is itself freer, looser, more obvious, occasionally more raunchy and not afraid to vary from past work. It is also sung with extraordinary beauty, from first note to last." (70)

And the *Village Voice* 1974 annual Pazz and Jop [sic] Critic's Poll ranked *Court and Spark* the number 1 album that year. It came in first place ahead of Steely Dan's *Pretzel Logic*, Stevie Wonder's *Fullingness' First Finale*, the Rolling Stones' *It's Only Rock & Roll*, Bob Dylan and The Band's *Before the Flood*, Jackson Browne's *Late for the Sky*, and Linda Ronstadt's *Heart Like a Wheel*.

Several people in the music business found *Court and Spark* inspirational. A decade later, when Madonna was interviewed in *Billboard* magazine, she announced, "In high school I worshiped Joni Mitchell and sang everything from *Court and Spark*, my coming-of-age record." (71)

Not surprisingly, twenty-six years later, in 2000, Anthony DeCurtis wrote in *Rolling Stone* that *Court and Spark* was an enduring classic among Joni's albums. "*Court and Spark* [is] an album that not only represents the culmination of Mitchell's folk-rock period but also signals the many musical experiments in her future . . . Playing behind her, musicians like [Tom] Scott, guitarist Larry Carlton, drummer John Guerin and trumpeter Chuck Findley add colors and depth to songs that stretch melodies and vocal lines in surprising directions . . . That's why the criterion of 'standing the test of time' was invented—a standard that *Court and Spark* will always meet." (72)

Court and Spark was a huge coup for Joni, hitting number 2 on *Billboard* in the United States, where it remained for four weeks, selling into both gold and platinum figures. In Great Britain it peaked at number 14. This was also the most hit single–producing album of her career in the United States. The song "Raised on Robbery" was the first single from it, which hit number 65. Then, with "Help Me," Joni finally scored her first Top 10 hit, when it logged in at number 7. In September the song "Free Man in Paris" made it to number 22.

Joni confessed that she had zero role when it came to selecting what became a single release and what did not. "I have nothing to do with the choosing of tracks for singles. Generally speaking, I don't agree with the selections, and there are tracks that never get played on the radio that I regret won't get that exposure. So I like the idea of well-received singles and am sorry when they don't get a chance to happen. 'Car on a Hill' was one I thought would have become a good single; I wish that was circulating in the golden oldies department, because it has a vitality today, it would work. 'Trouble Child' too, and 'Just Like This Train,' which I'd rather hear on the radio than 'Raised on Robbery.' I like the song 'Big Yellow Taxi' better than I like my rendition of it. I don't think my version is definitive. 'Help Me' is a throwaway song, but it was a good radio record. My record companies always have a tendency to take my fastest songs on albums for singles, thinking they'd stand out because they did on the LPs. Meantime, I'd feel that the radio is crying for one of my ballads!" (51)

From March 24 to mid-April, Joni continued to tour with the L.A. Express. Her travels took her to Durham, Dallas, Houston, Memphis, and Nashville. Then it was on to England for the kick-off of the European leg of the Crosby, Stills, Nash, and Young tour. It opened on April 20 at the New Victoria Theater in London. It was the first performance of a three-day engagement there.

Rob Mackie, who reviewed the show in London for *Sounds* magazine, observed of Joni, "She looks a little harder and tougher, from folk waif to rock & roll lady." (73)

July and August were filled with more tour dates, including Ravinia Pavilion in Denver with CSNY; the Civic Arena in St. Paul; Pine Knob Music Theater in Clarkston, Michigan; Massey Hall in Toronto; the Universal Amphitheater in Los Angeles; Temple University Music in Ambler, Pennsylvania; the Music Shed at Tanglewood in Lenox, Massachusetts; and Nassau Coliseum in Uniondale, New York.

In September it was back to Denver to play the Denver Auditorium and then a huge concert at Roosevelt Raceway in Westbury, New York. Finally, on September 14, 1974, Joni performed with Crosby, Stills, Nash, and Young, The Band, and Jesse Colin Young at Wembley Stadium in London.

In a unique move, Asylum Records released a second Joni Mitchell album only seven months after her last one. A live-in-concert album capturing the songstress and her L.A. Express band in action, the fittingly entitled *Miles of Aisles*, stands up with the best live albums ever recorded. Rarely does a live album take previously recorded material and add so much more to each of the songs. And, astonishingly, when it was released in November 1974, it hit number 2 in the United States and number 34 in the

United Kingdom. It was such an anticipated hit that it was certified gold before it hit the stores. Furthermore, when the new live version of "Big Yellow Taxi" was released as a single, it became a bigger chart hit than her original version did.

She doesn't just play her older songs; she sonically reinvents them and infuses them with new rocky, jazzy excitement. Whereas other stars' "live" albums often replicate the performer's songs with little addition, here everything gets kicked up several notches. From "Big Yellow Taxi" to "Blue" to "Both Sides Now" Joni adds a lot of new excitement to the proceedings. For people who might have just have gotten turned on to Joni's music via *Court and Spark*, the album *Miles of Aisles* was the perfect way to catch up on the wonderful and insightful music that preceded it.

"Big Yellow Taxi" especially gets a new blast of energy, with Tom Scott taking a jazzy sax solo midsong. When the new live version of this song was released as a single, it hit number 24 in the United States, whereas the original studio version of this song made it only to number 67 in 1970. The same is true for "Woodstock." Joni's original version was more haunting and had a slower pace. Here the song is reinvented as a jazzy ballad.

Miles of Aisles was composed of songs from all of Mitchell's previous album releases, with the addition of two new tunes: "Jericho" and "Love or Money." In an effort not to take any of the thunder away from the sales of the *Court and Spark* album, only one of the songs from that disc was included here: "People's Parties." Here the album takes "Circle Game" and makes it a fun sing-along with her adoring audience. Poignant songs like "Cactus Tree," "Cold Blue Steel and Sweet Fire," and "Woman of Heart and Mind" are infused with a luminous new life as well.

The majority of the *Miles of Aisles* album was recorded August 14–17, 1974, at the Universal Amphitheater. The song "Cactus Tree" was recorded on March 4 at the L.A. Music Center, and "Real Good for Free" was recorded on March 2 at the Berkeley Community Center. The album also brought together many of Joni's other favorite tracks, including "You Turn Me On I'm a Radio," "Rainy Night House," "A Case of You," "All I Want," "Both Sides Now," "Carey," and "The Last Time I Saw Richard."

The cover photo/illustration on *Miles of Aisles* is part photograph and part illustration, both by Joni herself. It started out as a snapshot that she took of her own feet draped over the back of the empty seats at a Detroit-area outdoor concert venue, Pine Knob. The only part of her that is fully visible are her two feet in green sandals, with her red pedicured toenails prominently showing through. She took the photograph during the summer tour that yielded this album, and then she continued the top and sides of her view in marking pens.

To cap off the year, Joni was front-page news in *Time* magazine. According to the song by Dr. Hook, you really know when you've made it in the rock world when you see yourself on "the cover of *Rolling Stone*." However, making the cover of the December 16, 1974, issue of *Time* meant that she had really made it big in a mainstream way.

In the article, Joni came across like the true *artiste* she was. "I feel like I'm married to this guy named 'Art.' I'm responsible to my 'Art' above all else." (21)

Regarding her revealing songwriting style, she claimed, "The most important thing is to write in your own blood. I bare intimate feelings because people should know how other people feel." (21)

She likened her songs to children: "My family consists of pieces of work that go out in the world. Instead of hanging around for nineteen years they leave the nest early." (21)

By now she had moved out of David Geffen's house and bought her own sixteen-room place in the Bel Air area of Los Angeles. She was currently living with thirty-five-year-old John Guerin, the drummer in Tom Scott's L.A. Express. According to her, the couple liked to stay home and play cribbage. After a rocky relationship track record, at long last Joni had found a man who was much more her soul mate than her previous musician boyfriends.

As though the song she wrote for *Blue*, "For Free," had been a prophecy, just before Christmas 1974, Linda Ronstadt, Carly Simon, James Taylor, and Joni Mitchell found themselves in each other's company and they decided to go Christmas caroling door to door in Los Angeles. Some very startled onlookers were treated to the best free concert of the year.

10

The Hissing of Summer Lawns

In February 1975, Joni's live version of "Big Yellow Taxi" peaked on the pop charts in America, and both her *Miles of Aisles* and *Court and Spark* albums were still on the LP charts. Her career was at an all-time high. On March 1, she and Tom Scott together won a Grammy Award in the category of Best Arrangement Accompanying Vocalists for the song "Down to You," from *Court and Spark*. The presentation of this trophy at the seventeenth annual Grammy Awards further cemented Mitchell's stature on the current rock music scene. She had produced the two most accessible and successful albums of her career, and now she had to decide where her music and her muse were going to take her next.

Joni recalls that there was a certain amount of pressure at this point. Would she continue along this refreshingly popular fusion of rock and jazz? Would she continue her self-examining lyric poetry? Would she continue to compose catchy melodies that were upbeat and radio friendly? Actually the answers to these questions were, No, no, and no.

Instead, Joni did what she had always done: whatever she pleased. For her next three albums, Joni Mitchell went out on a limb and off on a tangent. She produced albums that seriously divided her fan base. One album was indulgently experimental, one was brilliantly executed, and one was so esoteric it seemed to miss almost everyone's taste.

Referring to this triumvirate of experimental albums—*The Hissing of Summer Lawns, Hejira,* and *Don Juan's Reckless Daughter*—Joni later explained, "People seem to have a problem after *Court and Spark*—everything was measured unfavorably against it." (55)

In the first part of 1975 Joni was busy recording her next studio album. According to her, "*The Hissing of Summer Lawns* is a suburban album. About the time that album came around I thought, 'I'm not going to be your sin eater any longer.' So I began to write social description as opposed to personal confession. I met with a tremendous amount of resentment. People thought suddenly that I was secure in my success, that I was being a snot and was attacking them. The basic theme of the album, which everybody thought was so abstract, was just any summer day in any neighborhood when people turn on their sprinklers on all up and down the block. It's just that hiss of suburbia." (9)

That same year Joni and Joan Baez teamed up for their only recorded collaboration. Joan sings the lead, and Joni provides a distinctive background vocal. The song, entitled "Di Da," was included on Joan's *Diamonds and Rust* disc, her most commercially successful album. The song consists of Baez singing the word "Di Da" over and over again to a jazzy track. In the final third of the song Joni chimes in her harmony vocal. "Di Da" is a beautiful recording, but it makes one wish that this female folk-star duo had gone all the way to record a full duet.

In November 1975 Joni's eighth album, *The Hissing of Summer Lawns,* was released. Although it was not filled with "radio-friendly" singles, it is a fascinating aural affair. Of all the songs included here, the opening track, "In France They Kiss on Main Street," sounds most like it belongs on *Court and Spark*. Its allusion is to the same Parisian energy that made "Free Man in Paris" such a delight. In fact, on the 2004 Joni compilation album, *Dreamland,* she sequenced those two French-themed songs together to further strengthen their association.

Although the song's chorus repeats the song title, "In France They Kiss on Main Street" is filled with images of her teenage years in Saskatchewan, where she dreamed romantically about Paris. Here she sings of an adolescence filled with kissing in darkened hallways and stairwells—as though it were a sin, while across the Atlantic, people openly kissed on the streets of France. On this song about reminiscing about love, Joni's background trio is composed of three former lovers—David Crosby, Graham Nash, and James Taylor. In addition, Jeff "Skunk" Baxter of Steely Dan and the Doobie Brothers is featured on electric guitar.

"The Jungle Line" is instantly distinguished by its unique African sound, propelled by the beat of authentic Burundi warrior drums. Joni's vivid imagery transports the listener to the lush green jungles of Africa. Like a snake slithering its way through society, drugs flow from the poppy fields of Europe and Asia, and from the coca plants of South America. Joni weaves an intoxicating song about poppy's poison, and cocaine's insidious snake-like nature. This song is a stunning social commentary and a musically rhythmic creation.

For "Edith and the Kingpin" Joni introduces us to an over-dressed pimp and his coterie of girls who are destined to become old years before their time. When they start to fade, the kingpin revives their energy by guiding their noses to the cocaine spoon. While the music flows around her, Joni tells an urban fairy tale of prostitution. Surrounded by the Jazz Crusaders—Joe Sample and Winton Felton—as well as Larry Carlton and John Guerin, Mitchell weaves a musical spell. Then the album starts to meander off track. The song "Don't Interrupt the Sorrow" is lovely but rambling, like poetry set to a beat. She sings of her muse while her band concocts a percolating conga-enhanced confection of music behind her. And on "Shades of Scarlett Conquering," Joni examines the myth of the southern belle—Scarlett O'Hara style. According to Joni, a woman commands and needs everything at her fingertips. Images of Clark Gable, Errol Flynn, and magnolia blossoms are characters in this song, which also sounds like a poetic reading set to a tune.

The song "The Hissing of Summer Lawns" takes on the myth of suburbia. Here Joni sings of the hissing sound of water sprinklers on lush front yards. Inside the ranch house is a living room full of furniture that no one ever sits in. Around the suburban housewife's neck hangs a diamond, and in the backyard is a lovely blue swimming pool. But is this stuff worth staking your life to preserve? That is the question Joni is asking here. On "The Boho Dance" Joni talks about looking for the inspiration for her art.

Again, singing in a freeform style, she tells of reading books about how noble it is to suffer for your art. What is this dance she is doing in her life, she wonders, with its cocktail hours and Paris dresses. Are society's goals worth chasing?

The really dazzling jazz piece from this album is the combined song "Harry's House"/"Centerpiece." The song "Harry's House" is another suburban tale set to music. In this case, Harry's wife has stuck around for years, living in Harry's house and taking her part of Harry's weekly paycheck. Now she is going to escape from Harry. One of the most colorful visions of opulence she sings of is that of a helicopter landing on New York City's Pan Am Building, resembling a graceful dragonfly in flight. The most fascinating piece comes in the middle, when she segues into a slowed-down, jazzy version of the Lambert, Hendricks, and Ross classic "Centerpiece." Joni sounds wonderful here, and Joe Sample's piano solo in the middle of "Centerpiece" is breathtaking.

Recalling her love of Lambert, Hendricks, and Ross, Joni recalls cherishing the trio's debut album as a teenager: "I learned every song off of it, and I don't think there's another album anywhere—including my own—on which I know every note and word of every song . . . I couldn't do 'Cloudburst,' because of some of the very fast scat singing, but I did record two numbers out of that set: 'Twisted,' which was in the *Court and Spark* album, and 'Centerpiece,' which was incorporated with 'Harry's House' in the *Hissing of Summer Lawns* album." (74)

The next song, "Sweet Bird," sounds more like a jazzy rendition of a song from the *Blue* era. Here she contemplates the concept of time and space in her life. She sings of the spinning Earth and wonders what it's all about. Her singing is delivered in a very light vocal fashion, backed by her own guitar and her own piano playing. This song too rambles a bit.

Finally the album ends with Joni's dramatic multitracked epic, "Shadows and Light." Backed by a chorus of her own voice, she pontificates about life and love, blindness and sight, hope and hopelessness. This song is something of a Gregorian chant of Joni-isms, taken from her readings in philosophy. Playing an Arp-Farfisa synthesizer behind her many voices, Mitchell preaches to her musical disciples on "Shadows and Light." She delivers a yin and yang view on life itself, in a highly dramatic fashion.

The cover art for *The Hissing of Summer Lawns* was, naturally, by Joni herself. It depicts a black-on-gray backdrop sketch of mid-town Manhattan. The city instantly borders on suburban houses, and in the foreground of the houses is an olive green expanse of grass or lawn. On this olive green mass are the dark silhouettes of six African hunters, dragging the carcass of a long python-like snake back to their village in the valley below and off to the far left. Joni used this unsettling piece of art to make a statement. It demonstrated how so many segments of culture can exist, all bordering on the same grassy expanse. On the original vinyl edition of the album, the figures of the African men were embossed, so that they stood out even more dramatically.

It was an album of jazz-infused vignettes that were actually social commentaries. Without drawing conclusions, on each song she shines a light on different segments of society, from the elite ("Harry's House") to the mean streets ("Edith and the Kingpin") to the wilds of the brush ("The Jungle Line").

On the inside was a full body photograph of Joni wearing a bikini in a swimming pool, placidly having a dip. Snapped mid-stroke while the famed troubadour swam on her back, the photo was taken by Norman Seeff.

It was a wonderful photograph, but not everyone loved the concept. "People thought it was very narcissistic of me to be swimming around in a pool, which I thought was an odd observation. It was a lot of activity. As opposed to sexual posturing, which runs through the business—nobody ever pointed a finger at narcissism there. I had stopped being confessional. I think they were ready to nail me anyway. They would have said, 'More morose, scathing introspection.' They were ready to get me; that's the way I figure it. It was my second year in office. The cartoonists had their fun. There weren't enough good jokes left, so it was time to throw me out of office and get a new president. It's politics," she explained. (9)

Across the water of the photo, Joni wrote her own liner notes: "This is a total work conceived graphically, musically, lyrically and accidentally—as a whole. The performances were guided by the given compositional structures and the audibly inspired beauty of every player. The whole unfolded like a mystery. It is not my intention to unravel that mystery for anyone, but rather to offer some additional clues. 'Centerpiece' is a Johnny Mandel/Jon Hendricks tune. John Guerin and I collaborated on 'The Hissing of

Summer Lawns.' 'The Boho Dance' is a Tom Wolfe-ism from the book *The Painted Word*." (75)

Explaining the difference between *Court and Spark* and *The Hissing of Summer Lawns*, Joni revealed, "I guided everything into place on *Court and Spark*—even though I didn't play it, I sang it, and then they played it from that and it was pretty much as writ. *Hissing of Summer Lawns* was a little looser—I let people stretch out, and as result of that it had a jazzier flavor, because they used their own harmonies instead of mine. People weren't really ready for jazz in pop music at that time—jazz singing." (7)

How was the creation of this album so much different than her previous work? According to Joni, it was a complete change in the perspective of her writing. "When I first started writing, I used to write more fictionally," she explains. "The first three albums were more or less characters, like 'March.' Like any fiction writer there was some basis in something that happened, but after the *Blue* album I went through a period where I wrote very personal songs. I did a series of self-portraits, scrapings of the soul and I went through that for a long time. By the time I got to *The Hissing of Summer Lawns* I was back to doing portraits again. By that point, people were used to me being a confessional artist and the result of that subtle change was a lot of people didn't like *Hissing* because if I was saying, 'I'm like this,' that 'I' could either be them—if they wanted it to be—or if it got too vulnerable, they could go, 'It's her.' But the moment I started doing portraits again, saying 'you,' a lot of people saw themselves more than they wanted to. Then they would get mad at me." (68)

Well, people didn't just dislike it, they hated it. The press reviews for *The Hissing of Summer Lawns* were blisteringly critical. Fans who had fallen in love with her early and more personally revealing songwriting were confounded. Since when did Joni Mitchell become a narrator, a spectator, or a musical reporter?

According to Stephen Holden's *Rolling Stone* review of this album, "With *The Hissing of Summer Lawns*, Joni Mitchell has moved beyond what has become personal confession into the realm of social philosophy . . . Since *Blue*, Mitchell's interest in melody has become increasingly eccentric, and she has relied more and more on lyrics and elaborate production . . . Four members of Tom Scott's L.A. Express are featured on *Hissing*, but their uninspired jazz-rock style completely opposes Mitchell's romantic style . . . ultimately a great collection of pop poems with a distracting soundtrack. Read it first. Then play it." (76)

In addition to critically trashing *The Hissing of Summer Lawns*, *Rolling Stone* called it the worst album of the year in its year-end roundup. According to Joni, "If they had just said they'd hated it, I could have taken it. When other publications picked up the same attitude, I thought, 'I'll finish up this contract and quit making records." (12) Of course, that wasn't about to happen.

She later said in her own defense, "This is the thing that *Rolling Stone*—when it made a diagram of broken hearts—was being very simplistic about. It was an easy target to slam me for my romantic alliances. That's human nature. That hurt, but not nearly so much as when they began to tear apart *The Hissing of Summer Lawns*. Ignorantly. I couldn't get it together, in any way; it being human nature to take the attacks that were given certain projects. I got very frustrated at the turning point, when the press began to turn against me." (9)

In the *Village Voice*, Robert Christgau wrote, "The transition from great songwriter to bad poet is always a difficult one, and Mitchell's talent and good sense are putting up a fight. But any record that is more interesting to read than to listen to has got to be in trouble." (77)

Lynn Kellermann in the *Music Gig* complained, "With *The Hissing of Summer Lawns* it is difficult to recover the artist of old among lines and lines of self-congratulatory, grandiose statements of upper-class complacency and suburban mediocrity. Joni constantly evades the reason for anger and impatience—her own submission to the societal disease her characters have already succumbed to . . . the instrumentation precise and professional as always, but gutless and formalized. Joni's voice, like a far-off ghost in a seance, loses its fullness and 'talky' vibrance—reminiscent of her beginnings when her records were filled with uncertainty." (54)

Mike Watts in *Melody Maker* found the album cryptic. Listening to it was "a delightful torture . . . primitive and sophisticated." (78)

But other recording artists appreciated *The Hissing of Summer Lawns* for the epic jazz/rock opera that it was. According to Joni, "I got a telegram from Paul and Linda McCartney that year saying 'We really liked it.'" (79)

Years later, Prince confessed that he ranked it as the all-time best

Joni album. "I was so pleased when Prince said *Hissing* was his favorite. You know, that album was called all sorts of awful names. Of all my 'children,' that was the one that really got beat up on the playground. So for him to say that in the same rag [*Rolling Stone*] that kind of started the war against it, was a treat for me. When I listen to it I don't see why it was so hated really, but one thing that I did was I changed 'I' to 'you.' Dylan sang a lot of personal things saying 'you.' As a male that's better. It's easier for a man to go 'you.' I'm sure that when he says 'you,' part of it is actually a 'you' and some of it is an 'I.' But I hadn't used that device. I had been writing 'I' this and 'I' that. And it was easier to stomach or something because when I started writing 'you,' people said, 'Who does she think she is?' And, 'Why is she taking pot shots at us?' This simple dramatic device became a large point of contention. That constituted an enormous change for some of my fans." (68)

Ironically, with *The Hissing of Summer Lawns*, Joni became the first innovative artist to delve into the rich palate of sounds in traditional African music. It is nowadays known as "world music." Joni was a decade ahead of Paul Simon's African-influenced *Graceland* or Sting's *Nothing Like the Sun*, on which he delved into South American sounds, or Linda Ronstadt suddenly singing traditional Mexican music on *Canciones de Mi Padre*. Joni opened the door for blending the music of many cultures, and she was critically stoned in the town square for it. According to her, the album was a bigger hit with black audiences than with white music critics because of the use of the black characters on the cover and the African drums on the tracks.

"There was a big stink about that," she recalls. "It was taboo, you see. I don't think I realized how culturally isolated we were until the release of that record. In white culture it was problematic, but it got good reviews in the black magazines, where it was accidentally reviewed because there was an illustration of a black person on the cover. I thought it was adventuresome, but it was shocking how frightened people were of it. I think the record was inadvertently holding up a mirror to a change that people were on the brink of in this hemisphere, and people were disturbed by the teetering they were experiencing. The Third World was becoming more important and they were disoriented." (51)

The Hissing of Summer Lawns made Joni a true innovator. She beat the pack of male rockers to the plate when it came to experimenting with the traditional music of African cultures and blending it with her own jazz/rock. "I never called myself a feminist," Mitchell claims. "I could agree with a lot of the men's point of view. There was something very noble in a woman being willing to swallow her own dreams and devote herself to caring for her husband. There was nobility in that. Not that I could ever have done it. I had this talent to feed. A Gypsy told me that this is my first life as a woman. In all my previous incarnations I was a man. I'm still getting used to it." (2)

After years of praise from the critics and fresh from her biggest-selling albums yet, it must have come as quite a surprise to be blasted by the critics. Did it make her want to pack her bags and quit? Claims Joni, "Inspiration can run out, you know. Laura Nyro made a choice that has tempted me on *many* occasions. And that was to lead an ordinary life. She married a carpenter, as I understand, and turned her back on it all. Which is brave and tough in its own way. Many, many times as a writer, I've come to a day where I say, 'None of this has any meaning.' If you maintain that point of view, if you hold onto it and possess it, that's *it* for you. There's a possibility that you can come firmly to that conclusion, as Rimbaud did, and give it up. I've always managed to move out of those pockets." (9)

Joni wasn't paying a lot of attention to what the critics were saying about *The Hissing of Summer Lawns*. She was already off on her newest adventure. She joined Bob Dylan's famed Rolling Thunder Revue that year. She began just hanging out in the wings as an onlooker but soon found herself performing at several of the concerts from 1975 to early 1976. This was Dylan's idea, to join with several of the old Bleecker Street characters he had been friends with years ago and have a big all-star revue with an evolving onstage lineup. Among the players on this tour were Joan Baez, Roger McGuinn of the Byrds, Ramblin' Jack Elliott, T-Bone Burnett, David Blue, Rick Danko of The Band, poet Allen Ginsberg, and even David Bowie's guitarist Mick Ronson. Large segments of the tour were filmed and became the four-hour slightly fictional semidocumentary epic *Renaldo and Clara*. Joni requested that her parts in the concert film be cut to a minimum.

According to Joni, "I joined Rolling Thunder as a spectator. I would have been content to follow it for three cities just as an observer, but since I was there I was asked to participate. Then for mystical reasons of my own, I made a pact with myself that I would stay on the thing until it was over. It was a trial of sorts for me. I went out in a foot soldier position. I made up songs onstage. I sang in French *badly*. I did a lot of things to prevent myself from getting in the way. What was in it for me hadn't anything to do with applause or the performing aspect. It was simply to be allowed to remain an observer and a witness to an incredible spectacle. As a result, the parts of the film that I was in . . . for all I know, it was powerful and interesting footage. But I preferred to be invisible. I've got my own reasons why." (9)

Mitchell and Dylan had a long history together at this point. She explains, "The first official meeting was the *Johnny Cash Show* in 1969. We played that together. Afterward Johnny had a party at his house. So we met briefly there. Over the years there were a series of brief encounters. Tests. Little art games. I always had an affection for him. At one point we were at a concert—whose concert was that? How soon we forget. Anyway, we're backstage at this concert. Bobby and Louie Kemp were holding up the wall. I went over there and opened up the conversation with painting. At that point I had an idea for a canvas that I wanted to do. I'd just come from New Mexico, and the color of the land there was still very much with me. I'd seen color combinations that had never occurred to me before. Lavender and wheat, like old-fashioned licorice, you know, when you bit into it and there's this peculiar, rich green and brown color? The soil was like that, and the foliage coming out of it was vivid in the context of this color of earth. Anyway, I was describing something like that, really getting carried away with all of the colors. And Bobby says to me: 'When you paint, do you use white?' And I said, 'Of course.' He said, "Cause if you don't use white, your paint gets muddy.' I thought, 'Aha, the boy's been taking art lessons.' The next time we had a brief conversation was when Paul McCartney had a party on the *Queen Mary*, and everybody left the table and Bobby and I were sitting there. After a long silence he said, 'If you were gonna paint this room, what would you paint?' I said, 'Well, let me think, I'd paint the mirrored ball spinning, I'd paint the women in the washroom, the band . . .' Later all the stuff came back to me as a part of a dream that became the song 'Paprika Plains.' I said, 'What would you paint?' He said, 'I'd paint this coffee cup.' Later he wrote, 'One More Cup of Coffee.'" (9)

Playwright Sam Shepard joined the Rolling Thunder Revue for a while and later wrote a backstage diary about the tour, *Rolling Thunder Logbook*. He observed, "Joni Mitchell is cross-legged on the floor, barefoot, writing something in a notebook. She bites her lip and looks over to Rick Danko, who's smashing the shit out of a pinball machine. The high spirit of competition has seized us all. Headlines in the paper seem like messages delivered from outside the walls. This feeling of separateness weasels its way into everything. You find yourself expanding to the smell of arrogant power or deflating to total depression. Then everything filters away to the elevators. To music. To another marathon right to the break of day." (80)

The first time Joni joined Bob Dylan's Rolling Thunder Revue was on November 13, at Veterans Memorial Coliseum in New Haven, Connecticut. There were some real misadventures on the Rolling Thunder road. One afternoon in December, the eclectic revue, with the addition of Roberta Flack, played a correctional institution in Clifton, New Jersey, before an audience of mainly black inmates. In the book *Bob Dylan: A Biography*, author Bob Spitz wrote, "The inmates couldn't relate at all to Joni Mitchell's creamy white pastorales. Two minutes into her set, hoots and cat-calls sailed up over the makeshift stage, thawing Joni's icy composure. That tom cat face of hers puckered into a wicked sneer. 'We came here to give you love,' she lectured them. 'If you can't handle it, that's your problem.'" (81) Some days the old Woodstock/peace sign route just doesn't work on the crowd.

Also in December 1975 was the five-hour Night of the Hurricane benefit concert in Madison Square Garden, with the Rolling Thunder Revue. The money went to the defense fund for arrested boxer Hurricane Carter. Joni had a four-song set in that particular show.

Mitchell, however, suddenly got the vibe that the cause they were there to defend was not exactly just. Since Carter was black, Dylan and Baez decided to paint their cause as a race issue. To accentuate the point, they covered their faces in white greasepaint. As Joni explains it, "Bobby and Joan Baez were in whiteface and they were going to rescue Hurricane Carter. I had talked to Hurricane on the phone several times, and I was alone in perceiving that he was a violent person and an opportunist. I thought, 'Oh my God, we're a bunch of white patsy liberals. This is a bad person. He's fakin' it.' So, when we got to the last show, at Madison Square Garden, Joan Baez asked me to introduce Muhammad Ali. I was in a cynical mood. I said, 'What I'll say is, "We're here tonight on behalf of one jive-ass nigger who could have been 'Champion of the World,' and I'd like to introduce you to another one who is."' She stared at me, and immediately removed me from this introductory role. Anyway, Hurricane was released from jail and the next day he brutally beat up this woman." (82) Joni's instincts served her well once again.

On the tour Joni engaged in some hilarious antics to entertain herself. She recalls, "For my own amusement on that tour, I had taken to ripping off cops. I would use my wits and try and get a piece of cop paraphernalia off 'em—I got hats and jackets and tie-clips and badges. One time I chased a cop and he wouldn't give me anything so I said, 'What if I get a gang and we pin you up against a wall and you tell your superior you were outnumbered?' The smile came over just one corner of his mouth and he said, 'Go get your gang.' It was really a charming game. I would introduce myself as 'Mademoiselle Oink,' the liaison officer between rock & roll and the cops." (82)

Meanwhile, in spite of what the reviewers thought of Joni's album *The Hissing of Summer Lawns*, her fans bought it on sight. In the United States it hit number 4 on the charts, and in the United Kingdom it was number 14. One single was released from it, "In France They Kiss on Main Street," which peaked at number 66 in the United States. The album was certified gold and platinum in spite of what music publications had to say about her latest musical bent. After all, she was Joni Mitchell, and her true fans knew that whatever it was she had to say musically, they wanted to hear it.

11

Hejira

The year 1976 was an active one for Joni. Between January and May she was busy on tour. She not only had her own concert tour with L.A. Express to complete, she also connected with Bob Dylan's Rolling Thunder Revue several times during that winter and spring. She was on hand on January 25 at the concert billed as Night of the Hurricane 2, which took place at the Houston Astrodome in Texas. She was also present onstage with Dylan and company on May 15 at the Gatesville State School for Boys in Gatesville, Texas.

With a full schedule of her own shows mixed in, Joni went across America to see her fans in the eastern and central parts of the United States. When a reviewer from *Rolling Stone* magazine showed up for one of the concerts, the publication made it clear that the war of the wills with Joni was still in full swing.

Catching Mitchell's show on February 23, 1976, at the New Haven Coliseum in New Haven, Connecticut, Kit Rachlis of *Rolling Stone* wrote a highly unflattering piece on the show, entitled "Joni Mitchell: The Hissing of Winter Concerts." The review claimed, "Her lack of melodic ideas and the cliché-ridden, cumbersome support of the L.A. Express are particularly disconcerting. She circumvented some of these problems by playing much of the *Summer Lawns* material solo or accompanied by a single instrumentalist. As a result, 'Shades of Scarlett Conquering' and

'Edith and the Kingpin,' with her voice in full command, fared much better than in the studio . . . with her music and her masks rarely in order, Mitchell failed to establish that listening to her concerts is remotely as satisfying as hearing her records." (83) Ouch!

When her U.S. touring schedule was complete, she headed off for Europe. On May 26 she headlined the Hammersmith Odeon in London, which was the first gig of a three-day engagement. On May 30 she played at the Apollo Centre in Glasgow, Scotland.

As the tour came to an end, she returned to the United States and contemplated what she was going to do next. Half of her wanted to run away from the music business—again—and the other half found her seeking inspiration. Ultimately she decided to take some time off. As she explains it, "*Hejira* came out of another of my sabbaticals, another time when I flipped out and quit show business for a time. This instance was in '76. I'd been out with Dylan's Rolling Thunder Revue, which was an amazing experience, studying mysticism and ego malformation like you wouldn't believe. Everybody took all of their vices to the Nth degree and came out of it born again, or into A.A." (51)

Another life transition was on her mind at that time as well. She had recently broken up with John Guerin and basically wanted to run away. Again her sense of independence had driven her to walk away from this relationship, which had once seemed so cozy. Being on tour with John and the other members of L.A. Express made her want to strike out on her own. Her lust for independence won out again.

She found inspiration while looking out at the Pacific Ocean during a visit to Neil Young's beach house. As she explains it, "After the end of my last tour, it was a case of waiting again. I had an idea: I knew I wanted to travel. I was sitting out at the beach at Neil's place and I was thinking, 'I want to travel, I don't know where and I don't know who with.' Two friends of mine came to the door and said, 'We're driving across country.' I said, 'I've been waiting for you; I'm gone.' So we drove across country, then we parted ways. It was my car, so I drove back alone. The *Hejira* album was written mostly while I was traveling in the car. That's why there were no piano songs." (9)

Once she arrived on the East Coast, she decided to set out on an adventure-filled journey of her own. Joni recalls, "Afterward, I drove back across the country by myself, and I used to stay in places like light-housekeeping units along the Gulf Coast. I gave up everything but smoking, and I'd run on the beach and hit health food stores. In New Orleans, I wore wigs and pawned myself off as somebody else. Meanwhile, nobody knew where I was. I'd do those disappearing acts. I'd pass through some seedy town with a pinball arcade, fall in with people who worked on the machines, people staying alive shoplifting, whatever. They don't know who you are: 'Why you driving that white Mercedes? Oh, you're driving it across the country for somebody else.' You know, make up some name and hang out. Great experiences, almost like the prince and the pauper. So, whenever possible during these breakdowns in my career I would pawn myself off as someone else, or go to some distant clime and intentionally seek out a strata of society I was sure I would never have gotten near otherwise." (51)

The songs began to pour out of her, and ultimately they became the basis for her most melancholy and jazziest album yet, *Hejira*. She was fascinated by the definition of that very word. According to her, "'Hejira' was an obscure word, but it said exactly what I wanted. Running away, honorably. It dealt with the leaving of a relationship, but without the sense of failure that accompanied the break-up of my previous relationships. I felt that it was not necessarily anybody's fault. It was a new attitude." (9)

Joni explained her writing process at the time: "When I know that I have to write a song for an album, I walk around with eyes and ears wide open, totally set on reception. Often it is a minor event that gives me the inspiration for complicated stories. My imagination gets a little push and everything else happens by itself." (28)

She wrote an incredible travel diary of songs, which were again vignettes of what she saw on the road. Now she wanted to take her music and her sound into some new areas and delve even further into the jazz realm. According to her, "I've always tried to remain true to my own compositional instincts by eliminating the producer, who laminates you to the popular sounds of your time. I've been in conflict with the popular sounds of my time, for the most time, for the most part. All through the '70s I never liked the sound of the bass or the drums, just on a sonic level, but I couldn't get any [drummers] to take the pillow out of their kick and I couldn't get [bassists] to put fresh strings on and give me a resonant sound, because they were scared to be unhip. Hip is a herd mentality, and it's very conservative, especially amongst the boys." (18)

However the solution to her mid-1970s musical dilemma came to her in the form of a new bass player. "Finally," she explains, "someone said, 'There's this kid in Florida named Jaco Pastorius. He's really weird; you'd probably like him.' So I sent for Jaco, and he had the sound I was looking for—big and fat and resonant." (18)

Hejira was the first album of Joni's to feature the sounds of Jaco Pastorius, and it is a sonic delight to behold. He was able to give Joni a moody, flowing bass line on which she could sing and soar.

Adjusting to Jaco's way of playing was not easy at first, but Joni learned how to utilize his talents to full advantage. She explains, "Although I wanted a wide bass sound, his was even wider, and he insisted that he be mixed up so that I was like his background singer. So to get enough meat to hold his sound, I doubled the guitar loosely—I just played it twice." (18)

In November 1976 Joni released her ninth album, *Hejira*. Some people thought it was her most brilliant-sounding album yet. Others hated the fact that she was now deeply entrenched in the jazz idiom. However, it was inarguable that what she came up with on *Hejira* was a unified and exciting new sound for herself. Analyzing what phase she was currently at in her career, Mitchell claimed that she was at a stage where "the poet took over the singer." (7)

Indeed, that is exactly what happened on this beautiful-sounding, unified concept album. Opening with the rhythmic and energetic "Coyote," Joni sings of a man who is pursuing her across Canada like a wild coyote on the prowl. With Jaco Pastorius's colorful bass playing, Bobbye Hall's percussion, and Larry Carlton's guitar, the effect is that Joni is singing this vibrant song to the accompaniment of a jazz trio.

The song "Amelia" is in part about fabled lost aviatrix Amelia Earhart. While driving down the road, Joni spots six jet planes in the open sky, and conjures up the ghost of Earhart and has a conversation with the pilot who seemed to vanish into thin air over the Pacific Ocean. A haunting guitar and vibes track guiding her, Joni weaves a touching story, using several colorful allusions to illustrate her own flight from society. One of these comes on her brilliant mention of the Greek legend of Icarus, who fell from the sky having flown too close to the sun. This is the most beautiful song on the *Hejira* album, slow and moody and full of emotion. Like Amelia, Joni was a woman who often flew alone in life.

One of the many characters Joni met on her cross-country journey was legendary bluesman Furry Lewis. This encounter on Memphis's equally legendary Beale Street serves for the narrative of "Furry Sings the Blues." While on Beale Street, Mitchell recalls, "Standing in front of one of the many pawn shops was a guy in a purplish-blue shirt, bald, smoking a stogie. He looks at me and says, 'Oh, Joni Mitchell?' I think, 'Culturally this is impossible.' I mentioned Furry Lewis and he says, 'Oh, sure, he's a friend of mine. Meet me tonight and we'll go over and see him. Bring a bottle of Jack Daniels and a carton of Pall Mall cigarettes.' Furry was in his eighties or nineties, and senile at this point. Lived in little shanty in the ghetto. It was quite a nice visit until I said to him—meaning to be close to him—'I play in open tunings too.' People must have ridiculed him, because he leaned upon the bed and said, 'Ah kin play in Spanish tonnin'.' Real defensive. Somehow or other I must have insulted him. He just said, 'I don't like her,' as I wrote in the song." (82)

With Neil Young guesting on harmonica, "Furry Sings the Blues" perfectly tells the story of this bluesman in his twilight years. Joni evokes the blues mood with her loving vocals, even parroting Furry's gruff voice when she quotes him in the song.

On the song "A Strange Boy" Joni sings of a boy on a yellow skateboard weaving his way along the sidewalk on a busy day. Here Mitchell analyzes his noninterest in growing up and wonders what he is all about. Against a scarce track featuring Carlton on guitar, Hall on percussion, and Joni's own unique rhythm guitar, she wonders why she gave her body, and gifts of clothes and jewelry, to him.

With Jaco's moody bass dominating, on the song "Hejira" Joni surveys the highway trip she is making. Listening to Benny Goodman on the radio, she wonders how she again arrived at this questioning point in her life. She has travel fever, and she finds a little piece of herself in each stranger she meets.

"Song for Sharon" finds Joni talking to a childhood friend in Maidstone and pondering where her life is going. In her lyric poem of a song, Joni keeps referring to seeing a wedding dress and wondering if she is destined to ever wear one again. The narrative of the song changes locales as she looks out at Wollman Skating Rink in Central Park and spies twenty-nine skaters spinning around on the ice. With her own voice backing her, and John Guerin's drumming, Joni is mesmerizing to listen to as she talks to Sharon—presumably on the phone. According to her, all she wants now is to find another lover—presumably because her love affair with Guerin is over.

By the time she gets to the fast-paced and rhythmic "Black Crow," Joni confesses in her lyrics that she is wondering where her travels will lead her. Will she just fly aimlessly around the sky like the crows she sees from her car window? On "Blue Motel Room" she slows down the pace to survey the place she is staying in Savannah, Georgia. She asks if she will still be loved when she gets back to Los Angeles. She has the blues again—coast to coast—because of the demise of her latest love. Can she get him back? Does she want him back? Or is she happier to stay solo in this blue motel room?

For "Refuge of the Roads" Joni describes what she saw on her voyage across America, from the Winn-Dixie grocery stores of the South to the highway service stations that she stopped in along the way. For her, this journey is spiritual as well as geographic.

During her spiritual quest she consulted the Tibetan lama Chogyam Trungpa. According to Joni, "He was the bad boy of Zen. I wrote a song about the visit I made to him called 'Refuge of the Roads.' I consider him one of my great teachers, even though I saw him only three times. Once I had a fifteen-minute audience with him in which we argued. He told me to quit analyzing. I told him, I couldn't—I'm an artist, you know. Then he induced in me a temporary state where the concept of 'I' was absent, which lasted for three days." (64)

The *Hejira* album was a gleaming creative venture for Joni. On the cover she is depicted in a stark black-and-white photograph by Norman Seeff, with a superimposed highway disappearing into her black shawl. She wears a beret on her head, and in her right hand is her trademark lit cigarette. The album also features a photo of her on ice skates, her arms stretched out like the black crow she sings of on this masterful album. Naturally the art concept of this evocative collage was conceived by Joni herself.

The reviews for *Hejira* were much warmer than they were for *The Hissing of Summer Lawns*. Even *Rolling Stone* was laudatory. In that publication Ariel Swartley wrote, "It is true that she has all but abandoned melodies anyone can whistle, and her brief fling with the standard bridge seems to be over. But if she has denied her listeners memorable tunes and conventional formats, Mitchell displays other musical charms: new, seductive rhythms (not funk, but nearly as enticing) and lush guitars . . . Mitchell avoids the self-conscious artiness that marred *The Hissing of Summer Lawns* . . . With *Hejira* she redefines the elements of her music with as much courage as when she scrutinizes her aims and motivations." (84)

Perry Meisel in the *Village Voice* called it "her best since *Court and Spark* . . . Recitive rather than swinging or rocking, the songs tend to hover low and somber over the flat and sometimes faceless surface of the back-up rhythms (most of them without drums), making Mitchell's declamatory voice the disc's sole object of attention." (85)

Ron Baron in *After Dark* reported, "Joni Mitchell, reigning lady poet of folk-rock . . . She has an almost fanatical cult of followers who enthusiastically share the experiences and insights that this perceptive melancholy woman of the world chronicles in her long string of best-selling albums currently culminating in *Hejira*." (86)

David Cleary wrote in the *All Music Guide*, "*Hejira* would be the last in an astonishingly long run of top-notch studio albums dating back to her debut . . . hip and cool but never smug or ice . . . 'Blue Motel Room' in particular is a prototypic slow jazz-club combo number, appropriately smooth, smoky and languorous . . . Mitchell's verses, many concerned with character portraits, are among the most polished of her career . . . This excellent album is a rewarding listen." (43)

In 1976, I was a reviewer for *Rock* Magazine, and I wrote an extensive article about Joni and *Hejira*. This is what I proclaimed in that publication at the time:

> Joni Mitchell is a willowy wildflower of a girl, intense and individualistic, while at the same time fragile and colorfully contemplative. She fluctuates in her lyrical perspective from philosophical ("Both Sides Now") and worldly ("Free Man in Paris"), to resigned

("Down to You") and insecure ("I Don't Know Where I Stand.") She is sensitive to change and alert in her observations. Joni has never been reluctant to verbalize embittered passions or to expose to the air the demons of her depression.

Joni has grown and developed into a singer and songwriter of wide and universal appeal and renown. We now have at hand *Hejira*, Mitchell's ninth and latest album of original songs. With it Joni reaches inward for misty emotions and smoke-colored sentiments that are penned from a complex and sophisticated viewpoint that we are used to hearing from her.

Three years ago, with the release of the L.P. *Court and Spark*, Joni established a unique stature for herself. It was her first highly successful and commercial offering. With it came Grammy nominations for both the album and the hit single "Help Me," and topped off with a cover story in *Time* magazine. Since then she has lived the life of a recording star, now that she is no longer struggling to carve herself an identity, but is busily working at shaping the one she already has. Oddly she is as perplexed by her stature as she was of her anonymity.

On *Hejira* are the same thoughty insecurities and dramatically deep self-wonderings that she has always expressed, but this time the verses are more complex and less general, while the music is of a bleak and sepia-toned mood. Like her last album, *Hissing of Summer Lawns*, with its broader statements and experimental rhythms, it is doubtful if any of the songs will find any degree of individual commercial potential. Each cut is rather a complicated and wordy vignette of road signs that she passes in this vehicle of life.

The title cut, "Hejira," seems to sum up what it is that is on her mind. She sees life, she steps back to objectively observe her role in it, and she finds herself maturing and tallying mileage on life's road, and seriously wonders if there is any sense to be made of it all.

With the basic knowledge that Joni has an artistic tendency to live her life in fast and fleeting quests of the heart, each song is easily recognizable as a separate love or lover. She sees each varied episode like a new adventure as though she were smoothly gliding across the icy surfaces of life in a pair of silver skates. Each song occupies a new setting like the careful examination of different locales on this frozen pond of reality.

She describes her "Blue Motel Room" in Savannah, sings of solo traveling to seek "The Refuge of the Roads," and ponders the personage of "A Strange Boy" who is able to touch the "fool" and the "child" that live within her.

This entire album is a log of Joni's journeys—a collection of impressions penned through a whirling rearview mirror. While the music is pleasurably crafted of new and familiar chords, and the examining probe keen in its focus, *Hejira* remains more a product of Mitchell's self-discovery than an identifiable unraveling or widespread enlightenment. It is as Joni best describes it: "a travelogue of picture-post-card-charms." (87)

Hejira peaked on the American album chart at number 13 and was certified gold and platinum. In Great Britain the album reached number 11. The song "Coyote" backed with "Blue Motel Room" was released in the United States as a single, but did not find its way to the pop music charts on either side of the Atlantic.

In November 1976 Joni made a couple of special appearances at benefits. On November 11 she sang at the Tower Theater in Philadelphia at a benefit for the Main Point Coffeehouse. She performed with her new band members Jaco Pastorious and Bobbye Hall. On November 20 she appeared at Memorial Auditorium in Sacramento as part of the California Celebrates the Whales Day benefit concert. Also on the bill that day were John Sebastian and Country Joe McDonald.

In 1976 Joni told writer-photographer Dagmar, "My life has totally reoriented itself around one center: music. It is in me and around me, always. I couldn't even have children because it would interfere with my work." (28)

Of her aspirations at the time, Mitchell claimed, "I'd like to write a film script sometime. When I was younger, I used to write fairy tales about the kingdom Fanta-Real, for example, where fantasy and reality bordered on each other. I love contrasts. I used to be more superstitious, more mystical but now I live in and with reality." (28) Joni's world is a place where fantasy overlaps with reality.

The big theatrical-release film that Joni appeared in that year was directed by none other than Martin Scorsese. It was a documentary about the final concert The Band was going to perform before the members went their creative separate ways. The event, the film, and the resulting album were all called *The Last Waltz*.

Taped at Winterland in San Francisco on November 25, 1976, *The Last Waltz* was the ultimate farewell concert for The Band, and it attracted several of their celebrity fans, who participated in the festivities and sang with the musicians. In addition to Joni, the event included Van Morrison, Neil Diamond, Ringo Starr, Dr. John, Bob Dylan, Neil Young, Muddy Waters, Eric Clapton, and Paul Butterfield.

In her set with The Band and guests, Joni opened with "Coyote" and followed with "Shadows and Light" and "Furry Sings the Blues." Then she and Neil Young sang background vocals to The Band on "Acadian Driftwood." She also provided Neil with background vocals on his song "Helpless."

Regardless of what her albums were or weren't doing on the record charts in any one given week, at this point in her career Joni was acknowledged as a bona fide rock superstar. What she did in public was instantly news and fodder for the press to discuss. This included her wardrobe. She might have been the high priestess of folk/jazz/rock, but she rarely ever dressed in the rock & roll style of blue jeans and a casual shirt. This often confounded her critics.

Speaking defensively about her clothing choices, Mitchell claimed, "I remember showing up at a Carole King concert in Central Park in a pair of Yves St. Laurent pants. And a good shirt. They were simple clothes, but they were of a good quality. And I felt . . . really uncomfortable. I felt there were certain things that I liked, that were a part of me, that were outside the hippie guard. Things that were a part of me from before this delicious part of the '60's when we were fresh and were thinking fresh things . . . It was a good time period. It was a healthy idea that we were working toward, but there came a time when it [blue denim jeans] had become a ritual, a flat-out style. I began to make this transition, under a lot of peer pressure. I remember seeing, even when I went to *The Last Waltz*, [a journalist wrote] 'Miss Mitchell showed up looking like a Beverly Hills housewife.' I was outside the uniform of rock & roll and it was annoying to some people. And as a reply to this prejudice, I wrote that song, 'The Boho Dance'—'Nothing is capsulized in me / In either side of town'—as a demand for liberty." (9)

In Great Britain's *Melody Maker* magazine in 1976, Joni Mitchell was voted by the readers of the publication as the number 1 female singer of the year. Following Joni were Kiki Dee, Diana Ross, Grace Slick, Sonja Kristina of Curved Air, Emmylou Harris, Patti Smith, Maggie Bell, Linda Ronstadt, and Karen Carpenter. Joni had also been ranked number 1 on the *Melody Maker* reader's poll lists in 1970, 1971, and 1972. Carly Simon topped the chart in 1973, but Joni was back at number 1 for 1974 and 1975 as well.

While her fans were clamoring for her to return to recording albums in the style of her two greatest achievements—*Blue* and *Court and Spark*—Joni had other things to do. She had not taken any U-turns in her career so far, and she wasn't about to do so now.

12

Don Juan's Reckless Daughter

At this phase in her musical career and her personal life, Joni Mitchell was a voyager, a reporter, and a style chameleon. She would basically let paths of opportunity unfold before her, like Alice on her way through Wonderland, and she would see what new forms of musical creativity would present themselves to her. This is exactly what happened to her when she set out to plan her tenth album release. She had already untethered herself from the constraints of whatever was going on in the popular music realm, and she could pretty much create whatever she liked. While the whole music industry seemed to be going disco, Joni heard a completely different beat.

On a trip to Carnival in Rio de Janeiro, Joni found her new muse for the album *Don Juan's Reckless Daughter*. She also had a new musical partner in crime—percussionist Don Alias. Not only did he play a plethora of musical instruments—from the bongos, congas, snare drum, and bass drum, to the shakers, ankle bells, and sandpaper—he also became Joni's new boyfriend. While *The Hissing of Summer Lawns* found some of its inspiration in the rhythms of Africa, this newest venture found much of its inspiration in South America.

Joni felt she had nothing to lose by stretching out musically. She had already been blasted by the critics for some of her musical choices. As she explains it, "Here's the thing: You have two options. You can stay the same and protect the formula that gave you your initial success. They're going to crucify you for staying the same. If you change, they're going to crucify you for changing. But staying the same is boring. And change is interesting. So of the two options, I'd rather be crucified for changing." (9)

There was a strong feeling—from both the press and the public—that Joni should throw herself into recording another *Blue* or another *Court and Spark*. According to Mitchell, this was not what she wanted to do—at all. "This is what I think about those people," she said with disdain. "They want, they want and they *want*. However, if I actually gave them what they wanted, then they'd just get sick of it." (14)

Even more succinctly she proclaimed, "Would you ask Picasso to repaint his 'Blue Period'?" (88) Joni wanted to deliver something fresh and different, and that was exactly what she did.

Gone was Tom Scott and the L.A. Express—with the exception of her ex-boyfriend John Guerin, whom she continued to use as her drummer. The full-time addition of Jaco Pastorius represented a major new sound for her. Now, with the exotic colorings that Don Alias added, Joni moved her music into a whole new rhythmic realm. To say that she was finished chasing a hit single as a goal was a complete understatement.

Pastorius was wild and out of control as a bass man, and in his personal life. Joni later stated, "Prior to Jaco, I was questioning the bass's role in music. I would hum melodies to bass players and ask them to play them, and they'd refuse me and say, 'That's not the root of the chord, Joni.' And then I'd say, 'Why does the bass have to play the root of the chord?' In a way, I feel like I dreamed Jaco. I mean, he was exactly what I was waiting for, sonically: the big round sound and the different approach to the bottom end of music. But I think when I met Jaco it was pre-cocaine, because cocaine was not a good drug for him. Disastrous, actually." (64) But for the time being, Joni felt liberated by Jaco's musical freedom in the studio and onstage.

During this era she announced in *Ampersand* magazine, "I'm not a jazz musician but I need that creative freedom. That's why I'm being sucked into jazz projects and working more and more with jazz musicians. I find I'm more understood there, and the heavier the player that I work with, the more easy it is to communicate. Because I'm literate; I don't have the number system nor do

I have the letter chord system, I don't understand it. I'm a painter, I like to speak in metaphor: 'play me some semi-trucks going by,' you know, 'here we have the waves coming in, the keyboards should break like a wave, here's the pressure point'—by emotion and by remembrances." (42)

Her entire approach to the music was much more loose and free. She explained at the time, "You see, the way I write songs now, is around a standard melody that nobody knows, because that way you can get your words to have their organic inflection so that when you emphasize something you go up or you go down. Or if you want to put ten syllables in a line that in the next verse is only going to have three syllables drawn out through those bars, you have that liberty. As a result you can't write one lead sheet and put the four verses on it, every verse has to be written out individually—it's all variation on a theme . . . So the improvisational, the spontaneous aspect of this creative process—still as a poet—is set to words and music, which is a hammer and chisel process. Sometimes it flows, but a lot of times it's blocked by concept. And if you're writing free consciousness—which I do once in a while just to remind myself that I can, you know, because I'm fitting little pieces of this puzzle together—the end result must flow as if it was spoken for the first time." (42)

There was also the influence of inner-city black America, which was infused onto the tracks of the *Don Juan's Reckless Daughter* album. According to Joni, she was walking down Hollywood Boulevard one day, shopping for a costume for a masquerade party, when "all of a sudden this black kid goes by with a New York walk—you know, the diddybop with one leg shorter than the other, and the hand curled back—and gave me this most radiant grin and said, 'Looking good sister.' It was such a genuine, sweet smile; it woke up the spirit in me. I began walking behind him imitating his walk. He just took me into this very fun-loving mood. So I thought, 'I'm going to this party not as him, but as his spirit." (89)

To escape from her shell, the artist formerly known as white folk singer Joni Mitchell was suddenly reborn as an inner-city black man. One of the most controversial things she did on the *Don Juan's Reckless Daughter* album was to use dark brown facial makeup and pose as a gentleman of color on the cover of the album. Years before Michael Jackson covered himself in white pancake makeup, Joni went the opposite route for this album, and in several photos of herself on this unique album package, she dressed as a ghetto pimp, like the one she had sung about on "Edith and the Kingpin."

Any other Caucasian performer in 1977 who dressed in an Afro wig and painted her skin a dark tan to visually change races would have been burned at the stake by the critics. But somehow, on the album cover and interior of *Don Juan's Reckless Daughter,* Joni did it several times with just enough of a "wink" of the eye to let people know that this was not a racial slur, but an homage to the darker and richer improvisational jazz style that she had become possessed by as of late.

For Joni, the year 1977 was not an era of concert touring. A planned European tour was canceled when Joni backed out, claiming exhaustion. Actually, she was absorbed in the creation of this new suite-like album of hers.

Having grown up in the rock & roll era, she was very observant of a milestone event that happened in the rock world that summer. On August 17, 1977, Elvis Presley died. His cause of death was directly attributable to the prescription drugs he lived on during the last seven years of his life. Bloated, overweight, and overmedicated, his heart finally gave out. "The King of Rock & Roll" was dead. For many die-hard fans, August 17, 1977, was truly "the day the music died."

At that time, and since that time, his vast catalog of recorded music has continued to sell at record numbers. Throughout the 1970s, while he was alive, his current recordings sold well, but he was clearly surpassed by the raft of new performers on the music scene—including Joni Mitchell.

Several years later, Joni looked back on this era and proclaimed, "When I started out, rock & roll was in small theaters. There was no arena rock. Woodstock had not happened. The possibility of mass exploitation had not occurred to anybody. It was a small, intimate forum with loyalties. Think of Elvis. I sold more records than Elvis. Not after his death. But when I was 'The Queen of Rock & Roll,' I sold more than he did when he was 'The King of Rock & Roll.'" (9) It was a true and apt observation.

Elvis Presley's sad end was a cautionary tale for many rock musicians who were heavily involved in drugs at the time. Elvis's slow suicide was an undignified end for a man who was so highly revered by so many. With regard to overindulging in drugs, Joni claimed, "I was never a big druggie, but I had my moments. I wrote some songs on cocaine, 'cause initially it can be a creative catalyst. In the end it'll fry you, kill the heart. I found it sent all the energy up my spine into the top of the brain. It kills the soul and gives you delusions of grandeur as it shuts down your emotional center. [Cocaine is the] perfect drug for a hit man, but not so good for a musician." (9)

In December 1977 Joni's epic tenth album, *Don Juan's Reckless Daughter,* was released. Again produced by herself, the bulk of it was recorded at A&M Recording Studios in Hollywood—the refurbished film studio that Charlie Chaplin once owned. Some of the musical passages, including those by the London Symphony Orchestra, were recorded at different locales.

The album opens up with an instrumental overture that leads into "Cotton Avenue." The music accompaniment here is just Joni and her guitar, John Guerin's drums, and Jaco's bass. In the basis of the song she sings of a street scene where poor boys hang out on street corners, and people come through at night on their way to dance halls where they do the latest dances.

"Talk to Me" is a lively plea to her lover to please communicate. She sings about getting drunk in a bar on tequila and urinating in the parking lot. This lively cut spotlights Joni in something of a party mood. Pleading for conversation, Joni claims she doesn't care what topic is discussed; she simply asks to be talked to— whether its about Ingmar Bergman's icy Scandinavian films or Chaplin's comedies. Here she claims she is talking all the time, and to drive that point further home, she actually cackles like a chicken. She also pays reverence to William Shakespeare, whom she refers to as "Willy" the "Shake."

In an interesting move, Joni takes one of her previously recorded compositions, "Jericho," which originally appeared on her *Miles of Aisles* album, and reinvents it. Here it gets a slow, cool, and thoughtful approach as she compares the wall around her heart to the walls of the fabled city of Jericho.

On the original configuration of the album, the sixteen-minute, nineteen-second epic number "Paprika Plains" occupied one whole side of the vinyl album. On this song she steps out to watch the rain and then begins to reminisce about life in her hometown. She sings of McGee's General Store, and how she would dress like an Indian and beat her toy drum. The lyrics of this song are basically a jumble of memories, and in the center is a lengthy orchestrated musical segment that slows down the action and allows Joni to have a sweeping piano solo, while the strings of the London Symphony Orchestra back her.

Explaining this complex number, Joni says, "Oh! A lot of shuffling went on. There were Indian grass chants in the middle of it, there were a hundred and one different ways that I approached that. More so than anything else on the album. The instrumental passage in the middle just poured out." (42)

One of the featured musicians on "Paprika Plains" is soprano sax player Wayne Shorter. According to Joni, "There was a smugness to studio musicians in the early days, and I was an illiterate rock musician who had none of the A-chord and B-chord languages. But you can imagine the thrill for me when I first met great musicians like Wayne Shorter, who spoke to me in my language of metaphors for a track like 'Paprika Plains' on *Don Juan's Reckless Daughter*. Before he started to play his sax, he said to me, 'It's like we're in Hyde Park, and there's a nanny with a baby in a boat on the pond, just nudging it, her hand's nudging it.' Or sometime's he'd say, 'I'm a string section now!'" (51)

The odd song "Otis and Marlena" is about an aging, over-tanned, and obnoxiously affluent couple in Miami. According to Joni's lyrics, their age-spotted hands are busy playing cards and enjoying fun in the sun. As a social counterpoint, Mitchell claims that Muslims are "sticking up" Washington, D.C. Apparently this is a reference to the mid-1970s fuel crisis, where oil-rich Middle Eastern countries supposedly raised the price of a barrel of oil—thus financially sticking up Washington.

In an uncharacteristic instrumental number, "The Tenth World," her assembled band members all contribute to this jam session. Taking equal songwriting credit on this pulsating number, Joni provides her haunting voice, while Don Alias (percussion), Manolo Badrena (percussion on congas and coffee cans), Alejandro Acuna (percussion and vocals), Airto (drums), and Jaco Pastorius (bass) jam. It has the feeling of a jungle campfire ritual, set to music.

The most stunning song on the *Don Juan* album is the rhythmic song "Dreamland." Sung by Joni over a sea of Don Alias's percussion effects, it is a calypso fantasy. Mitchell uses every exotic South American/Caribbean/jungle reference she can gather together in her passionate lyrics. She speaks of Dorothy Lamour sarongs, Sir Walter Raleigh, and even Christopher Columbus in this South of the Equator rhythm-and-rhyme confection. The song starts out with Joni saying that Rio is a long way from Canada, where her mother—Myrtle—has her front lawn in Saskatchewan covered in six-foot-high snowdrifts. Joni sounds like she is especially enjoying this exciting place-in-the-sun song. Her voice is cool and confident, as Alias plays the snare drum and sandpaper blocks, Pastorius clangs the cowbells, Alejandro Acuna handles the shakers, and Airto plays the Surdo—a snare drum. Joni has guest vocalist Chaka Khan lending her incredibly distinctive voice to this brilliantly evocative standout track.

The song "Don Juan's Reckless Daughter" has the jazzy feeling of *Hejira* and finds Joni singing about the contradictions of the American dream. She uses images of an eagle fighting against a serpent to make an analogy between good and evil in the land of the brave.

"Off Night Backstreet" perfectly journeys toward the blues. Here Joni sings to her lover, who has moved in a girlfriend to live with him. However, he still calls Mitchell to be his secret backstreet love affair. With her Asylum label mates Glen Frey of the Eagles and John David Souther, Joni performs the most vital love song on the album—a song of a love that is stuck on a dead-end backstreet.

The album ends with Joni's most *Blue*-like song, the cautionary "Silky Veils of Ardor." Singing to her lone guitar, Mitchell offers advice about not getting your heart broken. Addressing herself to young girls, she warns against giving up your heart to a man, only to have him leave you the next morning. A beautiful ballad, "Silky Veils of Ardor" is a lost gem, glistening like the old Joni of the folk days. It provides one of the many highlights of this highly experimental yet completely misunderstood album.

Since *Don Juan's Reckless Daughter* was originally a vinyl two-record set, this offered Joni more than twice the space on which to create a visually artistic mural. In a stylish photo montage, she used mainly elaborate photographs of herself (plus one unidentified little boy) either dressed as her female self—or as a handful of black men, in makeup, coarse black Afro wigs, and *au courant* inner-city fashions of the day. Joni essentially became a black man—both visually and in a musical jazz sense. Against a deep blue cardboard sky and mahogany-colored ground, Joni created her own set of multiethnic clones of herself. In addition, on one of the panels is a photo of Joni as a young girl, dressed up like a Native American, complete with feathers on her head and a blanket wrapped around her. Although she wore many disguises on the cover of this album, they represent different sides of Mitchell herself.

The press reviewers either lauded Joni's artistry on *Don Juan's Reckless Daughter* or were blisteringly caustic. Janet Maslin in *Rolling Stone* led the pack who hated this album. In a review headlined, "Don Juan's Reckless and Shapeless Daughter," Maslin claimed, "Now, for once she has gambled and lost. The best that can be said for *Don Juan's Reckless Daughter* is that it is an instructive failure. Since *Blue*, Mitchell has demonstrated an increasing fondness for formats that don't suit her . . . She has been inexplicably inclined to let her music become shapeless as she tries to incorporate jazz and calypso rhythms that eventually overpower her . . . there is nothing said here that she hasn't said better before, except those things she should have kept to herself." (90)

The reviewer for *Playboy* magazine also claimed, "Joni Mitchell makes the transition from major songwriter to minor poet. The words . . . are great, but the music got left behind. Mitchell continues the trend begun on her last album: relying on primitive rhythms to carry her words . . . Mitchell has abandoned the streamlined popular song, apparently feeling that it is not the proper vehicle to vent passion, approach the eternal mystery or fill a concert hall. She is a tourist lady gone native, trying to find release in the native rhythms." (91)

Jon Parales in *Creem* wrote, "Somewhere along the way, Mitchell's reverent audiences convinced her that her every thought is profound. Having concentrated on herself for so long, Mitchell's discrimination has eroded; she can't separate out the trivia anymore. Her intimacy has become exhaustive—she tells all, every flicker of ambivalence, every last rationalization, seemingly anything that pops into her head. You feel like you're drowning in her stream of consciousness . . . Despite the feverish intellectualizing of its lyrics, *Don Juan's Reckless Daughter* turns out to be soft at the center." (92)

Some reviewers were mixed in their own reviews, like Stephen Holden in the *Village Voice*, who wrote, "*Don Juan's Reckless Daughter*, Joni Mitchell's most ambitious album, is a four-sided epic poem in which her old themes of personal corruption, American decadence, and the fall of man come together in a conscious synthesis. The measure of her accomplishment is that she almost pulls it off . . . In 'Paprika Plains,' a 16-minute dream song occupying all of side two, Mitchell imagines a pre-colonial Eden, when Indians were the only prairie dwellers. It's center is a meandering symphonic meditation in which Mitchell twaddles around on the piano while the London Symphony Orchestra saws off a bad pastiche of Ives . . . *Don Juan's Restless Daughter* gets off the ground about half the time: As epics go, that's not half bad." (93)

Carl Arrington in the *New York Post* wrote, "Those who were hoping for a return to her simple, breathy folk style will be dismayed . . . Joni Mitchell is easily the most pioneering artist in rock today. Her assumptions are beyond the talent of her peers and apparently ahead of the record-buying public . . . Yet the album works like a good painting in the tradition of fine art: The more you study it, the more satisfying and appealing it becomes." (88)

Billboard rather liked it, claiming, "Mitchell's hypnotic lyrical and vocal style is maximized to its fullest on this double-pocket studio LP as she weaves songs filled with vivid images around her swirling ethereal-sounding vocals. Incorporated into the lavish orchestrations are Mitchell's tasty use of jazz backing . . . Her surrealistic images, among the writer's best, introduce a haunting tone." (94)

Wesley Strick in *Circus* magazine also liked it. According to him, "*Don Juan* is an all-studio double—but, at just under an hour, it runs only six minutes longer than '77's stunning *Hejira* single LP. *Don Juan* is only one song bigger than *Hejira's* nine, but what a song: the seventeen-minute autobiographical epic sprawled across Side Two, complete with full symphony orchestra, called 'Paprika Plains' . . . Her smoky, folky jazz will always make money for Mitchell and Asylum [Records], even should *Don Juan* take a tailspin in the year of 'You Light Up My Life.'" (95)

Joni found the reviews for her tenth album a bit daunting. As she explained in 1979, "If I experience any frustration, it's the frustration of being misunderstood. But that's what stardom is—a glamorous misunderstanding. All the way along I know that some of these projects are eccentric. I know that there are parts that are experimental, and some of them are half-baked. I certainly have been pushing the limits and—even for myself—not all of my experiments are completely successful. But they lay the groundwork for further developments. Sooner or later, some of those experiments will come to fruition. So I have to lay out a certain amount of my growing pains in public. I like the ideas that annually there is a place where I can distribute the art that I have collected for the year. That's the only thing that I feel I want to protect, really. And that means having a certain amount of commercial success." (9)

In spite of what the critics claimed, Joni's fans continued to buy her albums on sight. *Don Juan's Reckless Daughter* in the United States reached number 25 on the *Billboard* album charts. In England it made it to number 20.

Don Juan's Reckless Daughter had the distinction of being the last of Joni's albums to be awarded a gold record certification for sales in excess of 500,000 copies in the United States. After this album she was no longer guaranteed to be declared "a hit." According to her, "It's a credit to the people that have supported me in spite of the bad publicity of the last four years—the out-and-out panning of a lot of fine and unusual projects—that at least they felt this work had some moments of accessible beauty. If a reviewer sits down and he plays [her albums] two or three times, it's just going to sound freaky to him. There are moods I'm in when I can't stand to listen to some of my own music. I don't expect it to be appropriate. But come the right moment, where we're on the same wavelength, it might slip in on you." (9)

Joni Mitchell was never someone who could be told what to do, in life or in her music. She was unfazed by the odd and mixed reception that *Don Juan's Reckless Daughter* received. She was an artist—lost in her box of paints—and an artist doesn't have to follow the rules—anyone's rules. She had created a unique album and a fresh new sound. For her, innovation was an integral part of her music and her artistic expression.

13

Mingus

In 1978 Joni Mitchell did no touring and made few public appearances. On July 22 she was backstage at Madison Square Garden in Manhattan to see Crosby, Stills, and Nash, who were headlining a concert there. She made a special guest appearance singing harmony vocals on the trio's second encore performance of "Teach Your Children." In September she performed in Berkeley, California, as part of the two-day Bread and Roses Festival at the Greek Theatre. Instead of touring, she was occupied with her next recording project. Actually, it was a project that found her. And it was her most challenging, most misunderstood album yet.

As soon as *Don Juan's Reckless Daughter* hit the stores, it was time for her to plot her next course. According to her, "Every year, when I've completed a project, I ask myself, 'What am I going to do now?' In the process of asking myself that question, a lot of possibilities came up," she explained. (9)

Over the previous couple of years she had dabbled in the jazz idiom. It had started slowly with *For the Roses* and *Court and Spark*. Then on her last three albums it progressively permeated her sound. In fact, she had been to listening to more and more jazz records.

Her love of jazz dated back to her days in Canada. "[Charles]

Mingus, of course was a legend," she recalls. "Folk and jazz were overlapping in the cellars of New York, so I'd heard of Mingus for some time. In fact, I'd heard his name as far back as when I was listening to Lambert, Hendricks and Ross in Canada. I was in high school then, but my University friends spoke of these legendary people. That was in the early '60s." (17)

She claims, "I was also impressed by some of the Miles Davis albums; first *Sketches of Spain*, with Gil Evans and a large orchestra; but later, Miles' smaller combo things like *Nefertiti* and *In a Silent Way* became just about my all-time favorites in any field of music. They were my private music, the albums I loved to listen to on my own. I never thought of making that my kind of music." (74)

Charles Mingus was known in the jazz world as a master of the bass, and he was an accomplished pianist in the world of bop and avant-garde jazz sounds. According to legend, he was gruff in manner, often bullying and demanding of his fellow players. In the *All Music Guide,* Richard Ginell wrote, "He was the greatest bass-playing leader/composer jazz has ever known, one who always kept his ears and fingers on the pulse." (43) He had a great sense of melody, but he also liked to throw abrupt musical changes into his music as well, and was a true innovator.

Like the unraveling of a smoky film noir mystery, through the grapevine a message came to Joni. "I heard on the street that Charles was trying to contact me," she recalls. "He tried through normal channels and never made it. People thought it was too far-out to be true. They had all sorts of reasons for thinking it was an impossible or ridiculous combination. To me, it was fascinating. I was honored. I was curious." (9)

When Joni was made aware that Charles Mingus was trying to reach her, she was genuinely intrigued, and she took the next step toward contacting him. "Somehow or other he liked what I did," she recalls, "I got a message through a friend and I called him up." (42)

When they finally made contact, Joni found that Charles had a concept for an album he wanted to collaborate on with Mitchell. As she explains it, "He had an idea to make a piece of music based on T. S. Eliot's *Four Quartets*. And he wanted to do it with—this is how he described it—a full orchestra playing one kind of music and overlaid on that would be a bass and guitar playing another kind of music, and over that someone would read excerpts from Eliot in a very formal literary voice, and interspersed with that, he wanted me to distill T. S. Eliot down into street language, and sing it mixed in with this reader." (17)

She was flattered that he chose her to collaborate with. "It was an interesting idea. I think of music in a textural collage myself, so it fascinated me. But his expansion was like expanding a theme in the classical symphonic sense, and I just felt I couldn't do it," says Joni. (17)

However, she didn't think it was the right project for her at the time. "I called Charles back and told him I couldn't do it; it seemed like a kind of sacrilege." (74)

Mingus was determined to work with Joni, so he came up with another idea that they could collaborate on. "Some time went by," Mitchell explains, "and April of last year [1978] I got a call from Mingus saying that he'd written six songs for me and he wanted me to sing them and write the words for them. I went out to visit him and I liked him immediately. And he was devilishly challenging." (17)

There was an immediacy to his plan as Mingus had cancer and his health was deteriorating rapidly. According to Joni, "He was already sick and in a wheelchair, but still very vital and concerned. We started searching through his material, and he said, 'Now this one has five different melodies.' I said, 'You mean you want me to write five different sets of lyrics?' He said, 'Yes,' then put it on and it was the fastest, boogieing-est thing I'd ever heard, and it was impossible! So this was like a joke on me; he was testing and teasing me, but in good fun." (74)

How did Mingus become fascinated with Mitchell? "As I understand it," Joni explains, "somebody played him some of my records. There's a piece of music called 'Paprika Plains,' which was done in sections. It was first recorded in January, and by August, when I played the verses, the piano had been tuned many, many times. So it hits a splice where it goes from the January piano to the August piano. With a fine ear you can notice this. Charles was a stickler for true pitch and time, and he kept saying, 'It's out of tune, it's out of tune.' When the piece is over, he said that I had a lot of balls! So, whatever it was he didn't like, he also saw some strength and—certainly an adventuresome spirit, because I'd been pushing the limits of what constitutes a song for years. I keep trying to expand it—with an instrumental in the middle, with no prescribed length. I assume that if it will hold my interest that long, then it will at least hold the interest of a minority." (17)

After that, Joni was hooked on the idea of working with Mingus. His rapidly deteriorating health made the project all the more vital, and everything had to be done with a sense of diminishing time to complete it. Since Charles was living in New York City, Joni took up residence in an apartment at the Regency Hotel, and many of the sessions were recorded at Electric Lady Studios on Eighth Street in Greenwich Village.

Mitchell found him unique. According to her, "Charles was a very poetic character. He was a very open person. His nature had a larger spectrum of display than anybody I ever met. Now I met him when he was paralyzed and couldn't really do the violence he was capable of. But he was a very open person and very vulnerable. He cried easily and got angry easily and couldn't stand bullshit. If he thought a guy was faking his notes, playing jive, showing off, he was liable to come swinging at the guy right on the bandstand. He was very true in a certain way and kind of crazy because of it. That's my take on him, anyway. I may have romanticized it some because I was so fond of him." (68)

They got together and started working out ideas for the music he wanted Joni to record. "Immediately I felt this kind of sweet giddiness when I met him. Like I was in for some fun," she remembers, "He teased me a lot. He called me 'Hillbilly'; it was charming. We went through some of the old songs. 'Goodbye Pork Pie Hat' was one we decided on immediately. So there was this search for another one, and he played me a lot of material." (9)

This was such an exciting prospect for Joni. As she saw it, "I'm not a jazz musician, but I had the experience of being invited into an idiom with which I had been flirting." (51)

When she announced the Mingus project to her manager, Elliot Roberts, he thought she was crazy, and he did everything he could to dissuade her from doing this album. He felt it would be career suicide for her. If *The Hissing of Summer Lawns* and *Don Juan's Reckless Daughter* weren't alienating enough to her fan base, this project with Mingus would surely finish her reign as a popular artist. But Joni had made up her mind and there was no dissuading her.

One of the musicians she wanted to use on the album, which was ultimately entitled *Mingus*, was Jaco Pastorius. She discussed Jaco with Charles. "We talked about him at an early stage, but—you have to understand that Charles was ill, so I couldn't tell from his responses whether he knew Jaco's work. I knew that he was prejudiced against electrical instruments, but Jaco transcends them all. Charles felt that with an electrical instrument you couldn't get dynamics, but Jaco completely defies all that. He gets more dynamics than any bass player. He's phenomenal, he's an orchestra. He's a horn section, he's a string section, he's a French horn soloist." (17)

Amid the creative process of the *Mingus* album, Joni explained, "All of a sudden I'm finding myself now in a very interesting project with Charlie Mingus. He's given me eight of his songs to sing and set words to, which is odd because I've never set words to anyone else's music. He's given me a lot of arranging—choice of musicians—he's given me a lot of leeway. What I'm having to learn is the rudiments of be-bop and everything, and the off part of it is, the timing is so perfect, it's just natural to me. The songs are difficult to write, but the one and a half that I've finished are a more natural vehicle for me to sing, in some ways, than many of my old songs. His music is '40s, early '50s, that kind of idiom—ballads, very Billie Holiday-esque except they have a lot more range than she can sing. Some of them are about two and a half octaves—it's a lot of notes. There's a possibility that I might do some things with double-basses and voice and saxophone. I want to try in some way to take the piano and vocalist thing off of it, so that it'll have a new sound to it. It's such good music—you almost gotta trick it into being modern without being gimmicky in a way, so more people don't just see it as a stereotype and say 'Order me a vodka collins, it's a girl in a cocktail lounge.'" (42)

According to Joni, she liked the fact that, like herself, Mingus enjoyed making unexpected moves in his music. "Charlie's into cacophony, multiple melody and contrapuntal overlays, which I mess around with too," she recalls. "The first time I talked to him was so warm, there was no barrier at all. And when I got to know him and read his book I understood why. He's a romantic and very spiritual man—very eccentric with a big chip on his shoulder, which has kind of devoured him all his life. It's very bewildering, this combination, you know, but it's very beautiful." (42)

Immersed in the middle of the *Mingus* project, Joni claimed, "My goal is to get three songs written, by the end of this month [June 1978] and get in the studio with Charlie. I want him to be there, if not for the complete project, to see some of it going into actuality. Four of the songs are ballads, very slow—and then there's some real be-bop blues, it's the freakiest thing. Six of them he wrote directly for me and he even attempted in his idiom to include some of my musical idiosyncrasies; I mean he would say, 'This is like something you do,' and I couldn't see it was like anything that I do! It's very demanding, in every way. And it's also peculiar to be setting words to someone else's vocal rhythm. Everybody has their own rhythmic speech pattern—and the phrases are almost set up to be crooned, that's the kind of lyrics that were written for a lot of these old moon-June-croonisms, although there were some great old standards. But the problem is to take the knowledge of progressive pop writing and applying it to this old form." (42)

One of the most distinguishing aspects of working on the *Mingus* album was the fact that she had never created an album as a collaboration. "This was a unique position. I've never worked for somebody else before. Although in the treatment of the music, it was much more my version of jazz. As far as the music was finally recorded. He's more traditional in a way—antielectronics and anti-avant-garde. I'm looking to make modern American music. So I just hoped that he would like what I was doing. I was taking it someplace where I would be true to myself. It was never meant as a commemorative album while we were making it. I never really believed completely that he was going to die. His spirit was so strong." (9)

The *Mingus* recording sessions were as unpredictable as bebop. "As a matter of fact he said to me one time, 'Joni you've got to take more control of your sessions!' And right after that we had this session in New York with a great band: Don Alias on drums, John McLaughlin on guitar, Tony Williams on [drum] kit and Jaco. It was a great band! It was during the *Mingus* project, and there was *no* chemistry that night. Jaco was up on McLaughlin that night, playing in his ear. It was a duet as far as Jaco was concerned. I said to Alias, 'Watch this. Jaco says I've got to take command of the band.' So I went up and said right in his ear, 'Jaco!' Nothing. No response. I'm in his ear saying his name and he's still playing all his flashy licks for McLaughlin. At that point he was a monster. You couldn't get his attention. But I liked his playing enough, he was such an innovator, that in a way, I was proud to present him. Even though those mixes are awful because of it. It's his solo and I'm the background singer. And I allowed that to happen on my own date." (68)

Recording sessions for Joni's *Mingus* album were well under way when Charles's health took a turn for the worse. "Then, because he had become very seriously ill, he and his wife, Sue, went to Mexico, to a faith healer, and during that time I spent 10 days with them. At that point his speech had deteriorated severely. Every night he would say to me, 'I want to talk to you about the music,' and every day it would be too difficult. So some of what he had to tell me remained a mystery. Sue gave me a lot of tapes and interviews, and they were thrilling to me, because so much of what he felt and described was kindred to my own feelings. He articulated lessons that were laid on him by Fats Navarro, the trumpeter, and others." (74)

During the final weeks of his illness, was Joni there to comfort him? "No," she says, "that was up to him. You can't do too much to assuage someone of their fears. I wasn't in that personal a role that I was his comforter. It was a professional partnership with a lot of affection. But one day I called him up and I said, 'How are you Charles?' I never really asked him too much about his illness, but that day I did. And he said, 'Oh, I'm dying. I thought I knew how to do it, but now I'm not sure.' At that point I had three songs finished, and I thought, 'Oh boy, I want him to be in the studio when I start to cut them. I want his approval on this. I want him to like my direction.'" (9)

Charles Mingus got to hear five of the six songs that are included on the *Mingus* album, "He heard everything but 'God Must Be a Boogie Man,'" says Joni, "which he would have liked, since it is his point of view about himself." (9)

While Joni's album was still in the works, on January 5, 1979, Mingus passed away in Cuernavaca, Mexico. Explaining the irony of it, Mitchell explains, "Charles died at the age of 56 in Mexico. The following day he was cremated. That day, 56 whales beached themselves on a coast of Mexico, and not knowing what to do with them, the people there burned them. So 56 whales were cremated the same day as Charles." (17) Sue-Graham Mingus took Charles's ashes to India and scattered them in the Ganges River. According to Joni, "At his request . . . finding a place at the source of the Ganges River, where it ran turquoise and glinting with large fold carp, [she] released him, with flowers and prayers at the break of a new day." (96)

One the most fascinating things about the *Mingus* album was the fact that Joni recorded each song three or four times. For each different version, she invited different top-flight jazz musicians into the studio to jam with her core band. As Joni wrote in the liner notes of the album, "During these experimental recording dates, I had the opportunity to play with some great musicians." (96) Among those musicians were Eddie Gomez, Phil Woods, Gerry Mulligan, Tony Williams, John McLaughlin, Jan Hammer, and Stanley Clark. She also had her ex-boyfriend John Guerin on several of the tracks, which have never been released.

On the six-song album that was released, the players included Joni (guitar, vocals), Jaco Pastorius (bass), Wayne Shorter (soprano sax), Herbie Hancock (electric piano), Peter Erskine (drums), Don Alias (congas), and Emil Richards (percussion).

Joni's eleventh album, *Mingus*, was released in June 1979. Based on curiosity and Joni's strong fan base, the album hit number 17 in the United States and number 24 in the United Kingdom. It was Joni's first album *not* to be certified gold in the United States.

More than twenty years after its release, the *Mingus* album remains a curiosity in Joni's career. There are eleven tracks on it, and five of them are pieces of dialogue between Charles Mingus and his friends captured on a tape recorder and interspersed in the album. Although they are included for historical significance, they clearly stop the flow of the highly evocative music.

The album opens with a dialogue between Charles, his friend Swede, and his wife Sue. It is Charles's birthday in 1975, and the three of them argue about how old he is going to be. The piece is called a "rap" entitled "Happy Birthday 1975." It leads directly into the slow and somber song that Joni wrote herself, "God Must Be a Boogie Man."

Mingus wrote a book called *Beneath the Underdog* that was published by Knopf in 1971. Joni used some passages from it for one of the songs on this album. According to her, "'God Must Be a

Boogie Man' is based on the first four pages of his book. I tried to use the meter and everything of Charles' melodies, but the words wouldn't adhere. So then I let them have their own syncopation and wrote my own melody to it. The song is very much his self-description." (96)

The third track is another rap entitled "Funeral." It is another discussion between Swede and Mingus. This time they talk about Charles's funeral and the fact that—if nothing else—he intends to live longer than Duke Ellington did, so he should count his blessings. (In reality, Ellington lived to be seventy-seven, and Mingus died at fifty-six.)

With music by Mingus and words by Joni, "A Chair in the Sky" finds Mitchell singing about Charles reminiscing about the jazz club Birdland, and all of his friends who are gone. The song starts out very somber and picks up the pace several times. This is basically a song about death, and the limbo Mingus felt he was trapped in, being confined to a wheelchair in his high-rise Manhattan apartment.

"The Wolf That Lives in Lindsey" is the second of two songs penned by Joni solo. In this song, Joni comes out of the "death and dying" spell long enough to sing about a wild individual named Lindsey, whom she felt Charles would identify with. The song sounds like something that could be included in the *Hejira* album and is by far one of the most musically successful tracks on the album.

As Joni explains it, "I can only work from inspiration. I can not work only from craft. A piece that is merely craft doesn't mean anything to me. It has to be inspired. Of the six melodies he gave me, two of them I never could really get into. They were too idiomatic for me. The four Mingus melodies that I did complete were all inspired. Either I stumbled across pieces of poetry in the street or they came to me in mysterious ways—they were meant to be. That left me with a song I had been writing before I met Charles—'The Wolf That Lives in Lindsey'—that strange piece of music. I included it because I felt the wolves constituted part of Charles' musical concept of cacophony—natural, beautiful cacophony. The wolves sing in a chorus, they're hitting every note on the keyboard. But it transcends dissonance." (17)

"I's a Muggin'" is another of the improvisational rap sessions interspersed here. This one is only seven seconds long, and finds

Joni and Charles goofing around on the tape recorder. It precedes the eight-minute track called "Sweet Sucker Dance." Again using Mingus's music, Joni tries to express the thoughts that Mingus was having around the time the sessions for this album were recorded. It is a slow blues number with lots of improvisational jazz moments to it, and Joni sings her poetry over it.

The rap "Coin in the Pocket" is a solo snippet of monologue from Mingus, in which he claims that he basically had a good life and always had a few coins in his pocket. It fittingly precedes the song "The Dry Cleaner from Des Moines," which is about a man who gambles and consistently wins—at the slot machines and at life. Another of Mingus's melodies, Joni is truly in her prime here. This is the album's only joyous and amusing song. According to Mitchell's lyrics, "The Dry Cleaner from Des Moines" is so lucky that he can put a quarter in the door at a public men's room, and it will pay him back change.

The final rap, entitled "Lucky," precedes the album's true masterpiece, "Goodbye Pork Pie Hat." It all has to do with jazz legend Lester Young and the prejudice that he experienced in his life.

As Joni explains, "That was a very difficult one. I had to find my own phrasing for the notes. The real difficulty for me was that the only thing I can believe is what has happened to me firsthand, what I see and feel with my own eyes. I had a block for three months. It's hard for me to take someone else's story and tell only his story in a song. Charlie assailed me with historical information about Lester Young and his family background, concerning his early playing days. He used to tap dance in his family band with his father and mother. He was married to white woman, traveling through the South in a time when that was just taboo. A lot of great black musicians were forced into cellars or the chitlin' circuit. So I had all these details, but I still couldn't with any conscience, simply write a historical song." (9)

Finally she had a vision of where this slow and thoughtful song needed to go. "Then something magical happened," she recalls. "One night Don Alias and I—he plays congas on the album, and he and I have been very close for the period of the last two years—were on the subway, and we got off, I don't know why, two stops early. We came up into this cloud of steam coming out of a New York manhole. Two blocks ahead of us, under these orangeish New York lights, we see a crowd gathered. So we head toward the crowd. When we get up on it, it's a group of black men surrounding two small black boys. It's about midnight, and the two boys are dancing this very robot-like mime dance. One of the guys slaps his leg and says, 'Isn't that something? I thought tap dancing was gone forever.' Immediately, I'm thinking about Lester Young. They were dancing under one of those cloth awnings that goes out of the curb of the bar. I look up—and the name of the bar is the Pork Pie Hat. The music they were dancing to was jazz coming off of the jukebox inside. There were big blown-up pictures of Lester Young all around the place. It was wild. So that became the last verse of the song. In my mind, that filled in a piece of the puzzle. I had the past and the present, and the two boys represented the future, the next generation. To me, the song then had a life of its own." (9)

In was Joni's idea to insert the bits of dialogue and monologue between the songs. Explaining her rationale, she says, "Then there's the documentary footage in the album, which I think is extraordinarily important. Charles knew long before he became ill how he wanted his funeral to be carried out, what he wanted and didn't want. I had to include that. And I love the spirit of the birthday song—which established the year he was born in, and that's why I used it to open the album. And I also like Sue's presence on the tape because she is a wonderful woman. She was very, very giving with Charles." (17)

Speaking personally, I have always loved the music on the *Mingus* album. However, I have also hated the snippets of Charles Mingus dialogue in it—especially where he talks about dying and his funeral. In my mind, you can't simply put the *Mingus* album on the stereo and just enjoy the music. The talk breaks it up too much for me, and I am sure that many of Joni's fans feel the same way. I understand Mitchell wanting the sound of Charles's voice to be part of this album in a "documentary" sense. However, I think it mars the album.

Finally, in the twenty-first century, I was able to take a CD of the *Mingus* album and burn a copy that sequenced only the six songs from the album and play them back-to-back, and finally appreciate them on their own. Since Joni recorded three to four versions of the six songs on this album, all with different jazz combos, I have a suggestion for her as well. Why not do an album called *Mingus Revisited*, edit out all the Charles Mingus dialogue, and give the public a listen to the alternate takes on this album? I think this would bring her the kind of success she was looking for with the *Mingus* material. All are entitled to their own opinion, and that's mine.

The press reviewers found this album completely cryptic. No one seemed able to pinpoint whether or not this was a good move or a sheer misstep. Sam Sutherland in *High Fidelity* wrote, "At once more compact and ambitious than the rambling abstract *Don Juan's Reckless Daughter* . . . *Mingus* will strike a responsive chord among mainstream jazz fans and more adventurous pop listeners . . . Mitchell's own confessional mien and self-absorbed penchant for analysis shape the songs' perspectives, but the title character and central motif of a defiant black consciousness are not inventions. She is clearly aware of the dichotomy between the latter and her own lily-white folk origins . . . And despite the sharp imagery and precise mannerisms seen in her lyrics to 'Goodbye Pork Pie Hat,' Mingus' own elegy to saxophone giant Lester Young, the melody's sensitive emotional spectrum renders words—even these—unnecessary." (97)

In *Rolling Stone* magazine Ariel Swartley claimed, "Sometimes it seems as if the tensions Mitchell's courting start to drive her crazy . . . There are times, too, of consolation and even ecstacy—not many, maybe not enough. But then, what we've got here is a requiem for unbelievers . . . 'Sweet Sucker Dance' falls flat . . . she chooses narrative in 'The Dry Cleaner from Des Moines' and is left huffing and quavering behind the jumpy beat." (98)

One of the strongest aspects of the *Mingus* album was the fact that Joni was able to use its package to further promote her artwork. She painted three canvases of Mingus solo, and an abstract one of the two of them together, which graces the album cover.

There are two ways to look at the *Mingus* album. The first is to view it as a brilliant opportunity for Joni to work with top-notch jazz masters to create a musical eulogy to a music innovator, and to stretch out her wings. The second is to see it as the one album that threw her career so far off track that her once strong fan base didn't know what to think. Joni saw it in the former light.

It caused her to be very philosophical about her choices. According to her, "It's typical in this society that is so conscious of being Number One and winning; the most you can really get out of it is a four-year run, just the same as in the political arena. The first year, there's the courtship prior to the election—prior to, say, the first platinum album. Then suddenly you become the king or queen of rock & roll. You have, possibly, one favorable year of office, and then they start to tear you down. So if your goals end at a platinum album or being king or queen of your idiom, when you inevitably come down from that office, you're going to be heart-broken. Miserable. Nobody likes to have less then what he had before. My goals have been to constantly remain interested in the music. I see myself as a musical student. That's why this project with Charles [Mingus] was such a great opportunity. Here was a chance to learn, from a legitimately great artist, about a brand new idiom that I had only been flirting with before." (9)

In her mind, was it a success? "There are different kinds of success. *Mingus* to me is a successful project to my core, and yet it pretty much cost me my airplay, my radio presence," she claims. (51)

Looking back on the whole *Mingus* experience, Joni later stated, "In a certain way, I was the first to go into the forest of jazz from pop. They pressed about ten copies of the *Mingus* album, I think," she says sarcastically. "There was no outlet for it. With that album, I became a person without a country. I was considered an expatriate from pop music. Meanwhile, the jazz folks thought, 'Who is this white chick?' They saw me as an opportunist come to exploit Charles. Whereas, in fact, Charles sent for me. In jazz circles they still complain about it, that what we did was not Mingus's music. Well of course it wasn't, it was a collaboration. It was not mine either. We had to meet somewhere in the middle, with integrity." (14)

Artistically, Joni Mitchell's *Mingus* album was fantastic. From a sales standpoint, it was an expensive disaster. It made everyone in the music business wonder, "What the hell is she going to do next?" But in Joni's life, the only constant is her sheer unpredictability.

14

Shadows and Light

In 1979, as the *Mingus* album was being released, Joni Mitchell hit the concert road in the company of a hot new band with jazz and rock credentials. This turned out to be one of the most creative and exciting bands of her career. It included Pat Metheny (lead guitar), Lyle Mays (keyboards), Jaco Pastorius (bass), Michael Brecker (sax), Don Alias (drums and percussion), and the Persuasions (vocals). During this tour she recorded a live album that was her most exciting jazz recording yet. Joni had a brilliant chemistry with this particular band, and the resulting *Shadows and Light* album did an impressive job of blending her recent jazz singing with these first-class musicians. On this record Joni sounds cool, confident, and 100 percent connected with her recent jazz-oriented material.

On this tour she played exciting versions of her songs from *Mingus*, *Don Juan's Reckless Daughter*, *The Hissing of Summer Lawns*, and *Court and Spark*. The song "Woodstock" was the one reminder of her folk era. An exciting upbeat version to Frankie Lyman and the Teenagers' "Why Do Fools Fall in Love?" is the only new song exclusive to this tour.

On May 6, 1979, Joni performed in Washington, D.C., at a No Nukes concert rally. That year several No Nukes events were staged for rock artists to voice their opposition to the escalation of nuclear power plants in America. Several of her rock musician buddies—including Bonnie Raitt, Jackson Browne, James Taylor, the Doobie Brothers, Carly Simon, and Crosby, Stills, and Nash— were also involved in this cause. On May 27 she was at the Berkeley Jazz Festival in Berkeley, California. On this particular tour, Joni actively courted not only her folk/rock fans but a whole new jazz audience as well. She then performed as part of the annual Playboy Jazz Festival at the Hollywood Bowl on June 15.

Her summer 1979 Shadows and Light tour then took her to Madison Square Garden in New York City; the Civic Center in Providence, Rhode Island; the Zoo Amphitheater in Oklahoma City; Red Rocks Ampitheater outside of Denver; the Mississippi River Festival in Evansville, Indiana; Pine Knob in Clarkston, Michigan; Alpine Valley in East Troy, Wisconsin; the Minneapolis Auditorium; Tanglewood in Lenox, Massachusetts; Merriweather Post Pavilion in Columbia, Maryland; Forest Hills Tennis Stadium in Queens, New York; Robin Hood Dell West in Philadelphia; Pacific Coliseum in Vancouver; Memorial Coliseum in Portland, Oregon; and the Civic Auditorium in San Francisco.

At the time, Joni was very enthused about this tour and the music she was making with her new band. But, in her mind, was this a rock concert or a jazz show? According to her, "With these players, we're talking about young musicians who have no real musical or categorical preferences. We all love rock & roll. We all love folk music. And we all love jazz. If anything, we want to be considered a musical event. We're going to do some traditional African ceremonial drum pieces. I would like to get loose enough to dance. Jaco, you know, is a bass player, but he's also a fantastic keyboard player. In this band, we're going to try to switch instruments. It should be very creative." (9)

On this tour Joni had a brilliant opportunity to capture the music and this band on film, to create a Showtime cable TV special out of it. So, on September 9, 1979, the show at the Santa Barbara County Bowl was filmed from several angles and audiotaped for a potential live concert album.

From Santa Barbara, the tour went on to another outdoor arena, the Greek Theatre in the Hollywood Hills of Los Angeles, where she headlined for five days. The tour concluded there on September 12–16.

Joni was very happy with the audio from the Santa Barbara show and was convinced that it should be released. However, at the time there was a conflict of opinion between Joni and Asylum Records. She wanted to create a live concert album—essentially the soundtrack for the concert film she was working on, but Asylum didn't see it as a wise decision. Joni explained at the time, "From the record company point of view, they're not certain that my audience wants a live album of material that was not a great commercial success in the first place. I think it's just amazing music. It's a shame that it wouldn't be released. They weren't my biggest 'hits,' but some of my favorite music that I've ever made is from *The Hissing of Summer Lawns*, *Hejira* and *Don Juan's Reckless Daughter*. I think that when the film is completed they'll see how spectacular it is and they won't be so conservative. But these are very conservative times with the record companies; it's conservative everywhere." (90)

When her comments were printed in the *Los Angeles Times*, there was suddenly a buzz about this potentially suppressed live Joni Mitchell album. Now everyone really wanted to hear it. Ultimately Joni won out, and the double-disk set called *Shadows and Light* was planned as well.

On November 7, 1979, Joni celebrated her thirty-sixth birthday and was seriously examining where her life was and where it was going. Looking back on this era she claimed, "I really have an interesting life. My father said to me one time, 'Joan, you've had a hard life, one could say. One could say you've several lives in one. But let's face it, most women are old bags by the time they're 36.' That was the time I brought my black boyfriend [Don Alias] home to meet them. He sat in silence for an hour and a half and then came out with that, so I don't know really where he was coming from. But his wheels were turning." (2)

Where did she see herself going, and what did she see herself doing at the age of thirty-six? According to her at the time, "You know, in a few years, I'll be past a safe childbearing age. I don't see many women raising children successfully alone, and as yet I haven't been able to bond with a man who I could see myself with in constant company for the twenty years that're necessary to do a good job of that. I wouldn't just frivolously get pregnant and bring a child into this world, especially a world that has such a difficult future as the one we're facing. Also, the children of celebrities have been notoriously troubled. But when it comes to the business of raising children, I finally feel emotionally stable enough to deal with it. It's taken me this long, but it may be something that's denied me. It may be one of my little regrets in my old age. I still leave the future open, and given the right relationship, even if I thought the relationship had a potential longevity of say, six years, I might do it." (9)

For some reason, Joni decided to end her feud with *Rolling Stone* magazine. She had been upset with them since they had published her trail of broken hearts in their magazine several years earlier. She submitted to an extensive interview with writer Cameron Crowe—whose own story as a rock writer was later glorified on the silver screen in the film *Almost Famous*.

She told Crowe, "It's a funny thing about happiness. You can strive and strive to be happy, but happiness will sneak up on you in the most peculiar ways. I feel happy suddenly. I don't know why. Some days, the way the light strikes things. Or for some beautifully immature reason like finding myself running to the kitchen to make myself some toast. Happiness comes to me even on a bad day. In very, very strange ways. I'm very happy in my life right now." (9)

According to her, "I'm still a child. Sometimes I feel seven years old. I'll be standing in the kitchen and all of a sudden my body wants to jump around. For no reason at all. You've seen kids that suddenly just get a burst of energy? That part of my child is still alive. I don't repress those urges, except in certain company." (9)

She was philosophical about Asylum Records label mates like Jackson Browne and Linda Ronstadt. She said at the time, "The Eagles have really stretched out thematically. Jackson writes fine songs. Linda is very special. I'm a great appreciator of all those people." (9)

She also talked about her tri-coastal lifestyle. For her, having a place in Canada, a place in L.A., and a place in New York City worked. "I consider myself spread across this continent in a very disorganized manner," she explained. "I have three residences. One is wild and natural [Vancouver]. One is New York, which needs no description. California, to me, represents old friends, and health. I love to swim. If there's anything that I love about this place here, it's the luxury of being able to swim, which is like flying to me. I could get in the pool, float around for about two hours and never touch the sides. That's better than any psychiatrist to me. I'm working out my body, working out my lungs—the poor things are blackened with cigarette smoke—and looking at nature. You don't have that in New York. New York gives me an opportunity to flex a muscle that I don't really get to use; for instance, out there there is directness. I find that it makes me stronger. You don't have so many anonymous encounters out here. In New York, constantly, the street is challenging you to relate to it." (9)

In the credits of the *Shadows and Light* TV special, the executive producer is listed as her manager Elliot Rabinowitz [Roberts]. Joni Mitchell is credited as the director, and David Myers is the director of photography. Joni was also one of the two editors on this filmed version of her concert.

A great part of 1980 found Joni working as a film editor on her forthcoming *Shadows and Light* TV special and album. Sequestered in a New York City editing room, she took on a wonderful new creative challenge. Before filming this concert tour, Joni confessed that she didn't know the difference between 16 millimeter film stock, videotape, and 35 millimeter film. "It's a crash, on-the-spot education, and it's the best education I've ever had. Film is the most natural new medium for me that I've ever worked in. It's not nearly as difficult as it was setting words to Charles Mingus' material last year," she claimed. (99)

Regarding the film that was made, Mitchell explains, "We filmed in natural light beginning at the 'magic hour,' about 6:00 P.M., and by 8:00 P.M. we were into total darkness. We had incandescent lights to take over, so it doesn't have the usual spotlights or colored lights associated with a rock show. This gave us an interesting look, but I've found that any performance, no matter how definitive, doesn't hold up visually for an hour-and-a-half. So we began shooting very low-budget illustrations for some of the songs. The illustration is not too literal—I don't want to spoil anyone's imagination of the situation. I've tried to leave a certain amount of the performance there and illustrate certain sections of songs, so it's integrated with live performance." (99)

Use of new illustrative material in the film included historic newsreel footage of the real Amelia Earhart, amid the filmed concert version of the song "Amelia." Joni was reportedly so impressed with the way that sequence turned out that she went to her record company and asked for more money for the film and the live soundtrack album to be released from it.

Joni explained at the time, "When that worked, the purse strings loosened a little and I've been able to go out and do some specific shooting. For 'Coyote' we shot a hitchhiking episode with a coyote . . . Now I find when the band comes back onto the screen, I'm glad to see us." (99)

According to her, the film's edits perfectly complemented the music: "My poetry is a lot of fast, rapid edits, and film construction has become more like that over the last five years. When it came to cutting from one scene to another, I've already done that." (99)

One of her main challenges was getting the two-hour show edited down to the hour-and-a-half format that the time slot for the TV special allowed. She said during the editing process, "If I can get a good short version, it could go out on prime-time television. If I can't reduce it to my liking to less than an hour-and-a-half, it could go out late-night. It's just an exercise in my own attention span really, but it's turning out very beautiful." (99)

When she finished editing her TV special, and sequencing and remixing her new album, she was ready to present her latest artwork to the public. The *Shadows and Light* album was released in September 1980. It did quite well on the album charts, peaking at number 38 in the United States and at number 63 in the United Kingdom. Joni made few public appearances during 1980. On October 4–5 she performed at the annual Bread and Roses Festival of Music at the Greek Theatre in Berkeley, California. On December 2, 1980, Joni's *Shadows and Light* concert special ran on the Showtime cable television network.

There are some song differences between the full-length album, the original truncated one-disc American CD version of the album, the newer two-disc full-length version of the CD, and the TV special, which is now available on DVD. For instance, the DVD/TV special adds "Jaco's Solo" and a rousing version of "Raised on Robbery." It skips "Don's Solo," "God Must Be a Boogie Man," "Dreamland," and "Woodstock." When the CD was introduced in the United States, there was a shortened single-disc version available, and a rare Japanese disc that was complete. Then Joni's Asylum Records catalog was remastered and rereleased, and now the full version of *Shadows and Light* is available in America as a high-definition CD, which is much improved in sound quality and longer in length, and has a more extensive booklet.

The *Shadows and Light* program, album, and TV special all

open with Joni singing the beginning lyrics to the song "Shadows and Light," while on the projection screens a fiery scene from Joni's favorite coming-of-age movie—James Dean's *Rebel without a Cause*—plays with dialogue. Quick snippets of Dean confronting his father (Jim Backus) and his mother (Ann Doran) illustrate Mitchell's introduction to the world of teenage rebellion, and her first introduction to her love of rock & roll. While the sounds to Frankie Lyman and the Teenagers play, they sing the song "I'm Not a Juvenile Delinquent." Film footage from another 1950s movie about teen rebels—out of the *Blackboard Jungle* mode—is also used in this introductory video montage, which then cuts to archive footage of the group Frankie Lyman and the Teenagers singing the same song in their matching sweaters with a large varsity-style letter T emblazoned on the front. Then cut to footage from a 1950s juvenile delinquent film, then cut back to James Dean putting his foot through a stretched canvas portrait of his grandmother, and more *Rebel without a Cause* footage. Meanwhile the stage lights come up to reveal Joni Mitchell and her red-hot jazz ensemble on stage swinging into the opening number, "In France They Kiss on Main Street." It's a great multimedia way to kick off the album and the show. Throughout the Shadows and Light concert, different film footage is used to illustrate the images Joni sings about on stage.

The *Shadows and Light* album was a critical and creative hit for Joni. It took her jazz-influenced music and made it all so much more accessible, relevant, and lively. Whereas many live albums capture an artist's concert experience, they rarely add anything new to the music. However, here Joni and her fresh new band bring new life to songs like "Edith and the Kingpin," "Coyote," "Dreamland," and "The Dry Cleaner from Des Moines," and make them even more lively and relevant on this album than they were originally.

In the previous couple of years Joni had been accused in the press, and by her record company, of catering to only a fraction of her millions of fans with her excursions into the world of jazz. According to her, "I don't believe so much in compromise as I don't believe in art that has become so elitist that only fourteen people in the world can appreciate it. For instance on this project there was a possibility that people would have this prejudice—'Oh, it sounds like cocktail lounge music.' Or, 'That sounds like *Johnny*

Carson Show music.' I wanted somehow or other to make something that transcended that prejudice. I feel that I solved that problem. It remains to be seen, but I feel that the music, while being very modern, still contains an almost folk-music simplicity. I don't think that it's intimidating. Some people get intimidated by jazz. It's like higher mathematics to them." (9)

She proclaimed during this era, "Since I have been playing with more masterful players, that is to say, true artists who don't think in terms of commercial consideration, who just play gut-level and that's it, it's an entirely different experience. And since I began to play with them, I mean as a singer, I feel I am a much better singer. If I was a better singer last year than I was the year before, I'm five or six times better a singer this year for the work that I'm doing on Charlie's music. You know, I can go almost anywhere that my range will take me; my pitch has improved, my confidence has improved—I really feel free now as a singer. But I still don't have my facility on any instrument. They're, to me, just tools for setting up a reference for my voice to float on. I'll probably never master those instruments, although there is a growth. The guitar, especially, is growing. The piano—all of a sudden I went through a breakthrough period last year where I sat down and off the top of my head, I couldn't play anything wrong. What I mean by that is that if I hit what would be called a wrong note, a dissonance, I would repeat it and it would sound fantastic—like where a dissonance was simply another statement and was not a wrong note. You know, lay on it; you hit a dissonance—well lay on it!" (42)

On the highly satisfying *Shadows and Light* album, Joni was able to stitch together her favorite tracks from her newest albums in a fashion that she genuinely loved. She was able to sing her three songs about her jazz and blues idols in the same show: "Goodbye Pork Pie Hat" [about Lester Young], "Furry Sings the Blues" [about Furry Lewis], and "God Must Be a Boogie Man" [about Charles Mingus]. She had evolved into a brilliant storyteller.

One of the happiest collaborations came on her songs with the Persuasions: "Shadows and Light" and her rocking version of "Why Do Fools Fall in Love?" The latter track was the only Joni song exclusive to this album.

After the critics didn't know what to say about *Don Juan's Reck-*

less Daughter and *Mingus*, the reviews for the *Shadows and Light* album were suddenly glowing. It was as if she had worked whatever intimidating edges there were off of her jazz material and gave noncommercial songs like "Goodbye Pork Pie Hat" and "Edith and the Kingpin" an accessible rocking edge.

In the *New York Daily News* Hugh Wyatt claimed, "Joni Mitchell . . . is to my knowledge, the only pop vocalist to attempt to sing that music of the free-form players. On first hearing, she appears to be consumed by Mingus's style. A closer appraisal, however, reveals a former folk/rock singer who is subtly experimenting with free-form . . . The highlight of the album is her treatment of Mingus' 'Goodbye Pork Pie Hat,' where she skillfully melds the spirit of free-form with basic harmonic and structural patterns." (100)

Stephen Holden in *Rolling Stone* was in awe of Mitchell, calling the album both "a surprise and a triumph . . . The extraordinary power of *Shadows and Light*, of a handful of great live rock albums, took me by surprise . . . Mitchell has grown into a breathtakingly polished pop-jazz singer . . . she's created a brooding instrumental sound that's unique in popular music . . . what rock & roll standard could summarize more wittily Joni Mitchell's lifelong obsession with romance than 'Why Do Fools Fall in Love?' . . . more casually effusive than she's ever been in the studio . . . A dream band . . . this is the finest ensemble that Mitchell has worked with, and her exhilarating vocals reflect her complete confidence in these musicians." (101)

On the *Shadows and Light* TV special, Joni sports a shoulder-length curly hairdo. She wears a teal green pant suit of knickers and a matching jacket over a purple blouse. A red carnation is pinned to her left front lapel. She appears cool and confident, cooing her graceful and smooth poetry to an adoring crowd.

While "Coyote" plays, footage of a real coyote running around a snow-covered setting plays. There are also scenes of Joni skulking around in a stalking coyote fashion and finally petting the coyote.

There is also an ice skating scene that is run while she performs the song "Hejira." Skating star Toller Cranston is seen performing an ice ballet to the music, while Joni is also captured on ice, swirling around on her blades. She wears a black outfit, complete with a cape of fur tails, looking very much like the "Black Crow" she also sings about in this beautiful jazz-infused concert.

Midway in this show Joni removes her jacket to reveal a chic black beaded cummerbund around her waist. She looks great, and vocally she sounds incredibly happy and in good spirits. Her lone piece of artwork displayed on the special is a sketch that she did of herself and the Persuasions.

It is interesting to note that in this special, and in all of her live bands, there are no frilly background girls and no other women in the group. It is just Joni in her element as one of the guys in the band. According to her, "I believe in equality. I believe that I am male and I am female. Not that I am male and I am female. Not that I'm saying I'm bisexual—I believe in heterosexuality. I think ultimately it's the most difficult and nourishing of them all. But I do understand homosexuality in these times. It seems to be a peculiar, in many cases, necessary, alternative to this mess that's happening between the men and the women. I know a lot of women now who have come through the whole gamut and they're at the position where they almost don't want to deal with it anymore. They want to be celibate. Men are not at this place at all. The new woman is embracing this as a possibility. If there wasn't always this intense sexual competition between women, it might provide the climate for them to develop a camaraderie. In my observation, what passes for feminine camaraderie is conspiracy. I would love to make new women friends, but I hardly have time to do justice to the ones I have." (9)

After her 1979 *Shadows and Light* tour ended, her jazz band went off in different directions. Pat Metheny went on to record several influential albums of his own. Michael Brecker and his trumpet-playing sibling, Randy, recorded several Brecker Brothers jazz duet albums. They also opened their own jazz club in New York City called Seventh Avenue South. The Persuasions were frequent attractions there in the early 1980s.

Speaking of Jaco Pastorius's tenure in Joni's band, she later stated, "Jaco had at that time what I thought was a beautiful inflamed ego. He had a huge ego and it offended a lot of people, but I didn't mind it. He'd say things like, 'I'm the baddest! I ain't braggin', I'm just tellin' the truth!' He was one of the few other people I ever met who thought Nietzsche was funny. We used to laugh about 'Thus Spake Zarathustra.' Jaco was a good friend, I enjoyed his company. But as he got on the scene, he kind of went too far over the other way. He used to push his bass up in the mix. Everybody thought it was because he was my new boyfriend! They'd say, 'You can always tell who Joni's going with by who's loudest in the mix.' But he was just such an absolutely dominant male that I couldn't control him." (68)

Since she was at the height of her jazz era, who are her true jazz idols? According to her, "Funny, as a painter I have so many heroes. But as a musician I like one or two in each camp and then I don't like the rest. Like, I don't care for John Coltrane—many people think he's the greatest. Coltrane seems like he's on Valium to me. Charlie Parker, I see his greatness. Then Wayne Shorter is a genius—he's a tributary of 'Trane, but he's got so much more breadth and mysticism and with and passion and everything. So to me, Coltrane is kind of a stepping-off point to Wayne." (7)

Although one tends to think of Joni Mitchell fans as being mild-mannered "flower children," she too—like many stars—attracted some crazy fans as well. From 1976 to 1980 a stalker staked himself outside her Los Angeles house. Joni had to have a twenty-four-hour armed guard on the premises. However, the crazed fan suddenly disappeared two days after John Lennon's assassination in December 1980. "It's my opinion that he realized how disruptive he was to my privacy," she surmises. "Or maybe he left because I had been pleading with his parents to intervene and they finally did." (12)

As she explains it, "I've had a lot of stalkers in my career. I've had to live under armed guard. One guy saw me as the gateway to God, the voice of his dead sister, his wife-to-be. He also had really violent necrophilic fantasies, which he described in detail in writing. He lived in the bushes—literally, like Robinson Crusoe—out here for two years. Months would go by, and nothing would happen. The guards thought I was a neurotic, but they'd leave for fifteen minutes, and he'd come over the wall, climb up on the roof, and start screaming and shaking the windows." (6)

At this point in time, Mitchell's native country began to appreciate the singer as a national treasure. On February 5, 1981, Joni was inducted into Canada's prestigious Juno Hall of Fame. Canadian Prime Minister Pierre Trudeau made the actual induction.

The Juno Awards are the Canadian equivalent to the Grammy Awards in the United States.

The critical and chart success of the *Shadows and Light* album returned Joni to a mainstream market. She was sounding better than ever and was now ready to change course and redefine her 1980s sound.

15

Wild Things Run Fast

Throughout the year 1981, Joni was again reinventing herself and exploring new songwriting directions and fresh sounds. She made very few public appearances of note. According to her it was a necessary exercise of artistic solitude. She needed the time away from the spotlight to reassess where she was going with her music and her personal life.

For Joni, was this era a conscious disappearing act or was it just a creative sabbatical? According to her, "No, it's just a natural undulation. I've been to a lot of grand parties, and they're fairly predictable to me at this point. I go to parties not so much to be seen or to meet new people. I'd rather party with people I've known for a while whom I like. The rest of the time I go off on little photographic journeys. I like to drive cross-country by myself about every two years. I don't know why, some call of the wild. I'm at large—I walk around the streets wherever city I'm in. It's not as if I'm cloistered someplace. I just don't have my picture taken, and I don't do interviews. In the case of this album, it's very strong. I'm willing to promote it. The last few projects have been pretty esoteric. There was no reason to come real high profile for them." (102)

In fact, it was a big transition period for the whole record business, especially in America. Everyone was going through major changes when the 1980s began. There was first of all a giant shift in what was going on politically in the United States. With the 1980 election of President Ronald Reagan, the focus of the country shifted dramatically and the prevailing musical style changed too. The party-down giddiness of disco, which had dominated the music charts from 1976 to 1980, came to a crashing halt. The careers of Donna Summer, Gloria Gaynor, and the Village People suddenly hit a brick wall.

Several of the biggest musical hit makers of the 1970s found themselves chasing a new sound and rethinking their approach to the music. "New wave" and "punk" music was the new thing. Groups like the Sex Pistols and the Ramones were stripping away the sounds of the last decade, and suddenly everyone seemed to chasing a fresh back-to-basics rock & roll sound. To keep up with the times Linda Ronstadt abandoned her country/rock sound to produce the album *Mad Love*, featuring several bare-bones songs written by Elvis Costello. Bonnie Raitt stepped away from her blues/rock stylings, put together a hot rock band, and introduced her new sound with *Green Light*. Carly Simon smoothly made the transition from folk/pop with her harder edged rock album, *Spy*.

The album *Shadows and Light* had fulfilled Joni Mitchell's contract with Asylum Records. In the meantime, David Geffen sold Asylum Records and started his second record label, Geffen Records. Among the first people he signed were Elton John, Neil Young, Cher, and Joni Mitchell.

Joni was facing a whole new, decade-long, four-album phase of her career. During this tenure at Geffen Records, Mitchell released her return to rock & roll album (*Wild Things Run Fast*), her hippest, most experimental 1980s techno album (*Dog Eat Dog*), and some of the most masterful melodic music of her career (*Chalk Mark in a Rain Storm* and *Night Ride Home*).

This was not necessarily Joni's favorite period. According to Joni, "I made four albums for Geffen [Records]. For one reason or another, they were viewed as being out of sync with the '80s. But I was out of sync with the '80s. Thank God! To be in sync with these times, in my opinion, was to be degenerating both morally and artistically. Materialism became a virtue; greed was 'hip.' You heard the word 'victim' bandied about, but never the word 'victimizer.' It seemed like everyone was dressed in black everywhere. What were we mourning?" (103)

The first album of Joni's new recording contract was her return to writing very personal songs with a rock & roll sound. It was called *Wild Things Run Fast*. When it was originally released in 1982, she explained, "I've been recording this album for four years. I must have cut every song on it about four times using different personnel . . . It took me that long to find a band that had the sophistication harmonically and rhythmically—to play with a rock & roll feel, heavy on drums. I have the luxury of working that way." (102)

Among the musicians whom Joni used on the *Wild Things Run Fast* album were Larry Klein (bass), Vinnie Colaiuta (drums), Steve Lukather (electric piano), Larry Williams (Prophet synthesizer), Larry Carlton (electric guitar), Mike Laudau (electric guitar), John Guerin (drums), Russell Ferrante (Oberheim synthesizer), Victor Feldman (percussion), and Wayne Shorter (sax). Like the majority of her albums, this was primarily recorded at A&M Studios in Los Angeles. The exception is the song "Be Cool," recorded at Devonshire Studios in England. This album was responsible for bringing old friends back into her life, ending old relationships, and attracting a new love to her life.

Joni got into a dispute with her longtime manager, Elliot Roberts, during the recording of *Wild Things Run Fast*. She found him "too busy" to devote time to her, as he was occupied with other clients of his, so she fired him. It was the end of a long and fruitful working relationship. Not long afterward, she signed Peter Asher as her new manager. Asher, who first found fame as half of the 1960s hit-making act Peter and Gordon ("Lady Godiva"), later found success as the producer and manager of James Taylor and Linda Ronstadt. In other words, Joni now had a new record label, a new band, a new sound, a new manager, and soon she would have a new boyfriend too.

Since Joni was now working with agent/manager Peter Asher, who was also James's longtime manager, it was actually Asher who negotiated a truce between the two superstar troubadours.

Eleven years had passed since the end of Joni Mitchell's affair with James Taylor. A lot of water had flowed under the bridge, and finally in 1981 the pair reconciled as friends and—happily—as musical collaborators.

At first, the offered olive branch of peace came in the form of a couple of intense and emotion-charged telephone conversations between Joni and James. Finally a chance meeting in a Los Angeles recording studio culminated in a musical reunion on record between the former lovers.

It had been a long time since Taylor and Mitchell had met face to face. Finally in March 1981, at A&M Recording Studio, they ran into each other. James was in the studio to record background vocals on David Lasley's album, *Missing Twenty Grand*. While he was recording his vocal parts on Lasley's tracks in Studio A, directly across the hall, there was Joni, who was working on her latest album, *Wild Things Run Fast*. In a highly impromptu move, she asked James if he would sing on her album. He agreed and spent the rest of the day hopping back and forth between the David Lasley sessions and Joni's sessions. On the *Wild Things Run Fast* album James can be heard singing on the track entitled "Man to Man."

What is the one thing that will make a recording artist return to writing and recording love songs? Well, falling in love, of course! That is exactly what happened to Joni when she became acquainted with musician Larry Klein.

"We met on the *Wild Things Run Fast* album," she recalls. "He played bass for me. I was kind of lonely at the time. And I actually prayed . . . I don't pray that often. And I prayed an embarrassed prayer, I said, 'Look, God, I know I don't write, I don't call. However, I don't need that much. All I need is a real good kisser who likes to play pinball.' So two days later, Klein said to me, 'How would you like to go to the Santa Monica pier and play video games?' And I looked up at that sky and said, 'Close enough.' And he said, 'I beg your pardon?' And we never looked back. We've been together ever since. So I look at it as divine intervention." (14)

Mitchell remained philosophical about relationships in general. Since the divorce rate was rising during this era, she pondered the reasons why people tended to not stay together for very long—especially in the conservative 1980s. "I think they're seeing too many movies!" said Joni, of women's need for romance. "I can understand the reason for divorce. That an old couple out on a farm—she does the cooking, he does the farming. It's a symbiotic relationship; they need each other for survival. In the city, you need to couple for survival but it's not so cut and dried. Our problem is too much choice, an inability to stick to one person." (102)

What kind of a relationship was she having with Klein circa

1982? Was Klein good for her? "Yes, a good relationship," replied Joni at the time. "I'm living with someone quite happily. We get along well, play well, work well together. I'm happy, it's a good time for me right now. It's reflected in this album." (102)

In one of her most revolutionary moves in ages, on November 21, 1982, Joni Mitchell married Larry Klein. The ceremony took place at the Malibu home of her former manager, Elliot Roberts.

Wild Things Run Fast had four of Joni's lovers—past and present—involved in its creation. There was James Taylor lending his vocals. There was John Guerin playing drums on some of the tracks. There was Don Alias doing musical arrangements. And there was Larry Klein on the bass. Since many of the songs on the album dealt with the subject of love, the obvious question is, Which song represented which boyfriend? In reality, the majority of the songs on her thirteenth album represented her current affair with Klein, and the obvious love she felt for him.

In November 1982 she released her thirteenth album, *Wild Things Run Fast*. The album opens with Joni's song "Chinese Café," which she teams with a few lines of the classic rock song "Unchained Melody," which was originally a huge hit for the Righteous Brothers in the 1960s. According to Joni, when she was a teenager, she would go to one of two different cafés in Saskatoon. The one where she could hang out and smoke cigarettes was owned by two Chinese guys named Artie and Charlie Mack. That was the "Chinese café" depicted in the song. There she would listen to the jukebox and hear the songs of the day, like "Poison Ivy" and "Love Potion No. 9."

In the context of the song "Chinese Café," Joni is talking to her childhood friend "Carol" and reminiscing about the old days in Saskatchewan at the café, and realizing that they are now—in the 1980s—the age their parents were when she and Carol went to the Chinese café. The one question about this particular song kicking off the album is that it is perhaps too light and sentimental a song to get the disc rocking. It's a pleasant song, but the wrong one to start a return-to-rock album with.

Although "Chinese Café" was not musically dramatic, it dropped another autobiographical clue in the lyrics. According to Joni in this song, her own daughter was someone she bore but could not raise.

"Wild Things Run Fast," the second cut on the album, should

have been the album's first song to get things rolling. Rocking, fast paced—and a much better choice for a single—it shows off Joni with a spirited song about fast-paced attraction and lust.

The song "Ladies' Man" is about a smooth operator. She sings about longing to be loved by him, loved as much as he apparently loves cocaine. During this era, that could have been about almost any man in the record business! A catchy song, it was one of Joni's favorites on this album. According to her, "'Ladies' Man' is another song radio missed, and it's a song that Aretha Franklin could have sung. In fact, there's two little catches in my vocal that are out of admiration for her. I also have at least one note I got from Tony Bennett, who I liked as a kid. And there's a lot of the Andrews Sisters in my choral work, although my harmony is different from the harmony of that era." (51)

Like so much of this album, this song was rerecorded several times until it ended up the way Joni wanted it. She later explained, "I invited Don Henley to come in and sing with me on this one. After he left, when I was playing it back, I was amazed how similar our voices sounded. It took a while to even notice that a new singer had even been introduced. So I went across the hall to where Lionel Ritchie was recording, and I conscripted him. There was the contrast I wanted, so I replaced Don with Lionel. The old editing room floor routine." (103)

In the ballad "Moon at the Window," Joni discusses love in terms of lust and desire, but laments that people don't know how to love when it all comes down to emotions. Sometimes after love is over, all you are left with is the moon shining through the window.

"Solid Love" is clearly written about her newfound love for Larry Klein. According to her, "I was beginning to rethink partnering—rethinking what allows love to endure rather than being merely a sexual attraction. The intensity of that plays out in the first year in most relationships." (103)

On the jazzy song "Be Cool," Joni rethinks the desire in everyone to want to be considered "cool" and together. She was later to claim, "'Be Cool' is like a pep talk to myself. It's tongue-in-cheek. While you generally want to be 'cool,' it's a corset." (103)

Again taking one of the songs of her rock & roll youth, Joni interprets the Jerry Leiber and Mike Stoller song "(You're So Square) Baby, I Don't Care." This particular song was originally from the

Elvis Presley movie *Jailhouse Rock* in the 1950s. Joni included the song on this album as a love song to Larry Klein—whom she found just a little bit square, but obviously didn't care.

After singing songs about the beginnings of love, on the song "You Dream Flat Tires" she rhapsodizes about the end of love. And on the song "Man to Man," she sings about how a lot of good men have come in and gone out of her door, and now she hopes she finally has a man in her life who wants to stay. Explaining the song "Underneath the Streetlight," Joni revealed, "I had an apartment in New York. My living room windows looked down on Little Italy—when it was still Little Italy, before it became gentrified Soho. It was near the Lincoln Tunnel. Great traffic jam chords—impatient—like Mingus sometimes, all that brass, you know—cacophony. I sat in my window expecting a song would go by underneath the streetlight. These are some of the things I saw." (103)

Of the song "Love" she explained, "It's hard to pick a favorite. It changes with your mood. Some of them make you want to get up and dance, some of them have a kind of dry humor. The last one, 'Love,' is a summary of all the different themes on the album. The poetry is from the thirteenth chapter of First Corinthians. It's a really profound contemporary statement considering it's Biblical and ancient. That song's inspiring, the highest piece. Each song's got its own little personality. There's no dead wood on it." (102)

Did Joni consider the songs on *Wild Things Run Fast* autobiographical? "I would rather people see their own lives in it than mine," she claimed. "There has been too much focus on me and not enough on the work itself. So often reviewers get into the current state of my psyche and miss the point that there is something else happening. A lot of it isn't exactly my life. It's very personal but it's more a murmur of the ideas and feelings of the people around me. I still think that the one-to-one relationship is the great art in life. If the relationship between the man and woman is creative and going well, I think your dealings with all other people improve. I think it's the new church." (102)

The *Wild Things Run Fast* album signaled a new era for Joni's painting as well. She used several of her oil-on-canvas paintings for the artwork on this package. On the cover is one of her many self-portraits, in muted tones of beiges, browns, and black. Wearing pants and a jacket, she leans against a TV set, and on the TV

WILD THINGS RUN FAST

screen we see a team of wild horses running through a flowing stream of water.

During this same period of time Joni became friendly with the famed painter Georgia O'Keeffe. She went to New Mexico to hang out with O'Keeffe, who in her own era was something of a non-conformist and a feminist. According to Mitchell, O'Keeffe said to her, "Oh, I would've liked to be a musician too, but you can't do both." According to Joni, "It's a lot of work, you have to give up a certain amount of socializing." (7)

The reviews for this album were generally good. In the San Francisco publication *BAM* (*Bay Area Music*), reviewer Dave Zimmer wrote, "On *Wild Things Run Fast*, she sails back into striking pop-jazz-rock territory, but without diluting her muse. If anything, she broadens it and uses more of the colors on her musical palette . . . Joni Mitchell's in love. At least she was while writing and recording *Wild Things Run Fast*. You can hear it in the loose and easy nature of her vocal performances and the generally hopeful, positive music and lyrics . . . There is a tremendous quotient of youthful exuberance on this LP. Joni addresses the issues of aging and passage of time with a shrug instead of despair." (104)

When the *Wild Things Run Fast* album was released in November 1982, it hit number 25 in the United States and number 32 in the United Kingdom. The one hit single from the album, "(You're So Square) Baby, I Don't Care," made it to number 47 on the U.S. record charts.

Although it was a Top 40 album on the charts on both sides of the Atlantic, Joni found that she was largely ignored on the radio level. She complained, "I felt like [Greta] Garbo when they didn't want her to be in talkies." (15)

From the album *The Hissing of Summer Lawns*, to *Hejira*, to *Don Juan's Reckless Daughter*, to *Mingus*, to *Shadows and Light*, Joni had largely turned her back on current trends in popular music. Now, with *Wild Things Run Fast*, she decided to chase what was going on in the pop and rock music scene. But, much to her dismay, in 1982 and 1983, when she came back to court rock radio, she found that radio programmers couldn't care less. She wasn't actively disrespected in the press; instead—and even worse—she was ignored.

This seemed to completely confound her. "In the beginning,

when I first started, for the first five years I had no drums on my record, so I didn't go to AM radio—so even in the time when I was a young artist!" She complained, "You only get about five or six years before they're sick of you in the business generally, and they let you ride—they don't put any money or effort or interest into you, really. They just let you sit there like manure in the pasture, as a procurer of young artists at the label. But they don't help you get your product to market." (7)

Something else happened in the early 1980s that really changed the way hit records were promoted: music videos. The advent of all-video TV networks like MTV and VH1 in the United States and Much Music in Canada ushered in a new way to "break" a new album, a new single, or a new act to the public.

Looking back to this era, Joni surmised, "I lost some people when I went from singing 'I' to singing 'you.' I lost some people when I added a band. I lost some people when I cut the band a little slack. I even lost some people for a photograph of myself in a swimming pool that somehow made me look uppity. Another thing was that in the '80s we moved into a particularly unromantic period in music. Videos had just begun, and they had a tendency to feature cold women with dark lipstick and stilettos grinding men's hands into the ground. It was an anti-love period, and my work—*Wild Things Run Fast*, in particular—was a joyous celebration of love, which basically made people sick. Once I realized that I had fallen from favor, I decided to stretch out." (6)

In 1983 Joni put together a hot new rock & roll band that included keyboardist Russell Ferrante (of the Yellowjackets), guitarist Michael Landau, bassist Larry Klein, and drummer Vinnie Colaiuta. This adept ensemble smoothly wove together elements of jazz, pop, rock, and folk, while Mitchell beautifully presided over this musical buffet of tunes from all of her musical eras.

That year, Joni, revved up by her hot new rock touring band, hit the concert road for an extensive world tour. From February to May she headlined dates in Japan, Australia, New Zealand, England, Ireland, Scotland, Belgium, France, Germany, Italy, Sweden, Norway, and Denmark. Then from June to October she toured from coast to coast in the United States.

Joni was so thrilled with this particular rock band that when the tour was over, she went into a soundstage and taped the show for a VHS video package called *Refuge of the Roads*. In 2004 it was released on DVD for the first time. Some intimate home movies of Joni appear on this impressive rock & roll video as well.

The track listing from this video package includes "Wild Things Run Fast," "Raised on Robbery," "Refuge of the Roads," "(You're So Square) Baby, I Don't Care," "Solid Love," "You Dream Flat Tires," "Chinese Café," and "Underneath the Streetlight." Her one jazz song on this concert video was "God Must Be a Boogie Man." The older songs that represented her here were "Sweet Bird," "Banquet," and "For Free." The oldest song on this package was her signature song "Woodstock."

Joni was soundly back in the realm of rock & roll—but behind the curve. Now that she was being ignored by radio, the video networks, and the press, something new and revolutionary had to happen in her music to get her back into the mainstream. Joni took this as a challenge. The gauntlet had been thrown down, and she knew she had to respond. For the first time in her long career, the time had arrived for her to want to actively chase the market that attracted the record buyers.

16

Dog Eat Dog

In 1984 and 1985 the music industry suddenly became socially conscious for the first time since the Woodstock years. It was the time of "We Are the World," Live Aid, Ferry Aid, USA for Africa, Farm Aid, Band Aid, and other huge all-star events meant to raise social awareness and raise money for worthy causes. Like so many other high-profile stars in this unique time, Joni Mitchell found herself caught up in the causes. Not only did she get involved in several of the all-star events, but the spirit of social criticism and commentary spilled over into her controversial fourteenth album as well.

In society, the decade of the 1980s was a period of opulence and greed. Television shows like *Dallas* and *Dynasty* glorified over-the-top wealth and set the tone for high-fashion clothes with big shoulder pads, jewels, and furs. TV evangelists like Jimmy Swaggart, Jerry Falwell, and Jim Baker fleeced the gullible public of their money and used the Bible to pad their own pockets. And the media in general massaged the public's lust for beauty and financial gain.

From the White House, the Reagan administration made some of the most shortsighted decisions in American history. Government-funded mental institutions were abolished and genuine mentally challenged patients were turned out into the streets. Millions of dollars were allotted for Star Wars–style surveillance systems, and all eyes were turned to the starving citizens of Africa, particularly in Ethiopia. These events and happenings were on Joni's mind when she penned her most daring, dynamic, and misunderstood album yet.

After Michael Jackson and Lionel Ritchie composed the song "We Are the World" and made it a huge number 1 hit, it raised millions of dollars that were earmarked to buy food for the starving Ethiopians. When a *We Are the World* album was planned, one of the other all-star tracks included on that disc was the Canadian version of a similar all-star collaborative song called "Tears Are Not Enough." The music was composed by David Foster; Bryan Adams and Jim Vallance wrote the lyrics, and additional French lyrics were penned by Rachel Paiement, Paul Hyde, and Bob Rock.

The song "Tears Are Not Enough" was produced by David Foster on February 10, 1985, at Manta Sound studios in Toronto. Foster utilized an instrumental track previously recorded in Vancouver. Over fifty singers participated in the recording, and solo lines of the lyrics were sung by—in order of appearance—Gordon Lightfoot, Burton Cummings, Anne Murray, Joni Mitchell, Dan Hill, Neil Young, Bryan Adams, Corey Hart, Bruce Cockburn, Geddy Lee (of the group Rush), and Mike Reno (of the group Loverboy).

"Tears Are Not Enough" was released as a twelve-inch single by CBS Records in March 1985 and it hit number 1 on Canadian charts by late April of that year. As a single it ultimately sold more than 300,000 copies. A video of the recording of the song was shown frequently in 1985 on Canadian TV, and a ninety-minute documentary about the recording session was telecast on December 22, 1985, by the CBC. The documentary was also released as a video package.

The money raised was administered by the Northern Lights for Africa Society in Vancouver. Reportedly the proceeds from the sales of the records exceeded $3.2 million. Of the money, 10 percent went to Canadian assistance programs and the remainder of the funds went to Ethiopian famine relief organizations.

During this year Joni's concert appearances were limited to benefits and fund-raising events. On September 22, 1985, Joni was one of the performers at the first annual Farm Aid event, which was held at the Memorial Stadium in Champaign, Illinois. Farmers in the Midwestern states were having major financial problems, and Farm Aid was organized to assist them.

Inspired by all of this, Joni had begun penning music for her *Dog Eat Dog* album. "It was written after I did the Canadian Band-Aid thing," she explains. "'We Are the World' is a beautiful idea. I believe we are the world. It's a very idealistic idea, but a good one. I just felt that in singing the words that the general overtone of these anthems was self-congratulatory and that there's another way to look at 'We Are the World,' it can narrow down to simply 'we.' All this heroism. In the big charity events of the past—Bangladesh, No Nukes—a lot of self-congratulation went on, and everybody that appeared in these things was 'the new consciousness,' and inevitably it did all their careers some good and everything—and the money never got to the people. Never. It got stripped off by the government, by the inevitable expenses of presenting such a thing. It never got there. So, you say, 'Well, why do you go to those things?' You go there with optimism that if you gain an inch, it's worth it." (68)

Dog Eat Dog was unlike any album she had ever recorded—before or since. It was the product of sheer experimentation. According to her, "If you stop experimenting, you're dead. Picasso is my patron saint. If you hear something you like that is not at all what you're doing, you go into another experimental mode. You have to start from scratch and become a beginner all over again. You have to do your growing pains in public." (102)

Something had to be done to generate excitement in her recording career and in her overall sound. Much of the music of the 1980s was more aggressive and had a progressive synthesizer sound to it. Her manager and her record company wanted to bring in new influences to kick the music up several notches. She too realized that she needed a fresh approach. How about bringing in a coproducer to work with her?

At first, she wasn't too excited about the idea. Finally, it was decided that musician/producer Thomas Dolby should be hired to work with her as a producer. She was not excited about this change in game plan. Dolby was one of the hot new stars of the 1980s, having produced and sung his own huge international techno hit, "She Blinded Me with Science." He seemed like an inspired choice to bring Mitchell's music into the contemporary realm. "To think I need a producer makes me feel like a head of lettuce," griped Joni. However, of Dolby's talent she had to admit, "He's a creative person. So if I let him, he would have fleshed everything out, and it wouldn't have been my music." (12)

She didn't mind taking a few suggestions in the studio, but she was dead-set against having him come in as the overseeing "producer" on the project. She was not about to relinquish that much responsibility. According to her, "I was accused of pandering on *Dog Eat Dog*—and my manager told Thomas Dolby, who'd been hired as a 'colorist,' to give me colors and get away. And he was comfortable with that, or so he said—but behind my back, my manager thought that if Thomas was producing it would create some more excitement. And so they negotiated that, and it caused a lot of trouble. And people said I was selling out or pandering on that record. I wasn't." (7)

Not only was Dolby given coproducing credits on this album, but the songs she wrote were anything but the typical "Joni Mitchell" genre of subject matter. There is an aggressive edginess to the messages she sent out on *Dog Eat Dog*. Mitchell admitted, "It is an angry album, and I have felt more angry in the last year, I would say. Some of it's personal and some of it is general—that's what my antenna is picking up. I just noticed an increase in my outrage at the general direction of things. At the way the government dispenses authority and money, and the Star Wars insanity and all that business. It's an angry album." (68)

She found working with coproducers very challenging. "This was one of the most difficult albums I ever had to make," she claimed. "I had never done any kind of work with a committee where, instead of just going in with my natural enthusiasm for something, there were four strong opinions to consider—and a lot of opposition. But frequently, because of delay and irritation, just like sand in an oyster, a pearl is born." (13) And so it was with *Dog Eat Dog*.

Not only was Dolby on hand to give each of her songs a unique techno flavor, but she also chose some new guest stars to come into the studio to record with her. According to her at that time, "I think Billie Holiday was a very natural singer. In the context of opera, Maria Callas was an excellent singer. I think the lead singer from the Doobie Brothers [Michael McDonald] is a very natural singer." (9) And so Michael McDonald was brought in to appear on *Dog Eat Dog*.

Recalls McDonald, "I had met her once before, a long time ago. I came out to visit John Guerin, when her and John were living together out there in Bel Air. I had submitted a song for an O. C. Smith project, and—unbeknownst to her of course—here I am, sitting there talking to John, whom I had known a little bit. He had done some sessions for me, when I was first signed as an artist at RCA years ago. He was nice enough to ask me about this tune for O. C. Smith, and it was really one of the first major covers I had gotten. I remember, she was sitting at the kitchen table with her guitar, working on a lyric, and I'm sitting there talking to John, and of course, I couldn't stop looking at her and thinking, 'I'm sitting here, and Joni Mitchell—she's over there writing a song!' And, John was asking me something about the song I wrote, and I was a little embarrassed by this. I thought the song was kinda pop, and an O.K. tune. And as thrilled as I was that I was doing it, I was kinda embarrassed to play it in front of Joni Mitchell. I remember saying something like, 'It's an O.K. tune. My songs aren't great. They're just kinda light-hearted and stuff.' And, I remember thinking, 'Why did I say that in front of her? I really sort of insulted her without meaning to.' And, I can still see her sitting there with her guitar working on some song. And I just thought, 'How incredible is this?' It was a real moment for me." (105)

After Michael left the Doobie Brothers in the early 1980s, he married singer Amy Holland. During this era Holland was a Capitol Records recording artist, with solo albums of her own. Says Michael of Joni, "I've just loved her songs. And, who hasn't? My wife and I, that's the one great passion we share, is Joni Mitchell and her music. And, I think that's kinda how we met actually. We both kinda realized that we were huge Joni Mitchell fans. My wife knows every lyric to every song." (105)

How did Michael's involvement in *Dog Eat Dog* begin? "Her husband, Larry Klein, called me. They were producing the album with Thomas Dolby, and it was just great. I knew it was going to be great, because every one of her records is an ongoing evolution into her artistry. I just love that song, and it was just great." (105)

There was one particular song that Joni had in mind for McDonald to sing with her. When Michael was asked to be part of the *Dog Eat Dog* sessions, he was honored and thrilled. He recalls, "'Good Friends' was the name of the track. And it was a big thrill for me, because I was just a huge Joni Mitchell fan. Always have been. I admire her as much as a songwriter as a singer and artist. It was a brief moment in my life, but it was a wonderful one." (105)

McDonald laughingly explains, "Actually Amy was with me that night. She would not let me go by myself. I wasn't going alone, that's for sure," he laughs. "She got to meet Joni, and that was a big thrill for her. And it was just a big thrill for me. I was real nervous. But singing with her was an incredible moment. And of course, everyone I know was going, 'You dog! How did you get that job!?' I have no idea. I was just at the right place at the right time." (105)

In addition to having several solo lines to sing in the song "Good Friends," Michael and Amy were invited to add their voices to the song "Tax Free" as well.

According to McDonald, he is also a big fan of Joni's artwork. "I bought a painting from her too. I have to say, that I was kinda like her worst nightmare as a fan," he laughs. "She was very sweet about it. She spent a lot of time with me, showing me some stuff. I was buying it for my wife for her anniversary. Amy just loves that, she really does. But, it was great. It's just neat to be around people like that, whom you've admired for so long. I'm no different than anybody else. I think most artists are the same as any other fan, and the admiration that you have for the people you've grown up listening to." (105)

Because of his friendship with Joni, he also had the opportunity to add a couple pieces of her artwork to his personal collection. "She is just wonderful," McDonald proclaims, "And she really has delved into that career as much as anything else. She's really, really wonderful. I have a couple of her paintings. I purchased an 'artist's proof' of the *Mingus in Mexico*. And then, I bought that other oil painting from her, which are two of my favorite things." (105)

Concurrent with the recording sessions for *Dog Eat Dog* came a ruling by the California State Board of Equalization claiming that Joni, and several other famous musicians, owed additional taxes dating back to the years 1971–1976. When the ruling came down, Geffen Records slapped a lien on her songwriting royalty account in an effort to recoup funds that it had spent promoting her.

Mitchell venomously proclaimed, "Now I know firsthand what it is to be dealt an injustice by the government. I got my advance [on a new five-year Geffen recording contract], and the state of

California said, 'Thank you very much. That's exactly what you owe us.' I'm telling you, it was like finding out that Daddy goes to hookers . . . The government *is* crooked." (13)

Although she still owed Geffen Records two albums beyond *Dog Eat Dog*, Joni did not mince words publicly, when asked about her relationship with the label. According to her, "[It] has been very bad for me." (106)

However, an awakening came about during the creation of this album. She claimed, "It put me in touch with all the powerless and prosecuted. And it opened up a political anger that was not there before." (107) Now she *really* had a cause to profess.

In addition to the politically based songs she wrote for *Dog Eat Dog*, the overall sound of her music changed as well. Regarding her sudden switch from acoustic music to 1980s synthesizer instrumentals, Joni claimed, "The synthesizer was irresistible. It puts the whole orchestra at your fingertips." (36)

Just as she had embraced jazz, Joni had suddenly gone techno. "It was a different way to work," she proclaimed. "I started out singing with just voice and guitar. But I don't think I lost anything of myself on this record." (108)

Joni was also feeling the pressure of being a recording star in the middle of the new MTV era. Since music videos were now the key to promoting albums, and since Joni was not making the sex-infused Madonna/Cyndi Lauper–style music, she found new promotional challenges. As she saw it, "There was a lot of adjustment to be made to the music world. Because of video, a lot of it is geared to a very young audience." (108)

According to Joni, her *Dog Eat Dog* album was a work of politically aware passion. The world around her seemed to be totally off track, and she wrote songs about her newly sharpened political views to express her anger and her frustration. "I'm a melancholy Nordic, you know," she stated. "Midnight sun in all the genes. Writing is very confronting work. A strong emotion—either a misunderstanding or a need to comprehend something within yourself—drives you to sit up all night to plumb the depth of your being. It's only rewarding when the muse coughs up something that has the right sound, as well as confirmation and content. When that happens, or when you get lucky in the studio, man, there's not another job in the world you would want. Sometimes I start to feel that the gods are smiling. To a certain degree I have to feel that there are forces at work beyond me." (13)

For the first time ever, Joni Mitchell allowed outside producers to get involved in one of her albums. Not since the song "Tin Angel" from her *Clouds* album had she consented to such a move. In fact this whole album was recorded with the influence of Thomas Dolby hovering overhead. He is responsible for giving a whole new "edge" to her sound. Also involved in the process was her new husband, Larry Klein, and recording engineer Mike Shipley.

When the album was released in November 1985, people either disliked it or—as in my case—loved it. Joni fans who were looking for another *Blue* or *Court and Spark* barely recognized the Joni on this album. And in a way, that was exactly what she was aiming for. *Dog Eat Dog* is innovative, exciting, and commands a listening. Among Mitchell's body of work it is truly a creative masterpiece.

Still there was a strong resistance among many of her fans who still thought of her as a confessional folk singer. "It's the same as typecasting," she said at the time. "However you come into the game, they're going to try to hold you there. But I shouldn't be ashamed that I like a lot of different kinds of music. Once something's in your soul, it's got to come out in your music." (12)

She was finished writing songs about looking for love—she had found the great love of her life in Klein. As she explained it, "It's the normal outcome in the development of an adult. I feel mated now. All those looking-for-love, what-went-wrong songs are kind of out of the way." (108)

The *Dog Eat Dog* album kicks off to a throbbing, pulsating start with the song she recorded with Michael McDonald, "Good Friends." In the context of the song—which is essentially about Joni and Larry Klein—she speaks of being hit "broadside." In actuality she and Larry were involved in a head-on car accident in Santa Monica, California. They were driving onto the Pacific Coast Highway, when a drunken young driver hit their car, and the two of them were taken to the hospital. Joni's head hit the windshield and Larry required sixteen stitches in his tongue. This song was about two good friends surviving what life had to dish out—both intentional and accidental.

The song "Fiction," with its choppy lyric pattern, finds Joni wondering what to believe anymore. Since the public is bombarded from all sides by the media—according to this song—it is hard to know what is real anymore. Since the news is dished out on TV by pretty people, interspersed with commercial plugs for all the latest products that are available, she questions what is real and what is not real. Where does "fiction" end and "fact" begin? Amid a techno beat, Joni asks her listener to question what the actual facts are. Does anyone really know anymore?

She again questions the decay of society with the electronically undulating song "The Three Great Stimulants." According to Joni, "The three great stimulants of the morality decaying culture, as Nietzsche observed in Germany prior to World War II are artifice, brutality, and innocence, or should I say, the exploitation and corruption of innocence. Artifice increases as culture declines real emotion becomes rare." (103)

With regard to the sound she achieved on this song, Mitchell explained, "I made a super-8 movie of a wall of graffiti in SoHo. When I got the film back I couldn't believe what I heard in the background; there was a guy hammering and a burglar alarm going off in that natural amphitheatre of New York City. The concrete resonance gave it this incredible foreboding sound. So when we started putting together 'The Three Great Stimlants,' I wanted a five-beat punctuation with that sound: 'Deep in the Night,' Bam Bam Bam Bam. Everybody was critical of the fidelity of it but I thought, 'We'll be here for days diddling with machines and I'll never get that sound again.'" (68)

The most blistering social criticism came on the song "Tax Free," which she wrote with Larry Klein. The song questions how TV evangelists, who use the Bible to beg for money from the unsuspecting public, are not taxed by the government—because they are *supposedly* legitimate religious preachers.

Says Joni, "You take these evangelists with their tax-free [status]. The government doesn't take the cut, so the chances are if they were true benefactors, which is how they present themselves, that they are in a position where that would not happen. They have direct access to money and they can actually put it into effect without anybody stripping it off. But it gets stripped off in the production cost of the hundred and one million reels that are running and these things which are broadcasting their message all over the place. That's the truth and the irony of it." (68)

As she explains the evolution of the song, "I saw a pink and black billboard on Sunset Boulevard that read 'Rock & roll is the Devil' signed 'Jerry Falwell and "The Moral Majority."' I thought, 'Soon they'll be passing out armbands for us to wear. We're being scapegoated!' I took to watching television evangelists, keeping an eye on them." (103)

Academy Award–winning actor Rod Steiger (*In the Heat of the Night*, 1967) is featured on the song "Tax Free" as the venom-filled televangelist preaching for his own self-aggrandizement. Also featured on this track are the voices of Don Henley, James Taylor, Amy Holland, and Michael McDonald.

"Tax Free" is a blistering criticism of the whole system that ruffled a lot of feathers. Joni explains, "And when the record came out, it appeared that some of the churches had been keeping an eye on me. Pat Robertson challenged me to a debate on *The 700 Club*. The Church of England called me a 'doubtraiser.' The ministers of the Crystal Cathedral and Episcopalian churches wrote letters of congratulations." (103)

One of the most fascinating and truly unique songs on this album is "Smokin' (Empty, Try Another)" which is a staccato-sounding recording of a cigarette machine at the A&M Recording Studios. It is a tongue-in-cheek homage to Joni's penchant for chain-smoking tobacco cigarettes.

She explains, "On the last record [*Wild Things Run Fast*], three years ago, we were particularly bogged down in the studio. No progress. I went outside. They had a cigarette machine in the parking lot and the man who serviced it hadn't come very regularly and during the course of the record, first my favorite brand was out, then my next favorite brand, and then it was down to Camel plains and Kools. It got to be—even for a hard-core smoker—a disgusting choice. So one night we were bogged down and we needed to shake something up, so I said [to recording engineer Skip Cotrell], 'Skip, get the long extension cord. We're gonna tape the cigarette machine.' When you hit the open channel the light would come on and it would say, 'Empty, try another/make another selection,' and the gears made that sound. So that's not even a loop—we recorded four minutes just playing the cycle, and then Larry played bass on it, and I put this chant on it. It didn't fit on the last record, which was thematically kind of a romantic album, my 'love' album, so I decided to put it on this [album]." (68)

The title song, "Dog Eat Dog," summed up what Joni thought of where American society was heading. "As the first few lines imply, this was my political awakening," she says. "I was robbed by my bank, by the government of California, by everyone around me who could—all at once. I was the kid with the unguarded marbles. During the Reagan era, greed became fashionable. We had come through the optimism of the '60s, the apathy of the '70s, and finally the accelerated consumerism of the '80s—hippie, yippie, yuppie." (103)

On the songs "Dog Eat Dog" and "Shiny Toys," both James Taylor and Don Henley of the Eagles are featured singing background vocals with Joni. Taylor reportedly loved working with Joni in the studio again. He was also very impressed with the growth and development of her music. According to him, "Her music isn't whimsical, transitory, or momentary. When I worked on her album, I said to myself, 'That's the stuff!' It's very easy to repeat past successes. Joni hasn't done it, and that takes a lot of strength." (12)

On the song "Shiny Toys," Joni sings about standing in line in the grocery store, thumbing through the tabloid magazines and reading about the rich and famous and glamorous that fill its pages, all of them with money and flashy smiles. Joni sings of the "hunks" and the "honeys" we all seem to worship at the newsstand. She actively questions how these images of physical beauty are sold to the American public as an ideal.

Then Joni's focus turns toward the disastrous political injustices taking place in Africa. The song "Ethiopia" is a joyless and pensively glum tune that perfectly matched the situation in that country, which was bleak, embattled, and drought-ridden at the time. As in most internal political battles, it is the innocent citizens who end up suffering the most. Ethiopia's poor and starving population were struggling to stay alive amid a corrupt governmental regime. Joni's thought-provoking and touching song effectively illuminated the problem.

Regarding the slow and abrupt sound of the song, Joni explained, "My chords—nobody in coffeehouses ever played chords like those. And they're not jazz chords either. [Saxophone player] Wayne Shorter came in on—what song is that? 'Ethiopia.' And, he said, 'What are these chords? These are not piano chords and these are not guitar chords—what are these chords?' And he waded into it like a champ. But harmonically speaking, I'm in my own kind of world." (7)

Where was society heading? According to Joni on the song "Impossible Dreamer," what happens to those who really question the system? As she explains it, "This is a tribute to Martin Luther King, John Lennon and Robert Kennedy—to all those who gave us hope and were killed for it." (103)

On the last song on the album, "Lucky Girl," Joni sings the one song on this album of true optimism. It is about her love for Larry Klein, and how many losers she had to date before she found him. Although it is a song of love, it still has the edgy sound of the rest of the album. Icy rhythms and synthesized percussion sounds audibly swirl as she rhapsodizes about the "mission impossible" of looking for the right one to love.

At the time, her relationship with Klein was one of the most satisfying in her life. According to her, "Marriage frees me up in a lot of ways. I feel mated . . . Relationship is everything." (13)

The artwork for the *Dog Eat Dog* album really allowed Joni to open up with her visual creativity. Photos of her jumping and snarling, along with shots of a pack of hounds were colorized by her and given a stark graffiti look. Silver paint-pen squiggles gave the album art an exciting and splashy style. She also included a photo of the smashed car she and Klein were riding in when the drunk hit them. Originally Joni had painted a highly stylized panel of canine and dog fang patterns for the album. But its use was nixed in the end. She ended up using it in the interior of the booklet for the 2003 boxed set *The Complete Geffen Recordings*.

Speaking of the photos of her on this album, Joni later explained, "My face was distorted in an anguish because that's how I was feeling. Relationships had turned and people were coming at me at all times. Needless to say, that was an angry album. If you're angry about the direction that the world is going in and you want to have a conversation about it, I would suggest *Dog Eat Dog*." However, she admits, "If I had stayed that angry, I would be a basket-case today." (109)

Rock journalists were confounded by this new side of Joni. *Rolling Stone*, and its review by Rob Tannenbaum, led the critical outcry against the album's sudden sharp turn down Techno Lane: "It's not surprising that Joni can't unravel world politics in a couplet the way she could a romance, but it is disappointing that after a three-year silence, her social criticisms are merely the sort of bloodless liberal homilies you would expect from Rush," wrote Tannenbaum. "Mitchell declares herself for drag queens, punks and simple joys . . . and against big business, mercenary lawyers, Eighties hedonism and Reaganoid preachers . . . sensing the populist ripple of post-Band Aid activism, and knowing that most of her Woodstock peers are either dead or trying to get there . . . 'Ethiopia,' with its parched Japanese flute, choked imagery and painfully enunciated chorus . . . why is *Dog Eat Dog* such an unpleasant listen? . . . with the industrial clank of a synthesizer, courtesy of Thomas Dolby, the music simulates the soullessness of our 'culture in decline' without revealing anything new about it. While Joni's venom is an encouraging sign, its clumsy expression is unnerving." (110)

Alanna Nash of *Stereo Review* echoed her own discontent with Joni's social discontent by writing, "*Dog Eat Dog* is an angry album, one that fairly seethes with outrage as Mitchell surveys the general state of things and finds rampant moral decay: government intervention in private lives, Yuppie materialism, Moral Majority censorship, Star Wars sensibility, and a frightening symbiosis of politics and religion." (13)

On the charts, the *Dog Eat Dog* album reflected Joni's slipping ratings in the 1980s. It peaked at number 63 in the United States and number 57 in the United Kingdom. The one hit single from the album was the duet with Michael McDonald, "Good Friends," which made it to number 85 on the *Billboard* singles chart in the United States.

This was an album that should have been praised for its daring. Instead it seemed to get lost in the shuffle of "Wake Me Up Before You Go-Go," "Girls Just Wanna Have Fun" giddiness. Disappointed with the sales of *Dog Eat Dog*, Joni claimed, "In a way I don't blame people. It's a period of escape, like the early '50s were, although for a different reason. Even the cause-mindedness, to me, has a more frivolous nature now than it did in the '60s. I mean, with the causes this time you've got albums for them flashing on the screen. So, on one level, it's just a great party time. Like my manager said, 'I don't know about these songs, Joan. Don't you have anything about sex and parties?'" (13)

As Joni explained, "[*Dog Eat Dog*] sounded like the airplay of the time, the album was pretty much dismissed. It was considered negative to think politically at the time and sophomoric. It was the height of rah-rah Reaganism." (111)

In her own defense she pointed out, "My records sell steadily over a long period of time, more like books. I think I lost a few people with the more jazzy projects but gained others who couldn't get into my previous work." (107)

On June 15, 1986, Joni appeared on the bill of a massive all-day Amnesty International concert at the Meadowlands in New Jersey. Joni was sandwiched in between U2 and the Police. Instead of doing several of her greatest hits, she instead chose many of her lesser-known songs. The rowdy, drunken crowd gathered there that day threw things toward the stage while she sang.

Recalls Joni, "I went on as a pinch hitter. I was filling in for Pete Townshend. Well, the thing is, that crowd was throwing stuff all day. It just happened that by the time I got out there, they'd had a lot of practice. Their aim was better . . . I picked the perfect material—'The Three Great Stimulants,' which addressed the cause. Well, nobody's there for the cause. That's heartbreaking. And in the back room, the managers are squabbling over position. They're kicking U2 out of their rightful spot to put the Police on top with their reunion, and it's ugly. And I did a song called 'Number One' . . . And, in the middle of it—if you see the videotape— my face kind of lights up. I'm thinking, 'Holy shit, if they stone me now it will be great. It will be so fitting.' But those big charity shows always end up being competitive situations, and I'm not the sort of person who likes competing against other people. Me, I'd rather just compete with myself, you know. I'd rather play pinball." (14)

In March 1986, painting legend Georgia O'Keeffe died at the age of ninety-eight. The previous year she had been awarded a Medal of Freedom by President Reagan at the White House. In the graphic art realm, O'Keeffe was Mitchell's idol, as well as a close friend. Like Joni, Georgia was someone who lived her life exactly the way she wanted to, and was a unique and determined individual. She was also concerned for Joni's health. According to the chain-smoking Ms. Mitchell, "She once told me I should quit smoking. She added that she thought I should live—which I took as a high compliment." (107)

Continuing her sweep of aligning herself with worthy causes, Joni was one of the singing stars to appear on the bill for an environmental benefit concert held at the Long Beach Arena in California on August 28, 1986. During the event, which was entitled Get Tough on Toxics, she shared the bill with Neil Young and Warren Zevon. Among the songs she sang as part of her set was "Cool Water," which she was planning to include on her next album.

The following year she again made few public appearances. On August 29, 1987, she was featured on a Showtime TV show called *Coast-to-Coast*, hosted by Herbie Hancock. Joni was featured on it, jamming with several jazz greats, including Herbie, Bobby McFerrin, Wayne Shorter, and David Sanborn. Also accompanying Mitchell was her bass-playing husband, Larry Klein. Among the songs she was featured on was her own "Furry Sings the Blues," and a jazzed-up Latin-flavored rendition of "Hejira."

On September 11, 1987, thirty-five-year-old Jaco Pastorius, Joni's former bass player, was found face down in a pool of blood outside a bar, the victim of a fight. He died ten days later in a Fort Lauderdale, Florida, hospital. The cause of death was listed as head injuries sustained in the fight. His death was judged to be a homicide. A twenty-five-year-old private club manager was later arrested on aggravated battery charges.

In the seven years since he had left Joni Mitchell's band, Pastorius had one personal problem after another, including extreme substance abuse, erratic public behavior, and arrests on various charges. As ingenious a bass player as he was, his personal life disintegrated into a shattered mess.

In 1981 on a tour of Japan to support his Warner Bros. album, *Word of Mouth*, Jaco began displaying erratic tendencies. He threw tantrums in the Los Angeles International Airport and threatened not to get on the plane. On the second night of the tour, in Osaka, he suddenly walked off the stage in the middle of the show and never came back. One day on the bullet train in Japan he wrote all over his face in Magic Marker, and then proceeded to write on the walls of the train interior.

During a tour of Europe in 1982 he fell from a balcony in Italy and seriously injured his shoulder and arm. He required a steel pin in his arm to assist with the healing process. According to friends he participated in fifteen-hour partying binges. Although he still managed to play great music in the recording studio, on solo albums, with jazz buddies, and with the group Weather Report, he would pass out in Manhattan's Central Park, and several times had his bass stolen that way.

He was diagnosed as manic-depressive as well as alcoholic. In fact, he had spent much of the summer of 1986 in the psychiatric ward at Bellevue Hospital in New York City. The following year he went back to Florida to try to get himself together. However his drugging and drinking got worse and worse. He was arrested on quite a few occasions for charges ranging from breaking and entering, to driving around a jogging track in a stolen automobile. He reportedly had worn out his welcome staying with relatives and was sleeping in various Fort Lauderdale parks at the time of his death.

In one of his last interviews he proclaimed, "I'm not an alcoholic. I'm not a drug addict. I am a partier. I take chances." (112) On September 11, at Sunrise Musical Theater in the Fort Lauderdale area, at a Santana concert, Jaco suddenly leapt up on stage in the middle of Alfonso Johnson's bass solo. Security guards, who had no idea who he was, promptly threw him offstage and ejected him from the venue. Later that night he had the altercation with the manager of the Midnight Club and had been severely beaten and left for dead when an emergency medical staff arrived.

According to Joni, once Jaco got involved in cocaine, he didn't know when to stop. She had parted company with him when she moved from a jazz band to a rock band, at the time she recorded *Wild Things Run Fast*. Jaco Pastorius will always be remembered as a driving musical force on Mitchell's albums *Hejira*, *Don Juan's Reckless Daughter*, *Mingus*, and *Shadows and Light*. Unfortunately, like so many brilliant jazz musicians, he was a sad victim of his own excesses.

On October 27, 1987, Joni was onstage at the Pacific Amphitheater in Costa Mesa, California, for a benefit concert called Cowboys for Indians and Justice for Leonard Peltier. Also on the bill that day were Willie Nelson, Jackson Browne, and several other socially conscious musicians. Joni's band at this event included Larry Klein on bass and Wayne Shorter on saxophone.

Although her album *Dog Eat Dog* was not the sales or critical success she had hoped for, its influences were felt in all of her future work. She had her social consciousness awakened by the material she had included in it, and Joni would continue to infuse her writing with an eye for exposing social injustice and political wrongdoing. Because of her *Dog Eat Dog* experience, she would—from now on—become known as one of rock & roll's leading watchdog troubadours.

17

Chalk Mark in a Rain Storm

As the year 1988 began, Joni Mitchell hit another of her famous career crossroads. As per usual, she was questioning the whole game of a life in the arts. While in theory she found the whole game of fame repugnant, she also had to admit her own addiction to the "star-making machinery." Like Icarus ascending on his wax and feather wings, Joni too could not resist the temptation to fly closer and closer to the sun.

According to her at the time, "I started this star machinery 'that brings me things I really can't give up just yet.' That was the dilemma. And I threatened to quit all the time, but it's: 'Hey, you're in show business until you're in the poorhouse!'" she laughs, seeing the irony of it. "You either stay up there, or you begin your decline and the vultures come and pick the last little bit as you go down. As your money diminishes, so does your ability to buy good lawyers to fight the monsters. You wonder about people who made a fortune, and you always think they drank it up or they stuck it up their nose. That's not usually what brings on the decline. It's usually the battle to keep your creative child alive while keeping your business shark alive. You have to develop cunning, and shrewdness, and other things which are not well-suited to the arts." (51)

Yet a certain segment of her audience *still* longed for her to write another highly confessional version of *Blue*. They wanted her to be the self-suffering Madonna of folk and heartbreak. Joni was not buying that crap. She had other things on her mind and other stories to tell.

As she explained it, "If some people had their way, they'd just want me to weep and suffer for them for the rest of my life, because people live vicariously through their artists. And I had that grand theme for a long time: 'Where is my mate? Where *is* my mate?' I got rid of that one. For a while it was assumed that I was writing *women's* songs. Then men began to notice that they saw themselves in the songs, too. A good piece of art should be androgynous. I'm not a feminist. That's too divisional for me." (14)

Joni held her ground firmly. When fans came up to her and told her things that they thought were complimentary, she often balked at their arrogance. She recounted amusingly, "One guy come up to me and said, 'You're the best female singer/songwriter in the world.' I was thinking: 'What do you mean "female"?' That's like saying, 'You're the best Negro.' Don't put a lid on it: it transcends boundaries." (11)

Consistently people likened her style and her position in the music business to that of Carole King, Carly Simon, Melanie, Judy Collins, and Joan Baez. This did not exactly thrill her. Mitchell claimed, "This whole female singer/songwriter tag is strange. You know, my peers are not Carly Simon and these other women." (14)

According to her, the one person who actually understood her position was Bob Dylan. He even publicly proclaimed that Joni was not just one of "the girls." She explained, "He was talking about how he didn't like seeing women on-stage, how he hates to see them up there whoring themselves. So he was asked, 'Well, what about Joni Mitchell?' And he says something like, 'She's not really a woman. Joni's kind of like a man,'" she laughs. "The thing is, I came into the business quite feminine. But nobody has had so many battles to wage as me. I had to stand up for my own artistic rights. And it's probably good for my art ultimately. I remember early in my career somebody wrote that my work was 'effeminate,' which I thought was pretty odd. So over the years I think I've gotten more androgynous—and maybe become an honorary male, according to Bobby [Dylan]." (14)

In April 1988 Joni Mitchell released her fifteenth album, *Chalk Mark in a Rain Storm*. Guest stars on it included such varied personalities as Billy Idol, Willie Nelson, Peter Gabriel, Don Henley, Thomas Dolby, Wayne Shorter, and Tom Petty, as well as Wendy and Lisa—formerly of Prince's band, and ex-Cars member Benjamin Orr.

A unique aspect of this album is the fact that in the context of many of her songs, Joni actually tells several detailed narratives. And, within those story songs, she found guest stars to vocally perform the roles of these characters. As she explains it, "It's an idea I've had for a long time, to sing the narrative and cast my characters. 'Cause the songs have a lot of 'he said' and 'she said' in them. So I thought, 'Who would be the perfect Old Dan in "Cool Water"? Who would be the perfect bully in "Dancin' Clown"?' Then it became fun, and I just started calling people when I would think of them." (106)

According to Joni, the circumstances surrounding these guest star bits were quite amusing, and their performances were riveting. Willie Nelson pulled up at the recording studio in a Winnebago at 2:00 A.M. after a gig. Billy Idol stopped in the night after the Grammy Awards telecast and enthusiastically recruited his guitar player, Steve Stevens, for the song "Dancin' Clown." She claimed, "I've put musicians on my albums simply because of their proximity." (106)

Joni used her hand-selected musicians—a league of superstar background singers—and the stories she chose to tell to full advantage on *Chalk Mark in a Rain Storm*. The themes and influences in the songs she wrote for this beautifully produced album came from such diverse experiences as her parents' courtship and a concert she gave for soldiers about to go off to the Vietnam War in the early 1970s.

There was also a general theme to the songs she penned for this album. According to her at the time, "I feel these times are just pathetic. When I wrote this album, I was just hurting for the culture." (106)

Taking a totally different musical approach than she did on *Dog Eat Dog*, Joni claimed, "I have to keep my spirit high. And keep my creativity flowing. I've learned not to be afraid of failing—because out of the ashes of failure may come a great idea." (107)

Mitchell was excited by the scope of what was going on in the music industry. World music had finally—circa 1988—become universally embraced and was quite successful. Joni was nearly roasted for doing exactly that with her African influences on *Hissing of Summer Lawns* album just twelve years previously. Now Paul Simon's *Graceland* (1986) and Sting's *Nothing Like the Sun* (1987) had become recent successes. According to Joni, "It was really encouraging to hear good music being widely received. Music was very apartheid then [1976]. It's not as bad now as it was. Sting's flirtation with jazz hasn't cost him his airplay as mine did. That's a good sign for the barriers coming down." (109)

In April 1988 Joni released one of the most warmly received albums in her long, prolific career: *Chalk Mark in a Rain Storm*. It is a disc full of rich tunes, with a multilayered musical sound to each selection. Track after track of guitars, guest star appearances, and dreamy background vocals made this one of the most exciting albums of her highly varied catalog.

Unlike her thirteen previous releases, this one carried a blanket coproducing credit shared by two people: herself and Larry Klein. Not since David Crosby's "producer" role on her debut album had this happened. In actuality, the beginnings of *Chalk Mark in a Rain Storm* dated back several months, to when Mitchell was asked to record a pair of songs for use in another medium.

Filmmaker Albert Magnoli was planning a movie called *American Anthem* (1986), which told the story of a talented gymnast who gave up his love of the sport to work in his father's Colorado bicycle shop. Through a series of events, he rekindles his love of the competition and ends up getting ready to try out for the U.S. Olympic team. Magnoli needed a song for a scene in which the young gymnast and his girlfriend are driving on a mountain road in a bright red Jeep, against the backdrop of a forest of yellow aspen trees. Magnoli approached Joni Mitchell and asked her write a song for this particular scene, and he told her that he would love to see what she could come up with for the film's theme song as well. With those instructions and a synopsis of the film's plot, she set about to write "My Secret Place" for the Jeep drive sequence and the song "Number One" for the movie's theme.

Joni decided to make "My Secret Place" a duet. Since she was in England with Larry Klein, and Klein was playing bass on Peter Gabriel's *So* album, she asked Gabriel if he would sing the song with her, and he agreed. According to Joni, "Rather than a duet of a boy singing *to* a girl—or *at* a girl—it's the beginning of the optimistic one-mindedness at the start of a love affair. You're on the same wavelength. That's the time when you're liable to say the same thing at the same time, and giggle a lot about it. It's a psychic period of bonding. I prefer to see life as an undulating force—which is more an Oriental process of perception. I disagree with Western thought with its mind/body split, it's good/evil split. You have to cultivate a dialogue with life that's less judgmental, yet has a greater attention span. I'm still living in the days of radio; I'm not a channel-changer. I'll watch anything on TV because moving pictures fascinate me, as does conversation." (51)

Furthermore, she came up with a great idea for making the sound of "My Secret Place" unique. "I decided to use up one of the reels of the tape doubling the part 24 times," she explains. "'My Secret Place' is 24 guitars playing the same part. On that whole album, all of the guitars are played 24 or 16 times, not in order to get a [Phil] Spector [Wall of] Sound, but to get people to hear my guitar playing. I thought, 'Well, maybe it's just too thin and silvery sounding. If I beef it up and make a whole section of the guitars, maybe they'll notice how these chords are moving and stop calling it 'folk music.'" (18)

The other song she penned for the film was "Number One," which is about being in a competition and wanting to come in first. In the lyrics of the song, she questions whether the race to be "Number One" is worth the price. It was a well-thought-out argument about competition in general. On "Number One," Benjamin Orr of the Cars is heard singing background vocals behind Joni.

Both "My Secret Place" and "Number One" are effective, lush-sounding songs that beautifully begin her *Chalk Mark in a Rain Storm* album. The music is luxuriously atmospheric and jazzy, while the lyrics are insightful. On "My Secret Place" she and Peter Gabriel literally weave a beautiful story about hailing from New York City and settling in the Colorado mountains. And "Number One" is a thoughtful song about how competitive life is in general. The irony, however, is that when film director Magnoli heard this pair of beautiful new songs—he rejected both of them for his *American Anthem* film! Joni had the last laugh by including them on this highly satisfying disc.

The next song on the album, "Lakota," falls into Joni's new-found 1980s socially conscious mode. The lyrics find her singing an impassioned plea to preserve the lands given to the Native American people. Particular to this song was the concurrent battle over the Black Hills area of South Dakota, which were found to be rich in uranium and other minerals. According to Joni, "Governments are hassling Indians everywhere on this continent for their natural resources. I believe the Hopi prophecy: the uranium should not be taken out." (107)

To make the song even more appropriate to the cause of Native Americans, Joni decided to have a Native American singer add his voice to the song. In a chance meeting at an Indian artifact show at the Santa Monica Civic Center, she enlisted Iron Eyes Cody to put an authentic Indian chant on the track. In addition, Don Henley is also heard singing background vocals on "Lakota." It is one of the most effective songs on this album.

Of the song "The Tea Leaf Prophecy (Lay Down Your Arms)" Mitchell explains, "That song began as a music track that Larry wrote. For the lyric, I kept thinking about World War II and my parent's courtship, which was unusual in a prophetic way. My mother had been a country schoolteacher, and she had come to the town of Regina in Saskatchewan to work in a bank. It was wartime, and early [in the war] all the men in the town had been shipped overseas. So there weren't many prospects for her, and she was a good-looking woman, thirty years old—which was old for that time. There was a fancy hotel in that town that served high tea, and you had to wear hats and gloves in those days to get in. One day, when she and her girlfriend went over there just for the dress-up of it all. When they were finished, a gypsy came over and read her teacup and said, 'You will be married within a month, and you will have a child within the year—and you'll die a long and agonizing death.' The last part was a horrible and hideous thing for even a clairvoyant to tell anybody." (51)

According to Joni, "My mother laughed in her face. She said, 'This is ridiculous. Look at this town. There's no men left, just frail boys and babies.' Two weeks went by, and a friend of a friend had a friend from out of town, and they put my mother and father together on a blind date and it was instant chemistry. My father had two weeks' leave. He said, 'I know this is sudden Myrtle'—her name was Myrtle McKee; in the song it's Molly McKee—'but would you marry me?' So they ran off to Moose Jaw, Saskatchewan, and got hitched. I was born within the year, and to this day she feels a little funny about the rest of the prophecy, considering the odds of the other parts coming true. I said to her,

'Don't worry about the gypsy, Mom. Two out of three ain't bad.' The gypsy got it wrong. It's me who's gonna die the long and ago-nizing death, with my bad habits.' But I had to ask her, 'What made you marry Dad? You were so picky.' And she said, 'Because he looked so cute in his uniform.' So, that's in the song too." (51)

The story song "Dancin' Clown" is one of the lightest and most entertaining songs on this album. According to Joni, "Dylan heard 'Dancin' Clown' and liked it. 'How'd you write that song?' he asked. I told him, 'I wrote it off the racing form from the O.T.B. [offtrack horse race betting]. I saw a lot of poetry in the horse's names. "I had that idea,' he said. 'I thought it was a dumb idea.'" (103) However, it sure works here!

"Cool Water," which was written by Bob Nolan, was one of the few songs on this album that was not penned by Mitchell in whole or in part. It was a hit for the Sons of the Pioneers—Roy Rogers's background group in the 1930s to the 1950s. Although at face value this is an innocent song about finding water to drink, it is used here to make a political statement. According to Joni, "I al-ways loved the Sons of the Pioneers' classic cowboy music . . . I updated this song because water is another issue that people aren't paying enough attention to—like the radioactive waste that is rapidly leaching toward the Colorado River." (103)

Joni explains the title of the album, "It's an image of imperma-nence. It's also a line from the song 'The Beat of Black Wings.' A young soldier delivers it, and he's drunk in a tavern somewhere, talking to anyone who'll listen. Mainly he talks to the woman who is serving him his beer, and his outlook is pretty gloomy. He says he's never had anything in his life, so it's from that standpoint that he delivers the line, 'I'm just a chalk mark in a rain storm, I'm just the beat of black wings.' An individual is a kind of chalk mark in a rain storm in the view of the direction we've taken as non-ecologi-cal animals." (51)

According to her, "In the '60s, while all my friends were busily avoiding the draft in any way possible, I was playing a coffeehouse circuit on the Eastern Seaboard which took me down to Fort Bragg in North Carolina. I played for gung-ho boys coming and going from Vietnam. One person I met there introduced himself as 'Killer Kyle.' He was like a Tennessee Williams character, very young and short. I walked into the room, and he was red in the face, livid, his fists clinched, and he said to me in a drawl, 'You've got a lotta nerve sister, standing up there talking about love, because there ain't no love. Not where I come from. Love is gone, love is dead, and I'm gonna tell you where love went.' This was approximately the way he opened up, and he proceeded to tell me a terrible—but I guess typical—story of a Vietnam experience. For a while afterward he wrote to me, but basically all he wanted to do was get strong enough to get over his shell shock so he could go back and 'kill a Commie for God,' although that illusion was broken." (51)

Resurrecting the character of Killer Kyle also comes from one of Joni's first compositions. As she explains, "As a matter of fact, Killer Kyle is mentioned in 'Cactus Tree,' one of my earliest songs. I hadn't thought about him for many years until I started recording this album at Peter Gabriel's studio in the southwest of England, near Bath. On the other side of the valley from the studio is an army base, the base from which U.S. planes attacked Libya. So it crossed mind when we were recording that if there was retaliation, we might very well be the target. Also, the radiation from the Chernobyl accident was drifting toward us. It was very pensive time for Yanks in England, and gave everyone an awareness that this planet is a tiny place indeed. Accidents from one country and wars in another now affect us all." (51)

The catchy mid-tempo song "Snakes and Ladders" cleverly uses the children's board game of the same name as a simile for the ups and downs in the game of love. One is either climbing to the top of a ladder of ecstasy or falling in a snake-like fashion down to heartbreak. Joni uses this image to full advantage against a very catchy melody.

"The Reoccurring Dream" is Joni's criticism of the whole Madison Avenue mentality of selling beauty, desirability, and sex appeal via TV commercials, and advertising in general. She ridicules the whole notion that sexiness, glamour, and attraction can come from using a particular product—be it a shampoo, a toothpaste, or whatever. It is a legitimate denunciation of the silliness of this notion that a scent, a soap, or a mouthwash can wash away your troubles. She effectively intersperses her singing with several radio announcer–style voices, with Joni playing the role of the voice-overs throughout this clever song.

The album ends with the song "A Bird That Whistles," which is a new arrangement of the traditional song "Corrina, Corrina." Explaining the making of her new version of the song, Joni said, "Klein and I just jammed it up for the fun. We only took up three [recording] tracks so there were lots left over for [saxophone player] Wayne [Shorter] and [the sound of actual] birds. That's what I heard in my mind for this one: Wayne Shorter with birds. We had a tree in our backyard at the beach that was always full of birds. Birds of a feather aren't supposed to flock together but our tree defied this natural law. It was a regular bird Babylon. We ran a cord out into the yard and recorded the 'bird babble' and we had it in our files. When Wayne came into the session, the only instruction I gave him was, 'You're the bird.' He's the only musician that I ever played with that could take metaphorical instruction. Wayne plays pictures. I wish more people could see/hear them and delight in them the way I do. He is indispensable to my music." (103)

Outside influences are evident in this album. For the first time, her husband, Larry Klein, shares songwriting credits as well as co-production credits with her. The songs "Lakota," "The Tea Leaf Prophecy," and "Snakes and Ladders" were all credited to "Joni Michell and Larry Klein." He has remained a strong force in all of her recorded music from that point forward.

The reviews for *Chalk Mark in a Rain Storm* were absolutely glowing. Nicholas Jennings in *Maclean's* magazine proclaimed that it was "an artistic landmark that re-establishes Mitchell as one pop music's premier talents. Three years in the making, *Chalk Mark* features some of her strongest compositions in more than a decade. And not since *Court and Spark* . . . has the singer sounded so confident." (107)

John Milward in *USA Today* claimed, "*Chalk Mark* achieves an uneasy truce between mood and melody as well as between the high-tech and the homespun. Acknowledging this modern conflict, Mitchell concludes with a lovely updating of 'Corrina, Corrina,' titled 'A Bird That Whistles.' In those unfettered surroundings—the track includes only guitar, bass and Wayne Shorter's saxophones—Mitchell truly soars." (113)

And Alanna Nash in *Stereo Review* wrote, "A record that positively thrills in places—in the intelligent, original bend of her lyrics, in the shimmering quality of her voice, and in her facility with language and imagery. It is also mesmerizing in spots—particularly in 'The Reoccurring Dream,' an assault on Madison Avenue . . . Joni Mitchell again proves herself to be what she has always been—one of the most talented people in popular music." (114)

Joni, who could be quite aloof about granting press interviews, gave a record number of them in 1988 to promote *Chalk Mark in a Rain Storm*. One of the most interesting ones was in *Vogue*, as Joni spoke of feminism and the feminist movement of the late 1960s and early 1970s. According to Mitchell, "Some people were persecuted for sexual freedoms while the banner [of liberation] was still flying. Examples were made. Even I was made such an example at one point." (52)

With regard to eroticism in the media Joni pointed out, "I haven't seen every erotic film ever made, but what I have seen seems so ludicrous, because of what frequently passes for erotic emotion in the female is, frankly, the angst of overstimulation. In the whole scene, which is so dominantly interested in sexy and hot, neither male nor female seems to know that the sound used to depict the woman in the erotic act is the sound of a woman who is NOT getting off. Ha! Nine times out of ten! So men don't know. Women don't even know! Nobody knows." (52)

She also claimed that she thought of herself as "one of the guys" when it comes to having a sense of humor. Said Joni, "I like men's humor. I like to be around men in a way that I don't disturb their maleness, so they can be themselves. I don't like to put any coyness into the situation that might make them want to be more like men to a woman. I like locker-room talk." (52)

In addition she gave press interviews on BBC Radio 1 in London, a press conference in Saskatoon, an interview for *Avsminkat* that was broadcast in Sweden, several interviews for Australian radio programs including the *Album Show* and *National Album Review*. Also she appeared on the *Ray Martin Midday Show*, the *Sunday Program*, and the *Rock Arena Show,* all for Australian TV broadcast. She was on *Hubier on the Air* on KRO Radio Holland for FM broadcast. She was also a guest at the San Remo Songfest in San Remo, Italy, for an Italian RAI-TV broadcast.

Joni's promotional efforts paid off for her, as *Chalk Mark in a Rain Storm* found much more success on the charts than *Dog Eat Dog* had. In the United States it made it to a respectable number 45, and in England it hit number 26. It was considered a big critical success for her at the time.

In addition to her music, Mitchell continued to create her oil-on-canvas paintings. In fact she had created enough of her works to begin to have her own exhibits in different places around the world. On May 18, 1988, Joni opened an exhibit of her artwork in Tokyo. When she wasn't crafting songs, she was painting.

While promoting *Chalk Mark in a Rain Storm*, Joni did everything she could to see that the album made some favorable noise for her. However, people's compliments weren't always met warmly. Mitchell explained that the time, "When you've been around for 20 years, people say, 'Oh, I remember you from the '60s.' God, I only made one album in the '60s. I went to meet and greet some radio programmers the other day, and one D.J. said to me, 'I'm so glad you're making a comeback.' I said, 'A comeback? Where'd I go? Where am I coming back from?'" (106)

In actuality she recorded two albums in the 1960s [*Joni Mitchell*, 1968, and *Clouds*, 1969]. However, her point was well taken. How can you come back when you never really went away? Whichever way you want to look at it, Joni was obviously much more than just a folk singer from the 1960s. And thanks to the critical reception she received from *Chalk Mark in a Rain Storm*, she was creatively back on top of her game.

18

Night Ride Home

oni Mitchell's initial fame in the 1960s and 1970s came from telling detailed stories about her life and putting them to music. By the late 1980s she had expanded that concept into masterfully telling the stories of other people— real or imagined. As she put material together for her next album, she kept questing for new inspiration for her music.

She had developed into something of a reportive singer. Like a journalist and a troubadour at the same time, she found herself comfortably in a new niche. During this era she explained, "In a certain way, I do see myself as an eyewitness reporter. Some of my things are purely fictional, though, in that I begin from an eyewitness vignette to depict it. Then I find it won't rhyme, or it lacks a certain dramatic quality, and there's a necessity for exaggeration. We're talking about art's artifice here, and it has its own truth. It's not necessarily a literal truth. It's a creative truth, a large truth." (51)

As the 1990s approached, she was busy with various events. On March 3, 1989, she took part in the Rainforest Benefit in New York City. Joni was one of several stars on the recording "Spirit of the Forest," which was another all-star song, this time raising money and awareness to save the South American rain forests via the Earth Love Fund. Also on the recording were Rita Coolidge,

Bonnie Raitt, Ringo Starr, Fleetwood Mac, Thomas Dolby, Kate Bush, Olivia Newton-John, the Plasmatics, Donna Summer, and dozens of others.

On June 3, 1989, she took part in the Our Common Future benefit in New York City. Joni performed two songs live for worldwide broadcast. That evening she sang with Herbie Hancock, Larry Klein, Wayne Shorter, and Andy Summers. They were billed as Herbie Hancock's Super Band. On the credits she was billed as Joni Mitchell Klein.

In late 1989 Joni was a guest on an HBO Muppets program produced by Jim Henson. It was taped in Newcastle, England. According to her, "There was a television show in England, an offshoot of *Sesame Street* designed to introduce a wide variety of music to children. It was called *The Ghost of Faffner Hall* . . . In this house lived an assortment of characters . . . They created an episode where the mad impresario gets a letter from an old sweetheart—Joni Mitchell—who is coming to visit him . . . The scene between the impresario and me takes place in a pink Cadillac by midnight." (103)

In November 1989 a monumental and historic event took place in modern Germany: the Berlin Wall dividing East Berlin and West Berlin came down. For the first time since the end of World War II, the two halves of Germany were reunited. To celebrate, on July 21, 1990, Roger Waters of Pink Floyd invited an international all-star cast to take part in a theatrical resurrection of the group's rock opera, *The Wall*. Joni performed the song "Goodbye Blue Sky" in a cast that included Ute Lemper, Cyndi Lauper, the Scorpions, Van Morrison, Thomas Dolby, Tim Curry, Marianne Faithful, Albert Finney, Sinéad O'Connor, Jerry Hall, and many other rock and show business luminaries. A double album, a television special, and a video package were made of this presentation as *The Wall Live in Berlin*. Joni also had a couple of solo lines in the show's big finale number, "The Tide Is Turning."

A year later, on November 1, 1990, a musical revue called "The Joni Mitchell Project: A Theatrical Retrospective," opened at the Los Angeles Theater Center and played for a three-month run. Featuring a cast of three women and two men, as well as a five-piece band, it performed a program of all-Mitchell music. A few days later, the real Joni Mitchell showed up to witness this highly flattering tribute to her. Persuaded to join the cast onstage, she sang an impromptu and a capella version of a new song she had yet to release, "Cherokee Louise."

On December 10, 1990, at the *Billboard* Music Awards in Los Angeles, Joni presented Sinéad O'Connor with the Number One World Single award for "Nothing Compares to U."

The music business had changed dramatically since Joni made her debut. MTV and VH1 had certainly seen to that. They had helped make it more accessible, as well as more fickle and more disposable. According to Mitchell during this era, "Music has become burlesque over the last few years—video's done that. Every generation has to be more shocking than the last. But at a certain point you've got to reel it in because decadence ultimately isn't that hip. Our country is going down the tubes from it. It's rotten to the core. And I think women can be more than decorative. I mean, it's the same old thing actresses have been saying all along, that there are no good roles for women. Well there are women creating their own roles, but they're creating such shallow roles. I wonder why." (14)

Although Joni's recordings were no longer huge sellers, she had certain standards she set for her career. She turned down some lucrative offers because they didn't seem right for her. According to her, "I turned down $1 million to play in Las Vegas for one night because it was the kiss of death to me. It was a symbol of corruption. What happened was that no contemporary rock was going to Las Vegas. And the youth of that town—and there's a lot of money in that town—complained, 'Daddy, Daddy, no one is coming into our town,' so they built this big hall, but nobody would open it. So they figured if they could get [Bob] Dylan or me, the ice would be broken and everyone else would follow suit. I wouldn't do it." (14)

But Joni has never been one to follow trends or jump through hoops. "Playing the game is repulsive to me," she claims. "You're still gonna get dumped after a couple of years—then you're compromising yourself and you're dumped. The dumping is inevitable, so I'd rather not compromise. I'm in it for the musical adventure." (15)

At this time Joni continued to be managed by Peter Asher. Although she was very much in control of her own destiny, Asher guided her into some creative and lucrative avenues. For her first new album of the 1990s, she followed up *Chalk Mark in a Rain*

Storm with what was viewed as another critical masterpiece album.

Sharing production credits with her husband, Larry Klein, Joni released her sixteenth album, *Night Ride Home*. It was recorded at her own home studio—billed as the Kiva. However, additional recording on the album was done at her old haunt, A&M Studios.

Night Ride Home was released in March 1991. It found Mitchell in fine form, telling several songs about her life, her imagination, and her theories on the meaning of life and love. In the same way that *Hejira* and *Shadows and Light* had a consistent musical tone, this album takes a more somber stance, with unifying musical moods throughout.

It begins with the title track, which evokes the mood of a leisurely "night ride home." A light, guitar-led ballad, "Night Ride Home" evokes the mood of a sultry summer evening. A background track of chirping crickets sets the moonlight tone. Joni sings of Fourth of July fireworks, a big moon in the sky, sitting next to the man she loves, and the pleasure of the open road.

This song set the tone for the entire album, which conjured up memories of her earliest recordings. According to her, "I could see fairly soon after it was completed that it was viewed by friends as a kind of return to something that they wanted from me and that I perhaps hadn't given them for a while. I didn't much intend it as a return, though ultimately it doesn't really matter what I intended. I am slightly defensive about the last couple of projects because they were really underestimated. I tried to write for large choruses on them. Suppose I want to write musicals. If I went along doing only nice intimate little things, how would I ever learn how to write for a full stage?" (64)

Explaining her composition "Passion Play (When All the Slaves Are Free)," Joni says, "The song is basically my telling of the Easter story, but it morphs into contemporary ecological and sociological disasters. It is about crisis in the heart and healing of the heart. The 'I' perspective that I am singing form is that of Zachius [sic], the little tax collector. He was short. He was jumping up and down in the back row of a large crowd that gathered to witness the arrival of Jesus in the town of Jerusalem. He had climbed into a sycamore tree to get a better look." (103) This melodic, medium-paced tune poses an age-old question: Who does the dirty work in life, once all the slaves are freed?

"Cherokee Louise" is a thought-provoking song about being nine years old and having a childhood friend who is abused by her foster father. When the girl is raped, Joni takes the song to an emotional peak. "Any time a singer sings—any singer in the world—they're acting," she explains. "And sometimes in the course of performance something strikes against the actor's life, and it becomes vital. But art is artifice no matter how much of your life you put in. When I sang 'Cherokee Louise' I felt like I was nine. I had to 'punch in' in one place and couldn't get the feeling back; I was an adult pretending to be young. I went to hear The Joni Mitchell Project, this revue that does some of my songs. They called me up and I did 'Cherokee Louise' a cappella, dancing to keep the groove. I'm coming up on the rape scene and I'm like, highly mirthful. But it came off because people got feelings from it. Every time you sing it you don't relive it. An old song can die on you." (115)

On "The Windfall (Everything for Nothing)," Joni complains about someone who wants to receive a bounty of riches for little effort. She tackles the myth of rock & roll stardom and the types of people it attracts—particularly untalented hangers-on. Specifically she is referring to a live-in maid of hers who wanted to live like a star, while paying her way with nothing but a bit of dusting and vacuuming.

According to Joni, when she moved into her large Spanish-style house in 1974, she had so much space and no furniture that she had to find someone to clean it for her. "I had to hire somebody to help keep the dust and spiders down," she recalls. "Most of the people who came for the position were horrified because it was so Spartan. One person, a professional houseboy, asked, 'Where is your silver?' It was clearly beneath him to keep a house so poorly appointed. Finally there came a Guatemalan who spoke no English. She was smiley and kind of cute. She wore white patent leather go-go boots and a red miniskirt. Over the years she learned to speak English, and I finally moved her and her husband and their infant daughter into my house. For a few years, all was well. But she began to climb." (103)

In the context of this song Joni sings of how Elvis Presley bought his circle of employed buddies—the Memphis Mafia—their own Cadillacs. The person who lives in Joni's house exists in the lap of luxury, has access to a swimming pool, and still complains that she doesn't have enough free stuff. In the revealing lyrics Mitchell surveys the greed and lies she encountered from this live-in sponge.

Her ponderous song "Slouching towards Bethlehem" was based on a poem by W. B. Yeats. According to her, "I love Yeats. The Yeats poem that I set to music, though, I corrected . . . there were parts of it that I added; they let me do it, which was amazing. Because I think they sued Van Morrison for setting something. They just said, 'You have to put "adapted by."'" And, I think I did it pretty seamlessly because I understand his style—the third stanza is mine, and it's very much in the style of the first one, more so than his second stanza." (7)

"Come In from the Cold" is a slow and moody song, in which Joni sings of her teenage years, when having her arms around a boy at local dance was a big thrill. She claims they had to dance a foot apart for fear of the chaperones and teachers. In the multi-tracked chorus of this song, she says all she wants is to "come in from the cold."

She gets philosophical about life on "Nothing Can Be Done," where she expresses frustration that some things cannot be changed and urges making the best of situations in life. Here she laments that she is not young, but remembers that she is not old either. What can she change? As the song concludes: in reality, nothing.

When a journalist asked what the theme of the *Night Ride Home* album was, she answered it was composed of "middle-aged love songs." According to her, "I just said that flippantly, because it was only half-written at the time. And middle age does not come up in a song like 'Come In from the Cold.' And 'Nothing Can Be Done' has a passage from 'The Desiderata.' Like 'Desiderata' says, surrender gracefully the things of youth—which is good advice. But it's easy for him to say. He was a monk, you know. He wasn't in show business." (14)

The exotic song "The Only Joy in Town" finds Mitchell recounting a real episode from a European trip she took. She was visiting Rome with a friend named Gloria Boyce, and the two of them were walking up the Spanish Steps when they encountered several black men selling goods. She recalls that everyone that day seemed glum. "So we were climbing the steps. We were nearly to the top when we heard a voice call out, 'Ladies! Ladies!' with an

American accent. We turned to see this gorgeous black kid. It was the first day of spring and there were these big pots of fuchsias and he'd taken blossoms from them and stuck them in his Afro. His black hair was polka-dotted with hot pink like those garlands, those halos of flowers that Botticelli paints on heads." (103)

On "Ray's Dad's Cadillac" Joni sings another ballad about her teenage years. Here she reminisces about the steamy windows of Ray's dad's Cadillac car—which was pink and had huge tailfins. She sings of the blue lights of the airport runway, where she and "Ray" would park while Motown music poured out of the dashboard speakers.

The music for the last song on the album, "Two Grey Rooms," was written seven years before it had lyrics. She wasn't sure what she wanted to say in the song. According to Joni, "I finally found a story in some magazine about a German aristocrat, a homosexual and a friend of [film director Rainer Werner] Fassbinder who had a lover in his youth that he never got over. He lost track of him for many years. One day he discovered that his old flame was working on the docks. He moved out of his fancy digs and into a couple of dingy rooms that overlooked the route where, with his hard hat and his lunch pail, his ex-lover walked to work. He lived to glimpse him twice a day, coming and going. He never approached him." (103)

A somber and moody album, *Night Ride Home* has a slow jazziness to it and is filled with beautifully crafted melodies and insightful lyrics. It is permeated with a quiet, smooth tone throughout. With story songs ranging from pensive ("Night Ride Home"), to tragic ("Cherokee Louise"), to sentimental ("Ray's Dad's Cadillac"), to sad ("Two Grey Rooms"), Joni weaves a melancholy musical spell. There are no sudden launches into rock & roll, just a harmonious, sophisticated élan.

She proclaimed to be a storyteller but wanted her stories to evoke a mood and not be dissected for their literal meaning. "The people who will enjoy the record won't think about what I meant; they'll hold it up and it'll be like a mirror. Any time a singer sings—any singer in the world—they're acting. And sometimes in the course of performance something strikes against the actor's life, and it becomes vital. But art is artifice no matter how much of your life you put it." (116)

The reviews for the music contained on *Night Ride Home* were unanimously positive. Jay Cocks in *Time* magazine claimed, "Joni finds the way to her best record in a decade . . . *Night Ride Home* is Mitchell's first album in almost three years, and her best in 10. It's easy to like and hard to forget, and it shows that Mitchell, for all her restless musical experimentation, has an undiminished skill in navigating some of the deeper estuaries of the mainstream." (117)

Don Oullette in *Down Beat* found that on "*Night Ride Home* Mitchell returns to an acoustic guitar foundation while continuing to incisively probe the spiritual and social bankruptcy of our culture as well as to eloquently muse on romantic matters . . . another strong outing by one of pop's most thoughtful and articulate artists." (118)

Rolling Stone's Tom Sinclair offered both complaints and praise: "*Night Ride Home*, in spite of this low-key approach, occasionally winds up sounding overproduced. Partly this is due to the tastefulness of the playing, which sometimes recalls the blandness of New Age jazz at its most cloying, and partially to annoying touches like the crickets (or whatever they're supposed to be) that cheep through the title track . . . *Night Ride Home* contains a handful of Mitchell's prettiest melodies in years, and her lyrics are acute as ever . . . *Night Ride Home*, if not the masterpiece some might have hoped for, is a convincing demonstration of her continuing validity as an artist." (119)

In *Stereo Review* Ron Givens wrote, "Joni Mitchell—pop's most obsessed and daring romantic—muses against the dying of the light . . . She's begun to settle down, relatively speaking, to make her peace with mortality, and the result is the strongest recorded update on her life and times since 1976's underrated *Hejira*." However he also claimed, "Mitchell's voice [is] sounding a little the worse for wear. The honeyed soprano is no longer quite so sweet; it's deeper, even a little hoarse. Mitchell still sings with the same gorgeous jazz inflections, but the old ease is gone . . . in this remarkable and moving album, we hear it with a touch of sadness, too." (120)

On the album charts, *Night Ride Home* peaked at number 41 in the United States and number 25 in the United Kingdom. Although it did respectably well on the charts, it was not a huge sales success for Joni. Its completion signaled the end of her obligation to her recording contract with Geffen Records. David Geffen told Jim Farber of the *New York Daily News*, "Even though we lost money on every one of her records we always treated Joni as one of the most important artists in the world." (121)

Explaining her four-album tenure at Geffen Records, Joni said at the time, "All the records that I've made with Geffen have cost a lot of money, and they haven't recouped, which is dangerous, because you're maintaining the integrity of your product, but you're becoming indebted to the company store. And just before Christmas the worst happened—in the selling and reselling of the company, the accountant deemed that two of my albums hadn't sold and they dropped them: *Wild Things Run Fast* and *Dog Eat Dog*. I raised a bit of a stink, and with [president of Geffen Records] Eddie Rosenblatt's help—God bless him—they were reinstated. But they almost bit it because they had horrendous press. Unfortunately, the press influenced more than we would hope it would. There are people who are afraid to stick their necks out and like something without being told it's hip. And that's gotten increasingly worse over the last two generations. There has been a general decline of independent thinking and integrity . . . since they reinstated my two records, I'm happy. And the creative freedom has been a great luxury. I appreciate that. Because I don't think this stuff dates that much, you know. Probably the one that will date the most ultimately is *Dog Eat Dog*. That was me looking out at what was going on in the world because nobody else was." (14)

At this point in time Joni began receiving the rare distinction of being mentioned time and time again by new generations of singers who credit her as one of their greatest influences growing up. In *Rolling Stone* magazine, Prince cited Joni as one of his major musical heroes. He loved Mitchell's first totally misunderstood album, *The Hissing of Summer Lawns*. Explained Joni, "Prince has assimilated some of my harmony, which, because it comes out of my guitar tunings, is peculiar. A lot of times my chords depict complex emotions—Joni's weird chords. Prince saw me in concert when he was very young in Minneapolis, and I remember seeing him in the front row, because his eyes are so unusual. You know, they're like Egyptian . . . But I remember I played a lot to him because his eyes were so unusual. Every time the light would spill down there, and he'd kind of hide inside his coat and look up at me." (64)

Not everyone understood her hybrid combination of folk, jazz, and rock & roll. According to her, rock & roll will never die:

"People keep writing songs about how rock & roll died a long time ago. It never even made it into the '60s. The roll went out of it. What died was the push beat, the remnant from swing and boogie woogie. And when it died what was left was just rock—a more vertical beat. A certain joy went out of rock & roll, and what was left was militancy—which I guess makes sense because of the times." (64)

During this era, Joni began to look back at her career and survey the choices she had made along the way. "I paid a big price for doing what I've done," she said at the time. "I started working in a genre that was neither this nor that. People didn't know where I fit in anymore, so they didn't play me at all. And so I disappeared. I lost my ability to broadcast, my public access. It was worth it. I would do it all over again in a minute for the musical education. But, of *course*, it hurt. Your records are like your kids. And you want to say, 'Don't bloody my baby's nose when I send him to school, because he's a *nice* kid. You just don't *understand* him. He's a little different, but if you try, you'll like him.'" (14)

In the previous few years, Mitchell had been developing her painting skills. Her slightly cartoonish style—as exemplified on the cover of the Crosby, Stills, Nash, and Young *So Far* album in the 1970s—had grown into a distinctive impressionist flair. It was colorful and lively, and fell somewhere between the colors of van Gogh and the fluidity of Monet.

As an outgrowth of this, in 1991 Joni's art was exhibited in Europe. She explained, "I'm used to being a woman without a country, you know? All my life I've been that way. People don't like it when you switch camps. I've got paintings in Europe on exhibition, and one of the curators was nervous at first, because there's four different styles. Some of the people's written comments were funny: 'Don't quit your day job.' 'Nice frames.' But mostly they liked it. I guess it was brought on by the pop thing, but the woman who ran it said it was kind of a phenomenon; people would buy a poster and want to sit and talk about which paintings they liked, and why." (116)

Early that year, at a Santa Monica venue called McCabe's Guitar Shop, Joni and Larry Klein attended an Eric Andersen concert. Eric called Joni onstage and she proceeded to sing backup vocals on his song "Blue River." The crowd went wild to see her perform impromptu. The audience reaction caused Joni to perform two of her own songs that evening: "Cherokee Louise" and "How Do You Stop?"

Although she didn't do any concert touring in 1991, she made several appearances on radio and television. On March 1 she was a guest on the CBC-FM radio program *Swingin' on a Star* in Toronto. April 4 found her as a guest on ABC-TV's *Good Morning America*, and on April 12 she was interviewed on the TV program *A&E Revue*. Although she often claimed to be ignored by MTV and VH1, on April 28 VH1 showcased her on a *VH1 to 1* special called *Night Ride Home*.

This era was a great career high point for Joni Mitchell. Far from chasing after hit singles or a blockbuster rock & roll sound, she aimed to create eloquent and well-thought-out poetry set to music, and on those terms she succeeded perfectly. The magic she had in her as a musician and a performer was brilliantly crystallized on *Night Ride Home*. Her fans were thrilled, the critics loved it, and she proved once again that she still had plenty of magic to share with her audience.

19

Turbulent Indigo

The 1990s brought another era of sweeping change to Joni Mitchell's life. Several new relationships were formed, and several old ones were dissolved. In 1992 and early 1993, Joni made no concert appearances. Then she began to appear sporadically at a variety of venues. On June 5, 1993, at UCLA, Joni performed at an event called Troubadours of Folk, which was held at Drake Stadium. On July 12, 1993, she was at the Beverly Hilton Hotel in Beverly Hills, California, where she sang the song "Night Ride Home" at comic and TV legend Milton Berle's eighty-sixth birthday party. November 14, 1993, found her at the Willows Golf Resort in Saskatoon, where she received a Lifetime Achievement Award from the Saskatchewan Recording Industry Association. It was an emotional evening, since her parents and several of her former teachers attended the presentation. Joni gave an hour-long interview and sang a song from her next album entitled "The Magdalene Laundries."

From May 20 to 22, 1994, Joni was one of the performers at the Great Musical Experience at the Aionoshi Festival held at Todaiji Temple in Nara, Japan. And from August 4 to 7, she was at the Edmonton Folk Festival in Edmonton, Alberta. During this time she was busy working on recordings to be included on her forthcoming album.

Since Joni Mitchell had signed with Geffen Records—David

Geffen's record label—in 1982, many changes had occurred. Geffen was no longer actively running the label. He sold Geffen Records to MCA Records, and Joni felt lost in the shuffle. She was not very happy with the way her career was being handled there. After she completed the *Night Ride Home* album, her obligation to Geffen Records was over, and it was time for her to make a move.

Joni switched labels, signing with Reprise Records, a division of Warner Bros. She had recorded her first four albums in the late 1960s and early 1970s for Reprise. It was like a reunion, since she was welcomed back with open arms to the label that originally made her a star. Key to the new record deal was the enthusiasm of her old friend Mo Ostin, the Reprise executive who had originally signed her to the label in 1967.

In addition to her own solo album, which was released on Reprise Records, Joni was heard that year on the Warner Bros. album *Seal*, by the performer of the same name. On the album, Joni and Seal sang a beautiful duet called "If I Could." The disc included Seal's biggest hits: "Song for the Dying" and "Kiss from a Rose."

Joni's seventeenth album, *Turbulent Indigo*, was produced by Joni and her husband, Larry Klein. It was recorded in her home studio, the Kiva. She and Larry seemed like the perfect pop music couple. They were dedicated musicians who seemed to complement each other well. However, the marriage ended during the recording sessions for this album. Unlike so many show business couples who part company with a degree of rancor, they discontinued their marriage and remained good friends.

On October 24, 1994, Reprise Records threw a listening party for Joni's *Turbulent Indigo* album at the Ruth Bloom Art Gallery in Santa Monica, California. There was a "meet and greet" session with the troubadour herself, and several of her paintings were on display. While her music played on the gallery's stereo system, the press and invited guests browsed through Joni's art while listening to her latest musical compositions.

When *Turbulent Indigo* hit the stores in October 1994, it caused quite a stir. In many ways this album was a culmination of the sixteen albums that preceded it. It has a mellow tone to it, with touches of folk, rock, and jazz, tied together with the unmistakably insightful poetry that Joni's lyrics have always contained.

The album opens with the acoustic guitar driven "Sunny Sunday," a deceptively cheerful song. Joni sings of a Blanche DuBois–like beauty with a bit of Tennessee Williams craziness. On the sunny Sunday Joni speaks of, the woman packs a pistol and tries unsuccessfully to shoot out a streetlight on the nearby freeway. Day after day she shoots at the streetlight but always misses. Somehow, if she ever hits the streetlight, she will be able to close a chapter of the book of her life. "Sunny Sunday" is a jarring parable for unrealized goals.

"Sex Kills" is the album's most rocking number, sounding like the edgy techno material from the *Dog Eat Dog* album. In the lyrics of the song Joni surveys the irony of American society. While Madison Avenue uses sex and sexual energy to sell every-thing from toothpaste to deodorant, in reality—in the era of AIDS—sex can kill you. She also tackles the American preoccupa-tion with guns and violence. Gas leaks, oil spills, and doctor's bills all receive disdain in this thought-provoking song.

The song "How Do You Stop?" is a rare Joni cover version of a song by another songwriter—in this case Dan Hartman and Char-lie Midnight. The song, a brilliant fit for Joni's narrative style of singing, was originally written for a 1990s James Brown album. Here Mitchell adopts it to her mode of delivering songs that ques-tion the craziness of life in general. She proclaims that fame and fortune can't wrap their arms around you on a lonely night. But, how, she asks, can you stop the crazy cycle of unhappiness? She sings about another person who achieved notoriety but found it to be hollow. Seal is heard on this track providing his creamy har-mony vocals.

The title song, "Turbulent Indigo," is about Vincent van Gogh. In this ballad of genius and madness, Joni sings about the subjects of Vincent's greatest paintings—black crows flying over a yellow wheat field and turbulent blue skies overhead. She addresses the irony that in life van Gogh was shunned by society as a drunken neurotic, yet his paintings now hang on the walls of museums and rich people's homes. Did the affluent invite Vincent to their homes to hang out when he was alive? No. But nowadays they pay mil-lions to have one of his paintings on their walls. It is a perfect song for Joni—a troubadour who lives in a box of paints—to add to her masterful musical canvas of an album.

"Last Chance Lost" finds Joni contemplating a hero and hero-ine who cannot make changes. It is a somber ballad about being unable to compromise one's ideas and ideals, even to the point of one's own emotional detriment. Given what was going on in Joni's personal life at the time, it is easy to envision that this is about her breakup with Larry Klein.

For the most haunting song on this album, "The Magdalene Laundries," Joni turns to the headlines for stories of young girls who are emotionally victimized by nuns in convents and boarding schools. The root of this story is a group of Catholic nuns in Ireland who were accused of abusing their charges in a convent. Reveals Joni, "I carried that for a long time. There are images I carried for a long time before I find the artistic receptacle, the proper scenario to let them into. I never understood how the nuns could call themselves 'the brides of Jesus,' the compassionate one, and be so hostile. I was sickly and in hospitals a lot as a kid. I'm not Catholic, but I had a lot of interaction with nuns in hospitals, and some of them were brutal, you know." (2)

"Not to Blame" is a scalding song about the abuses women endure at the hands of men they love. There were two headline-grabbing cases that dominated the news in the early 1990s. One was the murder of Nicole Brown, allegedly at the hands of her ex-husband, O. J. Simpson. And the other one cut even closer to home—it was the physical fight between her old flame, Jackson Browne, and his then girlfriend, actress Daryl Hannah.

The first stanza is clearly about the Browne/Hannah fight. On this piano-based ballad, Joni sings about the blistering irony of a socially conscious celebrity—obviously Jackson Browne—and asks, How does it feel to have your fist marks on the face of the beauty you once loved?

When press interviewers asked Joni whether or not the Jackson Browne/Daryl Hannah fracas inspired this song, she at first tried to diffuse that idea—claiming it was about misogyny in general. However, in the end, she neither admitted nor denied it.

According to her at the time, "The new press is so irresponsible they print their assumptions without using the word. I don't think they know the word 'assume' exists. They print it as a bald-ass fact: 'When she wrote this, she meant this,' like bad poetry teachers. I'm still here, and it's getting me in a lot of trouble too. Especially if they name a person. 'Not to Blame' caused a lot of friction. Some people said it's about O. J. [Simpson], and some said it's about Jackson Browne, right? Well, it's about men who batter women—and it has some details that are specific and some that apply to a lot of different situations. It's about the kind of guy who goes around battering women—and 'if the shoe fits, wear it,' you know?" (7)

On the song "Borderline," Joni sings about the borderlines that stand between us all in society. There are political borders, national borders, and religious borders that throughout time have divided "us" and "them"—whoever "us" and "them" are in reality.

Explains Joni, "Borderlines—roads, fences, they're like cholesterol in the arteries. In terms of the psyche, my country is in a state of division. Every province wants to be its own country," she says in reference to a concurrent movement by the Canadian province of Quebec to break away from Canada and become its own entity. "In L.A. we're racially divided. We had the man and woman differences. Everybody seems to love to draw these lines. So, as we come to this millennium, everyone's a divisionist in some way. So, it was a contemplation of that." (20)

"Yvette in English" is the only song on this album that was cowritten, with ex-boyfriend and longtime buddy David Crosby. Punctuated by Wayne Shorter's dreamy soprano saxophone, it sounds like a jazzy number out of the *Hejira* mode. Here Joni sings of a girl named Yvette who sits in a French bistro along the Seine and flirts with men. She sings of smoking a cigarette and discussing Picasso's paintings. It is easy to suspect that Yvette is actually Joni Mitchell, smoking a Camel cigarette and wearing her trademark *Hejira* beret. This is the album's most romantic confection of a song.

"The Sire of Sorrow (Job's Sad Song)" is another of Joni's songs that borrow parables from classic poetry or the Bible, and she again applies it to modern-day situations. As she did on the songs "Slouching towards Bethlehem" and "Passion Play (When All the Slaves Are Free)," she questions why we tend to crucify the saints. She takes the example of her own fame and her lifelong battle with her critics and the press, and likens her fate to that of the martyrs of the Bible.

There is an enlightening overall musical tone to *Turbulent Indigo*. It features some of the best use of all of her now famous musical styles and crystallizes them into one wonderfully constructed, insightful album. It isn't a reprise of what she has done before but more of a somber juncture point where all of her strengths and her insights intersect beautifully. *Turbulent Indigo* is one of the most artistically successful releases of her entire five-decade career.

A beautiful CD package, the original run of this album was released in a six-paneled unfolding cardboard CD case that afforded Mitchell lots of space for her artwork, framed and set against a warm terra cotta brown background. Inside was a small booklet containing the lyrics in a brown, textured paper cover. For *Turbulent Indigo*, Joni made a unique move on the album cover. Unlike *Chalk Mark in a Rain Storm* and *Night Ride Home*, which featured photographs of Joni on the front, this album contained a self-portrait of Joni—with her right ear bandaged à la the Vincent van Gogh self-portrait.

"Van Gogh did several self-portraits after he cut his ear off, and the turbulence of his stroke is always association with madness. Madness is kind of a chaos, but the world is mad right now," said Joni. (20)

The album package contains six of Joni's oil paintings, including landscapes and still lifes. Why all the van Gogh-like paintings? According to her, "Partially because I wanted to get my chops up to do a spoof on van Gogh for the cover of *Turbulent Indigo*." (6)

"I am really a painter at heart," she claims. "Music was a hobby for me at art school, and art was serious. Art was always what I was going to do; I was going to be an artist. But the time that I went to art school was very disappointing—although I romanticized the time that van Gogh went to art school. I thought that to go to the French Academy at that particular time—even though as a female I would have been considered an associate no matter how good I was—was the best education you could get. And yet in van Gogh's letters to Bernard, he's begging him to get him out of there, saying, 'They're providing you with the subject matter—if they have their way, they'll make a mistress of your art, and you won't know your true love should you come upon it.' He was begging him to get out and just paint from his heart at that time. That was an eye-opener to me—when I read that, I thought, 'I'm going to give myself the art education: I'm going to paint the way I want to, never mind the art world. So I went back to painting landscapes and my friends and cats and not making a mistress of it—stop trying to be innovative and *moderne*, and painting the kind of paintings that I can't afford to buy that I want to have in my house." (7)

Entertainment Weekly named Joni Artist of the Week when the album came out and amusingly announced, "For the cover of her new album, *Turbulent Indigo*, the brush wielding singer/songwriter rendered this likeness of herself as Dutch Impressionist painter Vincent van Gogh. Must be her blue period." (122)

The music reviews for *Turbulent Indigo* were glowing from the very start. *Billboard* called it "one of the most commanding statements of a peerless, 17-album career." (2)

In *Rolling Stone*, John Milward wrote, "Plenty has been written about the rockers of the '60s hitting their 50s, but Mitchell is virtually the only female pop star to pass that mark with her artistry undiminished. *Turbulent Indigo* is Mitchell's best album since the mid-'70s and a work that is highly musical, poetic and very, very sad . . . The spine-tingling 'Sex Kills' profits from Mitchell's recent work with synthesizer textures. The lyrics to Mitchell's most famous songs evoke a confessional voice, but here she rips horror from the headlines . . . her own marriage to [Larry] Klein fell apart around the time she was working on *Turbulent Indigo*—and is living proof that art endures." (123)

And Guy Garcia in *Time* magazine claimed that "*Turbulent Indigo* . . . is steeped in an even darker shade of *Blue*. The hallmarks of Mitchell's signature sound are abundantly evident—the crystalline arrangements, the unorthodox guitar tunings, the fluid, bittersweet melodies. Her voice, which has taken on a smoky flavor, can still soar through clouds of bass and piano. There are flashes of wry humor—as in her depiction of a comically inept Lothario in 'Yvette in English' . . . Mitchell's melodies still soar." (124)

Turbulent Indigo was a hit among the critics. On the charts, in America the album hit number 47, and in England it peaked at number 53. However, it was a consistent high-profile album that continued to bring her favorable press—and eventually serious accolades—for months to come.

Around the time *Turbulent Indigo* was released, Joni did a lot of press interviews in hopes of boosting sales. Since the album package was so heavily laden with her own artwork, she spoke a lot about her painting. When she was asked if she sold a lot of her paintings, she replied, "Generally, I don't. I have exhibitions from time to time, usually in Europe. But I had one show in Japan because the record company at that time would not allow me to make videos, and I need to flex that creativity. So I went to Tokyo, and I sold $120,000 worth of paintings. And I plowed it back into two videos that no one ever saw. MTV won't play me, VH1 barely plays me. It's beyond my control." (20)

Why has she not exhibited her paintings in the United States? According to her, "No one asked me. In America they're uptight about twice—let alone thrice—gifted. Every time I exhibit here, I take a lot of flak for it. They call me a 'dilettante.'" (20)

A lot of people don't take her artwork seriously because she became well-known as a singer and song writer first. "I sold paintings when I was in high school to dentists, doctors—small time," she explained. "I'm an O.K. painter. But the art world is just the same [as the music business]. I was preparing a show to go to London, one of the curators comes over and he sees this stuff, and he begins to joke: 'There are four different styles. The critics are going to eat you alive over there.' I said, 'Look, don't worry about it.' So I'm holding his hand and I'm thinking: 'Wait a minute, I'm an artist; why an I holding the curator's hand here? He's worried because I'm painting four styles and there's something wrong with that? It's not a negative thing, it's a positive thing! It's an appreciation of a wide range and the possibility of a hybrid. I may be onto something.'" (14)

During a promotional tour, on November 13, 1994, Joni was in London where she was a guest on BBC-TV's *The Late Show*. She was interviewed and sang two songs from *Turbulent Indigo*: "Sunny Sunday" and "Sex Kills." That same evening she was at Queensgate Terrace in South Kensington, promoting her new album. Before an audience of press members and record company people, she was showcased in an hour set that included older songs "Refuge of the Roads" and "Night Ride Home," as well as two new songs, "The Crazy Cries of Love" and "Face Lift." From *Turbulent Indigo* she sang "Sex Kills," "Magdalene Laundries," and "Sunny Sunday."

As she introduced the song "Yvette in English," she announced that cowriter David Crosby was in a hospital in California, waiting for a liver transplant. David had done so many drugs since the 1960s, that his liver was completely shot. He lacked the will to stop drugging and drinking until he ended up in a Texas jail in the 1980s. After he was released he wrote a book in 1988 about his life in the fast lane, which was called *Long Time Gone,* written with his friend Carl Gottlieb. In the early 1990s he started having severe physical problems. He was in such bad shape that a liver transplant was his only chance. Not long after Joni made this announcement in London, David received the liver he was waiting for and has lived a normal life ever since.

On December 5, 1994, Joni attended a Shawn Colvin concert in Los Angeles. Since she was friends with Shawn, she was invited onstage and became that evening's unbilled guest star. She was on stage for approximately fifteen minutes of the show.

Now that her marriage to Larry Klein had dissolved, Joni's main companions were her cats. But she doesn't allow her cats in her painting studio: "Not when I'm painting, because they bang the brush and they wipe their tails. They get between you and the canvas and then they get paint all over themselves and the furniture: They turn into big paintbrushes." (5)

When Joni was asked in 1994 what kind of current artists excited her the most, she replied, "I'll tell you what's knocked my socks off: Edith Piaf, Billie Holiday, Miles Davis, Pablo Picasso, Chuck Berry." With regard to contemporary 1990s music, she claimed, "A lot of it's very derivative now. It's two and three generations away from greatness, and some of it is building off of what was mediocre in the first place! It's geared to a very young and undiscerning audience." (20)

How does she relax? At this time she spoke of "a little cottage up in British Columbia; I've had it since 1970. The last couple of years I had a weekly social event that kinda happened by accident. It was a potluck where people would drop by, and yeah, it was usually outside with candles and two strings of Camel lights. I smoked 150 packages of Camels and sent away for two strings of Camel [shaped] lights. You wouldn't believe how cheap the plastic on them is. The paint peeled off of it, and I'm really pissed off. Because that was a lot of smoking, and why couldn't they have sprung for real yellow plastic?" (20)

After thirty-seven years with Warner Bros. Records and its affiliated labels—including Reprise Records—Mo Ostin retired from the company on January 2, 1995. Since he was one of Joni's main allies at the company, what would happen to her standing in the company?

Explained Mitchell at the time, "I don't sell a lot of records. [David] Geffen carried me because he knows I'm gifted. He said,

'Joan, you can record with me till you're 70.' I hope Warner Brothers will extend the same courtesy to me. Mo used to be 'the man,' but now you have a corporate mystery man, and he's inherited me, and I'm not going to recoup. So, there's the possibility that I'll be dropped. Although I do feel some responsibility to my gift, my ace in the hole is that I don't care if they drop me. I'll just cash in my marbles and go paint." (6)

Joni began the new year with several high-profile appearances. On January 19, 1995, Joni was one of the celebrities to perform at the charity concert event known as Commitment to Life VIII, at the Universal Amphitheater. It was an all-star event that raised money for AIDS Project L.A., a California-based organization. That night the honorees onstage included Elton John and Tom Hanks.

On January 26, 1995, Joni performed at the Wells Fargo Theater in the Gene Autry Museum, which was a live FM radio broadcast. February 3 found her the guest of Jay Leno on NBC's *Tonight Show*. She performed the song "Sex Kills" and had a brief chat with Leno. On February 17 Joni attended the music industry's Gavin Convention in New Orleans. Mitchell met several record company and media people and did all she could to promote the *Turbulent Indigo* album and support efforts by Reprise Records to promote her.

In the April 11, 1995, issue of the tabloid *Star*, a story appeared entitled, "Singer Joni Mitchell Has Crippling Polio." Many of her fans had no idea that she was still battling the effects of this crippling affliction. The story was such scorching news at the time that the *Star* put her photo on the cover and bannered it "Joni Mitchell Battles Polio 42 Years After She Beat It as a Child." In the context of the article, the singer is quoted as saying, "It's like multiple sclerosis. It means your electrical system burns out and your muscles begin to atrophy. It means impending paraplegia. I have to guard my energy. Just like the bunnies in those battery commercials, I'm the one that's about to keel over. I'm not the one that's going and going." (125)

According to her, she even sought out the advice of several alternative medicine practitioners: "Basically what the American Medical Association says is, 'Lie down and die.' But over there in Mysteryland, where I've chosen my medical aid, there's hope. I'm in the hands of two kinds of occult types who give me energy transfusions by pointing their fingers at me. I've got this Chinese guy who's trying to address my DNA and tell it that nothing ever happened. Well, maybe he can do it. I give him full faith, because faith is luminous." (125)

Joni was not afraid to talk about her medical problem. When folk recording artist Victoria Williams was diagnosed with multiple sclerosis, she and Mitchell spoke with each other about their afflictions. Explained Joni in *Rolling Stone*, "I have post-polio syndrome, which is like multiple sclerosis. Victoria Williams and I were comparing notes, and the two diseases are very similar. It's a deterioration of the nervous system. We're still mobile, but depending on the rate of deterioration, the muscles seize up and just don't work. So it's a *Magical Mystery Tour*—you don't know what lies ahead of you. There's no cure. But you know, I'm all right. Like Neil [Young] says, 'It's better to burn out than to rust.' Well, I don't want to burn out, and I don't want to rust. There must be a third choice." (20)

She seemed to be in a good space emotionally, in spite of her split from Klein, and any stress that her postpolio pains caused. According to her in early 1995, "I'm 51, and I've just had one of the most enjoyable years of my life. My bleeding years are behind me. Now I have rich people's problems, and you can't make songs out of rich people's problems. A lot of the songs on *Turbulent Indigo* are like Shakespearean soliloquies in a way—they require almost Method acting to get into. And I feel lighter than I ever have right now. I want to write some songs that are less dramatic . . . I want to sing with a smile on my face." (6)

On April 24, Joni made a guest appearance on the *Late Show with David Letterman*. During the taping in New York City, she performed "Sex Kills." On May 5 she made her debut performance at the New Orleans Jazz and Heritage Festival New Orleans. This was one of the first times she used her new guitar, which utilized the VG-8 processor to store her tunings.

Joni's new guitar does not have to be hand-tuned between songs, since it is computer programmed. "This instrument is going to be my savior," Joni claimed when Fred Walecki at Westwood Music in Los Angeles came up with the custom-made guitar for her. It has a foot-pedal-controlled "computerized brain" in a digital Roland VG-8 unit. Before she discovered this instrument, Joni was contemplating halting all concert performances. They had simply become too taxing on her, physically.

Suddenly, in the spring of 1995, Joni publicly claimed that she was unhappy with giving press interviews. In true Mitchell form, she was considering a total press interview moratorium. According to her at the time, "I'm threatening to never do press again. They chop you up. I ran into people who threatened me like a criminal on this last leg, interrogated me like a criminal . . . Any cooperation with the artist is seen by [the reporter's] peer group as collaboration with the enemy. I really hate the interview process at this point. I think it's degrading, I think it's a glut of crap. Why, when libraries are full of all great words on pages, do people devour junk food?" (2) Because, dear Joni, as journalism expert Marshall McLuhan so brilliantly proclaimed, "The medium *is* the message." In other words, reading the magazine *is* the entertainment, as opposed to the entertainment being the information that is imparted.

Continuing her rant, she claimed, "I love making records and I hate talking to the press. It's how Chairman Mao brainwashed China: it's Oriental torture. You're supposed to be this icon that transcends everything. 'Well you should rise above that!' Nobody can rise above that! The cumulative psychological effect of being interrogated seven hours is how they break down hardened soldiers! Have dental work done at the same time and you're a prisoner of war." (2)

In reality, this announcement was to be taken as seriously as her semiannual announcement that she was quitting show business. She ranted and raved, and then ended up going right back to it.

In September Reprise Records released *Friends—The Album*, which featured songs that had been used as background music or performance numbers on the hit television series *Friends*. Joni is featured on a special remixed version of the song "Big Yellow Taxi." In addition, Reprise Records also released a single-disc CD of "Big Yellow Taxi" that included seven separate mixes of the song, including Joni's "Original A Cappella with Guitar," "Radio Mix," "Late Night Club Mix," and "Double Espresso NRG Mix." The dance mixes were great, and all of a sudden Joni was on an international hit album that was certified gold, and she became a hit on the dance music charts for the very first time.

On November 6, 1995, the day before Joni's fifty-second birthday, she made an unprecedented move and appeared at the small downstairs Greenwich Village nightclub, Fez. Located in the basement of the Time Café, it was a brilliant return to the small club setting that launched her career. Minimally promoted, it became the hottest ticket in town. Naturally, the audience of two hundred people ended up being a who's who of the show business world.

Carly Simon, Natalie Merchant, and Chrissie Hynde of the Pretenders were among the luminaries there that night. These pop/rock divas came to pay homage to the great Joni.

Reportedly Chrissie got drunk and boisterous, yelling out things like, "We love you Joni!" and "Joni you rock!" Not everyone was thrilled with Hynde's enthusiasm.

When Carly told Chrissie to shut up, Hynde wrapped her hands around Simon's neck. It was an official diva fight right there at Fez. Then Chrissie shouted to Carly, "*That*," referring to Joni, "is a real singer!" (2)

Carly left in a huff.

New Yorker magazine reported, "During certain songs, Mitchell rocked her hips back and forth, in a modified version of the Elvis swivel. Between songs, the only sound besides Mitchell's voice and the audience's applause, was Chrissie Hynde intermittently shouting 'Let it out Joni!" (126)

After Joni's show, Chrissie's exuberance continued backstage. According to Mitchell, Hynde "climbed me like a telephone pole." (2)

Interviewed later, Hynde admitted of that night, "I was a little in the bag, but she was fantastic, brilliant. I was probably going a little over-the-top because people speak of her in hushed tones . . . She's a great singer, she plays great. She's always looked fantastic, but never flashed her tits. The only thing she ever flaunted was her songs . . . I was yelling, 'Go for it bitch!' She's only human—everyone needs to be told they're loved." (2)

With regard to Joni's encounter with Hynde, Mitchell explained, "I went to see her play in New York, and she was going, 'I just played this concert in California, and damn women were screaming at me. I didn't get in this business to have damn women screaming at me.' Then Monday night I played Fez, in New York, Chrissie came down, and I forget what she was drinking—but it seemed like she consumed quite a lot of it—and all through the show she was like, 'Rock it Joni!' It was such an interesting juxtaposition—I loved it." (55)

Commenting on the Chrissie/Carly cat fight, Joni commented laughingly, "There was a bit of fur flying between her and Carly Simon. As I understand it, Carly told her to shut up, and she wrapped her hands around Carly's throat!" (55)

On November 7, 1995, Joni attended an Eric Andersen show at the Bottom Line in Greenwich Village. She ended up onstage making a guest appearance with her old friend Andersen. On November 27 she performed a short set at the Waldorf-Astoria in New York City, at a dinner held to honor political cartoonist Garry Trudeau. Her date that evening was drummer Brian Blade, whom she had met at the New Orleans Jazz Festival that past May.

On December 6, 1995, Joni Mitchell received *Billboard* magazine's Century Award for lifetime achievement in the music industry. Her compatriot Peter Gabriel took the stage to announce, "I'm here to honor one of the very few artists I believe has been a real pioneer . . . she has continuously and courageously experimented, putting substance before style, passion before packaging . . . she's been a major influence on my work, as she has on many other artists as diverse as Seal, Madonna, Sting, Natalie Merchant, Annie Lennox, and the Artist Formerly Known as the Artist Formerly Known As [Prince]." (2)

That evening, after a filmed biographical tribute to her, Joni took the stage to accept her prize. From the podium she announced, "I've been thinking a lot about arrogance and humility to bring to this situation. But I feel like I'm emerging from the Mc-Carthy era in a certain way. I never thought of it as difficult being a woman in this industry, but it has been pointed out to me in the last few days how few women there really were, and there were some strikes against us from the beginning." (2) Whatever obstacles faced Joni throughout the years, she had passed through them all—by her grace, her determination, or her defiance.

On December 12 she was again a guest on the *Tonight Show* with Jay Leno. Although she had claimed earlier in the year that she was finished doing press interviews, she obviously managed to

In the late 1970s Joni began to dabble heavily in the jazz realm. Her work with
jazz master Charles Mingus widened her musical horizons but
harmed her pop and rock popularity.

(Photo: Norman Seeff for Geffen Records/Photofest)

Joni was part of the film *The Last Waltz*, which was the staged farewell for the rock group The Band. Van Morrison, Neil Young, and Joni have a pensive moment between songs.

(Photo: Photofest)

Dr. John, Neil Diamond, Joni, Neil Young, Rick Danko (The Band), Van Morrison, Bob Dylan, and Robbie Robertson (The Band) in the film *The Last Waltz*.

(Photo: Photofest)

As part of *The Last Waltz*, with an all-star band, Joni performed live versions of her songs "Coyote," "Shadows and Light," and "Furry Sings the Blues."
(Photo: Photofest)

Neil Young, Joni, and Robbie Robertson in the film *The Last Waltz*, directed by Martin Scorsese.
(Photo: Photofest)

Joni's paintings are as important to her
expressive nature as her songs. She poses
in front of one of her works with Ron
Wood at an exhibit in a gallery.
(Photo: Photofest)

Rocker John Mayall was
among the many friends and
fans to show up at the
Vogual Gallery opening to
see Joni and celebrate her
colorful impressionistic
paintings.
(Photo: Photofest)

In 1991 Joni hit a new creative high with her beautiful and expressive album *Night Ride Home*. She sang of childhood conflict ("Cherokee Louise"), greed ("The Windfall"), and unrequited love ("Two Grey Rooms").

(Photo: Nicola Dill for Geffen Records/Photofest)

In 1994 Joni released the album *Turbulent Indigo*. The critics heralded it as a return to the brilliant style of her early work. She ended up winning two Grammy Awards for it. One award was for the music, and one award was for the painting she did of herself for the cover.

In the late 1990s Joni's life took a huge change for the better when she reconnected with the daughter she had given up for adoption over thirty years before. Their relationship allowed Joni to move forward with a new-found happiness.
(Photo: Gregory Heisler for Reprise Records/Photofest)

Joni's *Both Sides Now* album marked a new era for her. By interpreting classic jazz and pop standards like "Stormy Weather" and "At Last," she won another Grammy and fell in love with singing in front of a whole orchestra.
(Photo: Photofest)

"Joni Mitchell," a portrait by Mark Bego.

(Photo: 2004 Mark Bego)

patch up whatever differences she had with the media. In fact in several interviews she tended to become more revealing than ever before.

One of the subjects she was suddenly frank and verbal about was the daughter she gave up for adoption in the late 1960s. *Billboard* magazine quoted her in an interview as saying, "I've never seen the child since, although I've always thought of her. I know a lot of people who have looked for their parents, and parents who have looked for their children. The reactions to it could go either way. The foster parent who had her until she was adopted contacted me the last time I was in Toronto—she was an old woman at that time and ready to die; she said she recognized me on TV because of my bone structure—and gave me all the child's early baby pictures. For years I didn't talk about this because of my parents, although I did leak little things, little messages into my songs for the child, just to let her know I was thinking of her." (1)

Several other publications also carried the story of how Joni had been actively searching for her long-lost daughter. She suddenly had a burning need to reconcile for whatever mistakes she had made in the past. Something was desperately missing in her life, and she had to solve the mystery of what happened to the girl she had named Kelly Dale Anderson—"Little Green."

20

Hits, Misses, and Surprise Reunions

There are times in life when it is necessary to confront the past before it's possible to move ahead into the future. For Joni Mitchell one of these times came in 1996 and 1997. In her career Joni was about to reexamine her old music in a pair of "greatest hits" albums. The music industry was about to start lauding her with prizes and honors—both for cumulative and specific projects. And in her personal life, something long missing was about to make a monumental return.

On January 3, 1996, Mitchell was a guest on the morning news magazine–styled TV talk show *CBS This Morning*. She was interviewed and was seen in performance on the program. That same month it was announced that her *Turbulent Indigo* album was among the contenders nominated for the thirty-eighth annual Grammy Awards. Not only was it a huge hit with the critics, but it made a big impression on her peers in the music industry as well.

Joni arrived at the Shrine Auditorium in Los Angeles on the afternoon of February 28, 1996, for the Grammy Awards ceremony. She was accompanied by Larry Klein—also a nominee—and an assistant named Julie Larson. The first award she won that day was the Grammy for Best Recording Package, the art director's award. She and Robbie Cavolina received trophies for the controversial Joni-as-Vincent van Gogh self-portrait on *Turbulent Indigo*, and the whole classy-looking packaging that enclosed the CD.

The frosting on the cake came when it was time for the presentation of the award for the Best Pop Album of the Year. Among the other albums she was competing against were the latest releases by such artists as Madonna, Janet Jackson, and the Eagles. It had been a long time since she won a Grammy for her *Court and Spark* album. She was long out of favor with the "popular" side of the recording business. What were her chances of winning that night? Obviously very good. *Turbulent Indigo* demonstrated musical craft polished by a career of masterful music, and the voters of the National Academy of Recording Arts and Sciences fittingly recognized it, and Mitchell's vast talent.

No one was more surprised than Joni when her name was announced as the winner. As she and Larry Klein took the podium to accept her Grammy, she said with startled glee, "Gee, Klein . . . considering we made this album in a state of divorce."

Larry then voiced his gratitude to her "for 10 years of instruction in the arts." (2)

Joni later commented, "When everybody jumped to their feet at the *Billboard* ceremony it felt a little obligatory, but the Grammy was lovely. It was a sweet victory, it really was. 'Cause I'm a little guy in this business now." (2)

After years of struggling to have her creativity acknowledged, Joni's fortunes were caught up in a sudden upturn. In her personal life, Joni had a new boyfriend, Donald Freed. Her mother had introduced them, and they instantly hit it off. According to her at the time, "When we first met, we threw the *I Ching* [fortune-telling stones]. The [instruction] book said to 'remember the beginning,' so I kept the essence of the idea and restructured the words. It seemed like a blueprint for proper conduct through the beginning phases of any intense attraction." (15)

Mitchell explained that Freed "teaches mainly Indian reservation children to write songs. He's an interesting man with an interesting calling . . . It's been quite an extraordinary relationship." (127)

For Joni, the accolades continued to pour in as she was presented the Polar Music Prize from Sweden. It was awarded to her and her fellow honoree, conductor Pierre Boulez, by King Carl Gustav at Brewald Hall in Stockholm on May 8, 1996. She and Boulez also split a cash gift of a million Swedish kronar. According to Joni, "They're trying to have a kind of Pulitzer Prize for music over there. It's fairly new. [Paul] McCartney had been a recipient and Quincy Jones, and they have a pop and classical category." (7)

Although the royal family of Sweden is steeped in tradition and carries on the traditional formalities, family members are actually very hip and personable. (I feel justified in saying this because I have met the very charming Royal Princess Christina—the king's sister—and her husband.) When Joni and her boyfriend, Don Freed, went to Sweden so that she could be honored by the king, she found that they hit it off as friends.

"It was fun. I enjoyed the King," Joni proclaimed. "I really enjoyed his company, he was a character—kind of a hippie playboy guy . . . He let me smoke, so that was good. I had to ask his permission, though. He smoked with me. He'd say he had to keep pace with me. So sometimes he'd say 'yes' and sometimes he'd say 'no.' 'Can I smoke now?' 'No.' 'Well, when can I smoke next?' 'I'll tell you.' And, he had a silver cigarette case, and he'd say 'O.K., we will smoke now.'" (7)

When Joni and His Royal Highness were signaled to enter the royal banquet room, he commented to the singer, "This is good marching music." (2) Not to miss a beat, Joni mimicked the king's arm-swinging march. However, she marched right by the main table, in the direction of the kitchen. The king comically grabbed her by the dress and stopped her from marching out of the room. When Joni cracked up in gales of laughter, the king joined in, as did the slightly startled guests at this usually formal royal event. Needless to say, Joni was a huge hit in Sweden that spring. (2)

Among Joni's dearest friends at this time were her four cats: Nietzsche, Pansy, El Café, and Mojo. As she explained, "I love to have them around and they love to be around. Nietzsche, in particular, is very vocal. As soon as the guitar stops, he starts talking. But the moment the guitar starts up again, he stops. I wrote a song inspired by Nietzsche called 'Man from Mars.' The night I started, Nietzsche disappeared for eighteen days. I wrote the song in seventeen days, and on the eighteenth day, he came back. When I played the song for him, he stood on his hind legs and danced, so he recognized it somehow." (5)

Joni penned the song "Man from Mars" for the soundtrack of the film *Grace of My Heart*. The film was directed by Allison Anders, and Larry Klein was the musical director. Mitchell was to appear in the film, as was her recording of the song "Man from Mars."

The film stars Ileana Douglas, and it is about a female song-writer in the 1960s and 1970s in the famed Brill Building in New York City. The character Douglas plays in *Grace of My Heart* is a thinly veiled version of the life of Carole King—who had started out as a songwriter but later emerged as a singing star as well. The big hit song that emerged from this film was "God Give Me Strength," written by Elvis Costello and Burt Bacharach.

The film went through several changes as it was being made, and ultimately Allison Anders decided to use Vristen Vigard's recording of the song "Man from Mars" in the film because hers was the singing voice used for Ileana Douglas. Regardless, they were still going to use Joni's recording of "Man from Mars" on the *Grace of My Heart* soundtrack album. But Mitchell protested this and wanted herself removed from it. Unfortunately several thou-sand copies of the *Grace of My Heart* album containing Joni's vocal rendition of the song had already been pressed and distributed.

Reportedly, on September 9, 1996, MCA Records recalled 40,000 copies of the soundtrack album to *Grace of My Heart* con-taining Joni. The copies that managed to hit the stores are now considered collector's items and show up on auction-style web-sites like eBay quite often. Ultimately it was not Joni who ap-peared in the film but her friend Shawn Colvin—as a folk singer strumming her guitar in an outdoor scene.

In Joni's nearly thirty-year recording career, she had never re-leased a "greatest hits" album—a staple of the music industry. Collecting music from all of Joni's eras onto one disc and still hav-ing something of a cohesive album would be hard. She had been through her folk, rock, jazz/rock, pure jazz, techno, and hybrid phases.

Of her career-long musical attitude dancing, Joni admitted, "There's a certain kind of restlessness that not many artists are cursed or blessed with, depending on how you look at it. Craving change, craving growth, seeing always room for improvement in your work." (18)

Joni never had a long string of Top 10 hits. She was an album artist first and foremost. "For years, people have been recom-mending or pushing me toward releasing a *Hits* album," she ex-plained, "but in my case, there weren't enough hits technically to fill an album—by that, I mean a single that rides the chart well up into the small numbers. I also felt like [a *Hits* package] would kill my catalog. The only reason I'm doing the *Hits* is to show I didn't die after 1973." (65)

What she came up with—to please both the album company and herself as a creative person—was to release two separate albums. She would call one of them *Hits*, and it would contain all of the obvious singles and songwriter top hits. She would simultaneously release a second album called *Misses*, and it would cull together the tracks Joni really loved and thought should have been hits—but never were.

According to her, "Once I got the idea for the *Misses*, my enthusiasm came in, because there was something in it for me. This way, it would give me a chance to run some of this overlooked material by the public again." (65)

She would allow her record company to release a "greatest hits" album only if she was totally involved and had the final say as to what went on the albums. "There aren't that many album artists," says Joni. "It used to be that albums had a couple of good songs in the one, two, and three slots and then a lot of filler, so that if you took the hits off them, there's not a lot left. But I think the albums as a form, I did from the beginning. The Beatles did. Brian Wilson did with *Pet Sounds*. That's why I hate to tear them apart. That was a hump I had to get over; to take them out of a chronology that was carefully constructed at the time." (65) Ultimately this is exactly what she did.

When it came time to release the *Hits* and *Misses* albums, Joni did some advance publicity to create anticipation. On November 3, 1996, she was a guest on the *Late Show with David Letterman*. And five days later she appeared on as a guest on the *Rosie O'Donnell Show*. Both programs were taped in New York City.

Finally on November 16, Joni's eighteenth and nineteenth albums—*Hits* and *Misses*—were released. The *Hits* album, the more successful of the two packages, opens with Joni's recording of the song "Urge for Going," never previously released. It was recorded in 1967 for her debut album, *Joni Mitchell*, but at the last minute was not included. The song was most famous for having been recorded by Tom Rush. Joni sounds great on this track, and it was well worth the wait.

"Urge for Going" is followed by "Chelsea Morning," "Big Yellow Taxi," "Woodstock," and "The Circle Game." These songs basically define Joni's folk and early hippie era songs. Regarding "The Circle Game," Joni explained, "[It] was never a hit, but it did replace 'Old McDonald Had a Farm' at summer camp as a standard. It slipped into the culture in an unorthodox way. It didn't get radio airplay, it didn't climb the charts, but many people said, 'You have to put it on there. I sang it at summer camp.'" (111) Indeed, it has been a campfire staple for years.

The songs "Carey," "California," "You Turn Me On I'm a Radio," "Raised on Robbery," "Help Me," "Free Man in Paris," and "River" define her *Blue* and post-*Blue* jazz/rock periods. Regarding "Car on a Hill," Mitchell proclaims, "I wanted to release it as a single, and [the record company] fought me on it. Instead, 'Free Man in Paris' was released, which never sounded like a single to me." (111)

"Chinese Café"/"Unchained Melody" and "Come In from the Cold" represent her work in the 1980s and 1990s, respectively. The album ends with the fifteenth cut, her signature song to end them all—"Both Sides Now"—which was a hit for Judy Collins but not Joni.

Then came the work she culled together to form her most fascinating but most experimental work, which was included on the *Misses* album. According to Joni, these songs were "not of what I consider my best work, but things that were commercially viable. Most of them are things that I would have chosen as singles. These are songs of experience, as opposed to the younger songs of *Hits*." (65)

As she saw it, "I've taken chapters from 10 books and built a new book. I think it's a whole new album, not just a collection of songs." (65)

She claimed that she was not allowed the creative freedom to do something like this until she was at Reprise Records. "Elektra and Geffen didn't want this out [*Misses*]. They didn't want to be associated with the *Misses*. I'm proud to be," she proclaimed. (65)

"The Arrangement" from *Ladies of the Canyon*, "Harry's House" from *Hissing of Summer Lawns*, "The Reoccuring Dream" from *Chalk Mark in a Rain Storm*, "The Windfall" from *Night Ride Home*, and "For the Roses" from the album of the same name were songs Joni favored as potential singles when their respective discs were released. Her thoughts on the subject were ignored.

The *Misses* album opens with "Passion Play (When All the Slaves Are Free)" and "Nothing Can Be Done." Of the latter song, from the *Night Ride Home* album, Joni explains, "This was a regional hit in Miami. Radio stations were asking for it. There was a video, but the company didn't move on it." (111)

They are followed by "A Case of You," which by that time was a trademark career song but was never a hit single on the charts. Joni couldn't decide which of these two albums it was going to go on: "[It kept] bouncing from the *Hits* to the *Misses*. It was my choice off of *Blue* to release as a single, but I never had any control over what was released." (111)

Next comes "The Beat of Black Wings," from *Chalk Mark in a Rain Storm*. According to Joni, "Basically, I was in the game, but I may as well have been dead. I went to Tokyo and sold $120,000 worth of paintings and took the money and made a number of videos. In this one, I played a black soldier, drunk in the alley, and no one knew it was me." (111)

The other tracks on this album include "Dog Eat Dog," "The Wolf That Lives in Lindsey," "The Magdalene Laundries," "Impossible Dreamer" "Sex Kills," "The Reoccurring Dream," "Harry's House"/"Centerpiece," "The Arrangement," "For the Roses," and "Hejira," which spanned twenty-two years of experimentation from *For the Roses* (1973) to *Turbulent Indigo* (1995).

Surprisingly, Joni did not write any notes or messages in the lyric booklets that were included in *Hits* or *Misses*. As she explains it, "I tried to write the liner notes, but I couldn't get the right amount of levity. There was too much pain involved. I feel a certain amount of levity at this time in my life, but then, my time was rocked with slings and arrows of outrageous fortune. I wrote and wrote and then abandoned the notes." (65)

Now that she was a Grammy Award–winning art director as well as a recording artist, Joni took full advantage of her artistic nature by creating similar-themed album cover art for *Hits* and *Misses*. Using her own slightly off-center sense of humor, Joni interpreted the words "hits" and "misses" to be tied with society's fascination with gun-related violence. On the cover of her *Hits* albums, an unseen gunman has successfully "hit" Joni, and she is seen as the casualty of this act of violence. She is depicted as a dead body in the middle of the street, surrounded on the asphalt by a police officer's white chalk mark outline. In the background is an automobile, parked at a curb not far behind her. "It's very fashionable to have gore on album covers right now. But I didn't. The only concession is that [the word] 'Hits' is in red," she said with a smile. (65)

On the cover of the *Misses* album, Joni is seen, bent over, butt to the camera—in a "full moon" fashion—escaping to her car. In other words, the unknown gunman has "missed" his mark. "I'm fully dressed, but this is a 'moon' shot. It's kind of a 'kiss my ass' shot. Reprise loves it," Joni laughed at the time. (65)

Just like *Turbulent Indigo*, the original runs of the *Hits* and *Misses* albums came in six-paneled cardboard cases that opened away from the middle, with little pockets slit into the interior panels, in which the lyric booklet and the CD are fit. Again Joni shared art director duties with Robbie Cavolina.

After all the years of waiting for Joni to put out a "greatest hits"–style package, this pair of retrospective concept compilations did not produce a huge sales success. *Hits* peaked at number 161 on the *Billboard* charts in the United States. And *Misses* failed to make the chart altogether. However, in the decade since its release, *Hits* has continued to be a steady seller for Joni, serving as a worthy single-disc introduction to her body of work.

On December 11, 1996, Joni was at the Regent Beverly Wilshire Hotel in Los Angeles, where she was presented with a Lifetime Achievement Award from the National Academy of Songwriters. This, in addition to two Grammys and a Swedish Polar Music Prize, had made 1996 Joni's most accolade-filled year in decades. Hastened by the retrospective focus on her—which the *Hits* and *Misses* albums brought along with them—the public was seeing Joni as a classic creative genius and not an out-of-touch experimental risk taker.

The next major accolade to come to Joni Mitchell was induction into the Rock & Roll Hall of Fame in 1997. However, Joni reacted in a much different way to receiving this "honor." There were definite politics involved in this decision.

In recent years, Joni's name had been bandied about for inclusion on this prestigious list of rock honorees. However, each year when it came time to announce the inductees, Joni found herself left out. Part of this—it is surmised—is the fact that the Rock & Roll Hall of Fame was devised and run by the founder of *Rolling Stone* magazine, Jan Wenner. Given the on-again/off-again relationship that she had experienced with *Rolling Stone* and Wenner over the years, Joni decided that she would not be attending the award ceremony.

This whole affair with the Rock & Roll Hall of Fame really set her off. "All of a sudden I'm getting these awards, but nobody really understands why—only that it should be done," she complained. "It was lip service: the speeches didn't illuminate what was, I thought, important about my work—they were kind of half-assed. I wish I was more simple-minded so that I could just say, 'Thank you for this symbol of achievement in my industry,' but I know too much about the manipulation that goes on behind the scenes. I also know what honor is—and I have been honored. For instance, a black, blind piano player in a restaurant once said to me, 'Joni, you make raceless, genderless music.' That to me, was an honor." (15)

She found there was a certain arrogance attached to who was inducted, and who was not. According to her, "If you're genuinely honored, it humbles you. But when you're getting arrogant, those things begin to ring hollow." (27)

Joni admitted openly, "Well, I'm a little bitter. I'm too underrated for the caliber of work I produce. I've been treated like I'm dead for twenty years by the industry, and people would be called 'the new Joni Mitchell' when they weren't as good as me—then they would turn against me! So I'm trying to heal . . . but I've still got some stuff I've got to spit out." (15)

Even her longtime friend and ex-boyfriend Graham Nash tried to get her to attend the ceremony. "Graham has a very good attitude about the Rock & Roll Hall of Fame," claimed Mitchell. "My father would have the same attitude. Unfortunately, I do not have a good attitude about the Rock & Roll Hall of Fame . . . It was a dubious honor—in that they held me out conspicuously for three years. To go, 'Oh, thank you, thank you,' I mean, having conspicuously ostracized me for a few projects, how can I be gracious, really? And the other complaint that I had is that it was gonna cost about $20 grand to take my family—that they charge, and they get a free concert out of you. It's exploitative, I'm sorry. [Her friend] Brian calls it 'the Hall of Shame,' and in a certain way I think it is. It's mercenary, and they're putting everybody in [it]—so the honor is dubious on that level. It's not correcting history as it should be. There's a lot that's in there that's great but . . . ." (7)

On the subject, her ex-husband Larry Klein said, "I think a lot of times she's been too truthful. I think she doesn't have any choice but to be absolutely honest. That's just the way that she has been shaped . . . She tells too much truth, and it's interpreted as arrogance, as bitterness, as a lot of other things. Not to say that at times she is not an arrogant person; she is. And at times she is a bitter person. But she is a relentlessly honest person. And I think in our world that is something that people misunderstand. One thing Joan is not is a diplomat. But the further I go along in life the more I value pure unadulterated honesty. I remember many times where we'd be out somewhere having a conversation with someone and afterward she would be mourning the fact that she had revealed too much of herself: 'God, I think I really fucked up by telling this person this and that.' Or in some instances a person would use some piece of intimate information Joan gave him to stab her with later." (2)

British rock singer Morrissey conducted an interview with Joni Mitchell that was published in the March 7, 1997, issue of *Rolling Stone* magazine. It was headlined as "Melancholy Meets the Infinite Sadness." The legendary British singer was obviously fascinated with the mysterious Miss Mitchell.

Morrissey asked her if she had any guilt about smoking cigarettes.

She replied, "Oh, no, no, no. I'm a smoker, for better or worse."

Then he said to her scoldingly, "It does kill a lot of people, doesn't it?"

Without missing a beat, Joni snapped back at him a defiant "So what?" (55)

As a vegetarian, he asked her why our society is cruel to animals. Joni's answer was, "Let's look at our culture. If the Western world's guided by anything, it's by the Bible. Our origin story puts the emphasis on the woman screwed by the snake, which is a pretty stupid interpretation of the story." (55)

On March 13, 1997, a most miraculous thing happened: for the first time since she had given her up for adoption, Joni Mitchell met her daughter. Joni was accused of getting the ball rolling by leaking it to the press that she was searching for the missing-from-her-life baby of "Little Green" fame. Insisted Mitchell, it was not she who leaked news like that: "I didn't let it out of the bag. They went snooping around. In a couple of songs I left a trail for the kid to follow, and it caught up with me. It's juicy in this yellow day and age. A tabloid did this 'SONGBIRD SEARCHES FOR LOVE CHILD' and my friends in Saskatchewan . . . sold me out. I will tell you, I did the right thing with the child. I had no money to buy diapers or anything. You don't want to flirt with this without telling the whole story, and that is really worse than *The Perils of Pauline*. To be a broke young woman in that position is Dickensian. You really don't want to know the details of how we were treated, young women at that time. It's just disgusting." (2)

The child whom Joni named Kelly Dale Anderson had grown up to become a beautiful professional model named Kilauren Gibb. Joni and Kilauren were not reunited sooner because Kilauren's adoptive parents didn't tell her she was adopted until she was twenty-seven years old. Why did they keep the knowledge of her adoption from their child? According to Kilauren, "Because they loved me. They wanted me to be comfortable." (19)

At that point Kilauren had gone to Canada's Children's Aid Society and received a limited amount of information about her birth mother. She learned that her mother was from Saskatoon, that she had polio as a child, and that she was a singer by profession. At the urging of friends who had read in the tabloids that Joni Mitchell was simultaneously looking for her lost daughter, Kilauren logged onto Joni's website and was startled by the similarities. She was pleasantly surprised to find that the singer's long-hidden unwed pregnancy paralleled her own birth date. There also seemed to be a close resemblance, especially in the cheekbones and other facial features. She contacted Joni's management company—which was now S. L. Feldman and Associates in Vancouver, British Columbia—only to learn that she was one of some thirty other woman who had also called, claiming that Joni was their mother.

When it became conclusive that Kilauren was indeed Joni's daughter, it was a cause for celebrating. All of a sudden, Joni was not only a mother, she was a grandmother as well! It was a case of going from being a single woman to having an instant family. Kilauren was the mother of a four-year-old son whom she had named Marlin.

In the British newspaper the *Express*, a man named Brad McMath claimed to be the father of Joni Mitchell's love child. According to him, as he broke his thirty-year silence, "I was a bum, a hippie. I wasn't ready for parenthood. Joni came to stay with me in Regina, but as soon as she arrived she met an old boyfriend and moved in with him . . . She just split. I never wanted to speak to her again after that." (128) That was the end of their relationship.

Joni's side of the story was somewhat different. She later claimed, "My daughter's father left me three months pregnant in an attic room with no money and winter coming on, and only a fireplace for heat. The spindles of the banister were gap toothed—fuel for last winter's occupants. He left behind a doodle of a pregnant woman seated at a window looking at a crescent moon and on it he wrote, 'The thief left it behind, the moon at the window.'" (103) This note inspired the song Joni wrote called "Moon at the Window" which appeared on her *Wild Things Run Fast* album.

She was thrilled to have Kilauren back in her life. Several months after their reunion, Joni said, "Her adoptive parents are very like my parents, so her rebellion—I think, and I'm just getting to know her, it's only been a year—is quite similar to my own. I was difficult to raise in my teens, and she was too. Both of us wanted to stretch out and see the world. She took off at 14 with her brother as a chaperone, and modeled quite extensively, 'til [the age of] 27, all around the world. And she's going through a second rebellion as we speak, you know against me, trying to shock me. Well, it's harder to shock me than it was the kids, because they're more like my parents, you know? I loved the experience, everything with the difficulty and all. We'll be fine. But it's an odd situation and there's much that has to be worked through." (7)

Their path toward finding each other was a long one. Throughout the years, Joni had left clues in her music alluding to the fact that she had a daughter who was given up for adoption. The song "Little Green" basically told the whole story. Then in the 1982 song "Chinese Café," Joni sang that of her own daughter, she was the one who "bore" her, but she could not "raise" her. According to Joni, "I just wanted to keep her in the pulse of my life—these mentions that I was thinking of her. And she said, 'Joan, these things are so subtle, I would never have known it was about me.'" (127)

Kilauren Gibb was then a thirty-three-year-old model residing in Toronto. Interestingly enough, a photograph of Gibb's face appeared on the label of European Evian facial spritzer bottles. According to Joni, "I don't know how many times I borrowed my best friend Gloria's spritzer when we were doing press runs through Europe, and sprayed my face with my fingers over my daughter's face." (127)

In April 1997 Joni proclaimed, "I met her three weeks ago. She's been looking for years. The agency gave her my bio but wouldn't release my name. All of this ugly press actually turned around in our favor. Somebody suggested to her, 'Joni Mitchell's looking for her daughter, wouldn't it be funny . . .' So she double-checked the bio that she had against my Web site and started jumping up and down with excitement . . . She's a kindred spirit. The press is already exaggerating, saying she looks like a young me. She doesn't—she looks like a young [version of] my mother. She's got my high cheekbones. She's tall—five foot nine, beautiful—she's been a professional model. She is highly educated. She's been a champion swimmer." (2)

According to Mitchell, "Surprisingly, there's less of a gap than there was between my mother and I. My mother thinks I'm immoral. I've searched diligently for a morality that applied to the times that I lived in. I keep saying to my mother, 'Think of me as a Catholic priest that drinks a little with the dock workers.' I just don't want to get that *clean*." (7)

Kilauren was quoted as saying that reuniting with Joni "made me feel complete." (19) And she attested that she has smoothed over the awkwardness with her adoptive parents.

Joni explains, "We worked through all of that, I'm totally grateful to them, and Kilauren hasn't forgotten about them." (11)

This event changed the whole dynamic of how she felt about herself. "It's tricky to mother someone who's a grown woman," she said trying to explain her feelings. "We've had a couple of skirmishes already. We worked our way through them. She was going through second teenage rebellion with me. It's interesting." (129)

They had to go through a period of adjustment. "It's hard," said Joni at the time. "Our situation is abnormal. We have a general affinity, but there are pockets of adjustments, and we've had a couple of skirmishes. But we've had some beautiful times, and yes, it's working. It's going along beautifully. I love my kid and my grandson. It's thrilling." (127)

News of Joni and her daughter reuniting was read at the annual American Adoption Congress convention in Dallas, Texas, in April 1997. The news was applauded with a standing ovation.

One of the most interesting albums that Joni Mitchell had appeared on in a long time was singer Janet Jackson's 1997 release, *The Velvet Rope*. Janet had long admired Joni and asked for permission from Mitchell to sample the song "Big Yellow Taxi" and use it as the chorus of a new song called "Got 'Til It's Gone." This move brought a new appreciation of Joni's music and exposed her to Janet Jackson's millions of worldwide fans—a whole new audience for her.

In the early 1990s Joni had signed a three-book deal with Random House/Crown in New York City. At the time, I was signed to the company to write a biography of Madonna called *Madonna: Blonde Ambition* (1993). When I found out that Joni was signed to the same house, I tried my best to get involved in Joni's publication deal and—at very least—become the ghost writer on the deal.

I was informed by my editor, Kathy Belden, "Joni is insisting on doing it all herself, so you can forget about that. To fulfill part of her contract, we are going to publish a book full of her lyrics, because we haven't seen a word of the autobiography she is supposed to be writing." (130)

With that, I decided to write an unauthorized biography of Joni, since she was going to write her own. Ten years later, her autobiography has yet to be written. In the meantime, Random House/Crown released the book *Joni Mitchell: Collected Lyrics*, in 1997. It is a book of sepia-colored photographs of her and the lyrics to her most famous songs. The book hit the stores in time for that Christmas season.

On December 12, the Record Industry Association of America (RIAA) announced that Joni's album *Court and Spark* had been officially certified double platinum for over 2 million copies sold in the United States.

At the time, Joni was asked to name the people who were her greatest influences. According to her, "Miles [Davis] was a fine, fine sonic innovator. And some of the music of the bands he inspired and kicked into gear, that's some of the finest music I've ever heard . . . The later stuff I think he had less inspiration. It took him longer to play. It seems like he stood around more. He was so pure. He really waited until he heard something that he felt. I'm in that place now, in a way. I'm almost too picky to go on. I'm still making music, and I've got some new ideas. But you get narrower, in a way. It takes more and more to get you off. Mingus, at the end, couldn't stand anything except a couple of Charlie Parker records. He couldn't stand his own music. He'd go, 'He's falsifying his emotion. That ain't shit.' He heard all the effort people put forth and very little purity and sincerity. I get that way sometimes. My jive detector gets too sensitive and music just sounds awful to me. All of it . . . In a certain way, we do most of our enthusiastic listening in our youth. It's the backdrop for our courtships, and you stow it and you're sentimental. The songs with the [Sons of the] Pioneers, Roy Rogers' backup band, I'm just thrilled listening to those old songs. That's the music of my pre-teens. It's much better music than I realized as a child. Sentimental, kind of cornball, classic cowboy stuff. I never was much of a country and western fan, but I love listening to that. It swings. It's got that element of jazz to it." (131)

Being a true artiste has taken its toll on Joni Mitchell. She continued to make music that expressed her soul and consistently turned her back on convention. When she finally returned to the kind of music that stood up well next to the commercial high points of her *Court and Spark* era—with the albums *Night Ride Home* and *Chalk Mark in a Rain Storm*—she found that the times had drastically changed around her. *Vanity Fair* magazine in 1997 claimed that she had not made money on any of her albums since the late 1970s—during the era of *Don Juan's Reckless Daughter*.

She paid bills to lawyers, doctors, record company disputes, and business deals gone sour. Still, she never pandered her craft just to be "popular" or "cool." She made decisions based on what she wanted to do, not what might have made more financial sense.

According to her in the late 1990s, "A lot of my real grief and bitterness in the last 15 years has been career-oriented. It's been rich people problems. The really deeply soul-disturbing things I've gone through would get no public sympathy. People like vulnerable artists. Why do they love Marilyn [Monroe]? People like balancing acts. There was a time in my life when I was a balancing act, but I stabilized, thank God. But people had to get used to dealing with more powerful women." (2)

Joni was in a feisty mood and wasn't going to take any crap from anyone. She had reached the age where she had new priorities in her life. Having gotten her daughter back in her life had changed her profoundly. She was finished wasting her time on things that didn't matter, and she felt that she had truly entered still another new phase in her life.

21

Taming the Tiger

The year 1998 was a magical one for Joni Mitchell fans. It brought a new album, an exciting new tour, a beautifully filmed TV special, and several new jazz-oriented performances and recordings—many of them in surprising places. When all of these events were put together, they spelled exciting moves in fresh directions for the woman who penned the song "Woodstock." And, speaking of Woodstock, three decades after the most famous rock festival of all, Joni at long last played a highly successful concert on the site of the original event.

The funny thing was that—according to Joni—a year before she had again seriously contemplated quitting the music business. She had been discouraged and frustrated. She was mad at the Rock & Roll Hall of Fame. She was tired of fighting with her record company. She was sick of reviewers constantly saying that they missed the "old" Joni Mitchell of the Woodstock days. As she had done so many times before, she considered just packing it in, walling herself up in her Bel Air home, and painting like a recluse.

She found sounding boards for this idea in unusual places. As she later explained, "I was sitting here in the Daily Grill in Brentwood, California, and I told the waitress I was going to quit. She burst into tears and told me how much she loved my music and used it to articulate her feelings when she couldn't find the words.

That made me feel good. People on the street have always been where I got my good reviews. It helped me to realize I still had things to say." (132)

Then several things happened that helped her gain resolve. Having her daughter back in her life signaled a whole new era of happiness for Joni—she felt that she was complete again. She was able to look back at 1997 and call it "an exhilarating year. A fairy tale." (2)

When Joni decided that she was *not* quitting the music business, she made the decision that she was "coming back" *big time* in 1998. With that, she went all the way, committing herself to a year's worth of touring and recording. Once again, she had developed a new attitude. "My prejudices against popularity are many, but I'm trying to get bigger," she claimed that year. (132)

What caused her to change her mind about her late 1990s threat to quit the music business? She explained at time, "I guess things started to take off in the last five years mainly because of the *Billboard* award. After that, it was a series of sort of copycat crimes, where people remembered me and I was the recipient of a lot of awards in a row. And then I won a Grammy—well, two Grammys, one for the artwork, which also pleased me very much." (7)

She felt encouraged by the warm reception she was suddenly receiving in the music business as well as by her new electronically tuned guitar. On March 27, 1998, Joni was a guest on *Morning Becomes Eclectic* from radio station KCRW-FM in Santa Monica, California. She was interviewed by Chris Douridas. She told him, "I'd gotten to the point where the process of making records is still enjoyable to me. I still have growth potential but the business and the marketing have become unbearable. And I've painted myself into a corner where the tunings wreak havoc on the neck of an acoustic instrument. I spend tremendous amounts of time in concert tuning, tuning, tuning. I just felt I didn't want to do it anymore, and I wanted out of the business. I'm a painter first anyway. I got seduced into [music] in art school. I felt at this particular time that the energy had gone back into the painting. I wanted for the music, I wasn't inspired." (133)

According to Mitchell, "This new guitar that I'm working with eliminated a certain amount of problems that I had with the acoustic guitar. *Problems* isn't even the right word; maddening frustration is more accurate. The guitar is intended to be played in standard tuning; the neck is calibrated and everything. Twiddling it around isn't good for the instrument, generally speaking. It's not good for the neck; it unsettles the intonation. I have very good pitch, so if I'm never quite in tune, that's frustrating." (18) Now that she had this new guitar, she decided to try it on a brand-new album, and on a high-profile concert tour that would take her across the United States. It would be her first major concert tour since 1983!

On April 16, Joni Mitchell was one of ten rock and show biz divas to headline a benefit concert at the Wiltern Theater. It was staged to raise money and awareness for Don Henley's pet cause, the Walden Woods Project, and the Thoreau Institute. Anyone who knows great American literature, knows of Walden Pond. In the twentieth century the land surrounding this area was in danger of falling into the hands of real estate developers, and Henley used his leverage as a founding member of the Eagles, and as a celebrity in his own right, to help save this delicate area.

The concept behind the concert was to have singing stars of the stature of Joni Mitchell, Sheryl Crow, Gwen Stefani, Stevie Nicks, Trisha Yearwood, Natalie Cole, and Björk sing classic jazz and pop standards, all accompanied by full orchestra. Vince Mendoza was hired to be the arranger/conductor, and Larry Klein was musical director of the event. It was an incredible evening of song, and it inspired Joni to come up with an album concept. Portions of this historic concert were later released on a promotional CD issued by AT&T, which was one of the project's corporate sponsors. Unfortunately that is the only publicly released record of this historic concert event. However, the album that was released is a true gem.

Joni recalls that the day of the event itself was something of an experience as well. For the first time in a long time, Joni was "one" of the stars on the bill, not the only star. According to her, "When I got to the hall that day, it was the first day that we went to our dressing room, and we'd been rehearsing with a bit of the orchestra, the central kind of little jazz group that was the centerpiece of the orchestra. It was the first time I'd gone to my dressing room, and there was a guy taking me up the stairs to my dressing room, and I was kind of huffing at the second landing, and I said, 'Why would you put the oldest one on the third floor and the young ones all down on the stage? It should be the other way around. So I put all my stuff down and came back down to the rehearsal, and I played with this big orchestra. I went back up to my dressing room, we started to do make-up, and when I looked at my face I was glowing—I realized I came up those three flights of stairs two-at-a-time after playing with that orchestra. That's how incredible it was. So I have to do that again." (7)

The experience began a renewed love affair between Mitchell and the classic songs of the 1930s, 1940s, and 1950s. She recalls, "They put together the orchestra, 60 pieces, and rounded up ten female singers, myself included. We all got to sing two songs. I sang a duet with Björk so she and I got three. One by one, women in beautiful evening gowns stood up like classic old band singers and sang with this big orchestra and it delighted us all. The experience of singing live with that big band is very powerful and exciting beyond words. When Charlie Parker got his taste of playing with classical orchestras he could barely stand to play anything else," explained Joni. (5)

That evening, the songbirds who performed included Stevie Nicks crooning a heartfelt "At Last," Sheryl Crow interpreting "Good Morning Heartache," Paula Cole jazzing up "But Beautiful," Shawn Colvin doing "You've Changed," Natalie Cole swinging on "They Can't Take That Away from Me," Björk's blues interpretation of "Gloomy Sunday," and actress Sandra Bernhardt's comically entertaining reading of the Peggy Lee classic "Is That All There Is?" Trisha Yearwood sang a torch version of "The Good Guy," Gwen Stefani lamented Elvis Costello's "Almost Blue," and Joni did a jazzed-up version of Marvin Gaye's "Trouble Man." Although these were contemporary numbers, they were sung with the same blues/jazz energy as the evening's classic pop and torch numbers. In addition to "Trouble Man," Joni also sang a lamentingly beautiful version of the Lena Horne trademark number, "Stormy Weather."

Speaking of that inspiring night of rock divas doing jazz standards with a full orchestra, Mitchell explained that there was very little interaction between the stars. "We didn't really—aside from the duet that I did—there wasn't that much commingling. People came—they kind of kept us apart in case the fur would fly, I don't know. I saw Stevie [Nicks] because she was before me, and Björk and I worked together. I love Björk. And I think we were all a little out of our idiom—it was hard work, everybody was a little nervous, it was just beautiful." (7)

Glowingly Joni proclaimed, "I loved it. I thought it was a beautiful night! People were talking about it for days afterwards. Which, of course, doesn't happen in this town [Los Angeles]. I've played with a big orchestra before, but never so comfortably. Maybe because I'm more comfortable, maybe because always I had to sing and play and play with them with very little rehearsal. This time I just had to stand up and sing, so I was liberated from having to plunk. And, I loved the arrangement. I sang 'Stormy Weather' with 60 pieces—the most beautiful arrangement we could find of it. Frank Sinatra had recorded it several times, but this one—I forget the arranger's name, but we just copped it—you couldn't beat it, it was so gorgeous. And to feel all those strings come rising up around you." (7)

Don Henley put together a full orchestra and augmented it with several of his music industry friends, including Michael McDonald. According to Michael, "I worked with her not too long ago, at Don Henley's benefit. She sang Marvin Gaye's 'Trouble Man.' She did a great job. It was great to hearing her singing that. She sings that song great!" (105)

A month later, Joni opened her new concert tour, which teamed her with her old friends Van Morrison and Bob Dylan. She wasn't exactly fond of touring anymore, but she made an exception for this particular three-ring attraction. As she explained it, "It took a great bill like that to get me on the road, because I don't have the appetite for applause anymore," Mitchell says. (132)

She hand-selected a great band, which included Brian Blade, Mark Isham, and Greg Leisz, and on bass was her ex-husband Larry Klein. This was going to be such an exciting tour that Larry claimed he literally begged her to be part of her band that year. How could she say no to such enthusiasm?

Amazingly, the fact that she and Larry were no longer romantically involved didn't hurt their friendship or their ability to work together. "Klein and I always had a broad ability to relate," she said. "Great discussions—that never went away. Playing music—that never went away. I said to Donald—Donald's my boyfriend—It's not like Klein and I are out of each other's life, we're just out of each other's hair." (7)

The tour opened at General Motors Place in Vancouver on May

14, 1998. Joni said of Dylan, "He greeted me after the show in Vancouver, he went on last that night, and it was a difficult show for me because I am not used to playing big sports arenas, and there was a lot of going for beer, and a lot of talking really loud through all of the shows. It seemed to be that that crowd had come for the beer and the event itself—not to listen, just to be at it, you know? And I thought that it was a shame. And you have three people that are really listened-to artists, it's O.K. if there's no lyrical text or something, but I assumed that this was gonna be a writer's tour, so I picked a set for Bobby. And I think he did for me too—because he put in one of the best line-ups of songs that I've seen him do for a long time." (7)

On May 16 and 17 they headlined the Gorge Amphitheater in George, Washington. On May 19, they were at San Jose Arena, May 21 and 22 at the Pauley Pavilion on the UCLA campus, and on May 23 at Arrowhead Pond Arena in Anaheim, California. One of the most enjoyable aspects of this tour for Joni was the fact that she was able to use her new VG-8 guitar. It enabled a technician offstage to automatically tune Joni's guitar for her between songs, without anyone touching the actual guitar. This freed Joni up to just relax and perform.

Another enjoyable aspect of the tour was the duo she shared the bill with. Joni had known Van Morrison for years, as they were both part of The Band's big *Last Waltz* album and film. But she was especially close to Bob Dylan. "I love Bobby," Joni claims. "I think Bobby thinks of himself as not friendly. I think he just thinks of himself that way. But I'm very fond of him, and over the years we had a lot of encounters, and most of the discussion has been about painting, actually. No, he can do whatever he wants as far as I'm concerned. He's one of those people like Miles [Davis], you know? Even if he wasn't up to it that night—or, I saw a performance where he just kinda 'cruised'—whatever it was, I would always be curious about the next. Because he's kind of untouchable in a lot of ways." (7)

Speaking of Dylan's slightly skewed way of thinking, Joni claims, "I don't think I'm prejudiced against any words per se, except the ones that come up psychology, because they've ruined the English language—neurotic, ego. Doctors love to levy neurotic at just about every woman who crosses their threshold. I had trouble with God for a while. I cornered Bob Dylan at a party one time and said, 'You're always throwing that "God" word in. What does "God" mean to you?' He said, 'It's just a word people use.' I said, 'Yeah, but you're using it. What does it mean?' And, he couldn't answer me. Then he went through his born-again thing about three years later and he came up to me: 'Joni, remember the time you asked me about God and the Devil? I'll tell you now.' And he launched into some real Christian rhetoric. I said, 'No, no. I didn't ask you about the Devil. It's God I was having problems with." (55)

Reviewing the show at Anaheim's Arrowhead Pond, Mikal Gilmore claimed in *Rolling Stone*, "All three rock & roll-era icons who have endured bouts of hard neglect and have come through those experiences with a solitary integrity and courage . . . Mitchell favored the pastel-toned sound that characterizes her more recent albums, *Night Ride Home* and *Turbulent Indigo* . . . this ascetic approach seemed tuneful and intimate, and presented Mitchell as a singer who is sensual yet reserved . . . It was a triumphant occasion—not just for Dylan, who has fought his way back from pop disdain to renewed critical and public acclaim, but also for Morrison and Mitchell . . . Dylan, Joni Mitchell and Van Morrison are artists who continue to make essential music and who still have the power to state their own terms and contexts for their art." (134)

As soon as this successful leg of the Mitchell/Dylan/Morrison tour was completed, there were already talks about doing another leg in the fall—which ultimately did happen. However, now that she was warmed up again by performing in front of tens of thousands of people each night, Joni was ready to stand in front of a more intimate audience and tape a TV special. It was staged for a very successful pay-per-view cable TV event, and it was later released on video, laser disc, and DVD as *Painting with Words and Music*.

The *Painting with Words and Music* special was taped on May 29–30, 1998, at Warner Bros. Studios, Stage 22, in Burbank, California. It was a theater-in-the-round stage setup, with Joni looking and sounding fresh, relaxed, and very lively. The audience was seated around her on sofas arranged on sequentially elevating risers. Among the celebrities and elite audience members present for the taping were actress Rosanna Arquette and ex-boyfriend Graham Nash. Joni included her career-spanning selections "Big Yellow Taxi," "Hejira," "Amelia," "Trouble Man," "Face Lift," "Moon at the Window," "Sex Kills," and "Just Like This Train" in her performance.

During the taped concert, right before she started singing "Woodstock," Graham stood up and came to the stage with something sticking out of a green plastic shopping bag in his hand. "I have a small present for Joan that I've been carrying around for almost a year," he announced to the audience. "She did not get into music to win awards," he said. "Millions of men's hearts maybe." (135)

After talking for several moments about his admiration of Joni, he took the item out of the plastic bag, and in front of the gathered crowd, he presented her with her trophy signifying her induction into the Rock & Roll Hall of Fame. As Nash announced that he had been inducted the same evening, she leaned toward her microphone and said, "But I was a no-show." (135)

"I'm sorry I didn't wrap this a little more genteelly," Graham said as he looked at the plastic bag with the black and gold trophy sticking out. Not missing a beat, Joni sarcastically chimed in, "It's perfect in a garbage bag," and emitted a wry laugh.

Graham announced, "On behalf of Jan Wenner and the people at the museum, into the Rock & Roll Hall of Fame goes Joni Mitchell." (135) With that, she received a standing ovation. It made for quite an amusing moment in the show. Her mixed feelings about the trophy showed on her face. Without skipping a beat, she went right back into her own introduction of the song "Woodstock."

She was still unhappy with the Rock & Roll Hall of Fame, and she often took pleasure in zapping it with criticism. She announced later that year of some of the accolades she had recently received, "That's what most of my honors felt like: They knew they had to do it but they . . . weren't quite sure what to [say to] illuminate in the work." (11)

Something monumental happened on August 15, 1998, when Joni finally appeared on the site of the original Woodstock music festival—the legendary Yasgur's Farm—twenty-nine years after the famed event that she immortalized in song. The anniversary event was entitled A Day in the Garden, and also on the bill that day were Woodstock alumni Melanie, Richie Havens, Donovan, and Pete Townshend [The Who], as well as two performers who did not play at the original event: Lou Reed and Joni. Lou took a

"Walk on the Wild Side," and Joni took her fans on a walk down the jazzy side.

In great voice and wonderful spirits that day, Joni enthralled the crowd, who casually smoked marijuana joints on the sloping hill that once housed the most famous rock music festival of all time. Said an amused Mitchell onstage at the Bethel, New York, event, "[It only] took thirty years to get here!" She performed several songs from her forthcoming album, *Taming the Tiger*, but when she launched into her signature song, "Woodstock," the crowd went into true Age of Aquarius ecstasy. The entire daylong event was a magical musical tour into Woodstock memories. It was a big treat to see how Woodstock legends Melanie, Havens, Donovan, and Townshend looked and sounded in the 1990s. And it was a huge thrill to finally see Joni on the stage she had so longed to grace in the summer of 1969.

The funny thing is that Joni is still saddled with the weight of the image she had when she first became a singing star. She is perceived as a folk diva extraordinaire, a sort of Woodstock/hippie goddess. This didn't always please her. As she explained it, "A lot of hippie politics were nonsense to me. I guess I found the idea of going from authority to no authority too extreme. And I was supposed to be the 'hippie queen,' so I had a sense of isolation about the whole thing. I've always had a different perspective—an artist is a sideliner, not a joiner; they must have a certain clarity and depth, which is burdensome and really inconvenient for fun." (15)

On September 9, Joni was interviewed by journalist Jody Denberg at Hotel Bel-Air in Los Angeles. It was broadcast on radio station KGSR-FM in Austin, Texas, the next month, and it was released as a promotional disc entitled *A Conversation with Joni Mitchell*. In addition to her other appearances during this era, on September 18, Joni performed a solo set during a fund-raising benefit for the Old Town School of Folk Music in Chicago.

One of the songs that Joni sang in concert throughout 1998 was the Marvin Gaye classic "Trouble Man," which was originally written as the theme song to a long-forgotten film of the same name. What remains is a moody and brilliantly written song by Gaye. "I love that song," Joni claimed. "I've played that song over and over. I'd only do the ones that I play over and over and over. I own them in a certain way because of my love of them. I love that song. I sang that at the Stormy Weather concert also." (7)

Joni made an outstanding appearance on Kyle Eastwood's jazz album debut, *From Here to There*. She can be heard singing her new, jazzy version of "Trouble Man" with Kyle's bass accompaniment. Eastwood is the son of actor/director Clint Eastwood and has appeared in his dad's films *The Bridges of Madison County*, *Honky Tonk Man*, *Bronco Billy*, and *The Outlaw Josie Wales*. His smoky-sounding jazz album, with Joni as one of the guest stars, was released on September 15, 1998.

Just when it looked like Joni had run out of new musical styles to explore, she managed to find a new "mood indigo" in which to pour all of her deepest, darkest thoughts on life and love. On *Taming the Tiger* Mitchell examines in song the subjects of love lost (her cat), love found (Kilauren), events from the headlines, the Rock & Roll Hall of Fame, and her ongoing relationship with her mother, and she even had a song with lyrics by then boyfriend Donald Freed.

According to her, "I like the way this record turned out, plus my stock has risen lately with Janet Jackson sampling me in her hit "Got 'Til It's Gone" and with my becoming a tabloider. More heads are turning at airports these days." (132)

Indeed, ever since the *Globe* ran the headline story entitled, "Songbird Joni Searches for Love Child" in its July 12, 1994, issue, Joni *was* big news. But oddly, in spite of the two Grammy Awards, a huge 1997 feature in *Vanity Fair* magazine, and her 1998 touring, she still wasn't selling records at a retail level. Of *Turbulent Indigo* she lamented, "The record didn't sell enough units to recoup the cost of making it." (133) Amazing to think about. Here she was at the top of her game, and she was being treated like a curious musical find from *Jurassic Park*.

Joni had plenty of new dragons to slay. She had to admit that year, "I'm not a typical artist of my generation, as my driving will isn't broken down. I haven't even peaked yet," Mitchell says. "I'm a serious musician in that I'm in it for the music. Unfortunately, this doesn't always make a record company happy. The pattern is to knock people for trying new things, and I've had my fair share of two-star reviews. I experiment because I'm restless and get bored easily . . . It's a racket, a business of wet dreams, and what chance in hell does that leave women in their 50s? Companies hang on to you for prestige but won't do anything to promote your work, especially if the public voice has criticized you. It's like being an athlete all suited up but sitting on the bench. It's hard to endure, but most artists will have to live it." (132)

Mitchell says the problem stems from constant pandering to whatever is currently "hip." She explains, "Instead of enthusiasm for something original, you hear, 'Well, what are we going to do with that?' The system trains people to be purchasers manipulated by hip, in and out, hot and not hot. But 'hip' is hindsight, so I stood my ground and plowed on. If you avoid doing what's cool, you won't have bell-bottom pants on your songs down the road." (132)

During 1998 Joni was busy working on her latest album. According to her, she was extremely happy with the way her new recordings had been turning out. "The last album I did was an attempt to express my contempt for music while creating a fresh approach to it, right?" she asks. "Who cares? So I thought this is a different way. Instead of trying to do it myself, let me display what I think was the best music of the century. 'See here? Remember this? This was music!' It just seemed like a reminder had to [be] made of what the bloody stuff is supposed to be—and who was great. Today, you see all these little puff creatures with unbelievably little talent. That's what the record company wants." (136)

During the recording process she proclaimed, "The music is coming out real fresh. It's not like I've hit a pocket—there's still growth going on; there's still excitement there. And the painting is really growing. But every time you put the brushes down you lose your chops. You go and do press and come back. Everything's always cooling off and heating up and cooling off. I've got 30 canvasses sitting in the garage, panoramic two-feet-by-six-feet shapes. And I'm just itching to do them. I know what they're going to be, but I need the time for execution." (2)

She also felt invigorated about the material she had created, and the way the compositions took form. "The writing is superior, really—but like rap," she said. "It's at the cost of melody to a certain degree. Although . . . it's more like jazz melody, it's conversational improvisation around a known melody. Except I don't really state the melody." (7)

Explaining her concurrent writing, she said, "When I sit down to write a song I have to introvert and introvert, because I like to scrape a little bit of how I'm feeling around me and all of that. But I'm tired of scraping my own soul because of what the press does to you. So I'm a little defensive in that way, yet I like it in the songs. It gives them depth. And I like the drama. I like to have the characters in an anti-heroic situation with a ray of light coming in." (2)

However, she did not hesitate to complain that "it's hard to write 10 good songs. I know the fellow that runs my website said, 'You used to put records out one a year.' And I did for a long time—and I think that the standard of writing on them is pretty even. People listen to it and for one year they've got three favorites, and then they put it on five years later and some of the ones they didn't even notice suddenly mean something, because they're all about different themes. So either you've experienced that—and if you have, then you're closer to the songs, so you know. But music now is so disposable. Like this new album [*Taming the Tiger*]—I'm very proud of it, I think the standard is high, I'm very proud of the composition, the tools were available. I play nearly everything." (7)

As the release date approached, Joni prepared herself for whatever reception *Taming the Tiger* was welcomed with. It seemed that jazz artists often accepted her the most readily. For example, sax master Joshua Redman covered her song "I Had a King" on his 1998 *Timeless Tales* album. "I don't have a false modesty. I know the work is good, but I appreciate the compliment that covers are. You can never hear enough nice things," said Joni. She also claimed she was tired of being "told I'm poop when I'm great, and great when I'm poop, by the looming public voice. Not that anyone should feel sorry for me," she adds. "I'm not a starving artist, and my career let me meet great people and see the world. I've had a hankering to explore my painting more. After all, my music bought a lot of oil paint." (132)

On September 29, 1998, Reprise Records released Joni Mitchell's twentieth album, *Taming the Tiger*. Many unique elements distinguish this album from its predecessor. Now divorced from Larry Klein, she resumed producing her songs by herself for this disc. And she was able to use her new self-tuning guitar on the tracks. The packaging for *Taming the Tiger* gave Joni enough room to display a dozen of her paintings on nice high-gloss stock paper on the cover and throughout the enclosed lyric booklet. On the cover of the album is a self-portrait of Joni with one of her cats. On her head she wears a large yellow straw hat. It too is reminiscent of Vincent Van Gogh in pose and execution.

The album opens with "Harlem in Havana," an exotic musical story about being underage and sneaking into a titillating traveling carnival sideshow. Joni's amusing lyrics enliven this tale of a girlie spectacle, starring women of color dancing seductively to a Cuban beat. The track has a sparse and hauntingly forbidden sound to it, with Larry Klein playing the bass, Brian Blade on drums, and Wayne Shorter's slinky sax. Femi Jiya is heard as the circus barker. They all work intricately together toward bringing it vibrantly to life. Joni is heard on the multitracked guitar part, which here is accredited as the "guitar orchestra."

The first song Joni composed entirely on the VG-8 was the first track on this album. She explained, "You'd never know it was in standard tuning because I haven't played in standard tuning for 30 years. I don't know how to play in standard tuning, so I treated standard tuning like it was a new tuning and used my repertoire of shapes. It's that I'm using a strange piece of music. The guitar sound that I'm using is like a marimba, but it's not like any marimba part you've ever heard because it's fingerpicked. The bass string is almost atonal and sounds almost like a didgeridoo. But off of it I'm building huge horn sections, and the poem that's going to it is about two little girls in my hometown getting into this black revue called Harlem in Havana, which was an Afro-Cuban burlesque kind of show that you weren't supposed to stand in front of, let alone go in." (18)

"Man from Mars" is a stark and slinky lament about Joni's pet on the run, with snappy snare drums, that communicates heartfelt sadness over the loss of a friend. Delving further into the *Grace of My Heart* saga, Mitchell explains the bizarre history of the song. First Allison Anders asked Joni to write a song for a grieving scene in the film *Grace of My Heart*.

According to Joni, "'I told her, 'I want to do it, but I'm not a hack. I can't write on cue, and the only song I have in me now is "I hate show biz." She told me to write that song and she'd fit it somewhere. Meanwhile, my cat Nietzsche, who my boyfriend called Man From Mars because he walks on two legs and looks like a classic Martian, had taken to piddling everywhere. I got mad and told him, 'If you want to act like an animal, you'll live like one.' I put him outside, and he gave me a look of betrayal before taking off. I was trying to write the song but was going through all the emotions of loss and guilt. I hung fliers and would search the neighborhood at night. After 17 days, I had written the grieving song Allison needed based on my loss." (132) The very next day, the cat she called "Man from Mars" returned home. The song was stripped from the *Grace of My Heart* soundtrack album but it finds the perfect home here.

"Love Puts on a New Face" is another song out of Joni's "I love France" series. A slow song that flows on Wayne Shorter's lilting saxophone touches, here the troubadour sings that in France they claim that every day "love puts on a new face." This fable-turned-song sounds like her long-distance love affair with Donald Freed. In the lyrics to the song, "he" longs for her to be there with him, and "she" tells him to send her pictures—till they meet again. This song is close to the kind of revealing diary-like music that made her *Blue* album so gripping and fascinating.

On "Lead Balloon" Joni gets to let the venom out of her many years worth of frustration with Jan Wenner's two enterprises: *Rolling Stone* magazine and now the Rock & Roll Hall of Fame. She really gets her message across, and this is the LP's only genuine rocker. It has a driving sound, like something out of her *Dog Eat Dog* genre of work.

As she explained it, "I've written a rock song. It's called 'Lead Balloon.' I wrote it for the Rock & Roll Hall of Fame. It begins, 'You can kiss my ass,'" proclaimed Joni. (2) Indeed, the guitars wail, as does Wayne Shorter's masterful sax. Here she complains that she is pissed at Jan Wenner and his sanctimonious position as head of the Rock & Roll Hall of Fame. She realized that if you are not on Wenner's good side, you can kiss your induction good-bye. The message of this song: Don't fuck with Joni!

Joni surveys the headlines in "No Apologies," and her findings are not positive. There was a highly publicized case in the news during this era, in which an American military man in Japan raped a little girl, and the military's reaction was basically "oops, sorry." It was a deplorable incident, and Joni doesn't mince words expressing her disgust. According to her, "The introspective artist is like a canary in a coal mine in that they are the first to feel things. If they are worth a salt, they should turn a jaundiced eye toward society and look for a vaccine. That's the difference between artists and stars. Stars are only concerned with twinkling." (132)

"No Apologies" lets Joni lament the decay in today's world. Following the senseless rape of the Japanese girl, she finds all of America being "laid to waste" at the hands of drug lords, crooked lawyers, and sleazy loan sharks.

The tiger Joni is wrestling with in "Taming the Tiger" is the record business itself. She had already logged thirty years in it, and try as she might, she can't seem to tame it. In the lyrics of this song she lets out her venom, casting herself as a "runaway" from the "biz." She disdainfully calls the kind of music that is proliferated on 1990s radio genuine "junk food" aimed at "juveniles."

The song "The Crazy Cries of Love" features music by Joni and lyrics by Don Freed. It is a song of love found that is accentuated by the sounds of Wayne Shorter's atmospheric saxophone. This song is every bit as good in sound and execution as anything found in *Hejira*. With Shorter's sax punctuating her singing, Joni weaves a jazzy, sexy spell about love and lovemaking. It is another highly revealing episode from her diary, and it is quintessential Joni.

"Stay in Touch" is a slow and somber song of love and hope written about Joni's boyfriend Donald. Joni's voice sounds like honey here, truly connecting with the meaning of every word, and cooing her lyrics longingly into the microphone. Again Shorter's sax is an integral part of the song. According to Mitchell, "Wayne is an undervalued, amazing talent. He crawls over notes and has a relationship with them. He is welcome to scribble all over my songs." (132)

There is a slight misconception about the meaning and inspiration for the song "Stay in Touch." Many assumed that it is about Joni's reunion with her daughter, Kilauren. It was Kilauren's boyfriend, Teddy, who perpetuated the erroneous assumption.

Explains Joni, "Speaking as a poet, I write a song, say 'Stay in Touch' on this album, and I know what I wrote it about. When my daughter and her boyfriend came, Teddy heard it and said, 'Kilauren, that's song's about you.' Well, it was—it was about the beginning unsteadiness in a very passionate new relationship. Any time I have a passionate new relationship, that song will come to life in a new way. If it's overly explained, you rob the people whose lives it brushes up against of their own interpretation and their own experience." (7)

According to Joni, someone will say something, and a perfect song lyric arises from an everyday sentence. "'Happiness is the best facelift,' for instance—I said that to my boyfriend one day, and he said 'Write that down'—or it would've gone up in the air, you know? I think that's a useful phrase," she recalls. (7)

The slow story song "Face Lift" is literally about Joni coming home to Saskatoon for Christmas and feuding with her mother. It seems that Joni had scandalously cavorted with her boyfriend Donald while staying in her parents' home. Caught up in one of those, "What will the neighbors think?" moments, Joni tells her mother to lighten up, as a smile is the world's best face-lift. Says Mitchell, "It's about a Romeo and Juliet situation. It's a love song between a mother and daughter. You know, parental disapproval." (1)

Joni found that still—in her mid-fifties—she was having disagreements with her mother, as though she were a teenager. "I think she's getting used to it," said Joni. "I keep saying, 'It's not our song, Mum, anymore.' This is so many people's story. This is a story of mothers and daughters; I can say now that I have my own back. There are bad Christmases from time to time. There's a big moral breach. Before I was separated from my husband, my mother introduced us to the man who later became my boyfriend. But the divorce had not come through; as far as she was concerned I was living in sin, flaunting my Hollywood ways in their faces, in their town—humiliating them. I said, 'Who am I humiliating you in front of? Your generation is all dead. There are no witnesses as far as I can see.' My generation is not as intolerant of this. So that's a generation gap song. The funny part of it is, that she's 86 and I'm 55—or 50 when the song occurred." (7)

"My Best to You" was written in 1942 by Gene Willadsen and Isham Jones for the Sons of the Pioneers. On this track Joni is accompanied by country pedal steel guitar wizard Greg Leisz, and it ends the album on a joyous note. It is the most bubbly and effervescent song on the album. With steel pedal guitar, and what sounds like a calliope of some sort, Joni delivers a parting message of optimism, with a cheery "Happy Trails" kind of message to it.

According to Joni, "The record just keeps sailing up this optimistic note. The last song on it is an old Sons of the Pioneers cover. It's a goodwill toast . . . It builds to optimism." (2)

Just when you think the album is over, after many long seconds of "dead air" a "hidden" last track comes onto the speakers. It is a song Joni calls "Tiger Bones," and it is an all-instrumental version of "Taming the Tiger," with her own voice stripped off the track. It is beautiful just to hear her play her guitar and keyboard. The album ends on a finely crafted note.

As she had done on *Turbulent Indigo*, for this album she placed one of her self-portraits on the front. The booklet that accompanied *Taming the Tiger* again became a showcase for several of her oil paintings, in a sort of minigallery. For the cover of this album Joni chose to use a portrait of herself in a straw hat, holding one of her cats, playing into the tongue-in-cheek feline-themed title of the album. In the liner notes Joni wrote, "And special thanks to Kilauren and Marlin just for being in the world." (137)

The reviews for *Taming the Tiger* were exceptionally glowing. In *Time* magazine Christopher John Farley proclaimed, "*Tiger* is composed of crystalline tones; breezy guitars that ring like wind chimes; crisp, jazzy vocals. A few of the songs attack pop radio ('Boring!' she sings). On other numbers Mitchell gets more personal, recounting her mother's disapproval of her live-in boyfriend . . . *Taming the Tiger*, whose title song was inspired by 18th Century poet William Blake, is a tough sell—unless you're selling it to fans of 18th Century English poetry. But Joni will be Joni when the trends have trended out. To paraphrase Blake, she still burns bright." (129)

Billboard illuminated, "The 11 tracks on *Taming The Tiger* are an extension of Mitchell's longtime love affair with smooth jazz, ambient new age soundscapes, layered sounds, and poetic lyrics chock-full of allusions and metaphors. Opener 'Harlem In Havana' invites listeners to step right up to a bouncy tune fashioned after traditional carnival-midway music . . . Next is Mitchell's lament for her lost cat, 'Man From Mars,' followed by a ballad of anguish and love called 'Love Puts On A New Face' . . . Mitchell picks up the pace for 'Lead Balloon' and delivers some of her folk-roots sound on 'Face Lift.'" (132)

And Neil Strauss in the *New York Times* wrote, "*Taming the Tiger* is a beautifully sung jazz, rock and classical fusion album, neatly extending Mitchell's body of work. In the tradition of *The Hissing of Summer Lawns* and *Hejira*, it is a self-produced, meticulous album that incorporates jazz musicians and harmonies, but stands on its own as a complete composition." (11)

In spite of the great reviews, *Taming the Tiger* didn't set the world on fire at the cash register. The album peaked in the United States at number 75; in the United Kingdom, it made number 57.

In mid-1998 Joni announced, "I'm going to record with Herbie Hancock, he's doing an album of Gershwin tunes. Stevie Wonder's going to be there too. I've got a choice of three songs. I think with Frank Sinatra's death and all, there's a resurgence of interest in that era. Of eras of music, I would say, I'm a swing baby. I love the swing beat. Even though my music doesn't reflect all kinds of music that I love, it eventually will." (7)

Released on October 30, 1998, the promised Herbie Hancock album composed of all George Gershwin tunes, *Gershwin's World*, featured Joni Mitchell on two masterful tracks. It is a delightful album of pure jazz, with several jazz masters playing on it, including Chick Corea, Ira Coleman, and Joni's dear friend Wayne Shorter. Mitchell and Wonder are the pop celebrities who make the album's most dazzling guest appearances. Stevie does a great vocal and harmonica version of "St. Louis Blues" with Hancock. And Joni sings lead vocal on two Gershwin classics: "Summertime" and "The Man I Love."

The *Gershwin's World* album went on to win a Grammy as the Best Jazz Instrumental Performance, Individual or Group, and the song "St. Louis Blues" won the Grammy for the Best Instrumental Arrangement Accompanying Vocal(s). Having sung jazz at the Walden Woods Event, having performed a jazz version of "Trouble Man" with Kyle Eastwood, and now having sung jazz with Herbie Hancock, Joni was in the right frame of mind to consider recording her own all-jazz standards album.

Meanwhile, Van Morrison, Joni Mitchell, and Bob Dylan embarked on a new eleven-date tour between October 23 and November 7, which took them to the Target Center in Minneapolis; United Arena in Chicago; Market Square Arena in Indianapolis; the Palace of Auburn Hills in the Detroit area; Maple Leaf Garden in Toronto; Corel Center in Kanata, Ontario; New York City's Madison Square Garden; War Memorial Arena in Syracuse, New York; Blue Cross Arena in Rochester; Cole Field House in College

Park, Maryland; and finally Alexander Arena in Atlanta. The last night coincided with Joni's fifty-fifth birthday. To commemorate it, her band brought a cake onstage at the end of the concert.

Although the tour was a triumphant one, not every press review was glowing. Not every critic was happy with the fact that Joni Mitchell was no longer the folk waif they once fell in love with. As she had predicted so long ago, she was now a multilayered, more complex version of the "women of heart and mind," whom she had once glorified in song. Yet many people still wanted her to be the folk troubadour of yore.

Reviewing her performance at Madison Square Garden—as well as the material included on *Taming the Tiger*—in the *Village Voice*, writer Steve Anderson complained, "Saskatoon, we have a problem: contentment, spreading its sly placation. Sure the album has vitriol—toward lawyers and military callousness in the Japanese rape case, or that ever-reliable Great Satan, the biz. But when Mitchell intends to be angry she ends up sounding perturbed . . . At the Garden, Mitchell avoided everything preceding 1974's jazzy renaissance, *Court and Spark*, except for two worn Earthshoes from *Ladies of the Canyon*, 'Big Yellow Taxi' and 'Woodstock.' What infuriates her now is her inability to elude the long shadow cast by her early albums, especially the back-to-back hippie twilight masterworks, *Blue* and *For the Roses* . . . the Yuletide numbness on 'Face Lift' can't touch the regret suffusing *Blue*'s ineffable 'River.' Likewise, the title cut's denunciation of current pop culture was more powerful on *For the Roses* . . . dulcimers can blow away a Roland VG-8 any old time." (138) Instead of being judged for her current merits, Joni often found herself competing with herself and the legend she created. Undaunted, she decided to forge ahead on the path she chose.

"I feel pregnant with creativity, and all that touring represents to me is a delay until I can be creative," Joni claimed at the time. "I'm responsible to the company, and the company wants me to tour. In the meantime I'm probably going to lose 20 songs, by being cooperative to the game. To be responsible to the creativity, I should go on strike right now and get into my pajamas. Most of my career right after I made an album I would run away; I'd go to Europe. I'm glad I did. While I was running away from the last record, I'd be writing the new one because I'd be having a life." (11)

There now was a strong connective thread between Joni's paint-ing and her music. More than ever before, since the mid-1990s Joni's albums have become showcases for her paintings, sketches, and other artwork. Comparing her musical sounds to her tech-nique with a paintbrush, she explained during this era, "It's like a wash. In painting, if I start a canvas now, to get rid of the vertigo of the blank page, I cover the whole thing in olive green, then start working the color into it. So every color is permeated with that green. It doesn't really green the colors out, but it antiques them, burnishes them. The drones kind of burnish the chord in the same way. That color remains as a wash. These other colors then drop in, but always against that wash." (18)

Several incidents during this era caused Joni to take a hard look at her long and exciting career. She was startled by female imper-sonator John Kelly's presentation of a whole act of Joni Mitchell music. At first it was a shock seeing a man dressed in drag, per-forming her songs as her. As she explained, "There are some things that I'm prejudiced against in my early work. I think they're the work of an ingénue, and I'm miscast in them now. I don't do them [in concert] for that reason. However, I saw this female im-personator, John Kelly, and he did a lot of my early work beauti-fully—from a spirit point of view, beautifully—and he's in his mid-thirties I think. And, in drag, to boot, and singing in a tenor voice, some of them, not even imitating me, just singing them with all his heart. He sang 'Night in the City,' which I think of as a child-like ditty, and like was a ghost at my own funeral I saw the audi-ence respond and I heard the song, it gave me some perspective on it that I never had. Not that in a limited show that I feel the need to include it. I'm out for a long time. What I felt when I put this show together, the necessity was to run by these songs that had become considered obscure and difficult." (7)

Although she was playing to sold-out audiences on the Mitchell/Dylan/Morrison tour and on the fall leg with Bob, she was still feeling abandoned by her current record company. "The [music] industry dropped me for 20 years. They wouldn't let me in. No matter what I did, they wouldn't let me on the radio [or] on MTV." (129) She wasn't going to take her discontent quietly ei-ther!

She loudly complained, "The last 20 years I've had no record company support, no radio support—the marketplace has been denied me, so I think a lot of those records, there's a bigger audience for it than it received. *Chalk Mark in a Rain Storm* really deserves a big audience, as big as anything the contemporary females have. It's not difficult music. I was disappointed that the company couldn't somehow or other—I was disappointed in the industry at large, that had closed me out from the marketplace, so to speak, that no one would allow me the normal venues that are open to announce that you have product out, with pride. Or that nobody saw. Except Janet Jackson saw it—and she touted it in her interview . . . The best review I got for that record was from Janet Jackson. Yeah, and it really please me, it touched me." (7)

It certainly wasn't that she had lost her muse. As she explained it, "I have to scrape my soul to write songs, and I had a lot of spiritual/material conflict at the time. I was trying to reconcile a climate that had a genuine leaning toward the spiritual and a stylish leaning toward the spiritual. That kind of thing is O.K. if you're a playwright, but not if you're a singer." (15)

Even though *Taming the Tiger* was a critical smash, she was still knocking her head against a brick wall when it came to getting noticed on the radio. By this point in musical history, pop and rock music was even more "throwaway," and stars were more dispensable than ever before. Record companies were now creating one-shot projects, not careers. Case in point: Hootie and the Blowfish had the hugest debut album of all time, but the group's next three albums were each less successful and more obscure than its predecessor. How was Joni going to compete in a market like this?

She lamented at the time, "When I did the *Mingus* project, I was advised what it would cost me. I took that seriously but I couldn't believe that I would lose my airplay. It kicked me right out of the game. It was a great experience, one of my fondest . . . I would do it today even knowing what it costs, but it certainly cost me. It took me some years to get back in it. And my work is still reviewed but radios stations don't play me. VH1 and MTV don't even touch me." (11)

Yet in the early 1990s, when the grunge movement came out of Seattle and Nirvana was the biggest thing since sliced bread, Joni sat in amazement. The frosting on the cake came when Nirvana's lead singer, Kurt Cobain, shot himself at the magical age of twenty-seven. Was this a coincidence or was it calculated? At twenty-seven, Jimi Hendrix, Janis Joplin, *and* Jim Morrison all perished and went on to rock immortality. Joni stated with disdain, "Everybody says Kurt Cobain was a great writer. I don't see it. Why is he a hero? Whining and killing yourself—I fail to see the heroism in that." (129)

One of the things that really got her goat was the fact that there was now—in the 1990s—a whole wave of female guitar-wielding performers who were all heralded as "the next Joni Mitchell." There was Tori Amos, Lisa Loeb, Alanis Morrisette, Joan Osbourne, and a whole raft of others. What the hell was wrong with playing music on the radio by the *real* Joni Mitchell? The pop/folk/rock/jazz diva was sick and tired of being "referred to as 'high-minded' and dismissed while watching cheap imitations use my name to launch careers and go Platinum. If you can like them, why can't you like me?" she says. "It's better for you and almost tastes the same. It's provocative and might take a little thinking, but the rewards are limitless when the product is good." (132)

Whenever Mitchell gets pinned as a "heritage artist," she gets really pissed off: "I have to compete with myself and often get panned for not playing my old stuff. I was careful to stay out of '60s and '70s repackaging so as not to be wrapped up and kissed off for early retirement. My chords reflect my complex life, which is why my simple old songs don't suit me. It's good folky pop music, but it's like primary colors when you like aubergine [deep purple]. It's hard to know who I'm addressing, knowing that my generation doesn't buy records and typical younger ones reject me as their parents' contemporary." (132)

In spite of throwing up much for her to complain about, the year 1998 was another magical one for Joni. She took time to reflect on all that she did have in her life. "I don't need more fame," she claimed. "I don't need more fortune, but I believe in the work. It's an altruistic thing. It's good for people, you know?" (127)

She was still marveling at having Kelly/Kilauren back in her life: "I'm involved with family and the socializing process, which is something very exciting and very different." (11)

She still had her writing sanctuary in British Columbia: "It's a place where I kind of restore my soul. I'm the gardener and the cook and the housekeeper, and I'm alone in nature. I've had some colorful adventures up in that particular place. I've battled with bears in my apple tree." (127)

And she still had her famous indulgences—cigarettes and liquor: "I still have a few vices. You can't get too clean and self-righteous. Every once in a while I like to go out and get really drunk." (127)

The year 1998 was a truly great and triumphant one for Joni Mitchell. Her millions of fans were thrilled that she had embarked on a high-profile concert tour. She received excellent reviews for *Taming the Tiger*. And, thanks to her participation in the Walden Woods Project event, she now had a fresh concept for her next album. No, she didn't exactly tame the monstrous "tiger," as she viewed the record business star-making machinery, but she sure gave it a big old kick in the ass! Witnessing her drive and creativity in 1998, what could one say but: "You *go*, Joni!"

22

Both Sides Now

In thirty years, Joni Mitchell released twenty unique albums. With rare exceptions, she did not record compositions she had not written. She used her albums to promote her own songwriting, and they became showcases for some of the most personal music of the rock era. Never once did Joni flirt with a foreign musical genre, if it required singing someone else's songs. There was never a *Joni Does Motown* album, or *Joni Sings the Patsy Cline Songbook*, or even a *Merry Christmas from Joni*. The closest she came was the *Mingus* album, and that was a collaborative effort.

What was the reason for this? According to her, it was never even a remote possibility. "I've never been able to. By contract. It was disallowed," she claims. (7) Her albums were designed as vehicles to promote her own music.

Larry Klein was instrumental in talking Joni into recording an entire album of pop and jazz standards. The Don Henley/Walden Woods event opened Joni's eyes to the possibilities. "I had to do some convincing," recalls Klein, "and I told her that once she sang with a large orchestra, she would want to do it some more. So she went ahead and did it and predictably loved it. After the event she came to me and said, 'God, I'd love to do a record like this.' A couple of the other singers who were involved in that show came to me and wanted to work with me on the same thing. So I told Joni that if she was going to do it, she should do it now, and together we began the long arduous task of producing it." (139)

One of the most alluring aspects of doing an all-jazz vocal album was the fact that it freed Joni from exploring her disdain for the music business and the state of the world. As she explained it, "I think it is in a horrible state. I don't even think of it as music anymore, but just the 'ic' business. It's 'icky' because the 'muse' is gone out of it. The divinity that it once contained is gone. Part of it is the capitalistic feeding frenzy. Music today is viewed [by corporations] as simply a [sales line] that is either going up or down . . . It's just a graph for shareholders. We don't even know who is at the top anymore of all these corporations. There used to be the chairman, who was as high up in a company as you could go, but now the chairman is just a 'piss-ant' in the larger corporation." (140)

She wasn't interested in delving into current headlines for inspiration this time around, "because my music is drawn from my [feelings] and I just didn't want to be a social commentator at this time. I feel these are difficult times and we all need to develop some type of . . . discipline or soul nourishment or strength to deal with all the problems facing the world, problems that are coming to a head in every department. Even I wouldn't want to hear an album of that stuff right now. I just feel my point of view is too realistic and reality is too bleak," she said. (140)

Since she seemed to hate the contemporary music she heard, this was a good time for her to record an album of old standards. "In a way I'd gotten to the point where I didn't like anything on the radio," Joni explains. "I hadn't really liked anything in the last 20 years, because in the '80s, when videos came along, the female began to be depicted basically as a hostile deadpan shrew in stiletto heels who wore black lipstick and ground men into the sidewalk. The early '80s was the most unromantic period ever—in terms of music. Some may like it. Some even think it got realer, but I think it lost something. I'm kind of realistic/romantic, I guess, but I do believe in the good heart. Then Foreigner came out with 'I Want to Know What Love Is,' with a video that was quite different from the trend. I loved that song. Anyway, the business has changed so much and the feminine stance in song now doesn't interest me as much as some of the '40s and '50s women." (5)

She found that music was being pumped out assembly line style. "The other thing I notice is music is being made by committees," she explains. "I received a lifetime achievement award recently from Sony and they played the year's big songs. They were horrible, one after the other . . . Drivel, commercial crap. And when people got up to receive the awards, you could see why: There were four to eight people getting up, and sometimes there was a businessman among them. A committee cannot make a work of art. Art is created by one person or two people working in unity." (140)

Furthermore, she needed to think of the new album in the works as her first album released in the twenty-first century. Did she want it to be one on which she complained about the state of the world? Obviously not. According to her, "I didn't want to think about the millennium when I wrote an album because I am too informed. I wanted a break from writing dark stuff. We're really in a terrible place as a species. If I went into the studio and did what I usually do—scrape my soul and sing about what I really think of the world—I didn't want to go through that process. I didn't want to think about how screwed up the world is, which is what would have happened if I would have gone in to write. *Taming the Tiger* had a romance to it, but it was against the backdrop of rotten lawyers, the stinking music business." (139)

She wanted to do something different and monumental. According to her, "This was an attempt to make a statement about music at the end of the 20th Century, when I feel that all away across the board that music has degenerated so disgustingly." (139)

Joni had certain ideas she wanted to incorporate into this new album. As she explained it, "I wanted to make a record that was a kind of synopsis of what I like best in twentieth-century music, but I also wanted to have an element of the modern. I wanted it to have a classical quality but I also wanted it to be cutting-edge jazz." (5)

She wanted to approach the recording of this album in a specific way. "The concept was to make an album that was a commentary on romantic love in the 20th Century," she said at the time. (136)

She had a certain sequence in mind for this concept album. According to Larry Klein, "As we began the process of selecting the songs for this record, Joni came up with the idea of having the record trace the arc of a modern romantic relationship. I thought that this idea was innovative, exciting and especially appropriate considering the focal point of her work has been an inquiry into the nature of modern love. The album would be a programmatic suite documenting a relationship from initial flirtation through optimistic consummation, metamorphosing into disillusionment, ironic despair, and finally resolving in the philosophical overview of acceptance and the possibility of the cycle repeating itself." (141)

One of the first songs Joni chose to include on the new album was Etta James's torchy ballad of finding love: "At Last." The song came to her in an unusual way: "I first heard that song, oddly enough, in a tampon commercial," she laughs. "Every time I'd hear it, I'd run towards the TV and crank it up because just as it was [fading] down in the first verse, she'd hit a couple of notes and all the hair on my arms would stand up and God came in and landed on her for four or five notes. Hardly any singers ever, no matter how good they are, get God to come in." (136)

As she began to explore other song possibilities, she got excited at the results she was having at just singing and getting into the meaning of someone else's words for a change. "I started doing these cover songs with my hands free, like I say—the liberty in it is just exciting, you know? I'd like to make a whole show out of Gershwin. The songs that I write, you see, they're not really so much for singing—they're more dramatic. Like Bob [Dylan]'s work, the prettiness of the singer, in the later work especially, is not the point—the point is to bring the words to life like a Shakespearean soliloquy. If you have to talk 'em, whatever it takes, you know? Whereas these old songs don't have a lot of words and there's plenty of time to ride the note and float, and they're real singerly material and I don't write stuff like that," she claimed. (7)

Joni came to view the making of this album as something of an acting assignment. She could use it to tap into another part of her psyche. According to her, "The '40s singers smiled and were elegant. They were drinking and having a high time, they really were more adult, there was a more graceful suffering going on. My generation was a generation of screamers, who were screaming over mountains of amplifiers—not myself per se. I was the only one on with an acoustic guitar." (7)

Other images swirled through her vivid imagination. "I love Edith Piaf and I love Billie Holiday," says Joni of her singing idols. "Ella Fitzgerald is a beautiful singer, she has perfect pitch and perfect time, but she doesn't illuminate the words—she just sings through them. 'S'wonderful, s'marvelous'—that's the way it's written, she sings through it. Whereas Billie Holiday makes you hear the content and the intent of every word that she sings—even at the expense of her pitch or tone. So of the two, Billie is the one that touches me the deepest, although I admire perfect pitch and perfect time." (7)

Speaking of her jazz master buddies, Joni explained that "Wayne and Herbie's contributions are definitely later 20th Century. I gave Wayne total liberty, because he knows how to join into my music so well. You see, what we did with this album was make something both retro and progressive. I was thinking that you would ask me about Linda Ronstadt and Carly Simon. If you see this as another girl making a cover album you are not musically informed. I hope to come in somewhere between Ella [Fitzgerald] and Billie [Holiday], and that I could bring something to the genre that very few did—to bring out the emotional readings on the text. Ella didn't really do that. As beautiful as her pitch and time were, she didn't seem to have the emotional palette of Billie. Billie lived so much, and has this warm transcendental resonation in her voice. It was distinctive. A lot of the women in the genre are hard to nail. They over-embellish. I'm actually not a huge fan of this genre. But what I love about it is the architecture, the melodic curve, the musicality of the chordal movement. But obviously, I abandoned that with the next wave." (139)

Joni was especially not accustomed to singing songs written by men. She explains, "Although a lot of the best-known songs from that era were written by men, the women who sang them tended to smile a little when they sang. That gave them a warm tone. They stood up in front of the bandstand and they were kind of decorative and they didn't talk much. They had a passive role in it. But that passive role had a grace and a dignity and a femininity and a warmth." (5)

She also found the romantic aspects of recording this album to be very alluring: "I think that romance, at least as depicted in my industry, has gotten less and less considerate. I frankly like my love affairs served up with kindness. And I think it's criminal if that's an old fashioned idea," she says. (7)

And she also felt the album was a natural move for her. "Sure this is new music for me on record, but I grew up with this. I was born in the '40's. Even when rock & roll came along, it was only on the radio from 4:00–6:00 P.M. Standards and country and western music were on the radio. So these are really my roots," claims Joni. (139)

According to Vince Mendoza, conductor and arranger for the album, "All of these songs were arranged with Joni's voice in mind. Her voice has changed a lot over the years ever since her first recording; it has gotten so much more interesting and colorful. Her delivery is so much more interesting. We see her breadth of experience now and the words mean more now than they ever did. I had her contemporary sound in my head. *Turbulent Indigo* is probably one of my most-valued albums—I know it backwards and forwards. I approached arranging every piece like a tone poem, like Strauss would write around a vocalist. Understanding the words and knowing when to move and when not to move, when to accentuate the lyrics and when not to. I learned a lot of that from Joni, how she writes and how she delivers the lyrics." (139)

Once the preproduction work was finished, the sessions for *Both Sides Now* came together quickly. The album was cut in three days in London, at George Martin's famed Air Studios. On separate days four of the songs were recorded with a full seventy-one-piece orchestra, four with a forty-two-piece ensemble, and four with a twenty-two-piece big band.

Klein said of the process, "Vince and I had been preparing the music for months, and it was quite emotional for me to hear them come to life. Her singing was just amazing. When we did 'A Case of You,' which is entirely her live vocal, the orchestra gave her a standing ovation, and half of them were weeping. It was quite amazing to see an English orchestra get that emotional." (139)

Recalls Joni, "I was surprised at how [the songs] affected the orchestra, like they jumped to their feet. A standing ovation on the first take of 'A Case of You.' They wept and blew their noses all the way through 'Both Sides Now.' That was very touching to me, because classical orchestras are typically jaded." (136)

She explained, "The goal was to keep [the album] from being a curio or merely a reflection of the past but make it progressive in some way. This is very different for me because I'm a freshness freak. And I'm pretty intolerant of copycats." (136)

Joni was very excited about the way the album was coming out. She told the *New York Times* prior to its release, "I don't like to make fluffy little songs, but now I want to make some light songs. I think that comedy comes from watching a lot of comedy. People will probably not enjoy it as much as the deep suffering that I've done in the past. And I don't even know if I can do it." (11)

While Joni was working on the *Both Sides Now* album in 1999, she stayed out of the public spotlight. On February 20 she was heard on a BBC Radio 1 broadcast entitled "Both Sides Now," being interviewed by Mary Black. On February 28 she appeared on *Musikbolaget* (Words + Music), a Swedish radio show.

On July 1, 1999, in Central Park, a tribute concert called Joni's Jazz was held. It featured an impressive list of musicians playing jazz versions of Mitchell's music. At the end of the show, Joni appeared onstage for an impromptu appearance with the musicians who had saluted her.

But the biggest thing by far to happen in Joni Mitchell's life that year was witnessing the birth of her second grandchild. "I saw Daisy when she was born. And I love my grandson. I just adore him. I don't like being a public person, especially at this time. It's the most unpleasant time in the history of the world to be famous." (20) Still, fame or no fame, she was thoroughly enjoying her new role as mother and grandmother.

The first debut of any of the material from Joni's new album came on the January 19, 2000, telecast of the TV series *Dawson's Creek*. On February 11, she was a guest on the CBC-TV series *Newsweek Magazine* from Toronto.

Prior to the release of the conventional album, Reprise Records issued a limited-edition exclusive CD version of *Both Sides Now*, in a round brown satin-covered box, resembling a hat box or a very exclusive box of chocolates. It hit the stores just in time for Valentine's Day 2000. What could be more appropriate for Valentine's Day than a satin box full of romance from Joni Mitchell? Inside the box, the album's liner notes are printed on individual square cards of lush paper stock. Also included are a quartet of four small lithographs of Joni Mitchell paintings. The limited edition version retailed for $49.98 and was issued in a run of 15,000 copies.

Explaining the final sequencing of the album, Mitchell said, "First, you are smitten—which is the first song, 'You're My Thrill,' which was a Billie Holiday recording. Then you go through facets of pleading and making concessions along the way, then the romantic love goes away and the album ends with 'Both Sides Now,' which says you don't know love at all. It's interesting, because 'Both Sides Now,' which was one of the first songs I wrote, clearly has one foot in each camp . . . old songwriting and new songwriting. The old songs were very symbolic. They used the weather a lot because they were coming out of an agrarian culture. There was a tremendous amount of references to the sky to denote emotion . . . 'You Are My Sunshine,' 'Stormy Weather.'" (140)

The regular version of the album in a standard plastic jewel case was released on March 21, 2000. Joni's twenty-first album release, *Both Sides Now* was a beautiful masterpiece. Produced by Joni, along with Larry Klein, the album begins with the buoyant "You're My Thrill." Surrounded by a lush orchestral accompaniment, Joni sounds great. It is directly followed by the dramatic "At Last," which was written by Mack Gordon and Harry Warren, and became a huge hit for Etta James in the 1950s. Here Joni infuses the song with lots of torchy convection.

"Comes Love" finds Joni deeply, hopelessly in love. Joni sounds smooth and upbeat on this swinging number by Lew Brown, Sammy Stept, and Charles Tobias. The somber "You've Changed" shows Mitchell in the beginning of a love-gone-wrong mode. This song of disillusionment by Bill Carey and Carl Fischer was made famous by Billie Holiday, and Joni gives it the right kind of bittersweet fury.

"Answer Me, My Love," penned by Gerhard Winkler and Fred Rauch with English lyrics by Carl Sigman, finds Joni begging her lover to take her back. Mitchell takes the song to emotional depths to bring this message of heartbreak to life. She knows she's been done wrong, and her voice betrays her dejected sadness.

In an unusual move, in the middle of the album Joni chose to cast one of her own songs about love gone wrong, "A Case of You," as the segment of the album when she knows the affair is over. Slowed down to a snail's pace, she milks the words of all the pathos she wrote into the lyrics originally. Here the message is all the more poignant—she finds she is better off as a solitary artist existing in her box of paints.

The second half of the album comprises songs that define the deeper spectrum of the blues. "Don't Go to Strangers," "Sometimes I'm Happy," and "Don't Worry 'bout Me" find Joni trying to keep her chin up in the face of heartbreak. On "Don't Go to Strangers" she insists that she is fine with being someone's old standby. "Sometimes I'm Happy" is the most effervescent song on the album, raising Joni's spirits and delivery in upbeat jazz fashion. The frosting on the cake comes in the middle with a great jazz piano solo by Herbie Hancock. This is one of the finest arrangements on the whole album. By the time she gets to "Don't Worry 'bout Me," she is really blue. Finally on Ted Koehler and Harold Arlen's "Stormy Weather," she goes into emotional meltdown mode as the floodgates of tears open.

Then comes the recovery phase. She takes a lighter approach with the Rodgers and Hart classic, "I Wish I Were in Love Again." Here Joni proves that she can perfectly capture the mood of some of the most beautiful music written in the twentieth century.

The album ends with Joni's more somber, world-weary version of her own composition, "Both Sides Now." Whereas she used to sing it with bright-eyed optimism, here she takes it another direction and makes it the song of someone looking back on her whole life. It is the perfect song at the perfect time in this clever and highly effective album of standards.

On the cover of the conventional album is another of Joni's self-portraits. This time around she is seen as the jilted lover that many of these songs personify. She is smoking a cigarette in a dimly lit bar. The back of the album is a painting of a reverse view, showing Joni from the rear, playing with her hair while she smokes a cigarette. The other two paintings represented in this album are a bowl of yellow roses and a bizarre portrait of Joni French-kissing her boyfriend. They appear here like painted postcards from this love affair.

The press reviews for the album were highly positive. According to Tom Moon in *Rolling Stone*, "Deep down, Joni Mitchell has always been a jazz singer . . . On *Both Sides Now*, Mitchell applies that precision to tunes that have been famously blubbered over for decades (plus two of her own songs). Where Linda Ronstadt and other pop singers who have covered jazz standards tend to lean on oversize crooning (most recently and abhorrently, George Michael), Mitchell knows that the romance vanishes when the lines are exaggerated . . . Singing atop a velvety orchestra, sounding buoyant one minute and betrayed the next, Mitchell interprets 'At Last' with slurry, smeared-paint gestures and gives 'Don't Go to Strangers' a weary, Billie Holiday-worthy soul ache. It is Mitchell's emotional generosity, not the fabulous surroundings, that winds up mattering most: After years of spinning yarns heavily dependent on words, she's telling these stories with a repertoire of gingerly placed inflections and anguished sighs, tools she's always had but never flaunted." (142)

Elysa Gardner in the *Los Angeles Times* wrote, "Predictably, her selections on *Both Sides Now* . . . show great taste, as do the warm elegant arrangements. Her vocals, which have deepened and grown seductively dusky with age, avoid the stiff reverence many contemporary singers adopt when approaching standards . . . Mitchell's mix of playfulness and understated pathos hits just the right note." (143)

In *People* magazine Steve Dougherty claimed, "Fans accustomed to Joni's soaring soprano and the spare acoustic settings of her folk/rock albums are in for a shock. Here her voice has dropped an octave or so, and she sings 10 tunes from an earlier pop era (as well as two originals) as torch songs in a husky, smoke-cured alto . . . In places, however, the melodramatic, string-heavy orchestrations featured on tracks like 'Stormy Weather' make the songwriter . . . sound more like the kind of ermine-and-pearls lounge crooner her parents might have swooned for . . . the album highlight is a richly textured reinvention of the title tune . . . the song is rendered here as a melancholy, middle-aged woman's rumination on the mysteries of love." (144)

Joni thoroughly enjoyed recording *Both Sides Now*. Again, she didn't do it for the critics' benefit but for her own creative growth and a strong desire to express herself. She claimed of this album, "If I had written songs this time, I think I'd probably have written about how sick the culture is, and I didn't want to sing that. So the writer in me blocked, out of necessity. I told my inner writer to 'shut up.' I just wanted to be a singer. I wanted to borrow from Gil Evans and from Miles [Davis], who was always my major music beacon. Even though my music doesn't sound like that, it's very influenced by them. My father understood the difference. He said, 'It's a beautiful record, Joan, but the saxophones didn't sound like that back then.' I said, 'I know they didn't.'" (5) However, what she did create was a brilliant concept album that showed her vocal talents in a new light. The fact that her father liked it was perhaps the most valuable review of all.

When the album was released, Joni did all she could to promote it in the stores. On March 22 she was a guest on Canada's CBC-TV show *SpeakEasy*. On April 3 she was a guest on the *Late Show with David Letterman* on CBS-TV and performed the song "At Last." That same day she also taped an interview by Katie Couric for the *Today* show, broadcast on April 14. And on April 4, Joni taped the *Rosie O'Donnell Show* for ABC-TV for broadcast on April 10. Joni was interviewed by Rosie and performed the songs "Answer Me, My Love" and "Both Sides Now."

On April 16, 2000, TNT's Masters Series presented *An All-Star Tribute to Joni Mitchell*. The event was hosted by actress Ashley Judd. Among the guest stars paying homage to Joni in song were Chaka Khan, James Taylor, and Diana Krall. The show closed with Joni singing her new arrangement of "Both Sides Now." The finale found Mitchell inviting the other performers to join her on the chorus of her song "The Circle Game."

The following month, Joni embarked on her most unique concert tour yet: the Both Sides Now tour, in which she performed to the accompaniment of a full orchestra. The tour opened at the Greek Theatre in Los Angeles and then went on to the Concord Pavilion in Concord, California; Mars Music Amphitheater in West Palm Beach; the Chastain Park Amphitheatre in Atlanta; the Theater at Madison Square Garden; Merriweather Post Pavilion in Columbia, Maryland; SNET Oakdale Theater in Wallingford, Connecticut; FleetBoston Pavilion in Boston; the Rosemont Theater in Rosemont, Illinois; Pine Knob Music Theater in Clarkston, Michigan; and the Sony Music Entertainment Center in Camden, New Jersey.

Joni's Both Sides Now tour was a huge success. She seemed at ease playing with a full orchestra behind her. In concert she not only sang the entire *Both Sides Now* album, but also revisited several of her signature songs with full orchestra. The outdoor venues, especially the shows at the Greek Theatre in Los Angeles, were nothing short of magical. Joni was truly in her element.

Joni continued to promote her artwork with the same enthusiasm she put into her songwriting. On June 30, 2000, she appeared at a press conference and at the grand opening of an exhibit of her art at the Mendel Art Gallery in Saskatoon. Mendel Art Gallery also published a retrospective book of Joni's paintings called *Voices: The Work of Joni Mitchell*. Amid color plates of her paintings, Mitchell commented on what inspired each of these works.

Things went quite well for Joni in 2000. According to her, "I have a very good relationship with a man from my hometown. He still lives there. We get together and travel. We are old enough where we are comfortable with a long-distance romance. In our youth, I don't think we could have done it. It's a growing, flowering relationship of nearly seven years. Plus, I have really good friends who I love. I have cats I love. I have a daughter I love. I have grandchildren I love. These are all different kinds of love, but lasting love." (140)

On January 3, 2001, when nominations for the forty-third annual Grammy Awards were announced, Joni's *Both Sides Now* album was up for honors in three separate categories. In the Best Female Pop Vocal Performance category Joni was nominated for the song "Both Sides Now." She was competing against Christina Aguilera's "What a Girl Wants," Macy Gray's "I Try," Madonna's "Music," Aimee Mann's "Save Me," and Britney Spears's "Oops! . . . I Did It Again."

The *Both Sides Now* album was nominated in the category of Best Traditional Pop Vocal Album. Her competition was Bryan Ferry's *As Time Goes By*, Ricki Lee Jones's *It's Like This*, George Michael's *Songs from the Last Century*, and Barbra Streisand's *Timeless—Live in Concert*.

In addition, Vince Mendoza was nominated three times in the category of Best Instrumental Arrangement Accompanying a Vocalist(s). His arrangements of Joni's "A Case of You" and "Both Sides Now" competed with his collaboration with Björk and Guy Sigsworth on the song "I've Seen It All," from the album *Selmasongs*.

Later that month, VH1 presented a TV special called *The 100 Greatest Albums of Rock and Roll*, hosted by Jeff Bridges. On the telecast, Joni's *Blue* album was ranked as number 14. And when the Grammy Awards were given out on the evening of February

21, 2001, Joni won the fifth Grammy of her career, in the category of Best Traditional Pop Vocal Album for *Both Sides Now*. Vince Mendoza also won a Grammy for his arrangement of "Both Sides Now."

Although Joni's win was not telecast, she and Carlos Santana were the presenters of the trophy for Record of the Year. Joni was dressed in a striking green Issey Miyake gown, and was in a game mood. She laughingly announced to the international television audience that night, "Well, the great Carlos Santana and I are really representing all the other teen acts tonight!" Santana returned the compliment by proclaiming that it was "a joy and an honor to be here, and to be next to the gifted and talented Joni Mitchell." (145)

On October 16, 2001, Joni Mitchell was presented with a sidewalk star in Toronto's Walk of Fame. "I'd like that little spot on the sidewalk to be a place where you don't spit," joked Joni. (146)

She accepted her honors alongside noted Canadian author Margaret Atwood, and she received the key to the city. "What does it open?" Joni asked Toronto Mayor Mel Lastman as he presented her the key to Toronto. He answered, "It opens the hearts of all the people of Toronto, and it is given on behalf of all the people of Toronto." (146)

The granite star bearing Joni's name is part of the sidewalk in Toronto's theater district on King Street West. She announced at the ceremonies, "I'm not certain what committee or voting system brought me to this podium, but I'm very honored, I didn't have to pay for this star on the sidewalk. They buy them in Hollywood. This is not corrupt, so I'm very honored for that." (146) As the stars were unveiled, Joni's song "Chelsea Morning" played over the loudspeakers.

Seated in the VIP area were Donald Freed, Kilauren, Joni's grandchildren, her manager, and noted film directors Norman Jewison and David Croenenberg. "It's a warm support group," Joni announced to the media. "For my star, I hope if you're crossing over it, since the world is moving so fast and has gone so mad, that you would slow down a little bit as you would cross over it, think of something funny or something kind—think of someone you love. If you're thinking of someone that you don't love as you're crossing over it, put them out of mind . . . Just use it as a little contemplative place. Sit there and have a private chuckle, and that would make me very happy. That would make it practical and useful." (146)

Both Sides Now had proven a hugely successful project. Winning awards and eliciting glowing reviews, it was the perfect album at the perfect time. Through the creation of it, Joni grew excited at recording with a full orchestra. She was so enthused, in fact, that she was inspired to record another album of interpretive classics—again with full orchestra backing her. She had begun the new century by showing the chops to create a hit album. Now it was time for Joni to shift gears again and head back to the recording studio.

23

A Musical Travelogue

In 2002 Joni Mitchell began surveying her career from the perspective of the new century. She had loved rerecording her songs "Both Sides Now" and "A Case of You" with full orchestra for her last album and wondered what it would be like to give several of her other compositions the same treatment. There was only one way to find out. With that thought in mind, she went back into the recording studio and began work on what was to become her twenty-second album, a career retrospective she called *Travelogue*.

This album went through several mutations along the way to its creation. The name of it was especially malleable. As Mitchell explains it, "When I don't have a title, I always go back to *The Songs of the Sunday Painter*. Somebody said, 'Joni, you've had that title for the last five albums,' and I said, 'OK.' I had trouble getting to the essence of it, and it was really last-minute when I did. Making an album like this, it's like unloading the car on a holiday. You know, if *Hejira* hadn't already been used as a title, it would have been a good title for this, too." (8)

A look back at her own songs, *Travelogue* presented several challenges. First, it was not always easy for her to recapture the feelings she had when she originally wrote and recorded this material. As she explains, "Rerecording 'Chinese Café' for *Travelogue*, I just couldn't find the 'pocket' in the performance, the character.

The character was almost right, but there was something missing for me to deliver that particular song with sincerity, and I tried to think of a role model. I tried to imagine an actress delivering those lines spoken, and I couldn't think of a female. You know who I ended up thinking of? Jimmy Stewart. Because no matter how impassioned or angry Jimmy got, he always seemed to be on his center. He never was melodramatic. He was always light, even when he was heavy." (8)

She was also reminded of the stylistic stretching she was doing at the time of the original recording. This was especially true when she revisited songs from her more experimental albums, like *Don Juan's Reckless Daughter*. Although that album was originally misunderstood by the critics, it now made perfect sense. "It really surprised me," says Joni. "In retrospect, it doesn't surprise me at all. I listened to that album recently, 'cause I was going to rework 'Edith and the Kingpin.' I was surprised. I feel that the times have caught up with it. At that time, I was beginning to introduce—for lack of a better word—jazz overtones. Nobody was really doing that. In the two years that followed, it became more acceptable, and when Steely Dan finally made *Aja*, with some of the same sidemen, it was applauded as a great, if somewhat eccentric, work. I fail even to see the eccentricity of it, myself. Perhaps there was a weary tone in my voice that irritated people, but there was so much of it that was accessible." (9)

Like many artists, she often prefers her more obscure creations and finds herself unable to understand why her biggest hits became so popular. "I thought 'Both Sides Now' was a failure, so what do I know? I was not a good judge of my early material; none of it sounded all that good to me. That's why I wanted to keep moving forward," she claimed during this era. (147)

Regardless of the changes she went through while recording it, *Travelogue* is a beautifully recorded mixture of Joni's favorite songs, revisited and reinvented with a full orchestra and several of her favorite jazz musicians—including Herbie Hancock, Wayne Shorter, and Billy Preston. Larry Klein coproduced it with Joni and also served as the musical director. As he had done on *Both Sides Now*, Vince Mendoza arranged and conducted.

Travelogue, with its twenty-two tracks, takes exactly half of its selections from Joni's post-1980 compositions. Some critics complained that it ignores some of her most famous work. The eleven tracks from her classic 1960s and 1970s albums include "Woodstock," "For the Roses," "Trouble Child," "God Must Be a Boogie Man," "Just Like This Train," "Hejira," "The Dawntreader," "Judgment of the Moon and Stars (Ludwig's Tune)," "The Last Time I Saw Richard," "Refuge of the Roads," and "The Circle Game." Undoubtedly all have their own list of favorite Joni Mitchell songs. Personally, I would love to see what she could have done with such poignant songs as "Little Green," "Urge for Going," "Blue," "Ladies of the Canyon," "Tin Angel," "Roses Blue," "Woman of Heart and Mind," "River," "The Fiddle and the Drum," and "Car on a Hill." Perhaps one day she will give orchestral treatment to these songs as well.

Among the most beautifully executed songs on *Travelogue* are "Refuge of the Roads," "The Circle Game," "Hejira," and "You Dream Flat Tires." The seafaring song "Dawntreader" is especially wonderful and luxurious here, with its references to peridots and periwinkle blue medals. It is one song that totally benefits from the fresh new arrangement. On the whole, the songs included on *Travelogue* met with mixed results. Some songs, like "Be Cool," come across as especially jazzy here, while others, like "Cherokee Louise," seem a bit too homogenized compared to the original version. Others have been given a new lease on life, like the brilliant rethinking of "Sex Kills." However, whether you like the old version of these songs or the new orchestrated ones, you must admit that the music and Joni's vocal performances are thoughtful, exquisite, intricate, and emotion-filled.

For over thirty years, Joni Mitchell has threatened to quit music business altogether. Her first announcement came before she recorded her classic *For the Roses* album. However, in 2002, as *Travelogue* was about to be released, Joni publicly proclaimed that she was sick and tired of the whole business end of the music business. David Wild in *Rolling Stone* magazine, December 3, 2002, reported, "When Joni Mitchell recently described the music industry as 'a cesspool' in the pages of *Rolling Stone*, her remark showed up on CNN. This was shortly followed by the news that Mitchell intends her latest collection, the double-CD *Travelogue*, to be her last." (8) If *Travelogue* was to figuratively become known as "an epilogue" to her dazzling and peerless career, it was a classy way to go!

It was released on November 19, 2002, on a new record label

for Mitchell: Nonesuch Records. *Travelogue* comes in an impressively packaged case. Having another of Joni's self-portraits on the cover, it consists of an outer box and an inner cardboard case for the two discs. It also includes two separate booklets: one with sumptuous color plates of Joni's paintings and another one, in black and white, featuring lyrics to all of the included songs.

At the time of its release, the press reviews for *Travelogue* were highly mixed. Some reviewers were perplexed, while others absolutely adored it. According to James Hunter in *Rolling Stone*, "This bizarre two-disc recording finds the loftiest of singer-songwriters collaborating with a seventy-piece orchestra, revisiting her past work. The arrangements treat Mitchell's tunes as precious artifacts, making little attempt to seduce the listener; only on 'The Circle Game,' for example, do the strings provide the kind of romantic sonic brocades associated with great orchestral rock. Mitchell—in strong, ultraconfident voice—proceeds with her famous jazz inflections . . . But, the occasional sax flourish notwithstanding, the music does not swing or get loose. Sometimes the album sounds wrongly monumental, as on 'Woodstock'; other times, it misses the boat, as on 'The Last Time I Saw Richard,' which ignores the song's thrilling harmonics. *Travelogue* translates Joni Mitchell as a scrupulously constructed puzzle." (145)

Not everyone loved what she did musically. Claimed reviewer Betty Clark in England's *The Guardian*, "If the health warning isn't enough to put you off cigarettes, the nicotine-ravaged vocals of the once angelic, now gasping Joni Mitchell should. Mitchell's voice is a husky shadow of its former feather-light glory, mirroring how her joyful, playful attitude has dwindled to bitter dissatisfaction. Having announced that this is her final album, Mitchell has reappraised her work with a huge orchestral makeover. She has already explored such classical territory on 2000's *Both Sides Now*, and here she slides easily among the brass and crashing cymbals of the 70-piece orchestra. Songs from her jazz-fusion era adapt well: the venomous 'For the Roses' is now more scathing and the brooding drama of 'Just Like This Train' has become an attack. 'Sex Kills,' from 1994's *Turbulent Indigo*, proves her skills as social commentator remain sharp amid the screeching strings. But the blustering instrumentation kills her fragile poetry and the earthbound vocals negate any magic, rendering this double album a leaden memorial to a shining talent." (148)

However, some reviewers really liked the sound of Joni Mitchell reinventing her classic recordings. Darryl Sterdan in the *Winnipeg Sun* wrote, "Some artists know how to make an entrance. Joni Mitchell knows how to make an exit . . . Naturally, Joni's favourites might not be the same as yours—while 'Woodstock' and 'The Circle Game' make appearances, *Travelogue* ignores seemingly obvious picks like 'Big Yellow Taxi,' 'Raised on Robbery,' 'Help Me' and 'Both Sides Now' in favour of relative obscurities such as 'Otis and Marlena.' Still, Mitchell's exquisite voice (which has descended over the decades from a brash soprano to a smoky alto) and Mendoza's rich arrangements (which run the gamut from the lush orchestral landscape of *Wild Things Run Fast's* 'Love' to the moody jazz silhouettes of *Mingus'* 'God Must be a Boogie Man') just might convince you to add some of these to your own personal Mitchell best-of . . . Ultimately, whether you're glad to see Joni go or not, *Travelogue* sends her off in style." (149)

Although *Travelogue* garnered Joni a ton of press—some favorable, some not—it was not a huge sales hit when it was released. However, it has remained a steady seller internationally.

Hit record or no hit record, meanwhile, the legend of Joni Mitchell continued to grow. She has been part of the pop culture landscape for so long that she doesn't even have to be present to be treated like a guest star. In an episode of the hugely successful TV show *Will and Grace*, Joni was the subject of one of the program's comic misadventures. In this particular episode, the central characters Will and Grace become involved in a huge disagreement when tickets to a Joni Mitchell concert become available, but only one of them can attend due to a previous obligation. Naturally the duo fights bitterly about who goes to the Joni concert, and who does not.

In the year 2003, Joni Mitchell was a pivotal part of the plot of the film *Love Actually*. In the movie, Emma Thompson professes her love of Joni's music, and the song "River" is played in the background. Further into the film, Emma's husband, played by Alan Rickman, presents her a copy of Mitchell's *Both Sides Now* album for Christmas. The fact that he gave her the CD uncovers a secret flirtation with a female coworker. It seems that the coworker received the gold necklace that Thompson was expecting to be her gift. Joni's 2000 recording of the song "Both Sides Now" is heard playing over two intertwined sequences depicting the scorned wife and then the grateful would-be mistress. Mitchell's recording also appeared on the original soundtrack album of *Love Actually*.

On April 2, 2003, a new documentary about Joni's life, entitled *A Woman of Heart and Mind*, was first broadcast in the United States. Its actual debut came the previous month in her native Canada. It is an engrossing audiovisual look at Joni's life, with several fresh interviews with key people from her life, including Graham Nash, David Geffen, and Elliot Roberts. It was released in June 2003 on DVD and is a brilliant career-spanning look at Joni's life, loves, music, and artwork. Several sections of her personal life were skipped over, however, like the specifics of her affairs with David Crosby, James Taylor, and Jackson Browne. However, the rare footage of young Joni make this a priceless documentary overview to watch.

Over the course of the next year, three separate compilations of Joni's music were released, and she ended up having a creative hand in the release of all three of them. On September 23, 2003, Joni's twenty-third album, *The Complete Geffen Recordings*, hit the stores. Presented as a boxed set, it found a quartet of albums— *Wild Things Run Fast*, *Dog Eat Dog*, *Chalk Mark in a Rain Storm*, and *Night Ride Home*—packaged in cardboard sleeves printed with the original artwork and housed in an elaborate outer case.

Including a full booklet of lyrics and exclusive artwork, *The Complete Geffen Recordings* features three tracks never before released. Two of them were stripped-down demo versions of the songs "Good Friends" and "Two Grey Rooms." The one nearly completed bonus recording finds Joni singing Bob Dylan's "It's All Over Now, Baby Blue."

Amazing as it seemed at the time, on November 7, 2003, Joni Mitchell celebrated her sixtieth birthday. At times, in the public eye, she was still the same young girl who had looked back at her short life in the song "The Circle Game." It was hard to believe that she was about to begin her seventh decade of musical creativity.

On January 14, 2004, Joni's former boyfriend John Guerin died suddenly in Los Angeles of a heart attack. He was sixty-four years old. As a member of the L.A. Express, he had taken part in several of Mitchell's best-selling albums, starting with *Court and Spark*. As a noted session drummer, Guerin had played on albums by such varied artists as Frank Zappa, the Byrds, and Frank Sinatra. Joni remained friendly with him for many years, and she was saddened to hear of his passing.

When the Grammys were handed out in early 2004, Vince Mendoza won a trophy for his arrangement of the song "Woodstock" on *Travelogue*. During that same Grammy season, Joni's *Court and Spark* album was among the thirty-three additions to the Grammy Hall of Fame. Four years previously, Mitchell's *Blue* had been added to the list of cherished recordings.

On July 27, 2004, Joni released her twenty-fourth album, a unique compilation called *The Beginning of Survival* on Geffen Records. Joni again had full creative control over the material included and a hand in the packaging. Featuring another of her self-portraits on the cover, it also functioned as a showcase for her paintings.

All of the selections from this album were taken from what is perhaps her most musically rich period of time: 1985–1998. It includes no love songs but stitches together all of Joni's strongest songs of social injustice, political rage, and human rights issues.

Instead of writing an essay about what was going on in her life when she was creating this music, Joni reproduces a letter written by Chief Seattle in the 1850s and sent to the president of the United States, at a time when the U.S. government offered to buy two million acres of Indian land for $150,000. In the letter, Seattle asked what gives man the right to think that he can own the land, own the sky, own the water? It sets the tone for the kinds of social criticism offered by the songs contained in the album.

One selling point of *The Beginning of Survival* is that it features a wide assortment of guest stars, including Willie Nelson on "Cool Water" and Rod Steiger on "Tax Free." Also featured are Wayne Shorter, Thomas Dolby, Amy Holland, Michael McDonald, Iron Eyes Cody, James Taylor, and Don Henley.

On *The Beginning of Survival*, Joni draws together her most impassioned songs about Indian and human rights ("Lakota"), Madison Avenue ("The Reoccurring Dream"), AIDS ("Sex Kills"), war ("The Beat of Black Wings"), greed ("Tax Free"), and women's rights ("The Magdalene Laundries"), as well as the fight for food ("Ethiopia") and liquid resources ("Cool Water"). It ends with a song that wonders where all of this is going to lead: "Impossible Dreamer."

The Beginning of Survival puts the spotlight on Joni's career-long role as troubadour/social critic. According to her, "This generation seems to be the most celebrity-loving/celebrity-hating generation that ever lived. And nobody wants to do the mundane job. In my parent's generation, you got a job and you kept it. My father wanted to be a lawyer, but he was a grocery clerk and then the store manager. You got a job no matter what your dream job was. That was your dream job. Then my generation, which was a more affluent generation—no war to deal with, no Great Depression to deal with—saw through and became very critical of the powers that be. I don't know whether that's good or bad—like certainly the dope wars of Vietnam, the transparency of that, did not deserve the thwarting of the boys coming home. I used to play in Fort Bragg to soldiers, like Bob Hope. I figured I don't care whether it's an unjust war or not, soldiers need singers. So I disagreed with my own generation. I wasn't really of my own generation either. I wasn't an anarchist, I wasn't a nihilist—I never really could find my politics." (7)

She is also not fond of the mass media's role in purveying pornography. "It seems like all we have left this generation was shock value," she says with dismay. "And they're very, very concerned about bodily excretions, in terms of their art and what they say. It seems like that's all we left them or something." (7)

According to her, "We are drowning in images. We don't know fantasy from reality. Especially the generation coming up. Something happened. Anything that is so accessible becomes disposable: You sit in your living room and you drink your cola and you eat your pizza, and you just watch all of this, you know, pornography. It's not even music." (8)

On September 14, 2004, Joni released another compilation of her past recordings. Obviously it was planned to be a companion to *The Beginning of Survival*, as it did not repeat any of the tracks used on that album. Entitled *Dreamland*, this album is partially a "greatest hits" kind of compilation in that it spans her entire career—from "The Circle Game" to songs from *Both Sides Now* and *Travelogue*.

Comprising tracks from all of her record labels, *Dreamland* was released by Rhino. It is a compilation album that does justice to the whole spectrum of Joni Mitchell's music. This is the liveliest career-spanning collection of all of them. As a satisfying listening experience, it features more exciting selections than *Hits*. The effervescent "Dreamland," the rhythmic "Jungle Line," and the blues/jazz sound of "Furry Sings the Blues" make this a special delight. Joni's two most famous French-themed songs—"Free Man in Paris" and "In France They Kiss on Main Street"—are placed back to back, and they fittingly open the album. All of the requisite signature songs are interspersed here: "Big Yellow Taxi," "You Turn Me On I'm a Radio," "Help Me," and "The Circle Game." Furthermore, three songs—"Amelia," "For the Roses," and "Both Sides Now"—are represented by their twenty-first century orchestral versions. Cameron Crowe, who once interviewed Joni for *Rolling Stone* magazine, wrote the liner notes. If you purchase only one Joni compilation disk—this is it.

Although *Dreamland* contains all of her "greatest hits," Joni hates that term. "Let's call them the most gregarious of my children," she says. "'Big Yellow Taxi'—I like the life that it has. I didn't intend it to be a children's song, but it has become one. This third-grade teacher in New Jersey has his kids illustrate that song every year . . . 'Both Sides Now' is probably the song that's been the most gregarious. Bing Crosby and Frank Sinatra sang it. It's been recorded in many different genres and all around the world. I saw a translation of it come back through the Chinese. It has gone to China, been translated into Chinese calligraphy, then been translated back out into English. And it came out 'Joni's Theory of Relativity.' 'Circle Game' closes eighth-grade graduation exercises around the country, and that's a great function for it." (14)

The month *Dreamland* was released, longtime Joni-phile Robert Hillburn wrote a cover story for the *Los Angeles Times* Calendar section about her remarkable career. In listing his favorite Joni Mitchell songs, he chose "Amelia," "A Case of You," "For the Roses," "Big Yellow Taxi," and "Two Grey Rooms" as the five songs he found the most telling of Mitchell's many moods. According to Hillburn, the five Joni "albums for all ages" are *Blue*, *For the Roses*, *Court and Spark*, *Hejira*, and *Night Ride Home*.

Since different eras of Joni's music touch her fans in different ways, we all have our own favorites. If I were to send someone to the local record store to purchase Joni's essential albums, there would have to be seven of them: *Ladies of the Canyon*, *Blue*, *Court and Spark*, *Hejira*, *Shadows and Light*, *Dog Eat Dog*, and *Chalk Mark in a Rain Storm*.

With regard to her decision to quit the music business alto-gether, Joni told Hillburn in 2004, "In some ways, my gift for mu-sic and writing was born out of tragedy, really, and loss. When my daughter returned to me, the gift kind of went with it. The song-writing was almost like something I did while I was waiting for my daughter to come back." (147)

Throughout her life, one of Joni's key traits has been her ability to keep many of her ex-boyfriends actively in her life, especially Graham Nash, David Crosby, James Taylor, and Larry Klein. Ac-cording to Joni, "They're all wonderful men, though. Graham is a sweetheart—and we didn't part with animosity. A lot of pain—there's always pain in pulling apart. Graham needed a more tradi-tional female. He loved me dearly, and you can see there's still a fondness and everything, but he wanted a stay-at-home wife to raise his children. And I said that I could—a rash promise I made in my youth—and then I realized I couldn't. So it all worked out." (7)

She is still very critical about the music business in general. "It's the business I don't like," she claims. "The pigeonholing I don't like, the pitting me against every female that comes along, favorably and unfavorably. That I've had to do because there weren't that many women in the business. I don't like the idea that they make us both put on the gloves, they prod one of them until they say something snotty about me, then hit me over the head with the snotty thing that they said, then get a rise out of me. Rather than thinking of me as a bitter old fogey, like the young press would like to do, if they thought about it as a mature artist, if it was the old guild system, it would be respected that I knew something and that maybe my criticisms of these people who out-sell me 20-to-1, so they really are creating more public interest." (7)

Furthermore, she can't stand it when she gets mentioned in the press amid all the other female singers. According to her, "I'm sick of being lumped in with the women. Laura Nyro you can lump me in with, because Laura exerted an influence on me. I looked to her and took some direction from her. On account of her I started playing piano again. Some of the things she did were very fresh. Hers was a hybrid of black pop singers—Motown singers—and Broadway musicals, and I like some things also from both those camps." (7) At the mention of Nyro's classic album *New York Tendaberry*, Joni sighs, "Beautiful record. Beautiful!" (7)

And Sinéad O'Connor is someone Joni truly admires. "I like Sinéad," Joni says. "She's a passionate little singer. And I understand her saying, 'I hate this job.' It's a horrible job. People don't realize how horrible it is. Making music is great. The exploitation of it is horrible. And I think you've got to be hard as nails. Maybe it's where Madonna has the edge on us. Maybe she doesn't think it's horrible. I think it's degrading, humiliating—so does Sinéad. Whereas, Madonna's above being degraded or humiliated. She flirts with it. And perhaps that bravado is in some ways to be applauded; but at what cost her soul, is my question." (14)

Speaking of the blatant material girl, Madonna, Mitchell blasts, "What's the difference between her and a hard hooker, you know? Who's being exploited here? She's reveling in herself, too. But she can take it. I guess that's what it is. It's just being able to take it, you know . . . She's a great 'star.' She's got that whore/Madonna thing built in," Joni laughs. "She's like a living Barbie doll but a little bit on the blue side. There's always been that type of female. There's always been a market for it, but the danger is that she thinks she's a role model. And it's a terrible role model. It's death to all things real." (14)

Joni is not impressed with much of the music currently being released. "You've got all these assorted divas, like these sappy, romantic singers," she claims. "They are not tender like Nat 'King' Cole—they are overwrought. And it's very flashy, but it's soulless. You look into the eyes of these people, and you know they are looking at themselves in the mirror. There is nothing to them but their own image. There's just nothing   the only thing I heard in many years that I thought had greatness in it was the New Radicals. I loved that song 'You Get What You Give.' It was a big hit, and I said, 'Where did they go?' It turns out the guy [Gregg Alexander] quit. I thought, 'Good for him.' I knew he was my kind of guy." (8)

According to her, "As a painter I admire much. And it's been hard—like music, it's been hard to synthesize the many styles that I like. In art school I was criticized for painting in two or three schools at the same time. Music hybrids better than perhaps painting does immediately. I ended up kind of without a country." (7)

Since she is such a big fan of Bob Dylan's, what does she think of Springsteen? According to her, "That's folk carpentry. Bruce Springsteen is a very nice craftsperson." (14)

With regard to Prince, Joni claims, "An innovator must change what went before. Charlie Parker was an innovator. Jimi Hendrix was an innovator. Miles Davis was a sound innovator. I don't think Prince is an innovator. He's a great hybrid." (14)

On the other hand, there doesn't seem to be a singing star on the planet who doesn't have great respect for Joni Mitchell. Both as a person and as a musician, she has touched the lives of so many people. The following are only a few of the celebrities who appreciate her talent, her insights, her music, and her heart.

> *Graham Nash:* "When you fall for Joni, you fall all the way. She means a lot to a great number of people." (21)
>
> *Sting:* "When *Ladies of the Canyon* came out, I wore it out. I played those songs and played them and played them. Her ability as a storyteller is second to none. But she doesn't get sufficient credit as a musician. She's underrated. She's a fabulous guitarist, and everybody knows she's a great singer." (2)
>
> *Mary Wilson of the Supremes:* "I love her music, there is no songwriter like her!" (53)
>
> *Elvis Costello:* "She's compared to the wrong people . . . It's not just that she has no rivals among female singer/songwriters, she has very few peers among any songwriters." (2)
>
> *Angela Bowie:* "As a musician, Joni Mitchell is an extraordinarily unique creative person who is often imitated but never quire equaled." (62)
>
> *Wynonna Judd:* "She's my hero. I've known her music since I was 10—I can remember being in my room, grounded, and she was my escape." (27)
>
> *Chrissie Hynde:* "I think her authenticity combined with her age has interjected a whole new interest into the phenomenon of Joni Mitchell. People want her even more now. A lot of people make it in the music business fueled by just the exuberance of their youth. It's only time that shows you what the real substance of the man—or, in this case—the woman, is. And, in her case, she's got it." (2)

Linda Ronstadt: "Joni is the first woman to match any man on his own terms as a songwriter, guitar player or as an incredibly magnetic human being. (21)

Melissa Etheridge: "She is the greatest female singer/song-writer." (2)

Randy Jones of Village People: "No matter what kind of music she decides to play, Joni Mitchell never settles for less than excelling at it. I have loved her through her folk era, and I have followed her through her quest for jazz mastery, and her exciting rock explorations. There is only one Joni Mitchell." (150)

Me'Shell NdegeOcello: "I love Joni Mitchell. She just seems to be always trying something new. I think she's fucking amazing!" (2)

Stephen Stills: "Joni exorcizes her demons by writing these songs, and in so doing she reaches way down and grabs the essence of something very private and personal to women." (21)

Michael McDonald: "She is the artist of the century! She is just one of those artists who—of this whole era we grew up in—from the '60s til now, is probably one of the most important artists that has come along. She has created a whole genre, almost all by herself. If anyone really saw to it that the folk era evolved into that whole fusion of rock and jazz, it was really her—almost single-hand-edly." (105)

Strangers often come up to Joni and tell her how much her music means to them. This amazes her. She didn't set out to shape or color people's lives, but that is the effect her music often has. As she explains it, "People are always telling me that I saved their life or I changed their life. And lately I've taken to saying, 'How?' Because I have a funny look on my face, they go, 'Oh, you hear that so much.' And I say, 'No, the funny look on my face is because I'm wondering, "How?" Well, they always pull a different line. Some of them I wouldn't even think had that kind of power, but it's a little phrase stuck in there somewhere that was just the thing they needed to keep from drowning at a certain moment. I think you'd find it would be different things for different people." (7)

Who does she admire the most? "Picasso was restless," she

claims. "I mean, he just kept changing and changing and changing." She also mentions Miles Davis and then proclaims, "So those are my heroes. The ones that change a lot." (11)

Since her most celebrated confessional album is entitled *Blue*, and it is almost universally recognized as her career pinnacle, what music does she listen to when she finds herself feeling blue? According to Joni, "Some Billie Holiday, or Miles Davis' *In a Silent Way* or *Nefertiti*. I love that pocket of Miles' music. But it depends on which way you want to go. If I wanted to dig out of feeling blue, Thelonious Monk." (8)

In the time since 1995, Joni has been going back and forth between announcing that she is quitting the music business and then asserting that she has something more to say in her music. In 1998 she announced, "I'm a long distance runner. Miles was a long distance runner. And I'd have to look up his birth date, but there was always that restlessness to never rest upon your laurels and become a human jukebox. Miles, to the end, was moving forward, still searching and exploring, like Picasso. I belong to that restless camp, you know. Not everybody does. Probably because of the stars, something as simple as that—the moment you popped out. Go figure. But the industry . . . is basically designed to make of you something disposable. That's the way mercantilism in America works. And they get the new improved version of the product. The attention span in this country is shorter, I think, than most. In other countries, if something's good, they're loyal to it. But here, good or not, people get off at a certain point. It's because we're trained—even more so than ever, this batch of babies coming up with the TV—to fear not to be hip. Well hip is a herd mentality, so anything too adventuresome, people are afraid to be the first, or they'll stick out too much. And usually anything that's innovative is not hip, and the copycat gets it all. Once they've heard it the second time the copier gets the mass approval, because it's kind of familiar by that time. It's been run past them once already." (7)

In 2000, she claimed that she may be through writing all-new albums of music for release; but would she consider recording the music of other writers? "Not unless something comes along," she explained. "I'm a painter that got sidetracked. You know, recently I sensed my mortality, and the painting is not fully developed. The music is pretty much fully developed, and the [music] game up until recently kind of kicked me out. It kicked me out years ago. It excommunicated me for one reason or other. So seeing the best of your work designated into the obscure department doesn't make you have much hope for culture, you know what I mean?" (136)

That same year she announced that she wants to do an orchestral holiday package called *Have Yourself a Dreary Little Christmas*: "It will include four of my secular Christmas songs, and four carols. I want to make a play out of it." (136)

Of her announcements that she is quitting business, Joni explains, "I've been wanting to quit for all these many years. But I still stayed curious with it. I'd always feel I had another one in me." (8)

What are the chances of Joni doing an about-face and recording another album like *Lady of the Canyon* or *Blue* or *Court and Spark*? Somewhere between slim and none, according to her. She does not and will not pander to the demands of the marketplace. She does not want to paint the same painting again, and she certainly does not want to put her "car on the hill" in reverse and go backward.

As she explains it, "I never wanted to turn into a human jukebox. I haven't used all of my ideas yet. There's a possibility that I can continue to invent new music up into my eighties—like a legitimate composer. But I'm working in a pop field, and whether they're going to allow an older woman to do that is an open question. It requires a loyal, interested audience who believes in my talent." (14)

With a career history like hers and a loyal fan base like hers, there will always be an audience. True artist that she is, there will always be one more song that needs to be sung.

She also realizes what a throwaway society the current musical marketplace is—especially in hyperfickle America. Although her albums in the 1980s and early 1990s continued her quest to create and express herself, their lack of success upset her to a certain degree. *Dog Eat Dog* and *Chalk Mark in a Rain Storm* and *Night Ride Home* should have been successful albums. But they were not. How did that affect her focus and creativity? According to her, "The only way it affected me as an artist was that it made me recognize the inevitable—that the time comes for every artist when they fall out of favor. People get sick of your name. People get sick of your *face*. It doesn't matter what you do. Recognizing those times, I would go even further out. I figured they're going to get me anyway, so I may as well stretch out. I often thought if somehow I could have had a new name and a new face, people would have flipped for every one of those albums." (14)

Since she is as talented a painter as she is a singer, would she like to simply shift gears and market her artwork? No. "I don't want to get into merchandising them. I want nothing to do with galleries, even in terms of exhibitions. When money meets up with art, there is a lot of pain, and it's the pain of ignorance and I don't want to meet up with that ignorance again. My work is personal, too vulnerable. That's why I quit making records." (147)

While other singing stars are addicted to fame and pursue their careers into their eighties and nineties, can Joni put herself in exile when she is only in her sixties? According to her, "I'm not addicted to the roar of the crowd and don't understand why the show must go on. I did it my way. I learned early that I couldn't trust anybody's judgment but my own. And even that, only sometimes." (27)

She is someone who insists, "I never wanted to be a star. If anything, I've been trying to get out since I got in." (27)

Joni professes that she would rather be an anonymous craftsman than a glittering star in the rock horizon. In fact, she has a stubborn artist's mentality. According to her, "I believe a total unwillingness to cooperate is what is necessary to be an artist—not for perverse reasons, but to protect your vision. The considerations of a corporation, especially now, have nothing to do with art or music. That's why I spend my time now painting." (147)

As she has stated many times in the past twenty years, she is sick and tired of the "shoot 'em up" violence of today's society. Indeed, where is the romance? "There's not much room for subtleties today," she claims. "It's the shallow, flashy heart that grabs the attention; chase scenes, atrocities. Mass murder is probably the favorite entertainment of the American culture at this point." (147)

To this day Joni still lives in the large Mediterranean-style house in the Bel Air section of Los Angeles that she moved into more than thirty years ago. Since her affair with Donald Freed ended, her only constant companions are her Jack Russell terrier and her three cats. She has no problem with that. Like the person she wrote of in her song "A Case of You," she is a solitary painter, finding a perfectly fulfilling life in her box of paints. According to her in 2004, "I'm so happy. Such good friends. So much in love with life, but romantic love is over for me. I'm very happy about this leg of my life. I wish I were better at painting. Great thing, though, having a challenge—painting personal things, which have their own validity." (147)

On Sundays she often invites friends to her Bel Air home to hang out. They play pool and pinball. Insists Joni, "There's a lot of laughter, and I feel loved by a lot of people." (151)

She has no interest in dating and certainly isn't looking for casual sex. As she explains of herself, "I'm a serial monogamist. That's not that uncommon in my generation. Kind of horrifying to the last generation, where everybody stuck together. This generation, we're so worn down that nobody can stay in our company for any length of time. And in that way my trip was not that unique." (2)

Joni feels very complete in her personal life, especially now that her daughter and two grandchildren are actively part of her life. When Kilauren tracked down Mitchell, she also met her biological father, Brad MacMath. Says Joni of MacMath, "He has a daughter by one marriage and a son by another. We all go out together as a dysfunctional family." (151)

She is working on restoring the balance in her life. According to her, she wants it to be "Spiritual, ritualist, Taoistic, Tai Chi, yoga under a tree. I want to develop some good habits of saying grace in nature." (20)

Of her artistic expression these days she claims, "In painting, your brain empties out and there's not a word in it; it's like a deep meditation, like a trance. I could step on a tack and probably wouldn't know it when I'm painting. In writing it's kind of the opposite. That's why some people take stimulants. You stir up chaotic thoughts, then you pluck from this overactive mind. It's part of my process as a writer, being emotionally disturbed by something exterior someone said or something that is happening in society. It's on your mind, and it won't go away until you deal with it." (147)

According to Joni, she doesn't want to write songs about the world she sees around her these days. She finds it full of frustration and violence, and sees it with very little wonderment. "My goal as a writer is more to comfort than to disturb. Most of the art created in this particular culture is shallow and shocking and I can't create music for this social climate." (147)

Will she ever tour again? Who knows. Thinking of a role model for such midlife ambivalence she says, "Miles [Davis] was like that at the end. He wasn't trying to be rude on stage when he would wait for an hour and a half to find someone who inspired him to play two notes. His golden age and his period of exploration was behind him. I just don't want to do it anymore. So I'm painting privately with my private adjudication." (147)

She has no regrets about the choices she has made in her life. "It's been a rich experience," proclaims Joni. "The music has given me the ability to travel, to see the world, and to afford first-class art supplies." (2)

Whether or not she ever records another album, one fact will remain: there never has been a recording artist quite like Joni Mitchell. If she chooses to rest on her laurels from this point forward, the music she has created will forever be remembered as among the most touching, personal, revealing, and beautiful ever recorded.

Much to her protest, she will forever be saddled with the folk singer image she entered the business with. However, she clearly transcends such a generalization. She is a chronicler of some of the most dramatic social change in the past hundred years. She has bared her soul in her songs, and she has bled publicly in her lyrics. She has mastered rock & roll, jazz, and folk music. She has remained so chameleon-like that she is nearly undefinable.

Perhaps new musical genres or ideas will inspire Joni to return to recording, songwriting, and public performing. It is hard to imagine Mitchell satisfied being the "lonely" painter she once described herself as being. She is too vital, too creative, and too outspoken to willingly submit to an eternity of withdrawal. Like Picasso, Miles Davis, and Georgia O'Keeffe, Joni is someone who needs to go on creating as long as there is breath left in her body.

No matter in what direction she takes her creative life from this point, she is a unique woman of heart and mind. She is the voice of a generation—a generation that needs her insights, her viewpoints, her quirky social commentary, and her brilliant artistry. The trouble child, the troubadour, the masterful musician, the poignant writer, the jazz singer, the vivid painter—these are all terms that describe the distinctive, succinctly insightful woman we have come to know and love as someone who defies all labels: Joni Mitchell.

Quote Sources

(1) Timothy White, "A Portrait of the Artist," *Billboard,* December 9, 1995.

(2) Bill Flanagan, "Lady of the Canyon," *Vanity Fair,* June 1997.

(3) *Joni Mitchell: A Life Story/A Woman of Heart and Mind,* video, Eagle Rock Entertainment, 2003.

(4) Holly George-Warren, *Musicians in Tune: Seventy-Five Contemporary Musicians Discuss the Creative Process* (New York: Fireside, 1992).

(5) Joni Mitchell, interview by Ingrid Sischy, *Interview,* May 2000.

(6) David Handelman, "Triumph of the Will," *Vogue,* April 1995.

(7) Dave DiMartino, "The Unfiltered Joni Mitchell," *Mojo, The Music Magazine,* August 1998.

(8) David Wild, "Come In from the Cold," *Rolling Stone,* December 3, 2002.

(9) Cameron Crowe, "Joni Mitchell: Her First Interview in Ten Years," *Rolling Stone,* July 26, 1979.

(10) William Ruhlmann, "Joni Mitchell a-Gogh-Gogh," *Goldmine,* February 17, 1995.

(11) Neil Strauss, "The Hissing of a Living Legend," *New York Times Magazine,* October 4, 1998.

(12) Michael Small, "She's Looked at Love from Up and Down, So Joni Mitchell Has New Ways to Write about Both Sides Now," *People,* December 16, 1985.

(13) Alanna Nash, "Joni Mitchell," *Stereo Review,* March 1986.

(14) David Wild, "Conversation with Joni Mitchel," *Rolling Stone,* May 30, 1991.

(15) Steven Daly, "Rock & Roll," *Rolling Stone,* October 28, 1998.

(16) Joe Smith, *Off the Record: An Oral History of Pop Music* (New York: Warner Books, 1988).

(17) Leonard Feather, "Joni Mitchell Talks about Mingus," *Down Beat,* September 1979.

(18) Jeffery Pepper Rodgers, "The Guitar Odyssey of Joni Mitchell: My Secret Place," *Acoustic Guitar,* August 1996.

(19) Andrew Purvis, "Joni No Longer Blue," *Time,* April 21, 1997.

(20) Jancee Dunn, "Joni Mitchell: Q & A," *Rolling Stone,* December 15, 1994.

(21) "Rock & Roll's Leading Lady," *Time,* December 16, 1974.

(22) Irwin Stambler and Lyndon Stambler, *Folk and Blues: The Encyclopedia* (New York: Thomas Dunn, 2001).

(23) Judy Collins, *Trust Your Heart* (New York: Houghton Mifflin, 1987).

(24) Jac Holzman and Gavan Daws, *Follow the Music* (Santa Monica, Calif.: First Media Group, 1998).

(25) Tom King, *The Operator: David Geffen Builds, Buys, and Sells the New Hollywood* (New York: Broadway Books, 2001).

(26) David Crosby and Carl Gottlieb, *Long Time Gone: The Autobiography of David Crosby* (New York: Doubleday, 1988).

(27) Fred Goodman, "Joni Looks at Life," *TV Guide,* April 15, 2000.

(28) Dagmar, "Joni Mitchell: Soft Shades of Green and Delicate Layers," *Aquarian,* March 1976.

(29) Brian Hinton, *Joni Mitchell: Both Sides Now–The Biography* (London: Sanctuary, 1996).

(30) Karl Dallas, "Joni, the Seagull from Saskatoon," *Melody Maker,* September 28, 1968.

(31) David Cleary, review of *Joni Mitchell* album, *All Music Guide,* retrieved online, 2004.

(32) *Joni Mitchell,* album liner notes, Reprise Records, 1968.

(33) Jean Valley, John Skow, Edward J. Boyer, and David DeVoss, "Linda Ronstadt: Torchy Rock/Linda Down the Wind," *Time,* February 28, 1977.

(34) Rob Tannenbaum, "The Return of the Pretender," *GQ,* November 1993.

(35) Cameron Crowe, "A Child's Garden of Jackson Browne," *Rolling Stone,* May 23, 1974.

(36) Ian Halperin, *Fire and Rain: The James Taylor Story* (Edinburgh: Mainstream, 2001).

(37) Happy Traum, "Joni Mitchell," *Rolling Stone,* May 17, 1969.

(38) Micky Dolenz, interview by Mark Bego, June 29, 2004.

(39) *CSN,* boxed set album liner notes, Atlantic Records, 1991.

(40) Caroline Boucher, "My Personal Life Is a Shambles," *Disc,* January 10, 1970.

(41) Gerald Astor, "Joni Mitchell: Songs for Aging Children," *Look,* January 27, 1970.

(42) Anthony Fawcett, "Joni Mitchell," *Ampersand,* October 1978.

(43) *All Music Guide,* 4th ed. (New York: Backbeat Books, 2001).

(44) Dafydd Rees and Luke Crampton, *Rock Stars Encyclopedia* (New York: DK, 1999).

(45) Joni Mitchell, live in London, 1970.

(46) Nick Logan, "Joni Is Supreme," *New Music Express,* November 28, 1970.

(47) James Taylor, liner notes for Carole King, *Tapestry,* Ode/Epic Records, 1999 version.

(48) *Maclean's,* "Joni Mitchell," 1974, as quoted in Halpern, *Fire and Rain.*

(49) David Crosby, interview by Ben Fong-Torres, *Rolling Stone,* 1970.

(50) Rich Wiseman, *Jackson Browne: The Story of a Hold Out* (Garden City, N.Y.: Doubleday/Dolphin, 1982).

(51) Timothy White, *Rock Lives: Profiles and Interviews* (New York: Owl/Holt, 1991).

(52) Rory O'Connor, "Talking to Joni Mitchell," *Vogue,* August 1988.

(53) Mary Wilson, interview by Mark Bego, March 6, 2004.

(54) Lynn Kellermann, "Joni Mitchell: The Hissing of Resignation," *Music Gig*, March 1976.

(55) Morrissey, "Melancholy Meets the Infinite Silence," *Rolling Stone,* March 6, 1997.

(56) Jules Siegel, "Midnight in Babylon," *Rolling Stone,* February 18, 1971.

(57) Peter Herbst, "Jackson Browne," *Boston Phoenix*, 1972

(58) Jackson Browne, onstage at Stony Brook, 1972.

(59) Michael Watts, "Priestess Joni," *Melody Maker,* May 13, 1972.

(60) Joni Mitchell, live at the Troubadour, December 1972.

(61) Stephen Davis, review of *For the Roses, Rolling Stone,* January 4, 1973.

(62) Angela Bowie, interview by Mark Bego, July 30, 2004.

(63) Barney Hoskins, "Our Lady of Sorrows," *Mojo*, December 1994.

(64) Dimitri Ehrlich, "Joni Mitchell Must Love," *Interview,* April 1991.

(65) Melinda Newman, "Joni Mitchell Offers Hits and Misses," *Billboard*, August 24, 1996.

(66) Chuck Pulin, "Joni Mitchell," *Sounds,* February 23, 1974.

(67) Steve Lake, "Return of the Woodstock Spirit," *Melody Maker*, April 20, 1974.

(68) Bill Flanagan, "Joni Mitchell Loses Her Cool," *Musician*, December 1985.

(69) Michael Watts, review of *Court and Spark, Melody Maker,* January 26, 1974.

(70) Jon Landau, review of *Court and Spark, Rolling Stone,* February 28, 1974.

(71) Madonna, interview, *Billboard,* as quoted in Mark Bego, *Madonna: Blonde Ambition* (New York: Cooper Square, 2000).

(72) Anthony DeCurtis, "Hall of Fame," review of *Court and Spark, Rolling Stone,* June 22, 2000.

(73) Rob Mackie, "From Folk Waif to Rock & Roll Lady," *Sounds,* April 27, 1974.

(74) Leonard Feather, "Joni Mitchell Has Her Mojo Working," *Los Angeles Times,* June 10, 1979.

(75) Joni Mitchell, liner notes for *The Hissing of Summer Lawns*, Asylum Records, 1975.

(76) Stephen Holden, "The Hissing of Summer Verses," *Rolling Stone,* January 15, 1976.

(77) Robert Christgau, "Christgau's Consumer Guide," review of *The Hissing of Summer Lawns, Village Voice,* December 22, 1975.

(78) Mike Watts, "A Bigger Splash," *Melody Maker*, November 29, 1975.

(79) Alan Jackson, "Portrait of the Artist," *NME*, November 30, 1985.

(80) Sam Shepard, *Rolling Thunder Logbook* (New York: Viking, 1978).

(81) Bob Spitz, *Bob Dylan: A Biography* (New York: McGraw-Hill, 1989).

(82) Phil Sutcliffe, "The Q Interview: Don Juan's Reckless Daughter," *Q,* May 20, 1988.

(83) Kit Rachlis, "Performance/Joni Mitchell: The Hissing of Winter Concerts," *Rolling Stone,* April 8, 1976.

(84) Ariel Swartley, "Mitchell: The Siren and the Symbolist," *Rolling Stone,* February 10, 1977.

(85) "An End to Innocence," *Village Voice,* January 24, 1977.

(86) Ron Baron, "California's Gold Record Rush: Hollywood and

Vinyl," *After Dark*, April 1977.

(87) Mark Bego, review of *Hejira*, *Rock*, 1976.

(88) Perry Meisel, "Jackson and Joni Cross New Paths," *New York Post*, January 13, 1978.

(89) Mick Brown, "The Flowering of Joni Mitchell," *Telegraph*, February 23, 1991.

(90) Janet Maslin, "Joni Mitchell's Reckless and Shapeless Daughter," *Rolling Stone*, March 9, 1978.

(91) Review of *Don Juan's Reckless Daughter, Playboy*, 1978

(92) Jon Pareles, "Four Sides Now," *Creem*, 1978

(93) Stephen Holden, "RIFFS: Madam Joni Almost Pulls It Off," *Village Voice*, December 19, 1977.

(94) "Top Album Picks/Review of *Don Juan's Reckless Daughter,*" *Billboard*, December 24, 1977.

(95) Wesley Strick, "Joni Mitchell Meets Don Juan's Reckless Daughter," *Circus*, 1978

(96) Joni Mitchell, liner notes for *Mingus*, Asylum Records, 1979.

(97) Sam Sutherland, "Mitchell and Mingus," *Stereo Review*, September 1979.

(98) Ariel Swartley, review of *Mingus*, *Rolling Stone*, September 6, 1979.

(99) Joey Berlin, "Another Hyphen for Joni Mitchell," *Los Angeles Times*, January 13, 1980.

(100) Hugh Wyatt, "Record Spinoff," *New York Daily News*, September 26, 1980.

(101) Stephen Holden, "Joni Mitchell's Live Album Is a Surprise and a Triumph," *Rolling Stone*, November 13, 1980.

(102) "At 39, the Most Jubilant Joni Mitchell in Years," *Glamour*, January 1983.

(103) Joni Mitchell, liner notes for *The Complete Geffen Recordings*, Geffen Records/Universal, 2003.

(104) Dave Zimmer, review of *Wild Things Run Fast*, *BAM*, December 3, 1982.

(105) Michael McDonald, interview by Mark Bego, backstage at the Shrine Auditorium, Los Angeles, California, April 4, 2004.

(106) Steve Pond, "Mitchell 'Storms' Back," *Rolling Stone*, March 10, 1988.

(107) Nicholas Jennings, "Portrait of an Artist in Her Prime," *Maclean's*, April 4, 1988.

(108) Bill Barol with Michael Reese, "Grown-up James, Adult Joni," *Newsweek*, November 4, 1985.

(109) Jefferson Graham, "Mellower Mitchell Still Makes a Mark, *USA Today*, March 28, 1988.

(110) Rob Tannenbaum, *Rolling Stone*, review of *Dog Eat Dog*, *Rolling Stone*, 1985

(111) Melinda Newman, "*Hits* and *Misses*: Track by Track," *Billboard*, August 24, 1996.

(112) Stocc Benarde and Tom Moon, "Bassist Jaco Pastorius Dead at Thirty-Five," *Rolling Stone*, November 19, 1987.

(113) John Milward, "Joni's Softly Drawn Chalk," *USA Today*, March 28, 1988.

(114) Alanna Nash, "Joni Mitchell Makes a New Musical Mark," *Stereo Review*, July 1988.

(115) Matt Resnicoff, "Joni Mitchell: Front Woman," *Musician*, March 1991.

(116) "Joni Mitchell," *Musician*, March 1991.

(117) Jay Cocks, "Navigator of the Deep," *Time*, March 4, 1991.

(118) Dan Oullette, review of *Night Ride Home*, *Down Beat*, June 1991.

(119) Tom Sinclair, review of *Night Ride Home, Rolling Stone,* March 21, 1991.

(120) Ron Givens, "Joni Mitchell Updates Her Life and Times," *Stereo Review,* June 1991.

(121) David Farber, "David Geffen," *New York Daily News,* 1994.

(122) "Artist of the Week: Joni Mitchell," *Entertainment Weekly,* November 4, 1994.

(123) John Milward, review of *Turbulent Indigo, Rolling Stone,* December 15, 1994.

(124) Guy Garcia, "A Deeper Shade of Blue," *Time,* November 28, 1994.

(125) "Singer Joni Mitchell Has Crippling Polio," *Star,* April 11, 1995.

(126) "Birthday Suite," *New Yorker,* December 11, 1995.

(127) "Joni Mitchell Gives Peace a Chance," *US,* November 1998.

(128) Brad McGrath, interview, *Express,* 1997.

(129) Christopher John Farley, "Burning Bright," *Time,* October 12, 1998.

(130) Kathy Belden, Random House, conversation with Mark Bego, 1993.

(131) John Ephland, "Joni Mitchell and Cassandra Wilson: Alternate Tunings," *Down Beat,* December 1996.

(132) "Joni Mitchell Unleashes Tiger," *Billboard,* September 9, 1989.

(133) Joni Mitchell, interview by Chris Douridas, *Morning Becomes Eclectic,* KCRW-FM Radio, March 27, 1998.

(134) Mikal Gilmore, "Bash of the Titans," *Rolling Stone,* July 9–23, 1998.

(135) *Painting with Words and Music,* video, Image Entertainment, 1998.

(136) Melinda Newman, "Reprise's Mitchell Explores Romance," *Billboard,* February 12, 2000.

(137) Joni Mitchell, liner notes for *Taming the Tiger,* Reprise Records, 1998.

(138) Steve Anderson, "Urgency Emergency," *Village Voice,* November 17, 1998.

(139) Jason Koransky, "Jazz Romance," *Down Beat,* May 2000.

(140) Robert Hillburn, "All She Needs Is Love Songs," *Los Angeles Times,* February 6, 2000.

(141) Larry Klein, liner notes for *Both Sides Now,* Reprise Records, 2000.

(142) Tom Moon, review of *Both Sides Now, Rolling Stone,* March 16, 2000.

(143) Elysa Gardner, "Joni's Standard Approach to Singing," *Los Angeles Times,* February 6, 2000.

(144) Steve Dougherty, review of *Both Sides Now, People,* March 13, 2000.

(145) James Hunter, review of *Travelogue, Rolling Stone,* November 28, 2002.

(146) Karen Bliss, "Sidewalk Attraction," rollingstone.com, October 19, 2001.

(147) Robert Hillburn, "An Art Born of Pain, an Artist in Happy Exile," *Los Angeles Times,* September 5, 2004.

(148) Betty Clark, review of *Travelogue, Guardian,* November 22, 2002.

(149) Darryl Sterdan, review of *Travelogue, Winnipeg Sun,* November 28, 2002.

(150) Randy Jones, interview by Mark Bego, September 23, 2004.

(151) Steve Dougherty and Lyndon Stanbler, "Both Sides Now," *People,* March 20, 2000.

Bibliography

Bego, Mark. *Bonnie Raitt: Still in the Nick of Time*. New York: Cooper Square, 2003.

———. *Linda Ronstadt: It's So Easy*. Austin, Tex.: Eakin, 1990.

Bogdanov, Vladimir, Chris Woodstra, and Stephen Thomas Erlewine, eds. *All Music Guide to Rock*. 3rd ed. Ann Arbor, Mich.: Backbeat, 2002.

Crosby, David, and Carl Gottlieb. *Long Time Gone: The Autobiography of David Crosby*. Garden City, N.Y.: Doubleday, 1988.

Dolenz, Micky, and Mark Bego. *I'm a Believer: My Life of Monkees, Music, and Madness*. New York: Hyperion, 1993; New York: Taylor, 2004.

Halperin, Ian. *Fire and Rain: The James Taylor Story*. Edinburgh, Scotland: Mainstream, 2001; New York: Kensington, 2003.

Holzman, Jac, and Gavan Daws. *Follow the Music*. Santa Monica, Calif.: First Media Group, 1998.

King, Tom. *The Operator: David Geffen Builds, Buys, and Sells the New Hollywood*. New York: Random House, 2000.

Kort, Michelle. *Soul Picnic: The Music and Passion of Laura Nyro*. New York: Thomas Dunne, 2002.

Lillian Roxon's Rock Encyclopedia. New York: Grosset & Dunlap, Tempo, 1969.

Maltin, Leonard. *Leonard Maltin's 1998 Movie & Video Guide*. New York: Signet, 1997.

Rees, Dafydd, and Luke Crampton, *Rock Stars Encyclopedia*. New York: DK Publishing, 1999.

Smith, Joe. *Off the Record: An Oral History of Popular Music*. Edited by Mitchell Fink. New York: Warner Books, 1988.

Spitz, Bob. *Bob Dylan: A Biography*. New York: McGraw-Hill, 1989.

Tober, John. *This Day in Rock*. New York: Carol & Graff, 1993.

Whitburn, Joel. *Billboard Book of Top 40 Albums*. New York: Billboard Publications, 1995.

———. *Top Pop, 1955–1982*. Menomonee Falls, Wis.: Record Research, 1983.

———. *Top Pop Albums, 1955–1985*. Menomonee Falls, Wis.: Record Research, 1985.

Wiseman, Rich. *Jackson Browne: The Story of a Hold Out*. Garden City, N.Y.: Doubleday Dolphin, 1982.

Discography

ALBUMS

Note: The terms "gold" and "platinum" are used in this book to describe the sales figures for albums sold in the United States. These are tallied by the Record Industry Association of America (RIAA). "Gold" refers to an album that has sold in excess of 500,000 copies. "Platinum" refers to an album that has sold in excess of one million copies.

JONI MITCHELL (1968/Reprise Records)
Also known as *SONG TO A SEAGULL*
Produced by David Crosby

1. "I Had a King" 2:26
   (Joni Mitchell)
2. "Michael from Mountains" 3:38
   (Joni Mitchell)
3. "Night in the City" 3:35
   (Joni Mitchell)
4. "Marcie" 4:35
   (Joni Mitchell)
5. "Nathan La Franeer" 3:13
   (Joni Mitchell)
6. "Sisotowbell Lane" 4:00
   (Joni Mitchell)
7. "The Dawntreader" 4:50
   (Joni Mitchell)
8. "The Pirate of Penance" 2:40
   (Joni Mitchell)
9. "Song to a Seagull" 3:50
   (Joni Mitchell)
10. "Cactus Tree" 4:35
    (Joni Mitchell)

CLOUDS (1969/Reprise Records)
Produced by Joni Mitchell, except "Tin Angel" produced by Paul Rothchild

1. "Tin Angel" 4:06
   (Joni Mitchell)
2. "Chelsea Morning" 2:30
   (Joni Mitchell)
3. "I Don't Know Where I Stand" 3:10
   (Joni Mitchell)
4. "That Song about the Midway" 4:33
   (Joni Mitchell)
5. "Roses Blue" 3:47
   (Joni Mitchell)
6. "The Gallery" 4:06
   (Joni Mitchell)

7. "I Think I Understand" 4:22
(Joni Mitchell)
8. "Songs to Aging Children Come"
3:03
(Joni Mitchell)
9. "The Fiddle and the Drum" 2:45
(Joni Mitchell)
10. "Both Sides Now" 4:30
(Joni Mitchell)

LADIES OF THE CANYON
(1970/Reprise Records)
Produced by Joni Mitchell

1. "Morning Morgantown" 3:12
(Joni Mitchell)
2. "For Free" 4:31
(Joni Mitchell)
3. "Conversation" 4:21
(Joni Mitchell)
4. "Ladies of the Canyon" 3:32
(Joni Mitchell)
5. "Willy" 3:00
(Joni Mitchell)
6. "The Arrangement" 3:32
(Joni Mitchell)
7. "Rainy Night House" 3:22
(Joni Mitchell)
8. "The Priest" 3:39
(Joni Mitchell)
9. "Blue Boy" 2:53
(Joni Mitchell)
10. "Big Yellow Taxi" 2:16
(Joni Mitchell)
11. "Woodstock" 5:25
(Joni Mitchell)
12. "The Circle Game" 4:50
(Joni Mitchell)

BLUE (1971/Reprise Records)
Produced by Joni Mitchell

1. "All I Want" 3:32
(Joni Mitchell)

2. "My Old Man" 3:33
(Joni Mitchell)
3. "Little Green" 3:25
(Joni Mitchell)
4. "Carey" 3:00
(Joni Mitchell)
5. "Blue" 3:00
(Joni Mitchell)
6. "California" 3:48
(Joni Mitchell)
7. "This Flight Tonight" 2:50
(Joni Mitchell)
8. "River" 4:00
(Joni Mitchell)
9. "A Case of You" 4:20
(Joni Mitchell)
10. "The Last Time I Saw Richard"
4:13
(Joni Mitchell)

FOR THE ROSES (1972/Asylum
Records)
Produced by Joni Mitchell

1. "Banquet" 3:00
(Joni Mitchell)
2. "Cold Blue Steel and Sweet Fire"
4:17
(Joni Mitchell)
3. "Barangrill" 2:53
(Joni Mitchell)
4. "Lesson in Survival" 3:10
(Joni Mitchell)
5. "Let the Wind Carry Me" 3:55
(Joni Mitchell)
6. "For the Roses" 3:46
(Joni Mitchell)
7. "See You Sometime" 2:58
(Joni Mitchell)
8. "Electricity" 3:00
(Joni Mitchell)
9. "You Turn Me On I'm a Radio" 2:40
(Joni Mitchell)
10. "The Blonde in the Bleachers"
2:40
(Joni Mitchell)

11. "Woman of Heart and Mind" 2:36
(Joni Mitchell)
12. "Judgement of the Moon and
Stars (Ludwig's Tune)" 5:25
(Joni Mitchell)

COURT AND SPARK (1974/Asylum
Records)
Produced by Joni Mitchell

1. "Court and Spark" 2:46
(Joni Mitchell)
2. "Help Me" 3:22
(Joni Mitchell)
3. "Free Man in Paris" 3:02
(Joni Mitchell)
4. "People's Parties" 2:20
(Joni Mitchell)
5. "Same Situation" 3:05
(Joni Mitchell)
6. "Car on a Hill" 2:58
(Joni Mitchell)
7. "Down to You" 5:36
(Joni Mitchell)
8. "Just Like This Train" 4:23
(Joni Mitchell)
9. "Raised on Robbery" 3:05
(Joni Mitchell)
10. "Trouble Child" 3:57
(Joni Mitchell)
11. "Twisted" 2:18
(Annie Ross and Wardell Gray)

MILES OF AISLES (1974/Asylum
Records)
Produced by Joni Mitchell

1. "You Turn Me On I'm a Radio" 3:55
(Joni Mitchell)
2. "Big Yellow Taxi" 3:05
(Joni Mitchell)
3. "Rainy Night House" 4:00
(Joni Mitchell)
4. "Woodstock" 4:25
(Joni Mitchell)

5. "Cactus Tree" 4:50
(Joni Mitchell)
6. "Cold Blue Steel and Sweet Fire"
5:10
(Joni Mitchell)
7. "Woman of Heart and Mind"
3:30
(Joni Mitchell)
8. "A Case of You" 4:18
(Joni Mitchell)
9. "Blue" 2:40
(Joni Mitchell)
10. "The Circle Game" 5:20
(Joni Mitchell)
11. "People's Parties" 2:30
(Joni Mitchell)
12. "All I Want" 3:20
(Joni Mitchell)
13. "Real Good for Free" 4:15
(Joni Mitchell)
14. "Both Sides Now" 4:10
(Joni Mitchell)
15. "Carey" 3:20
(Joni Mitchell)
16. "The Last Time I Saw
Richard" 3:45
(Joni Mitchell)
17. "Jericho" 3:30
(Joni Mitchell)
18. "Love or Money" 4:48
(Joni Mitchell)

THE HISSING OF SUMMER
LAWNS
(1975/Asylum Records)
Produced by Joni Mitchell

1. "In France They Kiss on Main
Street" 3:17
(Joni Mitchell)
2. "The Jungle Line" 4:20
(Joni Mitchell)
3. "Edith and the Kingpin" 3:35
(Joni Mitchell)
4. "Don't Interrupt the Sorrow" 4:04
(Joni Mitchell)

5. "Shades of Scarlett Conquering" 4:57
(Joni Mitchell)
6. "The Hissing of Summer Lawns" 3:00
(Joni Mitchell)
7. "The Boho Dance" 3:56
(Joni Mitchell)
8. "Harry's House"/"Centerpiece" 6:52
(Joni Mitchell for "Harry's House";
Johnny Mandel and Jon Hendricks
for "Centerpiece")
9. "Sweet Bird" 4:10
(Joni Mitchell)
10. "Shadows and Light" 4:15
(Joni Mitchell)

HEJIRA (1976/Asylum Records)
Produced by Joni Mitchell

1. "Coyote" 5:00
(Joni Mitchell)
2. "Amelia" 6:00
(Joni Mitchell)
3. "Furry Sings the Blues" 5:03
(Joni Mitchell)
4. "A Strange Boy" 4:15
(Joni Mitchell)
5. "Hejira" 6:35
(Joni Mitchell)
6. "Song for Sharon" 8:30
(Joni Mitchell)
7. "Black Crow" 4:20
(Joni Mitchell)
8. "Blue Motel Room" 5:03
(Joni Mitchell)
9. "Refuge of the Roads" 6:37
(Joni Mitchell)

DON JUAN'S RECKLESS DAUGHTER
(1977/Asylum Records)
Produced by Joni Mitchell

1. "Overture/Cotton Avenue" 6:35
(Joni Mitchell)

2. "Talk to Me" 3:40
(Joni Mitchell)
3. "Jericho" 3:25
(Joni Mitchell)
4. "Paprika Plains" 16:19
(Joni Mitchell)
5. "Otis and Marlena" 4:05
(Joni Mitchell)
6. "The Tenth World" 6:45
(Joni Mitchell, Don Alias, Manolo
Badrena, Alejandro Acuna, Airto,
Jaco Pastorius)
7. "Dreamland" 4:37
(Joni Mitchell)
8. "Don Juan's Reckless Daughter" 6:40
(Joni Mitchell)
9. "Off Night Backstreet" 3:22
(Joni Mitchell)
10. "Silky Veils of Ardor" 4:02
(Joni Mitchell)

MINGUS (1979/Asylum Records)
Produced by Joni Mitchell

1. "Happy Birthday 1975" (rap) 0:57
(Improvisation)
2. "God Must Be a Boogie Man" 4:36
(Joni Mitchell)
3. "Funeral" (rap) 1:07
(Improvisation)
4. "A Chair in the Sky" 6:42
(Joni Mitchell and Charles Mingus)
5. "The Wolf That Lives in Lindsey" 6:34
(Joni Mitchell)
6. "I's a Muggin'" (rap) 0:07
(Improvisation)
7. "Sweet Sucker Dance" 8:05
(Joni Mitchell and Charles Mingus)
8. "Coin in the Pocket" (rap) 0:12
(Improvisation)
9. "The Dry Cleaner from Des
Moines" 3:22

(Joni Mitchell and Charles Mingus)
10. "Lucky" (rap) 0:04
(Improvisation)
11. "Goodbye Pork Pie Hat" (5:37)
(Joni Mitchell and Charles Mingus)

SHADOWS AND LIGHT (1980/Asy-
lum Records)
Produced by Joni Mitchell
Note: When this album originally became a single compact disc, three
songs were dropped, and other edits
took place. The length of songs here
are from the subsequent two-disc release.

DISC 1

1. "Introduction" 1:56
(Multimedia)
2. "In France They Kiss on Main
Street" 4:10
(Joni Mitchell)
3. "Edith and the Kingpen" 4:10
(Joni Mitchell)
4. "Coyote" 4:56
(Joni Mitchell)
5. "Goodbye Pork Pie Hat" 6:02
(Joni Mitchell and Charles Min-
gus)
6. "The Dry Cleaner from Des
Moines" 4:34
(Joni Mitchell and Charles Min-
gus)
7. "Amelia" 6:40
(Joni Mitchell)
8. "Pat's Solo" 3:06
(Pat Metheny)
9. "Hejira" 7:52
(Joni Mitchell)

DISC 2

1. "Black Crow" 3:52
(Joni Mitchell)

2. "Don's Solo" 3:56
(Don Alias)
3. "Dreamland" 4:50
(Joni Mitchell)
4. "Free Man in Paris" 3:22
(Joni Mitchell)
5. "Band Introduction" 0:50
(Joni Mitchell)
6. "Furry Sings the Blues" 6:36
(Joni Mitchell)
7. "Why Do Fools Fall in Love?" 2:26
(Frankie Lyman and Morris Levy)
8. "Shadows and Light" 6:27
(Joni Mitchell)
9. "God Must Be a Boogie Man" 6:04
(Joni Mitchell)
10. "Woodstock" 6:12
(Joni Mitchell)

WILD THINGS RUN FAST (1982/
Geffen Records)
Produced by Joni Mitchell

1. "Chinese Café"/"Unchained
Melody" 5:17
(Joni Mitchell for "Chinese
Café"; Hy Zaret and Alex
North for "Unchained
Melody")
2. "Wild Things Run Fast" 2:12
(Joni Mitchell)
3. "Ladies' Man" 2:37
(Joni Mitchell)
4. "Moon at the Window" 3:42
(Joni Mitchell)
5. "Solid Love" 2:57
(Joni Mitchell)
6. "Be Cool" 4:12
(Joni Mitchell)
7. "(You're So Square) Baby, I Don't
Care" 2:36
(Jerry Lieber and Mike Stoller)
8. "You Dream Flat Tires" 2:50
(Joni Mitchell)
9. "Man to Man" 3:42
(Joni Mitchell)

10. "Underneath the Streetlight" 2:14
(Joni Mitchell)
11. "Love" 3:46
(Joni Mitchell)

DOG EAT DOG (1985/Geffen
Records)
Produced by Joni Mitchell, Larry
Klein, Mike Shipley, and Thomas
Dolby
+ Produced by Joni Mitchell, Larry
Klein, and Mike Shipley
++ Produced by Joni Mitchell

1. "Good Friends" 4:25
(Joni Mitchell)
2. "Fiction" 4:14
(Joni Mitchell and Larry Klein)
3. "The Three Great Stimulants"
6:11 +
(Joni Mitchell)
4. "Tax Free" 4:19
(Joni Mitchell and Larry Klein)
5. "Smokin' (Empty, Try Another)"
1:43 ++
(Joni Mitchell)
6. "Dog Eat Dog" 4:41
(Joni Mitchell)
7. "Shiny Toys" 3:27
(Joni Mitchell)
8. "Ethiopia" 5:53 +
(Joni Mitchell)
9. "Impossible Dreamer" 4:30
(Joni Mitchell)
10. "Lucky Girl" 4:02
(Joni Mitchell)

CHALK MARK IN A RAIN STORM
(1988/Geffen Records)
Produced by Joni Mitchell and Larry
Klein

1. "My Secret Place" 5:01
(Joni Mitchell)
2. "Number One" 3:46
(Joni Mitchell)
3. "Lakota" 6:25
(Joni Mitchell and Larry Klein)
4. "The Tea Leaf Prophecy (Lay Down
Your Arms)" 4:49
(Joni Mitchell and Larry Klein)
5. "Dancin' Clown" 4:09
(Joni Mitchell)
6. "Cool Water" 5:25
(Bob Nolan)
7. "The Beat of Black Wings" 5:19
(Joni Mitchell)
8. "Snakes and Ladders" 5:37
(Joni Mitchell and Larry Klein)
9. "The Reoccurring Dream" 3:02
(Joni Mitchell)
10. "A Bird That Whistles" (Arrange-
ment of the traditional work
"Corrina, Corrina") 2:38
(Joni Mitchell)

NIGHT RIDE HOME (1991/Geffen
Records)
Produced by Joni Mitchell and Larry
Klein

1. "Night Ride Home" 3:21
(Joni Mitchell)
2. "Passion Play (When All the Slaves
Are Free)" 5:25
(Joni Mitchell)
3. "Cherokee Louise" 4:32
(Joni Mitchell)
4. "The Windfall (Everything for
Nothing)" 5:15
(Joni Mitchell)
5. "Slouching towards Bethlehem"
(Based on a poem by W. B. Yeats)
6:54
(Joni Mitchell)
6. "Come In from the Cold" 7:31
(Joni Mitchell)
7. "Nothing Can Be Done" 4:53
(Joni Mitchell)
8. "The Only Joy in Town" 5:11
(Joni Mitchell)

9. "Ray's Dad's Cadillac" 4:33
(Joni Mitchell)
10. "Two Grey Rooms" 3:57
(Joni Mitchell)

TURBULENT INDIGO (1994/Reprise
Records)
Produced by Joni Mitchell and Larry
Klein

1. "Sunny Sunday" 2:37
(Joni Mitchell)
2. "Sex Kills" 3:56
(Joni Mitchell)
3. "How Do You Stop?" 4:09
(Dan Hartman and Charlie Mid-
night)
4. "Turbulent Indigo" 3:34
(Joni Mitchell)
5. "Last Chance Lost" 3:14
(Joni Mitchell)
6. "The Magdalene Laundries" 4:02
(Joni Mitchell)
7. "Not to Blame" 4:18
(Joni Mitchell)
8. "Borderline" 4:48
(Joni Mitchell)
9. "Yvette in English" 5:16
(Joni Mitchell and David Crosby)
10. "The Sire of Sorrow (Job's Sad
Song)" 7:08
(Joni Mitchell)

HITS (1996/Reprise Records)
Produced by Joni Mitchell
+Produced by Joni Mitchell and Larry
Klein

1. "Urge for Going" 5:08
(Joni Mitchell)
2. "Chelsea Morning" 2:50
(Joni Mitchell)
3. "Big Yellow Taxi" 2:16
(Joni Mitchell)

4. "Woodstock" 5:25
(Joni Mitchell)
5. "The Circle Game" 4:50
(Joni Mitchell)
6. "Carey" 3:02
(Joni Mitchell)
7. "California" 3:48
(Joni Mitchell)
8. "You Turn Me On I'm a Radio" 2:40
(Joni Mitchell)
9. "Raised on Robbery" 3:05
(Joni Mitchell)
10. "Help Me" 3:22
(Joni Mitchell)
11. "Free Man in Paris" 3:02
(Joni Mitchell)
12. "River" 4:03
(Joni Mitchell)
13. "Chinese Café"/"Unchained
Melody" 5:18
(Joni Mitchell for "Chinese Café";
Hy Zaret and Alex North for "Un-
chained Melody")
14. "Come In from the Cold" 7:31 +
(Joni Mitchell)
15. "Both Sides Now" 4:30
(Joni Mitchell)

MISSES (1996/Reprise Records)
Produced by Joni Mitchell
+Produced by Joni Mitchell and Larry
Klein
++Produced by Joni Mitchell, Larry
Klein, and Mike Shipley

1. "Passion Play (When All the
Slaves Are Free)" 5:23 +
(Joni Mitchell)
2. "Nothing Can Be Done" 4:51 +
(Joni Mitchell and Larry Klein)
3. "A Case of You" 4:23
(Joni Mitchell)
4. "The Beat of Black Wings" 5:24
(Joni Mitchell)
5. "Dog Eat Dog" 4:42 ++
(Joni Mitchell)

6. "The Wolf That Lives in Lindsey" 6:35
(Joni Mitchell)
7. "The Magdalene Laundries" 4:03
(Joni Mitchell and Larry Klein) ++
8. "Impossible Dreamer" 4:31
(Joni Mitchell)
9. "Sex Kills" 3:56 +
(Joni Mitchell)
10. "The Reoccurring Dream" 3:04
(Joni Mitchell)
11. "Harry's House"/"Centerpiece" 6:47
(Joni Mitchell for "Harry's House"; Johnny Mandel and Jon Hendricks for "Centerpiece")
12. "The Arrangement" 3:34
(Joni Mitchell)
13. "For the Roses" 3:43
(Joni Mitchell)
14. "Hejira" 6:42
(Joni Mitchell)

TAMING THE TIGER (1998/Reprise Records)
Produced by Joni Mitchell

1. "Harlem In Havana" 4:25
(Joni Mitchell)
2. "Man from Mars" 4:09
(Joni Mitchell)
3. "Love Puts on a New Face" 3:46
(Joni Mitchell)
4. "Lead Balloon" 3:38
(Joni Mitchell)
5. "No Apologies" 4:17
(Joni Mitchell)
6. "Taming the Tiger" 4:18
(Joni Mitchell)
7. "The Crazy Cries of Love" 3:54
(Joni Mitchell and Don Freed)
8. "Stay in Touch" 2:59
(Joni Mitchell)
9. "Face Lift" 4:41
(Joni Mitchell)

10. "My Best to You" 2:52
(Gene Willaden and Isham Jones)
11. "Tiger Bones" 4:22
(Joni Mitchell)

BOTH SIDES NOW (2000/Reprise Records)
Produced by Joni Mitchell and Larry Klein

1. "You're My Thrill" 3:51
(Sidney Clare and Jay Gorney)
2. "At Last" 4:26
(Mack Gordon and Harry Warren)
3. "Comes Love" 4:28
(Lew Brown, Sammy Stept, and Charles Tobias)
4. "You've Changed" 4:59
(Bill Carey and Carl Fischer)
5. "Answer Me, My Love" 3:22
(Gerhard Winkler and Fred Rauch; English lyric by Carl Sigman)
6. "A Case of You" 5:50
(Joni Mitchell)
7. "Don't Go to Strangers" 4:09
(Redd Evans, Arthur Kent, and David Mann)
8. "Sometimes I'm Happy" 3:58
(Irving Caesar, Clifford Grey, and Vincent Youmans)
9. "Don't Worry 'bout Me" 3:48
(Rube Bloom and Ted Koehler)
10. "Stormy Weather" 3:07
(Ted Koehler and Harold Arlen)
11. "I Wish I Were In Love Again" 3:35
(Lorenz Hart and Richard Rodgers)
12. "Both Sides Now" 5:46
(Joni Mitchell)

TRAVELOGUE (2002/Nonesuch Records)
Produced by Joni Mitchell and Larry Klein

DISC 1

1. "Otis and Marlena" 3:52
(Joni Mitchell)
2. "Amelia" 6:46
(Joni Mitchell)
3. "You Dream Flat Tires" 3:46
(Joni Mitchell)
4. "Love" 5:38
(Joni Mitchell)
5. "Woodstock" 5:54
(Joni Mitchell)
6. "Slouching towards Bethlehem"
(Based on a poem by W. B. Yeats)
7:09
(Joni Mitchell)
7. "Judgment of the Moon and Stars
(Ludwig's Tune)" 5:20
(Joni Mitchell)
8. "The Sire of Sorrow (Job's Sad
Song)" 7:09
(Joni Mitchell)
9. "For the Roses" 7:28
(Joni Mitchell)
10. "Trouble Child" 5:02
(Joni Mitchell)
11. "God Must Be a Boogie Man" 3:56
(Joni Mitchell)

DISC 2

1. "Be Cool" 5:09
(Joni Mitchell)
2. "Just Like This Train" 5:04
(Joni Mitchell)
3. "Sex Kills" 3:57
(Joni Mitchell)
4. "Refuge of the Roads" 7:56
(Joni Mitchell)
5. "Hejira" 6:47
(Joni Mitchell)
6. "Chinese Café"/"Unchained
Melody" 5:41
(Joni Mitchell for "Chinese Café";
Hy Zaret and Alex North for "Un-
chained Melody")
7. "Cherokee Louise" 6:00
(Joni Mitchell)

8. "The Dawntreader" 5:38
(Joni Mitchell)
9. "The Last Time I Saw Richard"
4:58
(Joni Mitchell)
10. "Borderline" 6:23
(Joni Mitchell)
11. "The Circle Game" 6:50
(Joni Mitchell)

*THE COMPLETE GEFFEN RECORD-
INGS* (2003/Geffen Records)
(Four-disc boxed set with three
bonus tracks and new liner notes by
Joni Mitchell)

DISK 1

WILD THINGS RUN FAST (Originally
1982/Geffen Records)
Produced by Joni Mitchell

1. "Chinese Café"/"Unchained
Melody" 5:20
(Joni Mitchell for "Chinese Café";
Hy Zaret and Alex North for "Un-
chained Melody")
2. "Wild Things Run Fast" 2:17
(Joni Mitchell)
3. "Ladies' Man" 2:40
(Joni Mitchell)
4. "Moon at the Window" 3:43
(Joni Mitchell)
5. "Solid Love" 3:06
(Joni Mitchell)
6. "Be Cool" 4:13
(Joni Mitchell)
7. "(You're So Square) Baby, I Don't
Care" 2:40
(Jerry Leiber and Mike Stoller)
8. "You Dream Flat Tires" 2:53
(Joni Mitchell)
9. "Man to Man" 3:45
(Joni Mitchell)
10. "Underneath the Streetlight" 2:17
(Joni Mitchell)

11. "Love" 4:05
(Joni Mitchell)
12. "Two Grey Rooms" (bonus track,
demo version) 3:58
(Joni Mitchell)

DISC 2

DOG EAT DOG (Originally 1985/Geffen Records)
Produced by Joni Mitchell, Larry
Klein, Mike Shipley, and Thomas
Dolby
+ Produced by Joni Mitchell, Larry
Klein, Mike Shipley
++ Produced by Joni Mitchell

1. "Good Friends" 4:30
(Joni Mitchell)
2. "Fiction" 4:11
(Joni Mitchell and Larry Klein)
3. "The Three Great Stimulants"
6:15 +
(Joni Mitchell)
4. "Tax Free" 4:20
(Joni Mitchell and Larry Klein)
5. "Smokin' (Empty, Try Another)"
1:47 ++
(Joni Mitchell)
6. "Dog Eat Dog" 4:45
(Joni Mitchell)
7. "Shiny Toys" 3:29
(Joni Mitchell)
8. "Ethiopia" 5:52 +
(Joni Mitchell)
9. "Impossible Dreamer" 4:31
(Joni Mitchell)
10. "Lucky Girl" 4:17
(Joni Mitchell)
11. "Good Friend" (bonus track,
demo version) 4:04
(Joni Mitchell)

DISC 3

CHALK MARK IN A RAINSTORM
(Originally 1988/Geffen Records)
Produced by Joni Mitchell and Larry
Klein

1. "My Secret Place" 5:03
(Joni Mitchell)
2. "Number One" 3:49
(Joni Mitchell)
3. "Lakota" 6:28
(Joni Mitchell and Larry Klein)
4. "The Tea Leaf Prophecy (Lay Down
Your Arms)" 4:55
(Joni Mitchell and Larry Klein)
5. "Dancin' Clown" 3:56
(Joni Mitchell)
6. "Cool Water" 5:27
(Bob Nolan)
7. "The Beat of Black Wings" 5:26
(Joni Mitchell)
8. "Snakes and Ladders" 5:45
(Joni Mitchell and Larry Klein)
9. "The Reoccurring Dream" 3:06
(Joni Mitchell)
10. "A Bird That Whistles"
(Arrangement of the traditional
work "Corrina, Corrina") 2:38
(Joni Mitchell)

DISC 4

NIGHT RIDE HOME (Originally
1991/Geffen Records)
Produced by Joni Mitchell and
Larry Klein

1. "Night Ride Home" 3:22
(Joni Mitchell)
2. "Passion Play (When All the Slaves
Are Free)" 5:26
(Joni Mitchell)
3. "Cherokee Louise" 4:33
(Joni Mitchell)
4. "The Windfall (Everything for
Nothing)" 5:17
(Joni Mitchell)

5. "Slouching towards Bethlehem"
(Based on a poem by W. B. Yeats)
6:55
(Joni Mitchell)
6. "Come In from the Cold" 7:32
(Joni Mitchell)
7. "Nothing Can Be Done" 4:55
(Joni Mitchell)
8. "The Only Joy in Town" 5:13
(Joni Mitchell)
9. "Ray's Dad's Cadillac" 4:34
(Joni Mitchell)
10. "Two Grey Rooms" 4:42
(Joni Mitchell)
11. "It's All Over Now, Baby Blue"
(bonus track, demo version)
4:42
(Bob Dylan)

THE BEGINNING OF SURVIVAL
(2004/Geffen Records)
Compilation produced by Joni
Mitchell and Mike Regogna

1. "The Reoccurring Dream" 3:04
(Joni Mitchell)
2. "The Windfall (Everything for
Nothing)" 5:10
(Joni Mitchell)
3. "Slouching towards Bethlehem"
(Based on a poem by W. B. Yeats)
6:50
(Joni Mitchell)
4. "Dog Eat Dog" 4:28
(Joni Mitchell)
5. "Fiction" 4:11
(Joni Mitchell and Larry Klein)
6. "The Beat of Black Wings" 5:23
(Joni Mitchell)
7. "No Apologies" 4:18
(Joni Mitchell)
8. "Sex Kills" 3:57
(Joni Mitchell)
9. "The Three Great Stimulants" 6:07
(Joni Mitchell)

10. "Lakota" 6:26
(Joni Mitchell and Larry Klein)
11. "Ethiopia" 5:39
(Joni Mitchell)
12. "Cool Water" 5:26
(Bob Nolan)
13. "Tax Free" 4:18
(Joni Mitchell and Larry Klein)
14. "The Magdalene Laundries" 4:02
(Joni Mitchell and Larry Klein)
15. "Passion Play (When All the
Slaves Are Free)" 5:20
(Joni Mitchell)
16. "Impossible Dreamer" 4:31
(Joni Mitchell)

DREAMLAND (2004/Rhino Records)
Compilation produced by Joni
Mitchell

1. "Free Man in Paris"
(Joni Mitchell)
2. "In France They Kiss on Main
Street"
(Joni Mitchell)
3. "Dreamland"
(Joni Mitchell)
4. "The Jungle Line "
(Joni Mitchell)
5. "Furry Sings the Blues"
(Joni Mitchell)
6. "You Turn Me On I'm a Radio "
(Joni Mitchell)
7. "Carey"
(Joni Mitchell)
8. "Big Yellow Taxi"
(Joni Mitchell)
9. "California"
(Joni Mitchell)
10. "Help Me"
(Joni Mitchell)
11. "Nothing Can Be Done"
(Joni Mitchell)
12. "Dancin' Clown"
(Joni Mitchell)

13. "Come In from the Cold"
(Joni Mitchell)
14. "Amelia" [Orchestral Version, 2002]
(Joni Mitchell)
15. "For the Roses" [Orchestral Version, 2002]
(Joni Mitchell)
16. "Both Sides Now" [Orchestral Version, 2000]
(Joni Mitchell)
17. "The Circle Game"
(Joni Mitchell)

REMIX EP RELEASES

BIG YELLOW TAXI: The Remixes
(1996 Reprise Records)

1. "Big Yellow Taxi/Radio Mix" 4:10
(Joni Mitchell)
2 "Big Yellow Taxi/Friends Album Version" 3:57
(Joni Mitchell)
3 "Big Yellow Taxi/Late Night Club Mix" 7:47
(Joni Mitchell)
4. "Big Yellow Taxi/N.Y. Cab to Club Mix" 7:51
(Joni Mitchell)
5. "Big Yellow Taxi/Double Espresso N.G. Mix" 4:35
(Joni Mitchell)
6. "Big Yellow Taxi/Tribal Dub" 7:39
(Joni Mitchell)
7. "Big Yellow Taxi/Original A Capella with Guitar" 2:16
(Joni Mitchell)

SINGLES

1. "Big Yellow Taxi"
(1970/Reprise Records)

2. "Carey"
(1971/Reprise Records)

3. "California"
(1971/Reprise Records)

4. "You Turn Me On I'm a Radio"
(1972/Reprise Records)

5. "Raised on Robbery"
(1973/Asylum Records)

6. "Help Me"
(1974/Asylum Records)

7. "Free Man in Paris"
(1974/Asylum Records)

8. "Big Yellow Taxi" [live version]
(1974/Asylum Records)

9. "In France They Kiss on Main Street"
(1976/Asylum Records)

10. "Coyote"/"Blue Motel Room"
(1976/Asylum Records)

11. "(You're So Square) Baby, I Don't Care"
(1982/Geffen Records)

12. "Shiny Toys" [12-inch remit]
(1986 U.K./Geffen Records)

13. "Number One" [CD single remit]
(1988 Germany/Geffen Records)

14. "How Do You Stop?"/"Moon at the Window" [Live]
(1994/Geffen Records)

APPEARANCES ON OTHER ALBUMS AND SPECIAL SINGLES

1. "Will You Love Me Tomorrow"
Tapestry (1971/Ode Records)
by Carole King
Background vocals by Joni and

James Taylor, billed as "The
Mitchell/Taylor Boy-and-Girl
Choir"

2. "Love Has Brought Me Around"
"You've Got a Friend"
"Long Ago and Far Away"
*Mud Slide Slim and the Blue
Horizon* (1971/Warner Bros.
Records)
by James Taylor
Background vocals by Joni

3. "Sing My Songs to Me"
For Everyman (1973/Asylum
Records)
by Jackson Browne
Electric Piano by Joni

4. "Di Da"
Diamonds and Rust (1975/A&M
Records)
by Joan Baez
Duet between Joan Baez and Joni

5. "Coyote"
The Last Waltz (1978/Warner Bros.
Records)
by The Band (and Various Artists)
Joni solo performance tracks with
various members of the ensemble

6. "Tears Are Not Enough"
We Are the World (1985/Polygram
Records)
by Various Artists under the name
Northern Lights
Joni as one of the featured soloists
on the track

7. "Spirit of the Rainforest"
7-inch British single (1989)
by Various Artists
Joni as one of the featured soloists
on the track

8. "Goodbye Blue Sky"
The Wall (1990/Mercury Records)

by Roger Waters (and Various
Artists)
Joni solo song

9. "If I Could"
Seal (1994/Warner Bros. Records)
by Seal
Duet by Seal and Joni

10. "Big Yellow Taxi" (remix)
Friends [TV soundtrack]
(1995/Warner Bros. Records)
by Various Artists
Joni solo track

11. "Just Like This Train"
Rare on the Air Volume 2:
KCRW Live Performances
(1995/Mammoth
Records)
by Various Artists
Joni solo track

12. "The Circle Game"
Hand in Hand: Songs of Parenthood
(1995/Music Little People
Records)
by Various Artists
Joni solo track

13. "Big Yellow Taxi"
"Woodstock"
*Message to Love: The Isle of Wight
Festival* (1996/Castle Music
Records)
by Various Artists
Joni solo live concert tracks

14. "Got 'Til It's Gone"
Velvet Rope (1997/Virgin Records)
by Janet Jackson
Joni's "Big Yellow Taxi" vocals
are sampled on this track and
serve as the chorus line to the
song

15. "Stormy Weather" (live recording)
Stormy Weather (1998/AT&T

WorldNet Records)
by Various Artists
Joni solo track in concert for Don
Henley's charity the Walden Pond
Fund

16. "Summertime"
"The Man I Love"
Gershwin's World (1998/Polygram
Records)
by Herbie Hancock
Joni solo track with Herbie and
jazz ensemble

17. "Trouble Man"
From There to Here (1998/Sony
Records)

by Kyle Eastwood
Joni sings lead, Kyle plays bass

18. "Both Sides Now" (2000 version)
Love Actually [movie soundtrack]
(2003/J Records)
by Various Artists
Joni solo track

19. "Coyote"
"Shadows and Light"
"Furry Sings the Blues"
The Last Waltz: The Complete Sessions Boxed Set (2002/Rhino
Records)
by The Band (and Various Artists)
Joni solo performance tracks with
various members of the ensemble

Videocassettes and DVDs

Celebrations at Big Sur (1971). Theatrically released concert video

The Last Waltz (1978). Theatrically released concert video

Renaldo and Clara (1978). Theatrically released concert video

Shadows and Light (1980). Concert video

Love (1982). As "Paula"

Come In from the Cold (1994). Music videos

Message to Love: The Isle of Wight Festival (1996). Documentary concert video

Painting with Words (1999). Concert video

Joni Mitchell: A Woman of Heart and Mind (2003). Biographical documentary

Joni's Awards

Grammy winner: Joni Mitchell, artist
Genre: Folk
Grammy category: Best Folk Performance
Year: 1969, twelfth annual Grammy Awards
Title of work: *Clouds*
Artist performing work: Joni Mitchell

Grammy winner: Joni Mitchell and Tom Scott, arrangers
Genre: Arranging
Grammy category: Best Arrangement Accompanying Vocalists
Year: 1974, seventeenth annual Grammy Awards
Title of work: "Down to You" from the album *Court and Spark*
Artist performing work: Joni Mitchell

Grammy winner: Joni Mitchell and Robbie Cavolina, art directors
Genre: Packaging
Grammy category: Best Recording Package

Year: 1995, thirty-eighth annual Grammy Awards
Title of work: *Turbulent Indigo*
Artist performing work: Joni Mitchell

Grammy winner: Joni Mitchell, artist; Joni Mitchell and Larry Klein, producers
Genre: Pop
Grammy category: Best Pop Album
Year: 1995, thirty-eighth annual Grammy Awards
Title of work: *Turbulent Indigo*
Artist performing work: Joni Mitchell

Grammy winner: Joni Mitchell, artist; Allen Sides and Geoff Foster, engineers/mixers; Joni Mitchell and Larry Klein, producers
Genre: Traditional Pop
Grammy category: Best Traditional Pop Vocal Album
Year: 2000, forty-third annual Grammy Awards
Title of Work: *Both Sides Now*
Artist performing work: Joni Mitchell

BILLBOARD MAGAZINE'S CENTURY
AWARD

December 1995

ROCK & ROLL HALL
OF FAME

Joni was inducted into the Rock &
Roll Hall of Fame on May 6, 1997, at
the twelfth annual induction ceremony.

SWEDEN'S POLAR MUSIC PRIZE

CANADIAN GOVERNOR-GENERAL'S
PERFORMING ARTS AWARD

NATIONAL ACADEMY OF SONG-
WRITER'S LIFETIME ACHIEVE-
MENT AWARD

Index

About the Author

Mark Bego is the author of several best-selling books on rock & roll and show business. With over forty-eight books published and over 10 million books in print, he is acknowledged as the best-selling biographer in the rock and pop music field. His biographies have included the life stories of some of the biggest stars of rock, soul, pop, and country. His first Top 10 *New York Times* best-seller was *Michael!* about Michael Jackson (1984). Since that time he has written *Rock Hudson: Public and Private* (1986), *Aretha Franklin: Queen of Soul* (1989), *Jewel* (1998), *Madonna: Blonde Ambition* (2000), *Cher: If You Believe* (2001), *Bette Midler: Still Divine* (2002), *Bonnie Raitt: Still in the Nick of Time* (2003), *Tina Turner: Break Every Rule* (2003), and *Jackson Browne* (2005).

In the 1990s Bego branched out into country music books, writing *Country Hunks* (1994), *Country Gals* (1995), *I Fall to Pieces: The Music and the Life of Patsy Cline* (1995), *Alan Jackson: Gone Country* (1996), *George Strait: The Story of Country's Living Legend* (1997), *LeAnn Rimes* (1998), and *Vince Gill* (2000).

Bego has coauthored books with several rock stars, including *Dancing in the Street: Confessions of a Motown Diva*, with Martha Reeves, which spent five weeks on the *Chicago Tribune* best-seller list in 1994. He worked with Micky Dolenz of the Monkees (*I'm a Believer*, 1993; new updated edition, 2004), Jimmy Greenspoon of Three Dog Night (*One Is the Loneliest Number*, 1991), and Mary Wilson (*Dreamgirl: My Life as a Supreme*, 2000 edition).

His writing has also been featured in several record albums and compact discs. In 1982 he wrote the interior notes to the Columbia House five-record boxed set *The Motown Collection*. His liner notes can also be found in the CD collection *Mary Wilson: I Am Changing* (2000) and the Motown album *Martha Reeves and the Vandellas: Lost and Found* (2005).

In 1998 Mark wrote books about three of the hottest leading men in late-1990s cinema. His *Leonardo DiCaprio: Romantic Hero* spent six weeks on the *New York Times* best-seller list. He followed it up with *Matt Damon: Chasing a Dream* and *Will Smith: The Freshest Prince*. He has also written about the lives of actresses: *The Linda Gray Story* (1988) and *Julia Roberts: America's Sweetheart* (2003).

In 1998 Melitta Coffee launched Mark Bego: Romantic Hero Blend coffee as part of their Celebrity Series. He is currently developing his book *Rock & Roll Almanac* (1995) into a television series. Mark divides his time between New York City, Los Angeles, and Tucson, Arizona. Visit his website at: www.markbego.com.